CO-CCJ-858

TAXATION
AN INTERNATIONAL PERSPECTIVE

TAXATION
AN INTERNATIONAL PERSPECTIVE

Proceedings of an International Conference

Contributors include:
James M. Buchanan, Edgar L. Feige,
Sir Alan Walters, Assar Lindbeck

Walter Block and Michael Walker (Editors)

The Fraser Institute
1984

Proceedings of an International Symposium on Taxation held in Vancouver, British Columbia, Canada on August 27–29, 1980. This was part of the program of Liberty Fund Inc. under the direction of its President, Dr. Neil McLeod. This Symposium was managed by The Fraser Institute and organized by its Director, Dr. Michael Walker.

Canadian Cataloguing in Publication Data

Main entry under title:

Taxation, an international perspective

Includes index.
ISBN 0-88975-046-7

1. Taxation - Congresses. I. Buchanan, James M. II. Block, Walter, 1941- III. Walker, Michael, 1945- IV. Fraser Institute (Vancouver, B.C.)
HJ2240.T39 1984 336.2'009'04 C84-091221-8

Printed in Canada.

Contents

PARTICIPANTS

Armen Alchian, University of California at Los Angeles
Douglas Auld, University of Guelph, Ontario
Ernst Berndt, Massachusetts Institute of Technology, Cambridge
Walter Block, The Fraser Institute, Vancouver, British Columbia
Edgar K. Browning, University of Virginia, Charlottesville
James M. Buchanan, George Mason University, Fairfax, Virginia
Robert Clark, University of British Columbia, Vancouver
Thomas J. Courchene, University of Western Ontario, London
Donald Daly, York University, Downsview, Ontario
Arthur De Vany, University of Houston, Texas
Edgar L. Feige, Netherlands Institute for Advanced Study/University of Wisconsin, Madison
Malcolm R. Fisher, Australian Graduate School of Management, University of New South Wales
Herbert Giersch, Institut für Welwirtschaft an der Universität Kiel, Germany
Herbert Grubel, Simon Fraser University, Burnaby, British Columbia
William R. Johnson, University of Virginia, Charlottesville
Jonathan R. Kesselman, University of British Columbia, Vancouver
Keimei Kaizuka, University of Tokyo, Bunkyo-Ku
Assar Lindbeck, University of Stockholm, Sweden
Robert Newman, Louisiana State University, Baton Rouge
David Perry, Canadian Tax Foundation, Toronto, Ontario
Hans-Georg Petersen, Institut für Weltwirtschaft an der Universität Kiel, Germany/Johannes Kepler University Linz, Austria
Sergio Ricossa, Universita degli Studi di Torino, Italy
Arthur Seldon, Institute of Economic Affairs, Westminster, England
Lawrence B. Smith, University of Toronto, Ontario
Zane Spindler, Simon Fraser University, Burnaby, British Columbia
Charles Stuart, Lund Universitet, Sweden/University of California, Santa Barbara
Michael Walker, The Fraser Institute, Vancouver, British Columbia
Sir Alan Walters, Professor of Economics, John Hopkins University, Baltimore, Maryland/Personal Economic Adviser to Prime Minister Thatcher, London, England

PREFACE

This book contains papers which were presented at an International Symposium on Taxation held in Vancouver, Canada. The co-editors of this volume wish to express a debt of gratitude to Dr. A. Neil McLeod, Executive Director of the Liberty Fund, Indianapolis, Indiana for generous financial support and for aid with the design of the program. We also wish to thank Sally Pipes, Assistant Director of The Fraser Institute for flawlessly administering the Symposium and Dianne Aho, for supervising the production of this book.

The Fraser Institute has been pleased to support the work of the scholars reported in this volume. However, their views were arrived at independently and do not necessarily reflect the views of the members, trustees, or funding agencies of The Fraser Institute.

Walter Block
Michael Walker

Vancouver, Canada
March, 1984

PART ONE

THE ECONOMICS OF TAXATION

CHAPTER 1

TAXATION: INTERNATIONAL EVIDENCE

Walter Block and Michael Walker

Few subjects have captured public attention and professional interest in the past half decade like taxes and tax systems. While unheard of in the recent past, topics like "flat-rate tax," "supply-side effects," "underground economy" and others are now common components of everyday conversation. While some of that attention arises from the great budget debate which has raged in the United States, it is also a reflection of a growing interest in the size of, and financing of the activities of government. Not the least of the reasons for the interest is the fact that in most of the western industrialized nations, governments now tax away 40 to 50 cents out of every dollar earned.

Evidently, growth in the size of government and the corresponding increase in the appetite for tax revenue has not occurred without causing stresses and strains elsewhere in the economic system. It was to probe this impact of the tax system on the modern economy that The Fraser Institute held an International Symposium on Taxation. Economists examined the system of taxation in eight different countries—and its effects on social and economic behaviour. This book is composed of the studies given at the Symposium, along with a critical analysis of each, as well as the highlights of the discussions which followed each presentation. The book is organized as follows: Part One presents two theoretical studies of taxation; Part Two is devoted to a country-by-country analysis of tax systems, for North America, Europe, Asia, and Australia.

THE UNDERGROUND ECONOMY

In "Macroeconomics and the Unobserved Sector," the first of the theoretical examinations of tax policy, Edgar L. Feige puts forward the unobserved income hypothesis. This holds that the existence and growth of the hidden or underground economy has introduced systematic biases into official economic statistics, and that these biases have fundamentally distorted our view of economic reality.

An example of this distortion is the increasing inability of economists to predict or even forecast the future. And this is more than just passing curious at a time of improving computer technology, and increasing sophistication of theoretical macroeconomic models.

Nor is this bias of interest only to the academically minded economists. If shifts from the observed to the unobserved economy can induce the misperception of declining real income, rising unemployment, reduced productivity and higher prices, all sorts of unwise tax-related public policy decisions are likely to be made.

In order to understand this phenomena, Feige puts before us evidence he has uncovered, which shows significant correlations between this bias and a proxy variable for the unobserved economy, monetary transactions. Using this methodology, he conservatively estimates the underground economy as comprising in the neighbourhood of 20 per cent or so of total recorded economic activity for the U.S. and the U.K. As well, he cites a similar research conclusion for Canada. Ignoring this substantial bias in economic statistics, asserts Feige, accounts to some important degree for the failures of professional economists to come to grips with unemployment, recession, inflation, and most importantly, stagflation.

This is why the Feige analysis has been accorded so prominent a place in this study: unless and until the basic data upon which all empirical work rests is made as accurate as possible, all economic analysis is to that degree suspect.

CONSTITUTIONAL TAX LIMITATION

The second theoretical study is, "The Limits of Taxation" by James M. Buchanan. This study delves into the question of why taxes in the western democracies have been rising so fast as of late, and what if anything, can be done about it.

Buchanan begins his analysis with a critique of the now widespread "democratic fallacy." This is the view that the results of all free elections are automatically wise and efficient. As Buchanan rightly points out, this is quite a shift from political thought in the 18th century, when people were more properly suspicious of encroaching democratic goverment.

There are three theories which can account for the increase in taxing-spending levels. In "redistributionism," various pressure groups align with each other in an attempt to wrest money away from minority coalitions, and from the unorganized public. "Structuralism" points to the fact that since we all consume numerous items and produce only one or a few, we are more politically concentrated in the latter role and thus better organized as producers than consumers to make raids on the public purse.

The third theory is "monopolization," the view that government ought not be looked at as a disinterested party, above the fiscal hurly-burly, but rather as a profit seeking participant, much along the lines of the private monopolist.

Due to the lack of scientific status for interpersonal comparisons of utility, the latter two models, but not the first, can be used as a basis for determining the "proper" or the most "efficient" level of taxes, says Buchanan. For this reason a "constitutional opportunity for tax reform exists." It is important to emphasize that a constitutional change of the sort discussed by Buchanan would affect only the institutional structure under which taxing and spending decisions were made, but not the specific decisions themselves.

Constitutional limitations might include a senior law-making assembly which would be responsible only for taxes; the inauguration of greater than simple majority votes necessary to make changes in the law; a requirement for proportional, not progressive taxes; tax base limitations (increased "loopholes"); a balanced-budget amendment; tax ceilings based on income levels.

THE AD HOC TAX SYSTEM IN CANADA

North America is the first of the continents addressed in our country studies, and Douglas Auld leads off with an analysis of the Canadian tax system. In his view, the Canadian system of taxation resembles nothing so much as a crazy quilt design, with pieces hanging here and there, without rhyme or reason, "representing ad hoc short term political considerations, rather than long term economic goals."

Professor Auld points to five separate major watersheds in the corporate income tax in the last two decades, each of which has rendered the system more complex. In 1963 there was the introduction of the accelerated capital cost allowances; in 1966, the deferred allowances; in 1970, the increase in capital cost base; in 1972–1973, the accelerated allowance, complete with tax reduction; and in 1975, the investment tax credit. And the changes which followed in the wake of the 1981 MacEachen budget probably set an all-time record for vacillation and complexity, lending further support to Auld's thesis.

The personal income tax has undergone even more changes. There were more alterations in the 1970s than in the previous two decades, and the 1980s bode well for an acceleration of this trend. Says Auld, "the changes have been coming so rapidly that to assess the redistributive or allocative effects of the entire system is almost a waste of time."

PROPORTIONAL TAXES

What policy prescriptions follow from Auld's analysis?

Based on his work, Auld would have us consider replacing the jerry-built system of progressive taxes with a streamlined, simplified proportional tax system featuring a broader and more encompassing definition of income. He estimates that an income tax with a flat rate of

21.6 per cent would generate as much public revenue as at present, with advantages in the form of lower administrative costs (both public and private), less (and less complicated) tax shifting, no need for tax bracket indexations, and fewer inflationary pressures on wages.

Nor need redistribution goals be eschewed, asserts Professor Auld, by such a proportional tax system. They could still be met by guaranteed minimum incomes and tax credits.

Jon Kesselman, in his comments on Auld's paper, takes issue with several of the methodological assumptions underlying his account of indexing, and insists that a greater distinction be maintained between payroll and income taxes. He notes the importance of incorporating the effects of inflation into the analysis of Canadian taxes, and calls for the creation of a general equilibrium micro-simulation model of the Canadian economy. Finally, Kesselman supports Auld's description of the Canadian tax system as based on political expediency, and agrees with his call for a broad-based, proportional income tax.

TAX INCIDENCE

Edgar Browning and William Johnson then present their findings on the U.S. tax system. This study can best be characterized as an analysis of tax incidence, so before we proceed with our summary, let us review this phenomena.

When one deals with the incidence of taxation, one is asking "Who really pays the tax, in the final analysis?" not "Upon whom is the tax levied, in the tax law?" The two can sometimes be very different.

Suppose the parliament, in its wisdom, decides to impose a tax of 20 per cent on the retail price of hot dogs in order to "punish" hot dog merchants. This is a rather stiff tax, and the immediate effect will of course be visited on the hot dog vendors. If the price was previously 50¢, merchants will have to fork over 10¢ per hot dog sold to the revenuers. But this is not the end of our little story. For the merchants may well be able to raise the price, without disastrous loss of sales. If the price rises to 55¢, the hot dog vendors will still be liable for the tax (11¢ now). But with the extra 5¢ in revenue, they will have shifted forward, onto their customers, 5¢ out of the 11¢ tax bill now due. (The customers pay 5¢ extra, and thus bear this as their share of the incidence of the tax. The merchant must pay the full 11¢ tax; but with the extra 5¢ in hand, the incidence of tax on him is only the remaining 6¢.)

But the merchant may also be able to shift part of the tax incidence backward, onto his suppliers and employees. Let us suppose that he can accomplish this, at a rate equivalent to 4¢ per hot dog sold. Under the assumptions, then, 4¢ of the 11¢ tax on the retail sale of hot dogs will fall on factors of production (suppliers, employees), and 5¢ on customers, leaving only 2¢ to be paid by the merchant, the person aimed at by the MPs. The people actually paying most of the tax will be far removed from the merchants, the only ones required by law to pay the tax.

A PROGRESSIVE SYSTEM

According to Browning and Johnson, the incidence of taxation and income transfers in the U.S. is a very progressive one, falling heavily on the rich. They use a broad definition of income (inclusive of imputed rents on owner-occupied housing, retained corporate earnings). They assume fixed total supplies of factors of production, and an allocation of sales and excise taxes in proportion to labour and capital earnings (not in proportion to household consumption, the more usual approach). Their findings show that "before taxes and transfers, the income of the top quintile (the income earned by the richest 20 per cent of the population) was 131 times as great as the bottom quintile, while after taxes and transfers, the top quintile has only 5.4 times as much."

Among the other important findings unearthed by Professors Browning and Johnson are the following:

- The U.S. tax system is strongly biased against capital income, charging it at the average rate of 56.1 per cent, and in favour of labour income, levying it at the relatively low average rate of only 26.6 per cent.
- Marginal rates of taxation are 45.5 per cent, roughly 50 per cent higher than average rates, which are about 30 per cent. (Marginal rates refer to the tax due for a small increment in earnings, such as $1; average rates are obtained by dividing the total tax bill by total income. Marginal rates are usually assumed more significant in terms of encouraging—or, more to the point, discouraging—labour and other productive effort.)
- The tax-transfer system as a whole has managed to reduce initiatives and productivity by about 13 per cent in terms of total resource supplies—equivalent to no less than $300 billion, in 1980 prices. This is not a total loss to society, since "people gain leisure and present consumption when labour supply and saving are reduced," but misallocations of this magnitude are serious indeed.
- With labour supply elasticities in the 0.2 to 0.5 range, a general reduction in tax rates would *not* sufficiently stimulate economic activity so as to increase tax revenues. This implies that, in terms of the Laffer curve, present "tax rates in the U.S. are well below levels that would maximize total revenues."

A CRITIQUE

Edgar L. Feige subjects the Browning and Johnson paper to a thorough-going critique, strongly rejecting their unconventional incidence assumptions, their overstatement of the incomes of the poor and understatements of incomes of the rich, and their resultant findings of progressivity in the U.S. tax system.

Particularly, he objects to a lack of sensitivity analysis (of tax incidence), lack of specificity as to the precise definition of income use, and the choice of time period for the analysis. "In short, I see the Browning and Johnson exercise as making use of every possible assumption to give the impression of a highly progressive tax system, when indeed the system may well be proportional, as most earlier studies have found."

BROWNING AND JOHNSON'S REPLY

The difficulty with this charge, according to Browning and Johnson, is that while their contribution to the present volume was based on a longer work of theirs wherein all underlying assumptions, amendments, refinements, etc., were painstakingly spelled out, Feige read only the shorter study, which excluded these details, of necessity, but nevertheless complains of their absence.

In addition, Browning and Johnson accuse Feige of improper stringency regarding their income definitions, which he would not apply to numerous other studies. They reject his claim that they have deliberately rigged income measures so as to impart a spurious progressivity to their tax incidence findings. As well, Browning and Johnson claim Feige misinterprets their position on the allocation of sales and excise tax incidence and indexation to capital and labour.

BRITISH TAX SYSTEM "UNREPRESENTATIVE"

Seldon begins the series of studies of European tax systems with a monumental analysis of the United Kingdom. Touching on virtually every nook and cranny of the British tax system, Seldon comes to the following conclusions:

- British taxes are not being spent as a majority of British people would wish.
- To this degree, indirectly or nominally representative British government is not representative of public preferences.
- Preferences in tax expenditure on personal services are being frustrated and suppressed. The more government is enlarged, and the more it removes personal services from the market, the less representative it becomes, and the more coercive of minorities.

- Government that supplies personal services precipitates social conflict. Coerced minorities who cannot or will not escape ("voting with their feet") by emigration become the victims of majority tyranny.
- This unnecessary suppression and coercion could be removed by withdrawing government from financing personal services, and by returning the taxes. This would allow for direct "representation" of consumers in the market, where goods and services can be financed by pricing.
- So-called majority rule (a majority of representatives representing a minority of electors) is inefficient, defective and deceptive in the use of taxes.
- "Representative democracy" has become a misnomer for overruling individual decisions in the expenditure of income.

These remarkable (but exceedingly well-founded) conclusions are based on research which can be characterized as nothing short of brilliant.

In the private marketplace, there is no difficulty at all in determining whether people value the goods and services they purchase more than the price, or cost to them. If they make the purchase, we are entitled to deduce from this fact alone, at least at that time, that they ranked the good higher than the cost, either in terms of money, or in terms of alternatives foregone. (They may later become disappointed or disillusioned, and change these rankings, but that is an entirely different matter.)

What of the analogous question for goods supplied by government, through the tax system? Are these worth more than they cost? Here there *are* no voluntary purchases, by definition, so the previous type of deduction must be ruled out. Most attempts to unearth the real value that the public places on goods and services provided by government are subject to a fatal flaw: people are merely asked whether or not they value a particular good or service, without any mention of the cost involved. In contrast, Seldon's research shows not only that the average Briton is woefully ignorant of the true costs of government services, but that when he is properly appraised of them, he overwhelmingly rejects the suggestion that they are worth the necessary costs.

SCIENTIFIC OPINION POLLING

For example, those who supported additional government services "were promptly asked the *source* (and then amount) of the additional spending thereby made necessary by transfer. Should it be by transfer from other services on which less would be spent, or by paying higher taxes?" Says Seldon, "It was thus hoped to make each respondent think of spending his taxes *micro*-economically on services supplied by government in the same way as in spending his 'take-home' pay for services in the market."

And the results are truly staggering. Seldon reports that the traditional public opinion polls continually show an overwhelming 80–85 per cent approval rating of the National Health Service. But "*only 13 per cent* of the total sample were prepared to pay higher taxes for better state medical care." This failure of Britons to "put their money where their mouths are" (or even to *say* that they would be willing to do so) held true even for Labour party sympathizers, who would have been expected to be warm supporters of NHS. Only 16 per cent of them said they wanted more spent on the NHS—*and* expressed themselves as willing to pay for this. "Hardly a demonstration of mass support," says Seldon. Nor, as he so eloquently shows, an indication that government taxing and spending policies are in accordance with the true welfare of its citizens.

LOW TAXES AND INFLATION

Whereas Seldon found that government spending was too high for the welfare of the populace, and should be reduced, along with taxes, discussant Walters assumes the level of public expenditure as a given, and argues that taxes should be raised, in order to fully finance government outlays. Otherwise, states Thatcher's economic adviser, inflation will result. As far as this argument is concerned, there is little conflict between the two, each relying on a different basic premise.

When Walters turns his attention to "candidates for the axe," however, he is warmly supportive of Seldon's tax cutting proclivities. Walters spotlights the British Steel Corporation and British Rail as examples of unnecessary subsidies "which have grown explosively and have the potential for vast future calls on the treasury" and points to the Chilean experience in whittling down similar waste as an example to be emulated.

Seldon expresses disappointment, in his reply, that outstanding market-oriented economists, such as Walters, are so unappreciative of the powers of the market pricing system. He insists that the price mechanism would serve a disciplinary function on the ever increasing demand for government services. Thus, there is no *given,* to the present level of public expenditure, as assumed by Walters.

And there is another difficulty with Walters' suggestion of a tax increase so as to meet government spending levels without raising inflation, according to Seldon: "this strategy will flounder on the rock of public resistance," and continually increasing tax avoiding and evasion ("avoision"), leading to a more and more robust hidden economy—where no taxes at all are paid.

SWEDEN

For many years, the Swedish welfare state has been a beacon, an example of socialism "that works," providing progressives in many other countries with a model to be emulated. But now, according to the findings of Professor Charles Stuart, the Swedes themselves are starting to have second thoughts about their own system. The problem is that protracted high levels of government expenditure are invariably accompanied by increasing tax burdens—and the "longer term disincentive effect of high taxes" are beginning to make themselves felt.

Some indications of the crushing impact of the Swedish tax system include the following:

- the 264 per cent tax rate on new stock issues, dividend paid today
- the 213 per cent tax rate on new stock issues, dividend deferred
- a differential of "more than 300 per cent " between the low taxes on housing and consumer durables on the one hand, and the high rates on "corporate durables," on the other
- the high marginal tax rates on labour, which approach the 80 per cent levels
- the surge in the level of "hidden" tax increases, to 103.6 per cent of "non-hidden" tax rises, in the 1970–1977 period
- a tax rate of 233 per cent imposed on real returns to bonds and savings in banks
- a tax of 195 per cent for investments in non-stock companies.

The effects of these punishing tax rates, *higher* than those necessary to maximize tax revenues, have been enormous, according to Stuart. By considering the usual income effect attendant upon a wage change (tax increase), but also an income effect based upon eventual government expenditure of tax revenues, he shows that we may expect disincentive effects on labour supply. That this has not happened to a great degree yet—Stuart attributes to institutional inertia (40 hour work week legislation) and flaws in statistics reporting hours worked, due to the rise of the hidden economy.

But there is evidence showing that the Swedish tax system has reduced the equilibrium number of hours desired work per week (Stuart calculates this as a fall from 40 to 29.5 hours per week). There is the rise of the tax-evading black market, which may involve as much as 10 per cent of the Swedish economy; the widespread desire for a shorter working week, as shown in numerous recent polls; the shift (of some

3.4 per cent of the labour force in 1975–1979) from full-time to part-time work. In addition, there are indications of lower work intensity ("on-the-job leisure"), lowered motivation to move to high salaried jobs, to engage in higher education, and tendencies toward earlier retirement.

In his comment on the Stuart paper, Professor Assar Lindbeck addresses himself to three aspects of the Swedish tax system. First, he supplements Stuart's description by showing just how very redistributive is this system. Lindbeck also focuses on capital taxation. He points out that in combination with inflation, these taxes have had a devastating effect on incentives.

Secondly, our commentator objects to the practice of analyzing the income and substitution effects of tax changes, while ignoring alterations in government expenditures.

And thirdly, while praising Stuart's econometric work as a "worthwhile" and "pioneering" effort, Lindbeck urges caution about the conclusions. He is skeptical about Stuart's explanation that disincentive effects can explain half the decline in the Swedish growth rate in the 1970s, and urges consideration for alternative hypotheses, such as a wage explosion which priced that country's exports out of world markets.

Supplementing his review of Stuart, Lindbeck also offers an extensive analysis of his own on the Swedish tax system. He covers income redistribution, poverty, and the underground economy.

GERMANY

The mystery of declining growth rates in the western democracies in the mid-1970s — and their connection to tax policies — is explored by Hans-Georg Petersen. Concentrating on the case of the Federal Republic of Germany, Professor Petersen starts by studying the impact of taxation on the supply of work. Based on a summary of the empirical literature, he finds little support for the view that higher taxation reduces work effort. However, he sees little prospect that taxes can continue increasing indefinitely without serious repercussions in this regard. For example, according to one authoritative interview survey, 41.8 per cent of surgeons would work fewer hours in response to a 10 per cent income tax increase, while only 3.2 per cent would put forth greater efforts as a result of such a policy. As well, an astounding (and frightening) 73.8 per cent of these pillars of the community indicated they would step up their efforts at tax evasion through either legal or illegal means. Only 13.0 per cent of the tax consultants gave this response, but this does not indicate a greater dedication and allegiance to the principles of tax paying. Rather, it is evidence of the fact that most of these experts in taxation matters are *already* protecting themselves, quite nicely thank you, as well as they possibly can.

With regard to the impact of taxation on saving and investment (another important determinant of the over-all growth rate), Professor Petersen's own empirical (regression) analysis indicates a statistically significant, albeit "weak negative correlation between the growth rate of private household saving and social security taxes." In contrast, he found no link between private savings and taxes on private households.

"FISCAL DRAG"

But the effect of taxes on economic well-being can be measured directly, not only via their incidence on work effort and saving and investment behaviour. And when this is done, Petersen finds evidence of "fiscal drag." According to the West German economist, that country's tax system—especially direct taxes—acts as an anchor, or a "drag" against forward progress.

If the German tax system does not promote economic activity, it does not enhance redistribution of income toward the poor either. Based on the findings of our author, although West Germany is in principle dedicated to redistributionism, the actual practice falls far short of this goal. Direct (income) taxes do redistribute income in this direction, but the effect is very small. In contrast, although the evidence on the impact of indirect (sales) taxes is not as clear, the best indication is that the lower and middle classes pay 7 to 8 per cent, while the highest income bracket pays only 1 to 2 per cent. When both direct and indirect taxes are taken into account, there is little evidence that any redistributional effects at all have taken place.

Based on his findings, Hans-Georg Petersen recommends that:

- tax discrimination against investment in shares of corporate stock be ended
- "excess burdens" for productive assets in general be avoided
- extremely high marginal tax rates be ended since they may well have significant disincentive effects on the supply of effort
- government moderate its revenue demands since punitive taxes—of whatever type—encourage barter and other inefficient economic institutions
- the tax system take account of inflationary pressures through an indexation adjustment scheme
- declines in tax revenues be financed by abolition of many direct government subsidies.

"MORAL HAZARD"

In his formal comment on the Petersen contribution, Professor Herbert Grubel proposes a new methodological departure. Unhappy with the accuracy of the traditional analysis in measuring the effects of taxation and government expenditure on work effort, the Simon Fraser economist focuses attention on "moral hazard." According to this concept, programs such as unemployment insurance can actually promote unemployment itself, by making it economically more attractive. To the extent that this "hazard" is in operation, it adds to the actual decrease in work effort. Likewise, increased retirement benefits can retard savings—the private self-provision for old age. Government health-care schemes induce people to allocate a greater proportion of their incomes to medical treatment than they would otherwise have done.

All these effects reduce the allocational efficiency of an economy. But because they are so difficult to capture through statistical techniques, Grubel fears that the actual situation in the economy may well be worse than reported by Petersen; that a more accurate assessment would show even more reduction of work effort and efficiency loss. As well, one would have to take account of the effect of progressive taxation on altering the employment mix in favour of low-skilled and civil service occupations, at the cost of the more risky—but ultimately more productive—entrepreneurial positions.

ITALY

Sergio Ricossa's report on the Italian tax system is one of gloom and doom, with the prospect of even worse in the offing.

According to the Italian economist, the main problem with the system is the voraciousness of the tax collectors. Explicit taxation does not show this, placing Italy only eleventh highest of the western democracies in terms of collections, which are well below 40 per cent of GDP. But when implicit taxes, such as Italy's widespread use of rent control legislation is considered, contends Ricossa, the true tax burden is extreme.

However poorly constructed the tax system, Italy's raging inflation, barrelling along at a 15 to 20 per cent annual rate, exacerbates matters. For the progressive income tax is not indexed, and thus nudges people into higher tax brackets—even if their real incomes have not risen. Worse, taxes on savings apply even to negative real returns. Although unfair to the individuals concerned, this does not seem to have decimated the Italians' savings rate, because of very strongly embedded habits, especially in the older generations.

But the Italian budget deficit is another matter. Government borrowing reached 31 per cent of the national budget, and 16 per cent of GDP. A record surpassed by few other countries, this deficit has had serious repercussions on the Italian economy. The crowding out of private capital investment, the rise of interest rates, expansionary monetary policy (which only fuels the entire process) have all been the result. And along with high marginal income tax rates, this policy has unleashed upon Italy one of the strongest "underground" economies in the world.

The redistribution of income from rich to poor has been the popular justification for these policies on the part of the Italian politicians. But the actual results in this direction have been minimal, reports Ricossa, and may have been swamped by programs which favour the rich, such as subsidies for arts and culture, and bailouts of large corporations.

This attack on the private sector, and continual aggrandizement of the public sector, cannot long endure without a fundamental change in Italian institutions. Under present trends, Professor Ricossa foresees the replacement of a mixed economy by one featuring coercive central control by the state—with serious loss of economic efficiency and civil liberties.

AN INTIMATE CONNECTION

Zane Spindler is broadly supportive of Ricossa's findings. The Canadian economist also stresses the dangers of public sector deficits, bracket creep, excessive taxation, and crowding out the private marketplace. He points to the vicious circle of deficits, inflation, indexation, transfers, tax evasion, increased taxation, and further deficits.

Spindler also focuses on the intimate connection between the tax and expenditure systems. Given a government budget constraint, deficits may be reduced by *either* tax increases *or* expenditure *reductions;* a lesson ignored by the Italian authorities.

He sees an important and positive role for the underground economy—as a corrective for the fiscal irresponsibility perpetrated by the Italian fiscal system. However, due to increased transaction costs, the entire system, even with the hidden economy, can never be as efficient as it would have been in the absence of government failure in fiscal matters.

JAPAN

The Japanese economy, and the Japanese "economic miracle," have long been the envy of the rest of the world. The spirit of cooperation which exists between labour and management in this country, and the resulting increases in productivity levels have set a standard admired by other industrial nations. Under these conditions, every aspect of the Japanese economy needs to be subjected to complete and exhaustive analysis.

Given the situation, Professor Kaizuka's examination of the

Japanese tax system – and its relation to economic progress – comes as a particularly welcome addition to the present volume. Our author begins by dividing the recent economic history of his country into two epochs. In the pre-OPEC oil crisis decade (1965–1974), the Japanese economy registered an astounding 9.3 per cent average annual growth in real GNP. In the following five-year period, the rate of increase fell to 4.1 per cent, still an enviable record for western industrialized democracies. Apart from the impact of burgeoning fuel prices on an energy-short island community, Kaizuka cites a too-restrictive monetary policy as the causal element.

Also of great importance have been the huge budget deficits of the 1970s. Not only high by Japanese standards, they were roughly *double* the deficits, on a *per capita* basis, chalked up by the U.S., U.K., West Germany, and France during this decade. Professor Kaizuka attributes these deficits, in substantial part, to the failure of rising tax revenues to match the pace of even more quickly increased expenditure levels. And this, in turn, may be due to falling tax elasticities (the rate at which tax receipts move in step with rising incomes) which are themselves a product of slower economic growth.

SPECIAL TAX MEASURES

An important feature of the Japanese system is its declining use of special tax incentives. For example, Japan has tightened up on depreciation of acquisition costs of industrial equipment, limited write-offs for inventory losses, curtailed deductions for medical care and abolished separate taxation privileges for interest and dividend income. Professor Kaizuka calculates that tax revenue loss from these measures had fallen from about 11 per cent of the total in the mid-1960s, to below 6 per cent by the beginning of the 1980s.

Japan's introduction of a general sales tax has also been subjected to much analysis. Although justified by some commentators on grounds of horizontal equity, it may owe its birth to "tax illusion": the citizenry feels a lighter burden from the relatively more hidden sales tax than from the more open and blatant income tax.

LIMITED ROLE FOR GOVERNMENT

In his comment on the Kaizuka paper, Professor Don Daly draws our attention to a crucially important but little appreciated fact: Japan has the lowest ratio of taxes and government expenditures to GNP of all the countries studied in this volume and relatively speaking, the highest deficit. To the extent that the success of the Japanese economy is based on its fiscal policy, this would seem to indicate that the level of government activity is far more important than the presence or absence of a deficit. The implication is clear. Fiscal responsibility could better be attained through a low government budget even if accompanied by a budget deficit, than with a large scale public sector involvement, even if there were no tax revenue short-fall. When coupled with a policy of low and falling tariff and non-tariff barriers to trade, the Japanese economic "miracle" may be attributed to a policy of limited government.

As to the recent relative decline in Japanese rates of economic growth, Professor Daly rejects the Keynesian explanation, and instead adopts that of monetarism – supply-side models. On a more technical level, Daly takes issue with Kaizuka's analysis of falling individual income tax elasticities. Daly attributes this phenomenon to indexation and tax exemptions, and rejects Kaizuka's explanation in terms of a slower growth rate in money income.

AN AUSTRALIAN PERSPECTIVE

Professor Malcolm R. Fisher begins his consummate and thorough treatment of the Australian tax system with a presentation of the classical liberal position on political economy, with its emphasis on free enterprise, limited government, individual initiative and private property. He argues that this discussion is not tangential to taxes; that on the contrary an understanding of the proper size and scope of the public sector is crucial for an understanding of an optimal taxing and spending policy.

In the event, the Australian tax system is characterized by a heavy reliance on income taxes. Such taxes, levied on individuals and corporations, account for over half of total revenues taken in by government. The seven states greatly rely on these imposts indirectly, through Commonwealth grants. And local governments rely mainly on rates levied on property, plus grants from state and federal authorities. As well, there are numerous indirect levies, such as custom and excise duties, and taxes on liquor, gambling, stamps, and motor vehicles. But apart from exise duties (14.2 per cent), none of these sub-categories account for more than 6 per cent of the total.

Professor Fisher informs us that in the post-war period, the shift toward personal income taxes has been accentuated. Capital taxes have virtually disappeared from the Australian system. Taxation as a percentage of GDP has hovered just under the 30 per cent level, while in the decade of the 1970s, outlays of all public authorities – federal, state, and local – have risen from just over 30 per cent to just under 40 per cent.

There have been several studies of over-all incidence in Australia, treating all taxes and subsidies together. The conclusions which emerge are as follows:

- the income tax is the most progressive of the taxes, indeed really the only one
- indirect federal taxes are regressive; state and local taxes are especially so
- excise taxes fall most heavily on the middle income ranges.

Although the actual statistics are as difficult to estimate as in the size of the underground economy itself, it would appear that tax evasion and avoidance amounts to some 8 per cent of total collections. But this may be an underestimate, given an unofficial treasury report which put the cost of such activities at $3 billion.

VERTICAL IMBALANCE

Professor Thomas J. Courchene, in his comment on the Fisher paper, focuses attention on the financial relations between the different levels of government. He sees in the Australian situation a vertical imbalance, in that the central government collected 80 per cent of total tax revenues, while spending 32 per cent. The gap was bridged by a set of intergovernmental grants: $9.6 billion of the states' total revenues of $14.5 billion is given them by the Commonwealth.

But unless that level of government which spends the money is also responsible for raising it, Courchene sees a difficulty. Those who spend without much natural limit will have little incentive to place any ceilings on their own expenditures. As a result, such spending will increase by leaps and bounds—a charge that applies to Canada and Sweden as well as Australia. And if these federal to state grants are restricted by numerous limitations and conditions, this can effectively emasculate federalism. For without any serious initiative on the junior level, the states become mere appendages of the more senior level of government.

Courchene strikingly illustrates the principle with a non-tax example from Canada. Quebec has long had the highest minimum wage level of all the provinces, but was able to continue down this path without being forced to pay the costs. For the additional unemployment created by this foolhardy policy was met through greater equalization payments, increased unemployment insurance transfers, and stepped-up welfare benefits—all courtesy of the federal government. (Actually, of course, these payments came from a long-suffering citizenry, not from federal bureaucrats, but that is another story.) In this way Quebec was able to escape the worst result of its folly—and thus had little incentive to reconsider.

We would be remiss if in this introductory chapter we failed to mention the informal discussions which took place after the presentation of each paper and comment. These sessions were always thought-provoking, useful and informative. At times they were positively scintillating. They were an occasion upon which this group of world class public finance economists and theoreticians could relax, ponder the issues raised, and engage each other in heady, humorous and intellectual debate. In these sessions, perhaps as much as in the formal papers and comments themselves, is to be found the "spirit" of this Vancouver Tax Symposium. They will repay close study, and the highlights thereof can be found in this volume at the end of each forthcoming chapter.

CHAPTER 2

MACROECONOMICS AND THE UNOBSERVED SECTOR

Edgar L. Feige*

A growing number of macroeconomists sense that there is something terribly amiss with the state of the art of our profession.[1] The predictions of traditional macroeconomic theories are largely inconsistent with the combination of economic symptoms which many of the world's most developed economies appear to be experiencing. Official government statistics reveal that the past decade has been characterized by declining rates of growth in real output and productivity, accompanied by levels of unemployment which had been thought to be fatal to any government presiding over them. Yet at the very time when these classical symptoms of depression appear, inflation rates soar. It is this peculiar and conceptually inconsistent set of symptoms of economic malaise (now known as "stagflation") which baffles economists and policy makers alike. Stagflation is an economic disease whose etiology remains obscure, whose consequences disrupt the social fabric and whose cures remain to be discovered.

Other cracks are becoming apparent in the economist's professional veneer. Macroeconometric models produce forecasts of real growth and inflation that are so unreliable that they can no longer be regarded as an adequate basis for industrial or government planning. Careful studies of productivity declines conclude that they remain "a mystery."[2] Inflation remains stubborn in the face of monetary stringency and receding energy prices. Lemming-like rushes toward the unchartered seas of "supply side" economics have produced massive fiscal deficits and growth inhibiting interest rates. In short, we are witnessing a widening gap between the predictions of our traditional theories and the measured observations of economic activity. This cleavage has precipitated a rash of *ad hoc* efforts to patch up our leaky theories, but to date all too little attention has been paid to the jestful adage, "If the facts don't fit the theory, *check the facts.*"

*Research support from the Ford Foundation and the A. P. Sloan Foundations is gratefully acknowledged. This research was undertaken at the Netherlands Institute for Advanced Studies.

I. THE UNOBSERVED INCOME HYPOTHESIS

In the hope of stimulating an alternative direction for inquiry into our perceived economic maladies, I entertain the implications of the "unobserved income hypothesis." Most simply stated, the hypothesis suggests that systematic biases, unwittingly introduced into our official data bases, distort our perceptions of economic realities. The bias introduced into our official information system may be directly caused by a large and growing sector of economic activity which eludes governmental observation.

This unobserved sector (or as some may prefer, unmeasured, underground, untaxed, unofficial, or hidden sector) includes all economic activity which because of accounting conventions, non-reporting or underreporting, escapes the social measurement apparatus, most notably the GNP system of accounts. The observed sector consists of governmental and private economic activities which are captured by our national income accounting framework.

COMPONENTS OF THE UNOBSERVED ECONOMY

The unobserved sector consists of two components: a market sector that utilizes money as a medium of exchange in the production and distribution of goods and services; and, a non-monetary sector in which real goods and services are produced but are either directly consumed by the producing unit (*e.g.*, the farm, the household) or are informally exchanged through barter.

The monetary part of the unobserved sector includes the output of illegal production of goods and services, since these are, by accounting conventions, often excluded from the standard accounts. Much more significantly, this sector also comprises a wide range of legitimate income-producing activities, which for a variety of reasons, are not appropriately captured in the social accounting mechanism. Such activities include all incomes that are earned but are either not reported or underreported to the national income accountants.The motives for such non-reporting or misreporting are alleged to include tax evasion, regulatory evasion, avoidance of costs of compliance, or simply mistrust of government. Ultimately, the accuracy and coverage of any social accounting system, regardless of the ingenuity of its design, will depend upon the cooperation and honesty of the reporting units. Whether such cooperation is eroded by economic incentives inadvertently introduced in any system of governance, or by a growing alienation from the articulated legal and social values of a society, the first causality of reduced compliance is the social data base.

The non-monetary component of the unobserved sector consists of those vital economic activities of households, firms, and voluntary institutions which produce real outputs that are bartered. They are thus not fully reflected in conventional income accounts. Examples would include child-care, cooking, cleaning, education, owner-occupied rental income, "do it yourself" activities, and consumption services provided by business.[3]

STAGES OF GROWTH IN THE UNOBSERVED SECTOR

What kind of relationship might we expect to exist between the observed and unobserved sectors of the economy during different stages of economic development?

Abstracting for the moment from the intrusions of technological discoveries, natural or political calamities such as famines or wars, and business cycles, we can consider an economy whose total economic output grows at some constant rate. At the primitive stages of societal development all economic activity is of a subsistence type, being neither observed, nor monetized. Once the remarkable social contrivances of organized markets and a monetary medium of exchange are introduced, resources will shift from the non-monetary to the monetary sector. If we then introduce the social science observer, whose task is to measure the monetarized output of the "legal" sector of the economy, we will initially observe a growth rate far in excess of the growth rate of the entire economy. If we interpret this expansion as reflecting the true rate of growth of all economic activity, we will be sorely misled. Indeed, this first stage of societal observation will be characterized by an increasing ratio of observed to total output simply as a result of the enlargement and refinement of the measurement system itself.

The second stage of economic observation will be characterized by a roughly proportionate relationship between the observed sector and the total economic activity. We might label this stage the "golden age of economics," since it is during this phase that well conceived economic theories and models which are themselves rooted in the empirical observation of the period will have the highest chance of explaining and predicting economic behaviour accurately. In essence, predictions and explanations of economic events will be uncontaminated by the effects of significant shifts between observed and unobserved economic activity. As long as the observed sector of the economy remains roughly proportional to total economic activity, government policies based on at least proportionately accurate information signals have the highest chance of achieving stabilization goals. Unfortunately, it is highly unlikely that the economist will be permitted to dwell indefinitely in this intellectual Garden of Eden.

As economic and political institutions grow more complex, they create incentives to shift resources away from the sphere of observed economic activity. Rising taxation, increased regulation and higher costs of compliance with the societal measurement apparatus lead both to underreporting and to real shifts of resources into the unobserved sector of the economy. Non-market "do it yourself" activity provides a haven from both taxation and regulation in the non-monetary sector, and underreporting or non-reporting of output and income can give rise to a monetarized sector which escapes the purview of the national income accountant. If such an erosion in the fundamental data base leads to the misguided perception of economic hardship, governmental actions, however well intentioned, will become procyclical. As government itself is increasingly perceived to be inadequate in fulfilling its avowed societal responsibilities, this in turn leads to an increased mistrust of government and increased alienation from legitimately constituted authority. Such political effects further serve to erode the measurement apparatus and reinforce the decline in the ratio of observed to total output.

CONVENTIONAL MACROECONOMICS

Conventional Keynesian and post-Keynesian analysis sought to explain macroeconomic phenomena in terms of shifts between the government and private components of the observed sector. The unobserved income hypothesis suggests that a more comprehensive *total income* framework is required; one which focuses on shifts between the observed and unobserved sectors. Unfortunately, the statistics on the observed sector have become so closely identified with what we perceive to be economic reality, that we have blindly accepted the medium of observation as the substance of economic activity.

It is the official statistics which generate the questions economists feel compelled to answer. The same statistics are the fodder for our forecasting industry, our empirical tests and our policy prescriptions. Any systematic discrepancy between our measures of economic activity, and actual economic activity, will generate misguided questions and produce erroneous answers. The unobserved income hypothesis suggests that as a result of higher taxes, increased regulation and eroded confidence in governmental authority, individuals and firms have resorted to legal and illegal means of hiding a growing proportion of their total economic activity from governmental observers.

OBSERVER-SUBJECT FEEDBACK

This development is viewed as a consequence of a more general principle which is the social science analogue of the Heisenberg Principle in physics. Heisenberg recognized that measurements of physical phenomena would themselves be affected by the very process of observation. In the social sciences, the phenomenon being studied is human behaviour involving cognition and volition, rather than particles, unconscious of the presence of the observer. It is therefore not surprising that measurements of human behaviour, indeed the behaviour itself, will be strongly and systematically affected by the process of observation. When the observer is an agency of a government and the subject is liable to governmental taxation and regulation, the presence of the observer will induce distortions in the responses of the subject. When biased subject responses are aggregated to form summary economic indicators, which in turn become basic informational inputs for economic and political decisions, the system itself becomes contaminated and less stable. Rational decision makers utilizing distorted information, will undertake action which transforms initial statistical illusions into real economic maladies. Hence, *observer-subject feedback*.[4]

IMPLICATIONS OF THE UNOBSERVED INCOME HYPOTHESIS

If it is the case that many highly developed economies have passed unknowingly into an era where the unobserved sectors of the economy are expanding relative to the observed sectors, what are the implications that follow? First and foremost, our conventional economic indicators will give a more and more distorted picture of the true state of economic affairs. Official statistics will reveal a slowing rate of real output even when the total economy is growing at its normal pace. Official price statistics in centrally planned economies will grossly *understate* the true price level, whereas market oriented economies will produce official price figures that *overstate* both the actual level and rate of change in prices. If the unobserved sector grows rapidly, with employees in the observed sector searching for secondary, untaxed jobs or "off the books" work, official productivity measures will appear to decline as output is understated more rapidly than inputs are reduced.

Under social welfare systems with liberal unemployment benefits, official unemployment statistics may become temporarily bloated as people "out of work" find alternative jobs in the unobserved sector. Macroeconomic forecasts would tend to become systematically biased, overpredicting real growth rates of output and underestimating inflation. Finally, and perhaps most significantly, citizens and policy makers will respond systematically to false economic signals thus converting the perception of malaise into the reality of serious economic distress.

II. EMPIRICAL EVIDENCE ON THE SIZE AND GROWTH OF THE UNOBSERVED SECTOR

Since these conjectures correspond closely with the economic realities experienced by many developed economies, it seems important to examine the empirical hypothesis on which they are founded. We must test the view that in recent times there has been a dramatic growth in the unobserved sectors of the economy relative to the observed sectors.

It is obvious that any attempt to measure social phenomenon whose *raison d'etre* is to defy observation is fraught with complex conceptual and empirical difficulties. All estimates are likely to contain substantial errors.

THE SOURCES OF INFORMATION

Different sources of information are available to the researcher and each has an important role in the analysis. First, there is the large and suggestive body of anecdotal information, casually collected and not easy to analyze by the systematic procedures of modern quantitative methods. Such information is, however, highly relevant as a qualitative guide to both the frequency and nature of the phenomenon under investigation and can illuminate its manifestations in both individual and institutional behaviours. It provides a necessary starting point for any serious inquiry insofar as it serves to raise many key questions. It points the research in specific directions concerning both the sources and processes involved in unobserved economic activities.

More systematic information on unobserved activities is available from micro-data sources such as tax return audits, survey questionnaires and unemployment records. A recent Internal Revenue study examined the extent of underreporting of income on individual income tax returns by examining in detail a sample of 50,000 returns.[5] The IRS concluded that in 1976, $100–135 billion was underreported, representing between 9.3 and 12.6 per cent of total income reported. This official government study made no effort to include underreporting on corporation income taxes, and utilized various methods and assumptions which have led critics to argue that the report significantly underestimated the actual extent of unreported income. Yet, if one takes the IRS's low estimate at face value, it suggests that unreported income in the United States in 1976 amounted to almost 50 per cent of the total officially reported GNP of Canada.

Survey methods have also been employed to collect information on the extent of tax evasion. A Taxpayer Opinion Survey also conducted by the IRS revealed that at least 26 per cent of respondents admitted to purposely understating their tax liability, and a similar study conducted in Oregon concluded that one in four persons admitted that they engaged in income tax evasion.[5] While it is difficult to estimate the total amount of underreporting of income from such surveys, they do suggest that tax evasion is a widespread phenomenon. This conclusion is strengthened by the fact that survey respondents have direct incentives for understatement. Moreover, non-response rates on surveys often approach 30 per cent, and it is highly probable that non-respondents are a self-selected group with the most to hide. Survey evidence therefore is likely to lead to substantial underestimates. Given the costs of such direct measurement procedures and the absence of historically comparable data, these methods are unlikely to reveal information on the crucial question, "What is the rate of growth of unobserved activity?"

The final method for obtaining evidence on the unobserved sector relies upon macroeconomic data which are collected for reasons totally unrelated to the measurement of unobserved activities. Such an "indirect" approach to measurement has the major advantage that the data utilized in the analysis are uncontaminated by the phenomenon we are attempting to measure. Reliance on macroeconomic data has the added advantage that it permits not only estimates of the magnitude of unobserved monetary activity, but also allows temporal measurements of the growth of unobserved activity at relatively low cost.

MACRO-MEASURES

In an earlier report in *Challenge* magazine,[7] I sketched out a macro-measurement method capable of revealing both the size and growth rate of the monetarized unobserved sector of the economy. The method relies on the proposition that one can, in principle, derive fairly accurate measures of the total volume of monetary transactions in any society, given knowledge of the quantity of the medium of exchange, and knowledge of the speed (or velocity) with which the medium of exchange circulates within the economic system.

The volume of monetary transactions directly gives rise to both observed and unobserved income in the monetary sector. It is therefore only necessary to postulate the relationship between transactions and the income produced by those transactions in order to derive an indirect estimate of the proportion of total income thus produced which goes unobserved.

A key assumption utilized in the analysis is that the volume of transactions is roughly proportionate to the income produced by those transactions. This assumption has long been utilized by monetary economists and appears prominently in the works of Fisher, Keynes, and modern day monetarists. Indeed, this assumption is implicit in most empirical studies of the demand for money, and has gone essentially unchallenged for over one hundred years.

If transactions are indeed roughly proportional to total income, and if transactions can be measured accurately, while income is subject to the types of underreporting discussed earlier, then any growth in unobserved monetary income will be revealed by a rising ratio of transactions to measured income. The conceptual basis for this measurement procedure is thus straightforward. Its empirical application, on the other hand, requires considerable finesse since it depends heavily on institutional details often overlooked in empirical macro-studies.

Total transactions in a society can be usefully decomposed into those transactions associated with the production of final output (final plus intermediate transactions); transactions in which money is exchanged for existing assets, whether real or financial; and direct transfer payments. Given the possibilities of financial innovations that might accelerate purely financial transactions and of changing patterns of transfer payments, it is perhaps most reasonable to limit the assumption of proportionality between transactions and income to a transaction concept that nets out, to whatever extent possible, major financial transactions and transfers.

What remains are largely transactions undertaken in the production of total final output – *i.e.*, observed plus unobserved. Even here, the degree of integration or disintegration of the economy is likely to affect the ratio of adjusted transactions to income. The obvious growth of the service sector – which is a highly integrated sector – would lead to the prediction that the ratio of adjusted transactions to income should decline. Under these circumstances, the assumption of a constant ratio of adjusted transactions to income must be regarded as a conservative one, that is, leading to a downward-biased estimate of monetary unobserved income.

THE RESEARCH FINDINGS

The foregoing transactions method applied to both the economies of the United States and the United Kingdom, yielded preliminary estimates which are recorded in Figure 2.1. The major findings from these calculations are that the monetary unobserved sector is remarkably large in both countries, averaging about 15 per cent of GNP for the U.K. during the 1970s, and ranging between 16 and 27 per cent for the U.S. during the same period.[8] Comparable estimates undertaken for Canada by Smith and Mirus reveal an unobserved monetary sector between 19 and 22 per cent.[9] In all three countries, there was a remarkable growth in the absolute magnitude of the unobserved sector during the decade of the 1970s.

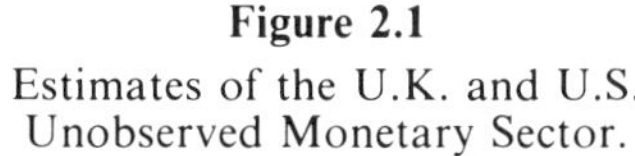

Figure 2.1
Estimates of the U.K. and U.S.
Unobserved Monetary Sector.

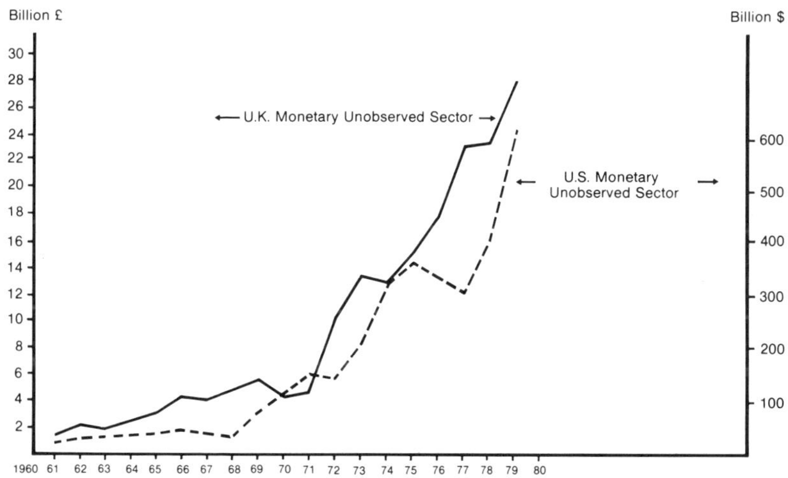

Source: Feige, Edgar L. "The U.K.'s Unobserved Economy" *Journal of Economic Affairs, Vol.1, No.4, July 1981.*

The former neglect of the unobserved sector was rooted in the belief that it was of relatively small magnitude and that it remained a fairly constant fraction of observed income. The three estimates cited above suggest that both of these former views require careful re-examination. For the estimates of the unobserved sector, while imprecise, suggest that the unobserved sector may be of major proportions and appears to have grown dramatically.

Given the inherent complexity of any effort to measure a phenomenon which seeks to defy description, these surprising preliminary results will hopefully stimulate a constructive discussion of means to improve the measurement procedures.

It would be unfortunate, however, if professional discussions were limited to that issue, since the major problem at hand is to achieve a better understanding of the complex macroeconomic morass in which we find ourselves. If the growth of the unobserved sector warrants the attention I believe it does, we must go further and inquire whether our current estimates of the phenomenon shed any light on the economic dilemmas of our times. Current and future estimates must be evaluated as well in terms of their ability to explain our current economic situation better than competing alternatives. While a rigorous testing of the full implications of the unobserved sector is beyond the scope of this paper, I present some preliminary evidence that is regarded as highly promising, though by no means definitive.

III. PRELIMINARY TESTS

STAGFLATION AND UNOBSERVED ACTIVITY

One of the important consequences of a growing monetary unobserved sector is that it may impart an upward bias to measured rates of inflation and measured rates of unemployment. It is therefore interesting to examine the relationship between year-to-year changes in a stagflation index (defined as the sum of the unemployment rate and the inflation rate) and the temporal estimates of the relative magnitude of the monetary unobserved sector.

Since stagflation is a complex phenomenon undoubtedly affected by a myriad of factors, such a simple relationship should not be given a causative interpretation. Nonetheless, it serves as a descriptive indicator of the potential promise of the hypothesis under consideration. When the unobserved monetary sector remains a fixed proportion of the observed sector, neither observed inflation rates nor observed unemployment rates will be affected. However, when the unobserved monetary sector rises relative to the observed sector we would expect such a resource shift to be associated with higher observed inflation rates and unemployment.

Prices in the unobserved sector may be as much as 20–40 per cent lower than in the observed sector, and such relative price differentials are likely to induce changes in consumption patterns toward the consumption of goods and services produced by the unobserved sector. The Consumer Price Index, a fixed weight index, can take no account of these changes in consumption patterns, and will therefore tend systematically to overstate the true price level for the entire economy.

Moreover, when the unobserved sector is rapidly growing and creating temporary disequilibria in observed markets, the supply of goods and services in the observed sector is likely to fall faster than the demand for these goods and services, thus temporarily forcing observed prices even higher. Many income payments are indexed to the CPI. Individuals base expectations of future inflation on published rates of current and past inflation. Therefore, even the short-term illusion of a burst of inflation, can readily induce behaviour that will produce the *reality* of future inflation.

Measured unemployment rates are also expected to be temporarily increased by shifts of resources into the unobserved sector. Workers finding employment opportunities in the unobserved sector are likely not to report them, and at least temporarily enjoy the benefits of unemployment insurance. Higher observed unemployment rates trigger both automatic and discretionary increases in government expenditures, which must be financed either by increases in the money supply or by higher taxes. The first policy response adds directly to further inflation; the second adds to it indirectly, by encouraging still more resources to escape to the unobserved sector, thereby accelerating the dynamically unstable stagflation.

In short, we would expect to find a positive relationship between changes in the stagflation index and measures of the relative growth and acceleration of the monetary unobserved sector.

Preliminary regression analysis reveals precisely such a relationship for the U.S. During the period 1953–1976, estimates of the relative growth and acceleration of the monetary unobserved sector "explain" 72 per cent of the yearly changes in the stagflation index. For the most recent period, 1970–1976, which encompasses the major oil "supply shock," 93 per cent of the stagflation variation is accounted for, even after energy prices are eliminated from the inflation series.

CAVEATS

While these findings are promising, they must not be misinterpreted. The evidence for the 1970s is based on very few observations, and must therefore be regarded with caution. Moreover, other variables which could directly influence the inflation series may be correlated with the measure of the unobserved sector, and thus its effect may be overstated. In particular, the strong relationship between the estimate of the unobserved sector and the rate of inflation might alternatively reflect a correct specification of monetary demand pressures on the observed economy.

Current "monetarist" explanations of inflation are in my view inadequate, since they focus solely on expansions in the money supply. They fail to take proper account of the medium of exchange functions of money. This is reflected not only in changes in the outstanding stock of money, but perhaps more importantly, by changes in the intensity of money use, that is, by increases in transaction velocity.

Since the measures of the unobserved sector incorporate estimates of transaction velocity increases, these may be partly responsible for the strong observed statistical relationship, particularly with inflation. It is not presently possible to distinguish between these two complementary hypotheses. These statistical results should not, therefore, be interpreted as cause-effect relationships. They simply describe a correspondence which is at least consistent with the maintained hypothesis.

PRODUCTIVITY

A stronger set of tests of measures of the monetary unobserved sector involves explanation of hitherto troublesome macroeconomic phenomena *after* conventional analysis has been brought to bear on the problems. One of the most puzzling macroeconomic issues of recent times has been the dramatic decline in observed rates of productivity growth. This is true not only in the United States, but also in other developed economies.

Edward Denison recently concluded his exhaustive search for an explanation of declining productivity in the United States with the candid admission, "What happened is, to be blunt, a mystery."[10] Denison's Brookings study explored seventeen reasons for the slowdown in productivity. He dismissed several of these suggested explanations, expressed skepticism about others, and found that even those he considered correct explained only a small fraction of the slowdown.

His residual series of unexplained variation in productivity, offers a tough nut to crack by any standard, since conventional explanations have been included, yet found wanting. The Unobserved Income Hypothesis(UIH) suggests that Denison's residual might be partially explained by the relative growth of the unobserved sector. As the unobserved sector grows, either as a result of underreporting of output in the observed sector or as a result of gradual shifts of resources into unobserved activities, measured productivity indices tend to decline.

Growth of the unobserved sector is likely to have a complex effect on factor inputs as well. Workers who utilize normal working time either to search for jobs in the unobserved sector, or actually to work in the unobserved sector, are likely to reduce their effectiveness in their normal employment. Anecdotal evidence suggests that firms may begin to underreport income for tax purposes, but when their profit picture becomes too gloomy, they often follow up by taking workers off the books so that their input-output relationship does not become too suspect. This pattern will eventually lead to practices of false invoicing that distort yet another aspect of the official data base.

In order to test this conjecture, I estimated regressions of the percentage changes in Denison's productivity residual on the relative level and growth of the monetary unobserved sector. For the period 1953–1976, the monetary unobserved sector explains 28 per cent of the year-to-year percentage changes in the productivity residual. The same measures explain 65 per cent of the residual variation during the crucial decade of the 1970s when the problem became acute.

OUTPUT LOSSES

From Denison's data, it is also possible to compute the percentage loss of potential output in the U.S. economy on a year-to-year basis. The

UIH predicts that a growing unobserved sector would be positively associated with the perception of a greater loss of potential output. The preliminary results confirm this conjecture. They explain 53 per cent of the loss in potential output for the period 1953–1976, and 80 per cent for the decade of the 1970s. These results provide tentative confirmation of both the importance of the unobserved sector, and the fact that its temporal profile has been reasonably captured by the estimation used to measure it.

MACROECONOMIC FORECASTING ERRORS

As an additional test of the Unobserved Income Hypothesis, I examined the explanatory power of my estimates in relation to forecast errors from major macroeconomic models. Large-scale macroeconometric models represent the formal embodiment of our profession's current state of the art. The forecasts from these models are the basic inputs to policy decisions. Given the supposed improvements over the past two decades in our data base, our computer technology, our theory, and our econometric estimation procedures, it would not be unreasonable to expect forecast errors from these models to have become smaller over time. Yet, the contrary has been the case.

Stephen McNees of the Federal Reserve Bank of Boston has chronicled the longest available consistent record of forecast errors for the President's Council of Economic Advisors Model of the United States economy, for the period 1961–1979.[11] The average of forecast errors reveals a systematic pattern of overprediction of real growth in output, and underprediction of the rate of inflation.

If one compares the forecast record of the period (1962–1969) with the forecast errors of the subsequent decade, the estimates reveal an 11 per cent increase in the avarage *overprediction* of real output and a 48 per cent increase in the average *underprediction* of the inflation rate. Analogous data reveal that during the period 1963–1969 the model tended to overpredict the percentage change in the unemployment rate by .74 per cent whereas in the later period the model on average *underpredicted* the percentage change in the unemployment rate by 1.78 per cent.

Thus, contrary to general expectations, not only have the predictions from this model seriously deteriorated during the past decade, but they have displayed a pattern consistent with that predicted by the UIH. Growth of the unobserved economy would lead to a systematic understatement of actual growth in real output and a systematic overstatement of actual inflation rates and unemployment rates. These effects, when ignored by the formulators of our econometric models, would result in forecast errors that are positive for real output changes and negative for inflation and unemployment rates. Moreover, a faster relative growth of the monetary unobserved sector would be expected to produce larger forecast errors.

In order to test this hypothesis more formally, forecast errors from the Council of Economic Advisors Model were regressed against the estimates of the relative growth of the monetary unobserved sector. The regression estimates reveal that the growth of the unobserved sector explains 35 per cent of the forecast error in real output, 46 per cent of the forecast error for the inflation rate, and 40 per cent of the forecast error of the unemployment rate. Each of the regression coefficients has the expected sign and is statistically significant. These findings suggest that the incorporation of the effects of the unobserved sector holds considerable promise for the improvement of macroeconomic forecasts. Policy decisions based on information that is free of the systematic biases resulting from the neglect of the unobserved sector, are thus likely to be improved.

The foregoing tests suggest that further study of the implications of the unobserved sector is likely to produce at least partial explanations of the paradoxes of stagflation, productivity slowdown, and macroeconomic forecast errors. By expanding the domain of study to the unobserved sector, we may yet be in a position to resuscitate traditional theory by simply generalizing its applicability to total economic activity including *both* observed and unobserved sectors.

IV. AN ALTERNATIVE PERSPECTIVE ON ECONOMIC MALAISE

I have attempted to present as simply as possible an overview of the present state of malaise that appears to afflict not only the world's developed economies, but also the economics profession itself. Our profession deems the economic patient to be sick on the basis of symptoms it measures with the thermometer of official government statistics. The readings are indeed ominous. Price indices are rising at accelerating rates, unemployment rates are approaching socially unacceptable levels, and indicators of real economic activity are falling dramatically.

The patient, in fact, appears to be suffering from a combination of symptoms that traditional theory insists cannot coexist. Inflation is a disease of long standing origin, whose causes and consequences economists believed they understood. Depression, too, is a well-known and easily recognized pathology, for which a variety of cures have been found to be successful. It is the simultaneous existence of the symptoms of both inflation and depression that has, however, become ubiquitous.

FIXING THE ECONOMIC THERMOMETER

The simple answer I propose to this puzzle is that the economic patient is much healthier than we imagine; it is the social thermometer that has gone awry. The problem may well lie with omission from our measurements of what I describe as the unobserved sectors of our economies.

Before too much solace is taken from the diagnosis, it is well to remember that the patient believes herself to be sick, and this impression of serious dysfunction is continually reinforced by swarms of academic, government, and journalistic economists mumbling "crisis" at her bedside. The continued reinforcement of the perception of malaise and the misguided administration of a variety of potent medications may yet result in the patient's total collapse. The repeated Cassandric prophesy may well become self-fulfilling.

What is now required is a serious re-evaluation of the patient's condition, taking direct account of the failures in our measurement apparatus, perhaps a more circumspect application of remedies, and most importantly, the re-establishment of the patient's self-perception of normalcy. This is a tall order. Yet, it is only under such conditions that we can look forward to a more hopeful prognosis.

The suggestion that a significant portion of our present day problems in both East and West is the result of a mere statistical artifact will strike some professionals as preposterous. To those in our economies who suffer the real tragedy of prolonged unemployment and poverty, this perspective may seem a cruel and callous hoax. It is essential, therefore, to make clear that I do not deny the reality of serious economic hardship among important segments of our population. Nor do I advocate the abandonment of governmental policies aimed at alleviating such chronic distress. It is clear, moreover, that we have entered a transitional period of reduced growth resulting from a shift in the balance of economic power in favour of energy exporting nations. Prices of many commonly consumed goods have in reality risen dramatically.

All this notwithstanding, I maintain that the extent and magnitude of these problems have been exaggerated in official statistics and, because economic actors have responded to these false signals, we have seriously exacerbated our difficulties. The economies of the United States and Western Europe, as seen from the perspective of official government statistics, give the impression that they are accelerating toward what I regard as an *avoidable* financial catastrophe. As presently constituted, these economies are inherently dynamically unstable. This instability derives from a fundamental misperception of the true state of economic life, which may be far healthier than is generally understood. Social science, however, teaches us that the mere perception of malaise and crisis is sufficient to produce the reality of crisis. This is why the foregoing conjectures should not be lightly dismissed. Unless perceptions of citizens and policy makers are brought back into conformity with underlying economic realities, we may be condemned to suffer economic and even political crises of serious proportions.

The hypothesis suggests that the growth of the unobserved sector (whether in response to higher rates of taxation, or growing mistrust of government) will produce the initial illusion of higher rates of inflation and unemployment, and the illusion of slower real growth and declining productivity. The perception of slow growth will lead well-intentioned policy makers to overstimulate the economy with misguided macro-policies. The perception of inflation will reinforce these policies' consequences by encouraging current consumption and forcing prices still higher. Indexed wages and social benefits in turn push individuals into higher marginal tax brackets and thus increase the burden of real taxation, which may also be raised by the expansionary efforts of governments to combat the perceived slowdown in growth. But then these effects will stimulate further shifts of resources into the unobserved sectors.

Growing frustration with the apparent inabilities of governments to manage their economies adequately will produce a deterioration in the social and political fabric, which manifests itself in a growing distrust of government. This is turn reduces compliance and honesty in both the tax system and the governmental data collection system, leading to yet further distortions in the basic information system on which our complex society relies. Unfortunately, this process has no automatic self-limiting mechanism. If I am correct, it will continue unabated unless we first recognize its existence—and then redress our information systems and our policies to reverse its debilitating effects.

NOTES

1. "The Crisis in Economic Theory," *The Public Interest*, Special Edition (1980).
2. Denison, E. *Accounting for Slower Economic Growth*, Washington D.C.: The Brookings Institution (1979).
3. National Accounts do attempt to make imputations for several categories of "in-kind income."
4. Feige, E.L. *Observer-Subject Feedback: The Dynamics of the Unobserved Economy*, Leiden University Press (1982).
5. *Estimates of Income Unreported on Individual Tax Returns,* Department of the Treasury, Internal Revenue Service, Publication 1104. September (1979).

6. *A General Taxpayer Opinion Survey*. Office of Planning and Research, Internal Revenue Service, March (1980) and Mason, R. and Calvin L. "A Study of Admitted Income Tax Evasion," *Law and Society Review*, 13:1 (1978).
7. Feige, E.L. "How Big is the Irregular Economy?" *Challenge*, November (1979).
8. Feige, E.L. "A New Perspective on Macro Economic Phenomena: The Theory and Measurement of the Unobserved Sector of the United States Economy," American Economics Association Meetings, Denver, Colorado, August (1980), and "The U.K.'s Unobserved Economy: A Preliminary Assessment," *Journal of Economic Affairs*, 1:4 (1981).
9. Mirus, R. and Smith, R. "Canada's Irregular Economy," *Canadian Public Policy*, 7:3 (1981).
10. Denison, E., op. cit.
11. McNees, S. "An Assessment of the Council of Economic Advisor's Forecasts of 1977," *New England Economic Review*, March-April (1977).

DISCUSSION

Edited by: Walter Block

The comments during the informal discussion of the Feige paper indicated widespread satisfaction with his contribution. Indeed, his presentation was greeted with warm congratulations from the entire assembly, and accorded a tumultuous ovation as well.

One topic of deliberation concerned the inefficiency of the underground economy, relative to that of the open economy. Giersch held that the hidden economy is subject to heavy costs in terms of inefficiency. Fisher supported this view, although he held that people in it are doing quite well, in many cases. Feige maintained that this was shown by, in large part, the sharp rises in the prices of antiques, gold, stamps, furniture, etc., which are part of the wealth effect. "These items are untaxed, the income is untaxed, and they are an obvious informal market in which heterogeneous goods can be exchanged for currency."

An obvious reason for the rise of the underground economy is an increasing distrust of government by the populace. But all countries are not alike in this regard. This theme was touched upon by Giersch, who pointed out the need for further research in Switzerland, Austria and Germany, and by Grubel, who related this phenomena to the acceleration of inflation. Feige heartily supported the call for more intensive study, and pointed out a University of Michigan study of measures of trust in the U.S. government.

Courchene raised a very important question about the policy implications of the underground (tax evading) economy for tax policy: "Suppose the rest of us who haven't taken the plunge into the non-market economy feel people in that sector ought to be sharing our burden of taxes. Have you thought about the changing structure of taxes?"

Feige's reply is worthy of recording, at some length: "There are two points of view about the unobserved sector. One group of people might regard this as—I think Milton Friedman would—a wonderful safety valve. It's a way out of regulation and government pressure. Others, particularly sociologists and political scientists, might regard this as a very dangerous and corrosive force, a force affecting, in a very negative way, the most fundamental institutions of our society. That's a normative issue. I try to avoid this because I don't want to divert attention from the positive analysis. But we could ask, what would be the most effective way of stamping out the underground sector. I don't think reducing taxes marginally is going to do the trick because there is a very complex interaction between the "trust in government" phenomenon and the monetary incentives to enter or leave the underground economy. Therefore, any policy designed to reduce the growth of this sector, or at least reduce it's acceleration, is going to have to be sufficiently broad. It will have to not only provide a new set of monetary incentives to leave that sector, but will also have to be politically imaginative enough to restore a sense of confidence in government. Now how do you do that? One solution might be to move towards a much more comprehensive income tax base, accompanied by a very dramatic cut in taxes.

"The effect of that is lovely. It reaches both of the problems we're talking about. The marginal incentive to go into the unobserved sector is reduced. At the same time, the public can be convinced of the wisdom of moving towards a broadly based comprehensive tax base. This would mean genuine tax reform, a simplification of the system so that people can understand it, and this would give show that the system is equitable and enforceable. That is the only way in which to effect, simultaneously, economic and important political and psychological variables. There may be other methods, but that's the one that appeals to me at this point from a policy point of view."

Smith raised a point about inflation: "I would like to know whether there may not be an overstatement of the effects of what you're talking about on something like increased inflation. It seems to me that the only way you're going to get any increased inflation through this, is in a movement from the observed to the unobserved. The unobserved has a lower price level, so you're getting the shift from a high to a low. But difficulties will arise with pretty close to parallel inflation rates within the observed and unobserved sectors of the economy."

And Feige's answer made an important contribution to our understanding of monetarism, and monetary theory: "Not if the unobserved is accelerating at an accelerating rate because there may be a dynamic effect: It takes longer to set up consumption habits in the unobserved economy. But your fundamental point, I think, is very well taken. I'll give you what I think is not a competing hypothesis but a complimentary one. This involves a fundamental critique of monetarism, as we've known it to date. My technique, after all, for measuring this phenomenon, has relied on what? On changes in the supply of money and changes in the velocity of circulation.

"Going back to Irving Fisher, which is where I believe we belong—I think our focusing on income and money as a store of value, rather than as a medium of exchange, has been a major digression from intellectual truth. I have included estimates of changes in the velocity of money, transactions velocity, not income velocity, in the measurement procedure. It may well be that, implicit in all of this, is a sort of supermonetarist theory. This says that inflation is definitely caused not just by changes in the money supply, but by changes in monetary pressure. This can be broken down into two parts: increases in the money supply and increases in the use to which money is put. There have been major changes in monetary velocities because of financial innovations that totally swamp any stock effects. This indicates how we can reconstruct monetarism. Not by looking at the monetary aggregates, but by starting to construct some serious debt figures which will tell us more about the velocity of demand deposits—and by finding more imaginative ways of getting a handle on the velocity of currency. I suspect that your observation is an appropriate one and I think that the answer to it is that there's an implicit strong monetarist story here—but it's quite different from the one we've been hearing for the last couple of years."

There were several other important discussions which flowed from the Feige paper.

DeVany pointed out that there is something akin to the Heisenberg uncertainty principle at work in economics. "The attempt to measure a particular phenomenon with ever greater accuracy introduces errors in the other measurements in the system. What's happened over time, I think, is that governments, through ever more persistent attempts to raise additional sources of revenue, have monitored the observed economy to an ever intensive degree and that has introduced larger and more systematic errors in the rest of the economy. The attempt to measure one parameter, with ever increasing accuracy, is obviously going to introduce errors into the other ones that we could measure."

He also reported, based on his research, an increase in the time component of costs for medical care (waiting for the doctor), with a consequent diminution in the proportion of money spent on these services.

This was put forth not as competitive with the underground theory hyphothesis, but as consistent with it.

And Grubel and Feige discussed the importance of the markets for marijuana and other illegal drugs, worth an estimated $35 billion in the U.S. But the underground economy is far from limited to these, or other Mafia-related activities. It is far bigger.

CHAPTER 3

THE LIMITS OF TAXATION*

James M. Buchanan

I. INTRODUCTION

The papers in Part Two survey the tax structures of different countries. Although the results differ substantially, country-by-country, the most striking common features are the explosive rates of growth in taxes (and government spending) in the years since World War II, along with the large share of taxes in national income or product. These facts prompt the general question: What are the limits of taxation? How high can taxes go? Are "democratic" electoral controls possible? If not, what about constitutional limits? Can anything be said about how high taxes should be? What sorts of constitutional limits might work? How should these limits be designed and enforced?

It may be useful to recall the struggles between the English crown and Parliament over the "power to tax," and the general sentiment toward taxation that prevailed throughout pre-modern times. Taxes were levied on the people; they were considered to be exactions against persons for the benefit of crown and clergy. As such, taxes were to be feared, opposed, and minimized. This prevailing sentiment or attitude carried over well after the commencement of the period when "the people," through the representative agencies of constitutional democracy, were considered and considered themselves to be ultimate masters of their own political fortunes. Power to topple governments was not equated with power of governments untoppled to do as they pleased. The American Founding Fathers considered themselves to be constructing a government from consent, but they also recognized that restrictions on the powers of governance were required. They sought to constrain government explicitly through a constitution that would act to insure against the imposition of burdensome taxes. The United States was indeed born in a spirit of tax revolt.

What has happened in the relatively short span of two centuries? Where is the 18th and early 19th century wisdom?

---

*I am indebted to my colleague, H. Geoffrey Brennan, for helpful suggestions.

THE DEMOCRATIC FALLACY

We know very little about how ideas change, and about how public attitudes shift. But somewhere between "then" and "now," we lost our bearings. And by "we" I refer to members of the body politic, in the United States, in Canada, in Great Britain, and in most of the Western world. In part, but perhaps only in part, we (including our political philosophers) were caught up in and by "the fallacy of free elections," perhaps the most serious error ever accepted as truth by leaders of opinion. This "electoral fallacy" presumes that governments can be and are effectively controlled as long as politicians and parties submit their records to the voters in periodic elections. Constitutional constraints are deemed sufficient if elections are open and free; if politicians "represent" the people, the level of taxation (and public spending) cannot rise seriously beyond limits desired by the citizenry at large.

The 18th century philosophers and the American Founders knew better. They recognized that "democracy" could work only if government is tightly constrained within constitutional limits. A few citations are illustrative:[1]

> If men were angels, no government would be necessary. If angels were to govern men, neither external nor internal controls would be necessary. In forming a government which is to be administered by men over men, the great difficulty lies in this: you must first enable the government to control the governed; and in the next place oblige it to control itself.
>
> James Madison, *The Federalist, No. 51*

> It is better to keep the wolf from the fold, than to trust to drawing his teeth and claws after he shall have entered.
>
> Thomas Jefferson, *Notes on Virginia*

> In constraining any system of government, and fixing the several checks and controls of the constitution, every man ought to be supposed a knave, and to have no other end, in all his actions, than private interest.
>
> David Hume, *Essays, Moral, Political and Literary*

> No doubt the raising of a very exorbitant tax, as the raising as much in peace as in war, or even the half or even the fifth of the wealth of the nation, would, as well as any gross abuse of power, justify resistance in the people.
>
> Adam Smith, *Lectures on Jurisprudence*

> The interest of the government is to tax heavily; that of the community is to be as little taxed as the necessary expenses of government permit.
>
> J.S. Mill, *Considerations on Representative Government*

> ... the very principle of constitutional government requires it to be assumed that political power will be abused to promote the particular purposes of the holder; not because it is always so, but because such is the natural tendency of things, to guard against which is the especial use of free institutions.
>
> J.S. Mill, *Considerations on Representative Government*

A SHIFT IN ATTITUDES

The attitude expressed in these citations was largely lost to Western consciousness for more than a century. The challenge before us is to reconstruct a modern equivalent. In the leisure of our ivory towers, this challenge has spurred us on, and we can now begin to express some pride in the shift in public attitudes that has been discernible for at least a decade. The electoral fallacy is no longer accepted universally. Government, politics, bureaucracy—these institutions are now seen "warts and all" by many observers. Skeptical views about politics have filtered down to the members of the thinking public. Furthermore, increasing concern is being expressed, in all countries, about the negative consequences of oppressive taxation, as indeed the studies in this book attest.

But is there time for the slowly maturing shift in attitudes to work its will? How can such a turnaround in attitudes be channelled in support of a dismantling of the governmental Leviathan we encounter at every behavioural nook and cranny? The critically important bridge to be crossed is that between the increasingly realistic view about what government is, what it can and cannot do, and the actual translation of these ideas into institutional reality. How can we unscramble the eggs?

II. WHY ARE TAXES SO HIGH, AND HOW MUCH HIGHER CAN THEY GO?

Why are taxes so high? How much higher can they go?

To answer these questions we require a *positive* theory of how government operates, of how taxing and spending decisions are made.[2] Why has government grown so rapidly?

I shall introduce three explanatory approaches or "models," without claiming to exhaust the possible listings. Each of the three models has some explanatory potential.

REDISTRIBUTIONISM

The first broad explanation can be called "redistributionist." It explains observed taxing-spending levels exclusively in democratic electoral terms. The fiscal process is conceived basically as a transfer mechanism, with successful majority coalitions levying taxes for the purpose of transferring incomes to specific groups. In this model of government, there is no breakdown in the democratic electoral process; indeed what we observe is just what might have been predicted to occur under unchecked majoritarian democracy.

There are several variants within the redistributionist model that have been used to explain the accelerating growth of taxation in this century. Professor Sam Peltzman suggests that the transfer process tends to increase as the variance in the pre-tax income distribution is reduced, *i.e.*, as income differences are lessened.[3] Professors Allen Meltzer and Scott Richard, on the other hand, suggest that the transfer potential tends to increase as the median income diverges increasingly from the mean income.[4]

STRUCTURALISM

A second broad category of explanation for the observed high levels of taxation involves analysis of the institutional structure through which political decisions are reached. Of special interest are the possible biases in patterns of outcomes. One familiar bias highlighted is the asymmetry between tax incidence and benefit incidence, as these are translated into pressures on political representatives. Beneficiary groups, recipients of direct transfers or of governmentally-financed programs tend to be concentrated, organized, and capable of exerting influence over elected politicians. By contrast, those who pay taxes tend to be widely dispersed and, indeed, tend to include almost everyone in society. This is due to the fact that taxes are general rather than specific. As a result of the asymmetry, it becomes easier for political decision-makers to expand budgets than to contract them. There is a structural bias toward expanded levels of taxation and spending, and this bias has become increasingly pronounced as governments have invented and discovered new ways of spending.[5]

Within the budget itself, there is a comparable bias toward outlays providing direct benefits to concentrated groups, as opposed to outlays (*e.g.*, national defense) that confer benefits to the entire citizenry.

Other structural biases are perhaps more evident. If governments are allowed to spend, and to finance this spending either by public debt issue or by money creation, the true costs tend to be concealed. In a sense, of course, "taxes" must always be paid when government uses resources, paid either in some future period (under debt financing) or paid via inflation (under money creation). But the deficit-financing instrument allows politicians to generate fiscal illusions that bias decisions toward spending.[6]

Much the same sort of bias exists when the base for taxation allows for growth-related automatic revenue increments. Perhaps the single most powerful explanatory factor for the growth of the United States federal government in this century is the 16th Amendment, adopted in 1913. This allowed the central government to levy income taxes at progressive rates. It gave the government access to a revenue source that, with a given rate structure, generates automatic increases in real tax revenues as the economy grows, either in real or in purely monetary terms. The automatic increases in real tax rates generated by economic growth or by inflation tend to be concealed from the public, allowing the politicians additional revenues in the seeming absence of additional taxes.

MONOPOLIZATION

Both the redistributionist and the structuralist models for explaining the high and increasing levels of taxation and spending are incomplete. They suffer by their exclusive emphasis on demand-side elements in the fiscal process. The redistributionist model operates "as if" all voters come together in a gigantic town meeting during which a majority coalition forms and takes money away from members of the minority. The structuralist model operates in the same way, except that it allows for the expenditure of at least some part of tax revenues on real goods and services that may be beneficial to all voters.

But, of course, politics cannot be described as a gigantic town meeting, even at the level of analytical abstraction allowed to the ivory-tower economist. Even in the most "democratic" of settings, the political-fiscal process involves "demanders," the voters, "purchasing" goods and/or transfers from "suppliers," who make up "government" itself. The active role of government, as an entity separate and apart from the citizenry, must be incorporated into any explanatory model of the taxing-spending process.

Once this elementary point is recognized, supply-side explanatory elements emerge to supplement and possibly to dominate those already suggested above. For any given political jurisdiction, there is, by definition, only one government. The economic-theory analogue is monopoly, and analysis must commence with the potential for exercise of monopoly power rather than with competitive limits. Once the monopoly nature of government is accepted, we need only to look at how a government might try to squeeze out maximum "surplus" (akin to the monopoly profit of a firm) in order to explain many features of what we observe all around us in modern politics.

The monopoly-government model gives us some handles on the question about how high taxes might go. The economist's theory of monopoly can be directly utilized. In this construction, taxes will tend to be increased to that level at which the government's "surplus" of revenues over required or obligated spending is maximized.

MAXIMUM TAX LEVELS

This level of taxation is conceptually determinate once we specify the sources the government is empowered to tax, and the degree to which taxpayers can substitute between taxable and non-taxable sources of income or expenditure. As well, part of total revenues collected must be returned to the citizenry in program benefits and/or transfers. We must therefore also specify the constraints on government that define these pay-out ratios.

Other elements drawn from the economic theory of monopoly may be applied in differing institutional settings. "Democratic" controls over budget size can be allowed to be operative, with the monopoly government acting to influence the conditions of "trade" between the citizenry and the state. This can be accomplished by appropriate agenda manipulation, by tie-in or bundling arrangements within the budget. Legislative majorities can be presented with biased options that generate budgets substantially in excess of those that might be approved in the absence of monopoly power. Such biases in the decision-making process are similar to those discussed under the structuralist models described briefly above. But the difference lies in the fact that, here, the biases are deliberately introduced by the monopoly government for the purpose of exploiting the fiscal potential of the community.

The monopolist model explains the modern growth of taxing and spending levels in terms of the increasing centralization, and hence monopolization, of the governmental sector. Monopoly thrives in the absence of competition, actual or potential, and intra-governmental competition effectively constrains taxing powers when fiscal authority is decentralized. In a federalism, with separate states or provinces possessing independent taxing powers, there are built-in checks on the exercise of monopoly powers. To the extent that the central government assumes larger relative shares in the overall tax-spending mix, monopoly power necessarily increases.

III. THE MODELS COMPARED

There are explanatory-predictive powers in each one of these three models, both in general and in specific detail. Nonetheless, there is one distinctive difference between the *redistributionist* model on the one hand and the *structuralist* and/or *monopolist* models on the other. This is worthy of some emphasis here, and especially with respect to possible controls over levels of taxation.

Both the structuralist and the monopolist models yield "solutions" for levels of taxation and spending (for the relative size of the public or governmental sector in the economy) that are *inefficient* in the economists' usual meaning of this term. This result allows us to say "scientifically," as it were, that the levels of taxation and spending are "too high." And as I shall note below, this result allows very different and important conclusions to be reached concerning prospects for reform or improvement.

By dramatic contrast, the purely redistributionist model does not allow such a "scientific" statement to be made. The equilibrium result in this model, on any variant, defines the marginal trade-off between additional transfers and incentives to generate product. But the result cannot be labelled "inefficient" in the economists' ordinary meaning of this term. To members of the majority coalition, the fiscal process is being utilized efficiently. Only those who find themselves in the exploited minority are dissatisfied. But there is no basis for equating mere dissatisfaction of one group with overall inefficiency.

REFORM

This distinction becomes critically important when the issue of reform is addressed. To those who accept the redistributionist model, "improvement" can only mean some change in the make-up of the majority coalition. The basic political game is necessarily viewed as one of pure conflict, essentially zero-sum. There can be no conception of generally agreed-on changes that might be expected to lead to improvement in the positions of *all* groups in the economy. Applied to levels of taxation, "improvement" for the exploited minority can only take the form of "defeating" the now-dominant majority, through either electoral victory or through revolution. Another way of putting this is to say that there is no genuinely "constitutional" avenue for reform that is offered by the redistributionist model.

For both the structuralist and the monopolist models, in contrast, such a "constitutional" opportunity for tax reform exists, necessarily. In labelling existing taxes "too high," and "inefficient," the analyst is indirectly demonstrating that changes can be made in such a way as to yield improvements for the positions of *all* groups in society, poor, middle, and rich alike. The observed exploitative levels of taxation can be reduced to the benefit of *all* voters-taxpayers-beneficiaries. Consensus can be established on genuinely constitutional changes that will reduce levels of spending and taxes, and, more significantly, will keep rates of growth in such aggregates within defined constraints or limits. To use game-theoretic terminology, both the structuralist and the monopolist models of explanation diagnose the observed fiscal setting as one variety of the n-person prisoners' dilemma. There exists hope for genuine change from political consensus; revolution does not offer the only avenue of radical reform.

IV. HOW HIGH SHOULD TAXES BE?

Those who use the redistributionist model exclusively to explain the growth and level of taxation cannot answer the normative question: How high should taxes be?, except in terms of their own privately-held moralities or their personal preferences. By contrast, for those whose analysis-diagnosis allows them to say that taxes are "inefficiently high," or simply "too high," the "should" question becomes a meaningful scientific issue. If taxes are "too high" in terms of some determinate standard other than my own personal preferences, we can try to determine by how much they should be cut.

In approaching this question, we must take care not to slip too readily into the romantic absurdities of modern-day anarchists, even those of our friends who call themselves anarcho-capitalists. It is perhaps self-satisfying in some sense to argue, quasi-seriously, that the optimal level of taxation is zero, and that any taxation at all is inefficient and undesirable. But any plausibly realistic assessment of human interaction as we know it must suggest that life in genuine anarchy would be just as Thomas Hobbes described it, "poor, nasty, brutish, and short." Government is a necessary element of viable social order, and government must be financed. The questions are: How much government? How much finance? How much spending? How much taxation? And of what sort?

It is essential at this stage of the discussion to separate *constitutional* questions and *political* questions. The first set involve general rules, the framework for political decision-making, within which the second set, ordinary political action, takes place. It seems clear, for example, that most of us would allow for ordinary political representatives in our legislatures to set levels of taxation if we could be sure there were some constitutional constraints that prevented excessive use of the taxing power. Recall both the structuralist and the monopolist models of politics discussed above. If constitutional constraints could correct for the high tax-high spending biases, then year-to-year levels of revenues and outlays might well be left to legislative assemblies. And, recognizing that there will be attempts to use monopoly powers, government might be limited in its access to exploitable revenue sources by constitutional constraints.

V. INDIRECT CONTROLS VIA CONSTITUTIONAL CHANGE

At this point it will be useful to list, and to discuss briefly, each of several constitutional proposals designed to limit levels of taxation and/or spending. These proposals are of two sorts, those that seek to control taxing-spending levels indirectly by changing constitutional procedures and those that seek to control these levels directly.

TAX SHARES AND TAX RATES

Professor F.A. Hayek[7] has suggested that the constitutional structure be modified, so that a specially-selected and "senior" law-making assembly be granted powers of decision over the basic structure of taxation and over the distribution of tax shares among individuals and groups. This tax structure would presumably remain in place quasi-permanently, and would not be expected to change from year to year with shifting political winds. Within such a tax structure, ordinary governmental majorities would then be allowed to decide on levels of tax rates and on budget size. Hayek's particular proposal in this respect was made, it seems, largely with reference to a parliamentary system of government, but the general idea warrants consideration in any setting.

QUALIFIED MAJORITY REQUIREMENTS

Knut Wicksell,[8] as early as 1896, called for qualified, larger-than-simple majorities, in order to guarantee that taxing-spending proposals are efficient and generally beneficial. He spoke of a five-sixths majority requirement in a legislature. Some modern advocates (*e.g.*, Alan Greenspan) have called for a constitutional requirement that three-fifths or two-thirds of both houses of the United States Congress be required to pass fiscal legislation. One of the neglected parts of Proposition 13, adopted as a constitutional amendment by California in 1978, is the requirement that new taxes be approved by two-thirds majorities in the state legislature.

PROPORTIONAL AND PROGRESSIVE TAXATION

Professor Hayek argued in his earlier treatise[9] that progressive rates of income taxation violate the basic rule of law. By implication if not explicitly, Hayek's argument lends support to constitutional restrictions against the imposition of progressive taxes, or, in the United States setting, to repeal of the 16th Amendment. More recently Milton and Rose Friedman[10] have also called for a repeal of the 16th Amendment and a constitutional stipulation of rate proportionality in income taxation.

A constitutional prohibition of progression in tax rates would dramatically modify the distribution of tax shares among different individuals and groups in the economy. It is not at all clear, however, what the direction of effect on total tax revenue, and spending, would be. From a given tax base, government can always extract more revenue under a proportional than under a progressive rate structure.

LIMITATION OF TAX BASES

In the work that Geoffrey Brennan and I have published[11] in which we utilize essentially the monopoly model of government described briefly above, we emphasize constitutional restriction of the bases or sources of revenue allowed to governments. If, through constitutional means, the taxing power can be limited to specified bases or sources, overall revenue extractions can be kept within bounds, regardless of the success or failure to modify year-by-year budgetary decisions.

From this perspective, our analysis lends strong support to the proposed *budget-balance amendment* to the United States constitution or, more generally, to constitutional requirements for budget balance. If the central government could, in fact, be required to maintain budget balance as a normal rule, the debt-creation and money-creation options for raising revenues are ruled out. In general, both of these options involve "taxation," and such a constitutional reform amounts to a denial of access to these two "tax" sources.

Our analysis also suggests that governments should never be granted access to capital or wealth taxation since this source for revenue (like public debt) allows government to extend its powers of fiscal exploitation beyond the "natural" limits dictated by gross income produced in a single time period.

TAX LOOPHOLES

Any recognition of independent supply-side behaviour by government as a part of the fiscal process lends support to arguments for constitutional limits on the exercise of the fiscal power. Restrictions of allowable tax bases are suggested, but, tax bases themselves may be so broadly defined as to make such restrictions meaningless.

One means of reducing the maximum revenue potential of government is to define allowable bases for tax narrowly enough so as to allow potentially exploited taxpayers access to substitutable non-taxable options. This is a positive argument for the deliberate introduction of constitutional guarantees for "loopholes" or "escapes" from tax pressures. If governments know that excessively high tax rates will shrink the taxable base, then this knowledge, in itself, will cause governments to keep such rates within limits. An example may be useful.

Suppose that the constitution allows government to tax wine, but not beer. We can then be sure that the tax on wine will not become overly burdensom, for the simple reason that the base for tax falls with every increase in rate as potential taxpayers switch to beer, the non-taxed option. With personal income taxes, restriction of the tax base to money income receipts will insure ceilings on rates that are related to the ability of persons to shift into non-money, non-taxable options.[12] I should point out that the argument here runs directly counter to the normative tax orthodoxy which elevates "comprehensiveness" in tax base to a position of an ideal, and especially with the income tax.

VI. DIRECT CONTROLS VIA CONSTITUTIONAL CHANGE

The various proposals listed above have the advantage of allowing governments to make taxing and spending decisions through ordinary political process, while this process itself is controlled by constitutional limits. In none of the schemes suggested is there any attempt to specify directly what the level of tax rates (and spending) shall be. Government is allowed to respond to the pressures of citizens and to its own revenue-spending needs as conditions dictate. The constitutional checks are designed only to prevent excessive exploitation of the taxing power.

A second, and quite different, set of proposed constitutional constraints on the fiscal authority of governments involves much more direct controls.

THE TAX RATIO

There are constitutional proposals which involve a definition of a ratio between total tax revenues (or total spending) and total product or income, either in terms of levels or rates of increase. The most familiar of these proposals involves constitutional limits on the share in total product or income in the relevant jurisdiction that may be collected in taxes or used in governmental outlays or on rates of increase in this share. This type of constraint first gained prominence in the United States in 1973 with Governor Reagan's Proposition 1, which was soundly defeated in California. After the success of Proposition 13 in 1978, however, several American states[13] incorporated ratio-type limits in their constitutions, and, in late 1979, an amendment to the United States Constitution was proposed which limits rates of increase in federal government outlays to rates of increase in gross national product.

The advantage of these direct constitutional controls lies in their specificity; the proposals put definitive ceilings on total tax revenues or on total spending. The disadvantage lies, however, in the same features; because they are quite specific, the flexibility of response of governments in the face of changing fiscal pressures is reduced. In recognition of this disadvantage, almost all proposals of this type have escape clauses incorporated. These clauses allow the specified ratio to be waived in emergencies, with emergencies defined by a qualified majority of the legislative assemblies. Through these escape clauses, the direct control proposals collapse into the indirect controls noted earlier.

TAX RATE CEILINGS

The most prominent feature of Proposition 13 in California was the constitutional ceiling placed on the rate of tax on real property. It was probably this feature more than any other that insured the overwhelming success of the proposition. Voters were able to predict the results directly, in terms of their own tax bills. The major disadvantage of such specific limits, however, lies in the incentive that such limits provide to government to shift to non-limited tax sources and to higher-level governmental sources of revenues. Unless constitutional ceilings are placed on rates of *all* taxes, there is no assurance that overall levels of taxes will be reduced.

VII. TAX LIMITS IN THE 1980s

I have listed and described briefly different proposals for constitutional change that have emerged in the tax-revolt climate of the late 1970s in the United States. The motivation and support for each one of these proposals arises from the conviction that existing levels of taxing (and spending) are "too high," and that ordinary electoral politics are unlikely to correct the situation. Electing "better" politicians and "better" political parties may not have much effect in modifying results, given the structural features of the fiscal process and the inherent monopoly powers of modern government.

It is natural in the United States setting (and to some extent in the Canadian) to turn to *constitutional reform* as a means of controlling government that is independent of the direct electoral process. In this respect, my discussion in this paper is relevant primarily in the United States context. Constitutional history and constitutional attitudes are different in European nations and in Japan. Imposing limits on government's power to tax will obviously not take on identical characteristics in different constitutional settings. And, to the extent that explicit constitutional constraint is not an important part of a nation's political heritage, tax limitation may prove more difficult.

Even in the American setting, the potential effectiveness of constitutional reform may be questioned. I have suggested elsewhere[14] that our situation may be described as one of "constitutional anarchy," given the continuing erosion of meaning in our traditional constitutional precepts. It is tempting to conclude that modern Leviathan government is simply out of control and that we are tilting at windmills in all discussions of constitutional checks.

It seems to me, however, that those of us who care about liberty and who think about the structure of society have a moral obligation. And this is to build on the faith that the people can change the structure of their political order by constitutional means, and that politicians will honour the rules laid down, at least within some limits of tolerance. Personally, I was excited and encouraged by the post-Proposition 13 climate of opinion in the United States.

Relative to 1979, 1980 was a disappointment. My own assessment is that the tax-limit advocates failed to "seize the day." The opportunity that seemed to be available during a few months in 1978 and 1979 may now all but have disappeared. The external events of late 1979 and early 1980 have shifted attention toward the needs for major increases in military spending. This shift in priorities may have precluded short-term success for any proposed fiscal limits. Honest prediction suggests a ratchet-like increase in the federal governmental budget in the United States, with consequent increases in the size of the deficits, and in the rate of inflation. Real tax rates seem more likely to rise than to fall in the early 1980s. Once again we seem to be on the threshold of a period when military priorities may generate a permanent shift upward in the size of the governmental sector.

THE FISCAL RATCHET

Such a shift does not, of course, modify the basic diagnosis. Nor does it mitigate the urgency of seeking some means of imposing fiscal limits. Indeed, the problem becomes worse with each upward move in the ratchet. But the attention span of the public is severely limited, and the whole tax-revolt package of notions may be placed on the back burner while the U.S. concerns itself with shoring up its defenses. In this setting, it becomes critically important to prevent the United States central government access to yet a *new* major revenue source, such as the proposed *value-added tax*. Enactment of legislation authorizing utilization of this tax base would be a tragedy of major proportions and would guarantee that real tax rates increase very substantially and to permanently higher levels.

It is also important to recognize more fully the hidden tax that inflation represents, and the automatic increases in real rates of income tax that inflation generates. In this respect, Canada and a few other countries have taken the lead in introducing at least partial tax indexing. If conceived to be a permanent *constitutional* feature, such tax indexing might be included among the procedural constraints listed earlier.

A TAX MOST UNJUST

It is also important to recognize that the military draft is best interpreted as a very unjust tax on those who are conscripted, a tax that would not pass the constitutional tests of equity if called by such a name. Finally, the set of costs arbitrarily imposed in blunderbuss political attempts at preventing inflation directly amount to taxes that produce no revenues.

My diagnosis, which seems to be amply supported by the studies in this book, is that taxes in most Western countries are already "too high," and that the disparity between what taxes should be and what they are will increase as real rates go up. For the United States at least, I am convinced that constitutional limits on the taxing and spending power of government can be effective. The events of 1980 suggest that future implementation of constitutional reform will be more difficult than it seemed in 1979.

A constitutionally imposed and defined fiscal and monetary framework is a necessary requirement for the viability of a tolerably free society. There is now more agreement on this statement of normative principle than at any time during my three and one-half decades of reflections on such matters. This fact alone provides grounds for optimism. Ideas are changing; institutional change will follow unless we have passed the point of no return.

NOTES

1. These quotes are used as chapter-heading citations in James M. Buchanan and Geoffrey Brennan, *The Power to Tax: Analytical Foundations of a Fiscal Constitution,* Cambridge University Press (1980).
2. I have already suggested that, in my view, governments in this century, and throughout the Western world, have grown in size and scope beyond the limits that would have allowed us to explain their operation in terms of what we may call the traditional or orthodox model. For purposes of discussion here, we can label this model as that of the *productive state*. In this perspective, governmental activity is explained as the observed response to the emerging demands of the citizenry. The activity is productive in that desired "public goods" are supplied. Viewed in this light, there is no diagnosed breakdown or failure in political process. There is no cause for

concern or alarm about taxes, or spending, being "too high" or about how high they may go. As I noted, my view is that any such productive state model fails utterly to explain the growth of government in this century and notably during the decades of the 1960s and 1970s. We need, therefore, alternative positive theories of how government operates so as to move beyond any conceivable boundaries of "productive" activity.

3. See "The Growth of Government," Working Paper 001, Center for Study of the Economy and the State, University of Chicago (1979).
4. See Allan H. Meltzer and Scott Richard, "A Rational Theory of the Size of Government," Mimeographed, Carnegie-Mellon University, April (1979).
5. For an extended discussion, see James M. Buchanan and Gordon Tullock, *The Calculus of Consent,* Ann Arbor: University of Michigan Press (1962).
6. See James M. Buchanan and Richard E. Wagner, *Democracy in Deficit,* New York: Academic Press (1977).
7. F.A. Hayek. *Law, Legislation, and Liberty,* Vol. III, University of Chicago Press (1979).
8. Knut Wicksell. *Finanztheorietische Untersuchungen,* Jena: Gustav Fischer (1896).
9. F.A. Hayek. *The Constitution of Liberty,* University of Chicago Press (1960).
10. Milton and Rose Friedman. *Free to Choose,* New York: Harcourt, Brace Jovanovich, (1980).
11. James M. Buchanan and Geoffrey Brennan, *The Power to Tax,* Cambridge University Press (1980).
12. Viewed in this perspective, the increasing quantitative importance of the "underground" or "unobserved" economy, discussed by E. Feige in his study "Macroeconomics and the Unobserved Sector," (pages 21-37 in this volume), has the effect of keeping income tax rates *lower* than might otherwise be the case. Hence, rather than being looked upon as "immoral" tax evaders, those who shift to underground activities may be applauded as benefactors to ordinary taxpayers.
13. Tennesee, Michigan.
14. James M. Buchanan, *The Limits of Liberty,* University of Chicago Press (1975).

DISCUSSION

Edited by: Walter Block

The discussion following the Buchanan paper was fast and furious, indicative of the great enthusiasm generated by his presentation.

BALANCED BUDGET

Auld agreed that a constitutional requirement for a balanced budget might make sense for current expenditure, but doubted whether this made sense on the capital account. Buchanan pointed out that as long as capital items are rolling along at more or less a constant rate, Auld's distinction was not too important. Alchian continued this line of reasoning, by explaining that in a well functioning capital market, the distinction between current and capital account wouldn't make any difference anyway.

The balanced budget theme was next taken up by Lindbeck, who expressed himself as "skeptical" on this subject. Said Lindbeck, "Look for instance at the rules of balanced budgets. First of all, there are good reasons for loan finance or government investment. Second, such a rule would have perverse effects on short-term economic trends. I don't mean that the balanced budget rules would make discretionary counter-cyclical policy completely impossible, but if there is a balanced budget rule, the government would often be forced into perverse economic policy. As soon as the tax base goes down, the government would be forced to raise the tax rate and drive the economy even further down." Buchanan thought there would be a great deal of mileage in a balanced budget rule, if it tied a spending item to a specific tax. He supported the balanced budget rule because people easily understand it.

His own version of the balanced budget would not be destabilizing, Buchanan claimed, nor would it require residual balancing. How would this work? "At the time the final budget resolution is passed by Congress, they would have to have projections that would match the two sides of the account. Now, obviously, the two sides might not end up being matched, if something happened in the internal economic process.

"Re-balancing would not be required, although there would have to be some penalties for consistent violations. There would be an honest attempt to carry out this plan. The perverse effects mentioned by Lindbeck might ensue, particularly if the plan was not accompanied by some sort of constitutional monitor. That is why these things have to be considered as a package. To treat them completely independently is a little bit artificial."

THE GERMAN CASE

Giersch discussed the annually balanced budget, an actual amendment to the German constitution. "First of all, during the initial pre-balanced budget period, as a result of high tax incomes during the German economic miracle, and low expenditure as a result of the behaviour of the finance minister, excess reserves were piled up. But later on they were distributed. A lot of behaviour of government, under the rule of a balanced budget, will depend upon tax estimates for the future, and that starts immediately. There is a second necessary addition. Not only must the tax schedules be indexed, but there must also be a provision that, with a progressive tax system, the schedule would have to be lowered from year to year. Otherwise there are automatic increases in tax receipts as a result of economic growth. So, it has to be made inflation-proof and growth-proof.

"Another exception in the German constitution, which is a Keynesian one, is that in periods of recession, a deficit may be run. You may say, 'That should not be written into the constitution, because the kind of recession which one may have under a pre-announced monetary policy, would be something which could be cured by itself. Therefore anti-cyclical fiscal policy isn't necessary.' I quite agree. But a provision about monetary policy would certainly have to be added to the German constitution in order to make it workable.

"The German constitution hasn't been very workable because of the absence of these kinds of supplementary rules. They do not exist, and have not been written into the constitution or into any law."

Spindler focused on the role of political parties in linking tax and expenditure policies, and thus controlling government expansion. He pointed to the Swiss example, where government as a proportion of gross canton product is inversely related to the extent to which referenda provisions are available to the citizens of each canton.

Block objected to the balanced budget amendment as a means of reining in rising government expenditure levels. He called attention to the fact that a tax-expenditure link could be set at any height whatsoever, even, in the limiting case, at 100 per cent of the GNP. Those who favoured unlimited government expansion thus need not oppose a balanced budget amendment.

EDUCATION NEEDED

Grubel was worried about canny bureaucrats and politicians who would attempt to circumvent all constitutional restrictions placed on public sector growth. "They are all too familar with accounting tricks of passing on expenditures, hiding them, using tax concessions to achieve essentially the same thing as if they were expenditure. In Canada, a favourite technique is to create Crown corporations. I'm sure that if we left the bureaucrats with enough time, they would come up with an infinite variety of ways of circumventing constitutional limitations." He proposed a stepped-up effort to "educate the public on what is going on so that they will be more wise in their choice of the people they elect."

Courchene warmly supported Grubel's call for greater educational efforts, alluding to the "continually rising expectations on the part of the citizenry," for "the government to do something."

Alchian focused attention on the precise kind of education required:

"There was a game of basketball in which after every point there is a toss-up. The team with the tallest man almost automatically won. The basketball players, even the tallest, didn't like that. There are a lot of games we play where the rules are such that the players of the game, even those that are winning, don't like that game. The rules destroy the game.

"In like manner, Buchanan's* premise is that there are enough people in the United States and Canada who don't like the outcome of the fiscal game. They understand the game, but they don't like the outcome. He's saying there must be some thought given to changing the rules that we all agree to. They need not be educated, because Buchanan is assuming they already think the government too large.

CHANGING THE RULES

"The trick is to find some rule they can all agree to. One that will, in fact, reduce the size of that game. The education required is not to change their minds, but to let them perceive some new rules that will change the outcome. Education which is merely an attempt to proselytize, to make people change their minds about politics, to make them see the world as we see it, is, I think, a mistake. We can't tell them what is the right kind of world. This role is reserved for God, not economists.

"People already believe that the size of government is too large. If we all pay for our dinner by splitting the total bill equally, we're all going to order too much. We don't like that rule so we devise another one. If we pay only for what we buy, the system can run more reasonably. Buchanan is suggesting not a constitution written in stone, that can't be changed, but rather some more sensible rules.

"I repeat: it is a mistake to think that we have to change people's opinions, teach them that government is too large. We're not going to change their preferences. We've got to change the way in which their preferences get revealed and get turned into activity."

THE CANNY BUREAUCRAT

Seldon was concerned with the same type of bureaucratic evasiveness, mentioned by Grubel, which took place in Great Britain. "Margaret Thatcher inherited the problem of excessive government spending. She has tried to change this. In her first year, she made use of constraints of a macroeconomic type: cash limits or ceilings on expenditure. Each

*All conference participants invariably referred to each other by their first names. For ease of identification, however, this has been changed to surnames—ed.

department was told it may not spend more than 5 per cent or 10 per cent less than last year. But all that happened was that the power of allocating public funds was left in the hands of public officials, or politicians, or local government officials. They decided where government will spend its lower ceilings and how much taxes were required.

"Worse than that, they not only kept their jobs going, but made reductions precisely in the services that the public, if there were a market, would prefer to be maintained. They have no knowledge of where the public would prefer cuts, nor incentive to accede to them. The bureaucrats have made cuts in all sorts of services that the public would rather keep going. The people might even want to have more spent on some services like school lunches or hospital nurses and so on. If civil servants retain the power of deciding where to cut expenditure, and therefore how much taxes are needed, there will be a distorted range of cuts."

But Seldon's solution to the problem was far different than that of several other participants: "The only way, it seems to me, to modify government expenditure and therefore total taxes is to pass the decisions (of where to cut) to the taxpayer. And this is technically feasible with the creation of a range of market prices, for all government services except public goods. This would cover fuel, transport, health, education, housing, and a wide range of total authority services. They could be placed on the market by returning taxes.

"This is a method that Ed Feige seems to have overlooked. In fact, most economists seem to have forgotten that there are vast potential markets in government services. A far better plan is to return substantial tax revenues, and to say to the public, 'You can now have all the health services, or the housing services, or the school services that you want and will pay for.' In this way, the public would get as large a range of tax reductions as it wanted. Moreover, those reductions would be made where the public, suitably informed, would like the cuts. They would be made with less damage and more benefit.

"I see no reason to continually exclude the scope for the use of market pricing for a wide range of government services. I'm sure this is true of Canada as well. Richard Berndt has written a book which discusses charging for public services where he explains why economists are still ignoring the constraining power of pricing."

POLITICAL POWER

There was continued refrain, mentioned by several of the participants, concerning the reciprocal relationship between constitutional change and political power. Paradoxically, if the political power necessary to effect constitutional change is already available, then the constitutional change is itself unnecessary. If an electorate is ready and willing to incorporate limits on government growth in the constitution, it can certainly be counted upon to support these ends in the non-constitutional, more ordinary political process.

Alternatively, if the voters are not politically motivated to rein in government expansion, that is when a constitutional amendment is most needed—and precisely when it is least likely to be attained. For if the public will not elect politicians to support a limited role for government, how can it be expected to enact constitutional changes toward this end? In short, as Grubel said, "If you can persuade the public then you don't need the constitution."

Variations on this theme were sounded by Lindbeck, Clark, Giersch, Grubel, and Kaizuka.

Buchanan's constitutional position also came under sharp and very able attack from Walters. He argued eloquently that however important is the constitutional tradition in the U.S., there were numerous other countries in the world that had managed quite well, thank you, to preserve their free institutions without such documents. "Throughout the nineteenth century there was price stability in Britain. British budgets were subject to great rectitude throughout the whole of that period. Gladstone was terribly embarrassed about any suggestion that he'd run a deficit. Even Disraeli took the view that deficits were immoral.

NO CONSTITUTIONS PLEASE, WE'RE BRITISH

"The point is, this was all done without the formal constitution at all. We find it very difficult, in Britain, to believe that formal constitutions make any difference. We look at countries like, for instance, Honduras, which has more constitutions than years of independence. It's a joke! We believe that what really kept Britain, and what keeps many countries, on the straight and narrow, with respect to both monetary and fiscal policy, was the ever present threat of the flight of capital. This held even during the difficult period of the Crimean War. During this period Great Britain even set up its Colonies with balanced budgets and currency board systems; the state sector was depoliticized both with respect to money and with respect to overall financing arrangements. This external discipline worked quite well during the nineteenth century. We want to depoliticize our monetary institutions so they are subject to these external disciplines, and our fiscal institutions, too. I should say that the Chileans, with no constitution whatsoever, have gone quite a way towards this already, in a period as short as four years. Would one recommend that they put into effect a constitution? I would never do that.

"Constitutions, as we know, in Latin America, have disappeared with the rapidity of snow falling on a summer shore. There's just no point in trying to do it. It's all very well to revere constitutions in America. Americans are very fortunate to have one of the most outstanding political documents ever written as their constitution. But it's just luck. So please be indulgent with your poor European cousins. We're not stupid and we're not unappreciative."

BUCHANAN REPLIES

However challenging these positions, Buchanan was not without answers of his own. He supported Seldon's call for market prices instead of taxes. "If you are advising Mrs. Thatcher to introduce prices in various sectors of the public services, well and good, that's fine. I encourage you to do it and I join you, and would sign a petition to that effect. My only worry is that there's a limited value in this. For then somebody else comes in, a labour government for example, and knocks prices out again. A temporary persuasion of politicians in one particular party is a useful exercise, but it is not structural reform."

On Latin American constitutional history: "But the Chileans are desperately searching around for a constitution that they can, in fact, now impose. They are talking about it despite the history of the Latin American type constitution. And I wouldn't deny for a minute that it's this sort of ethos that really matters."

On circumvention: "I don't deny for a minute that any constitutional procedure could be circumvented by determined people. On the other hand, it seems to me that if you had the kind of politically supportive movement that would be required to pass a genuine constitutional amendment in the first place, then, because of the ethos of politics, it would be much more difficult to circumvent."

And on the nineteenth century: "America had the same experience regarding the balanced budget in those years. We never had the balanced budget written into our formal constitution, and yet I would argue that the balanced budget rule was in effect a part of our constitution up until the 1930s. So you can have unwritten rules that people honour and respect. But, my point is, at least in the American context, and maybe in the British context too, that because you've had people like Hailsham and Robbins recently talking about that, you must have a constitution in the British situation.

"In the American context, the only way we're going to revive trust in government is with some sort of major symbolic shield. And a constitutional amendment would do this. It's the only thing that I can see that would do it. I don't see how just by electing different people, or by educating the people to change their policies, this can be accomplished."

PERMANENCY

But Buchanan's major thrust was that the constitutional amendment is more permanent than any other conceivable alternative. True, one cannot achieve anything on the constitutional level without the political power that would enable much else to be accomplished, as well. The point is, that if such power can but be mobilized, even for a short time, it is far better to direct it into the (relatively) permanent constitutional channel, than to fritter it away with other changes which can (more) easily be swept away by a change in the political tides.

Says Buchanan in this regard, "The constitutional amendment is one that outlasts ordinary political regimes, or at least is supposed to outlast ordinary political regimes. Of course, public attitudes must be changed in order to pass constitutional amendments. But surely, public attitude changes are only temporary; if the basic structure can be changed that's quite different, and much more important."

Despite his reservations from the Buchanan position, Lindbeck also supported constitutional rules, drawn, by analogy, from the realm of international trade. "I agree that we should also look at constitutions. Trade policy was mentioned, and there we have a constitution. The G.A.T.T.* rules have been very helpful in constraining governments against the protectionists because they've been able to blame the G.A.T.T. rules for their non-activity. I think the G.A.T.T. rule is a very good example of the usefulness of constitutional rules." As well, Giersch mentioned G.A.T.T. as a supra-national constitutional-type barrier which limited the options of sovereign countries.

---

*the General Agreement on Tariffs and Trade, an international agreement whose objectives are to gradually reduce government imposed barriers to trade. It was signed initially by 23 countries, including Canada, and went into effect in 1948 – ed.

PART TWO

COUNTRY STUDIES

CHAPTER 4

PUBLIC REVENUES AND PUBLIC POLICY: THE IMPACT ON THE CANADIAN ECONOMY

D.A.L. Auld

The growth of government expenditure in the post-war period has been paralleled by a similar growth in taxation. This growth, however, has not merely been a matter of increasing tax rates to keep pace with higher expenditures. New forms of taxation have emerged, old structures been reformed, tax bases expanded and eroded, and even the definition of taxable income has changed. These changes have affected the allocation of resources, the distribution of income and the ability to finance government.

An evaluation of the impact of the tax system on redistribution and resource allocation requires some prior information on the structure of the public revenue system. In Part I, we examine the principle forms of taxation and their relationship to total revenue; in Part II, recent trends in taxation. The allocation and stabilization aspects of tax policy are discussed in Part III while Part IV covers the all-important debate on taxes and income redistribution. Part V is a short analysis of public debt as an alternative to taxation. This is followed by our summary and conclusion in Part VI.

I. PRINCIPAL FORMS OF TAXATION AND THE RELATIONSHIP TO TOTAL REVENUE

The present Canadian tax system is characterized most dramatically by the proportion of revenue accounted for by the personal income tax. Using the data in Table 4.1 about 47 per cent of federal tax revenue, and 43 per cent of provincial tax revenue, is derived from that one source. Although there is no local personal income tax, this tax still accounts for 40 per cent of total tax revenue in Canada.

The second most important tax in terms of its share of tax revenue is the *ad valorem* sales tax, accounting for 16 per cent and 17 per cent respectively of tax revenue at the federal and provincial level, and slightly over 14 per cent of total tax revenue in Canada. The corporation

TABLE 4.1

Tax Revenues in Canada: 1979 ($ Billion)

	FEDERAL		PROVINCIAL		LOCAL		TOTAL			
Tax Revenue	Actual	Adjusted*	Actual	Adjusted*	Actual	Adjusted*	Actual	%	Adjusted	%
personal income	14.0	20.1	10.9	10.9	—	—	24.9	39.6	31.0	42.1
corporate income	6.3	6.3	2.5	2.5	—	—	8.8	14.0	8.8	11.9
sales (ad valorem)	4.7	4.7	4.4	5.6	—	—	9.1	14.5	10.3	14.0
property	—	—	—	—	6.7	—	6.7	10.7	6.7	9.1
customs duties	2.7	2.7	—	—	—	—	2.7	4.3	2.7	3.7
excises	1.9	1.9	2.2	5.7	—	—	4.1	6.5	7.6	10.3
death and gift	—	—	.1	.1	—	—	.1	0.2	0.1	0.1
health insurance premiums	—	—	1.4	1.4	—	—	1.4	2.2	1.4	1.9
social insurance levy	—	—	2.2	2.2	—	—	2.2	3.5	2.2	3.0
Quebec pension plan	—	—	—	—	—	—	—	—	—	—
other	—	—	1.7	1.7	1.2	1.2	2.9	4.6	2.9	3.9
Total Tax Revenue	29.6	35.7	25.4	30.1	7.9	7.9	62.9	100.0	73.7	100.0
Non-Tax Revenue										
post office	.9	.9	—	—	—	—	.9			
investment income	3.2	3.2	3.3	3.3	—	—	6.5			
resource revenue	—	—	4.8	1.3	—	—	4.8			
licenses, etc.	—	—	1.4	1.4	—	—	1.4			
profits (liquor boards)	—	—	1.2	0	—	—	1.2			
service charges (water)	—	—	1.0	1.0	1.4	1.4	2.4			
other	.5	.5	.5	.5	1.1	1.1	2.1			
Total Non-Tax Revenue	4.6	4.6	12.2	7.5	2.5	2.5	19.3			

TABLE 4.1 (continued)

	FEDERAL		PROVINCIAL		LOCAL		TOTAL			
Tax Revenue	Actual	Adjusted*	Actual	Adjusted*	Actual	Adjusted*	Actual	%	Adjusted	%
Non-Budget Revenue										
Canada Pension Plan(CPP)	2.1	0					2.1			
C.P.P. investment income	1.1	0					1.1			
unemployment insurance premiums	2 9	0					2.9			
other										
Total non-tax, "non-budget" revenue	10 7	4.6	12.2	7.5	2.5	2.5	25.4	14.6		
Total Own-Source Revenue	41.4		37.6		10.4		89.4	89.4		
Intergovernmental Transfers (net)	-10.1		+0.2		+9.9					

Source: Statistics Canada, *Local Government Finance* and *Provincial Government Finance*, 68-205; 68-203 and Public *Accounts, Budget Speech*, 1979.

* See text for adjustments.

income tax ranks a close third in importance representing 14 per cent of total tax revenue. At the federal level it accounts for 21 per cent of revenue and at the provincial level, 10 per cent.

The real property tax is the mainstay of local tax revenue, with almost 85 per cent of tax revenue derived from this source, making it the fourth most important source of tax revenue for total government. It accounts for over 10 per cent of the total tax revenue in Canada.

Depending upon the method by which budgetary revenues are classified and reported, tax revenue may account for only 71 per cent of the total revenue accruing to governments in Canada. The largest share of non-tax revenue occurs at the provincial level, 32 per cent, but even at the federal level, non-tax revenue (as defined in the budget accounts) is over 26 per cent of total revenue. Table 4.1 illustrates the breakdown by jurisdiction. According to the classification used by the sources of data, 28 per cent of total own-source revenue is non-tax.[1]

Surely, however, a number of these "non-tax" and "non-budget" revenue sources are very closely related to taxes and can be classified as such. For example, contributions to universal pension plans and unemployment insurance are not generically different from health insurance premiums, and we could easily classify *all* such contributions as personal taxes. Liquor board profits arise because the price is higher than it would be if such boards operated at zero profit. The profit is nothing more than an additional excise tax. Finally, resource revenues can be considered non-tax because there is no legally specified tax base to which a schedule of rates can be applied. For example, natural resource revenue includes the sale of leases to explore for oil, stumpage duty, licences to fish or trap game, and royalties. Royalties on oil and gas account for the bulk of natural resource revenue and they are not that different from an excise tax. At least $3.5B of the $4.8B resource revenue can be viewed in this manner.[2] If these adjustments are made to the revenue system classification, tax revenue accounts for 84 per cent of total own source revenue (see Table 4.1).

In a federal system such as Canada, it is most important to consider inter-governmental transfers. The federal government transferred almost $10B in own-source revenues it collected in 1979, most of it to the provinces in the form of equalization grants (a scheme to reduce regional disparity through payments to governments) and specific purpose grants, which together account for roughly two-thirds of the total transfers. The provinces, richer by almost $10B, then grant $9.6B in turn to local governments, in the form of general purpose transfers ($1.4B) and specific purpose transfers ($8.2B). As well, there are some minor ($0.2B) transfers from the federal to local governments.

PERSONAL INCOME TAX

Residents of Canada are liable for tax on all sources of income (including most transfer payments from government) except capital gains, where only one-half of the gain is included. From gross income, the taxpayer is permitted a wide range of deductions ranging from unemployment insurance contributions to registered retirement savings plans, up to specified limits which have been altered frequently. One thousand dollars of interest, dividend, or capital-gain income on Canadian investments is also deductible. From net income the taxpayer is permitted a variety of personal exemptions in order to arrive at a taxable income. Federal progressive rates of taxation in 1979 ranged from a 17 per cent rate on the first $1,765 of taxable income to 43 per cent on taxable income above $99,480.

Because of federal tax credits for low-income taxpayers and provincial tax thresholds, no tax is levied on a taxpayer until taxable income is slightly over $2,000. Selected taxable income brackets and federal rates of personal income tax are shown in Table 4.2.

TABLE 4.2

1980–1981 Federal Marginal Tax Rates

Taxable Income	Effective Marginal Rate (Federal)
1,765	17.
8,096	19.
12,062	23.
*17,361	22.75*
24,721	32.00
33,903	32.00
54,381	36.00
99,480	43.00

* The rate declines between 12,062 and 24,721 because of a 9% tax reduction with a minimum $200 and maximum $500.

Each province levies an income tax which is a percentage of basic federal income tax. These rates range from 38.5 per cent in Alberta to 58 per cent in Newfoundland. Thus, in 1980, a taxpayer in a federal tax

Figure 4.1
Federal Personal Income Tax
Paid as Per Cent of Assessed Income.

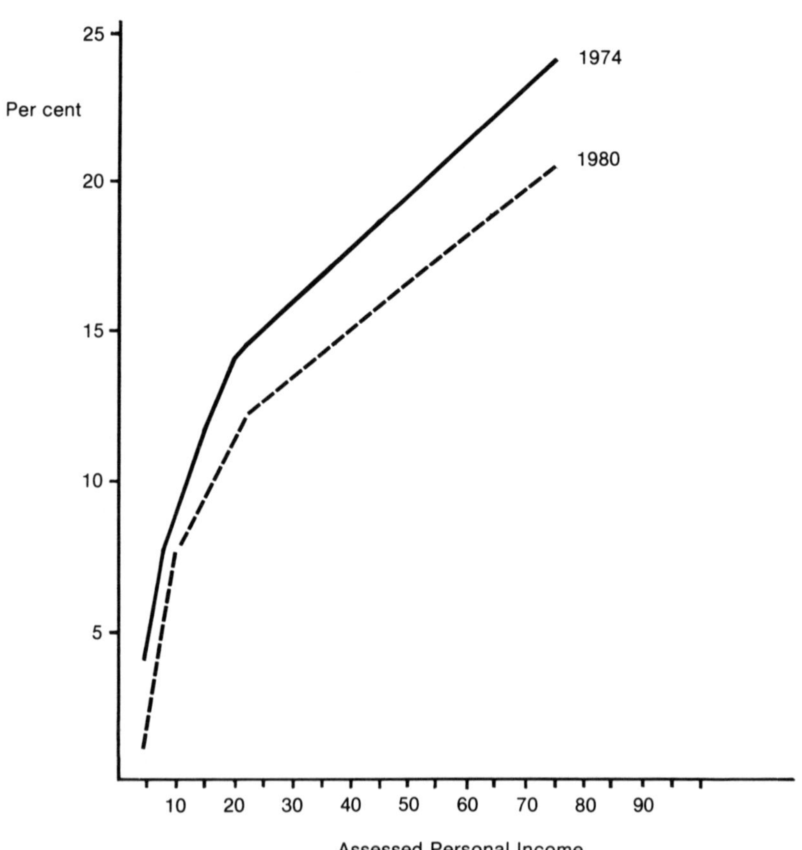

Source: Revenue Canada, *Taxation Statistics.*

bracket of 25 per cent in Alberta would pay a marginal tax rate of [25 + .385 (25)] = 34.6 per cent while in Newfoundland, the rate would be [25 + .58 (25)] = 39.5 per cent. Some idea of the actual progressivity of the rate structure for 1980 can be seen in Figure 4.1.[3]

One of the more unusual features of the personal income tax in Canada is that it has been indexed since 1974. The system used allows for indexing a portion of net taxable income as well as the tax rates themselves. How this indexation operates and how it affects the growth of personal income tax revenue can best be explained by using the concept of tax elasticity. We define elasticity e, as:

$$e = \frac{\Delta T/T}{\Delta Y/Y}$$

where T = tax revenue
Y = gross national income

This elasticity can then be disaggregated

$$e = \frac{\Delta T/T}{\Delta NB/NB} \bullet \frac{\Delta NB/NB}{\Delta B/B} \bullet \frac{\Delta B/B}{\Delta Y/Y}$$

where NB = net base or taxable income
B = gross tax base or total personal income

During a period of inflation, Y, B and NB can be viewed as having 'real' and inflationary components. For example, Y or current dollar GNP can be expressed as

$$Y = \bar{Y}(1 + P_Y)$$

where $\bar{Y}$ = real GNP
P_Y = inflationary component of GNP.

The net tax base or taxable income (NB) is roughly equal to B – XD where XD represents personal exemptions. Without indexation then

$$NB = \bar{B}(1 + P_B) - XD$$

where $\bar{B}$ represents the 'real' value of the gross tax base and P_B the inflation component based on the consumer price index. In a period of inflation, the net base or taxable income rises at the rate of inflation even if there is no increase in the real gross base. If the personal exemptions *are* indexed, then the indexed taxable income is:

$$NB^* = \bar{B}(1 + P_B) - XD(1 + P_B)$$

and taxable income only rises by the increase in *real* gross income. In Canada, the indexation factor is the rate of change in the consumer price index (CPI) in the year prior to the current tax year. Thus:

$$NB^* = \bar{B}(1 + \dot{CPI}) - XD(1 + \dot{CPI})$$

Since the inception of the law the indexation factors have had a noticeable impact on the nominal value of one exemption, as shown in Table 4.3.

TABLE 4.3

Indexation and the Nominal Value of the Personal Exemption

Year	Indexation Factor	Value of Personal Exemption For	
		Single Status	Married Status
1973	None	1,600	3,000
1974	6.6%	1,710	3,200
1975	10.1	1,880	3,520
1976	11.3	2,090	3,920
1977	8.6	2,270	4,260
1978	7.2	2,430	4,560
1979	9.0	2,650	4,970
1980	8.9	2,890	5,420

Source: *National Finances*, Canadian Tax Foundation, 1980.

Indexation in Canada does more than raise basic exemptions by lagged inflation rates; it also adjusts the marginal tax brackets by raising the ceiling at which the next marginal rate of taxation applies. For each ith taxpayer, total tax is

$$T_i = t_i (NB_i^*)$$

where t_i is the average effective tax rate. Since the rate structure is a progressive one, the average effective tax depends upon the size of the taxpayer's net tax base,

$$t_i = f(NB_i^*)$$

If the ceiling of the income bracket is adjusted upwards by the rate of inflation, that is equivalent to lowering the indexed net base by (approximately) the rate of inflation. The effective tax rate is therefore (in a completely indexed system):

$$t_i = f\left[\frac{NB_i^*}{(1 + \dot{CPI})}\right]$$

The average taxpayer (depending upon the province of residence) faced a marginal tax rate of slightly over 30 per cent during the 1975–1980 period. On the deduction for single status alone, the cumulative loss in tax revenue due to indexation over the 1974–1980 period amounted to just over three billion dollars, one-quarter of the1979–1980 federal deficit.

A final point about the personal income tax is that only personal exemptions are indexed. This leaves a number of special deductions with ceilings set in nominal terms subject to discretionary action. Additionally, the Canadian tax system provides no inflation adjustment for capital source income.

CORPORATE INCOME TAX

Like the personal income tax, corporate profits are subject to joint federal-provincial taxation. The basic rate of tax is 25 per cent of taxable income up to $150,000 (for private Canadian companies) with limits on the cumulative amount taxed at this low income. After that, the rate is 46 per cent. For manufacturing and processing companies the current rate of tax is 40 per cent. The provincial governments receive 10 per cent of a corporation's taxable income earned in that province and the federal rate is thereby lowered by this amount. The provincial rates can vary, however, and they range from 10 to 15 per cent. There are also different provincial rates for small businesses. The *combined* rates of tax may be as low as 15 per cent for a small manufacturing company (in Alberta) and as high as 51 per cent for large non-manufacturing/processing corporations (in Manitoba and British Columbia). Overall, in 1977, Canadian corporations paid $6.76B in income tax on taxable income of $18.2B, for an effective tax rate of 37.1 per cent. However, out of the 325,000 corporations which filed a tax return, just under 50 per cent of them reported taxable income.

SALES AND EXCISE TAXES

(a) Federal sales tax

The manufacturer's sales tax is applicable to all goods made in Canada or imported, unless specified as being exempt from the tax. Exemptions range from foodstuffs and insulation material to intermediate goods. The rate of tax applied to the manufacturer's selling price is inclusive of import duty and varies from 5 per cent on building material to 12 per cent on alcohol/tobacco, with an average rate of 9 per cent. It is not a value-added or federal retail sales tax. There are a few selected goods subject to additional special sales taxes, *e.g.*, a 10 per cent tax on watches with a value exceeding $50.

(b) Federal excise taxes and duties

In addition to the basic sales tax there are numerous additional excise and customs duties which provide for very heavy taxation of particular products. There is, for example, an excise of 3 cents per 5 cigarettes, and a customs duty of $6.00 per thousand. If the cigarettes are imported, the excise duty is waived, but a customs duty more than makes up for the difference. Wine and liquor are taxed differentially, based on their alcoholic content. Other taxes include a gasoline excise tax (1.5 cents per litre), a tax on oil exports, and a special air transportation tax.

Customs duties or tariffs are levied, broadly speaking, according to three schedules. The lowest tariffs are imposed on countries of the British Commonwealth. The General Tariff, incorporating the highest tariff schedule, is of little consequence since Canada has limited trade with countries covered by these tariffs. Most tariffs are therefore levied under the Most Favoured Nation status.

(c) Provincial sales taxes

With the exception of Alberta, all provinces levy a tax on the sale of goods and services subject to a variety of exemptions. The complexity of the retail sales tax system across Canada can perhaps best be seen in Table 4.4. A few exemptions such as food, prescription drugs, books, and farm machinery are universal. There is little pattern to the remainder of the exemptions. Newfoundland taxes magazines; Ontario exempts candy if it is less than 50 cents per unit; five provinces exempt certain thermal insulation material and Quebec exempts clothing under $500 per unit.

(d) Provincial alcohol and tobacco "taxation"

The word taxation is placed in quotations because the provinces do not have a special alcohol tax, but instead mark up the cost of alcoholic beverages through their monopoly on its sale and distribution. We saw earlier that such mark-ups produce a handsome profit for the provinces. Tobacco is taxed in the true sense of the word with rates on cigarettes varying from .3 cents to 1.6 cents; on cigars from 1 per cent to

TABLE 4.4

Provincial Retail Sales Tax Rates — 1979

Basis: retail selling price	Nfld.	P.E.I.	N.S.	N.B.	Que.	Ont.	Man.	Sask.	Alta.	B.C.
Goods (tangible personal property)	11%	8%	8%	8 %	8%	7%	5%	5%	nil	4%
Minimum taxable sale	26¢	26¢	16¢	26¢	26¢	21¢	26¢	26¢		15¢
Prepared meals	11%	8%	8%	8%	10%	10%	5%	nil	nil	nil
Minimum taxable meal	$3.00	$5.00	$3.00	$2.00	$3.25	$6.00	$4.00			
Alcoholic beverages	11%	10%	8%	8%	8%	10%	10%	10%	nil	7%
Taxable services										
Hotel and motel accommodation	11%	8%	8%	8%	nil	nil	5%	5%	nil	4%
Telecommunications other than telephone	11%	nil	nil	8%	8%	7%	5%	5%	nil	nil
Telephone services										
Local	11%	8%	8%	8%	8%	7%	5%	5%	nil	4%
Long distance	11%	nil		8%	8%	7%	5%	5%	nil	nil
Natural gas	11%	nil	nil	nil	8%	nil	5%	nil	nil	4%
Electricity:										
Residential uses	nil	nil	50¢/mo.	nil	8%	nil	5%	5%	nil	4%
Other	11%	nil	$1–$30/mo.	nil	8%	nil	5%	5%	nil	4%
Laundry and dry cleaning	11%	8%	nil	nil	nil	nil	5%	nil	nil	nil

Source: *Provincial and Local Finance*, Canadian Tax Foundation, 1979, p.79.

45 per cent of price after the first 9 cents; on tobacco, from 2 cents per ½ ounce to 30 per cent of price.

(e) Provincial fuel taxation

Only Alberta does not tax automobile motor fuel. In other provinces the rates vary from 17 to 27 cents per gallon. There are a variety of different systems for taxing fuel used in farming, fishing, commercial shipping, and industrial use across Canada.

SOCIAL INSURANCE PREMIUMS

The distinction between non-tax and tax revenue is blurred even in the most respectable sources of data. For example, the Canadian Tax Foundation excludes the Canadian Pension Plan and Unemployment Insurance Premiums from its analysis of federal tax revenue, but includes health and Quebec Pension Plan levies in the analysis of provincial taxation.

The major levies of this type are federal unemployment insurance fund contributions (employee and employer), the Canada and Quebec Pension Plans (employee and employer), health insurance premiums in three provinces (elsewhere health care is financed totally from general revenues) and other levies such as worker's compensation.

PROPERTY TAXATION

Real property, defined generally as the value of lands and buildings, forms the main tax base for virtually all local governments in Canada. The most significant change in recent years involves greater participation by provincial governments in the determination of the valuation of local property. In most municipalities, real property is assessed at its capital value. This capital value depends upon assessments which vary widely depending upon the year(s) selected for the assessment. For example, a re-assessment of real property value is underway in Saskatchewan whereby the value of property will be set at its 1961–1970 average. In Ontario, a province-wide assessment based on 1975 has been completed, but is not used yet in the tax base.

Exemptions, classification of property (residential, commercial, agricultural, etc.), tax rates (mill rates) and special provisions vary widely across Canada. Most provinces have attempted various programs of property tax reform designed to either equalize assessment, provide relief from property taxes for various income groups, or reduce the local government's reliance on property tax as a source of revenue. The latter effort has brought about a significant reduction in the ratio of property tax revenue to total municipal expenditures over the 1967–1977 period.

II. RECENT HISTORICAL TRENDS IN CANADIAN TAXATION

TAX REVENUES IN RELATION TO TAX BASES

The most noteworthy aspect of taxes in Canada during the last thirty years has been their growth—not just in absolute terms but as a share of national income as well. From a low of 21.2 per cent in 1949, tax revenue as a share of Gross National Expenditure (GNE) reached 33.0 per cent in 1974 and has declined, only slightly, to 32.0 per cent in 1979. This growth is illustrated in Figure 4.2. As we suggested, certain non-tax revenues can be classified as taxes for analytical purposes; the growth of these revenues would therefore indicate an even sharper growth rate of overall taxation.

Figure 4.2

Tax Revenue as a Per Cent of GNE.

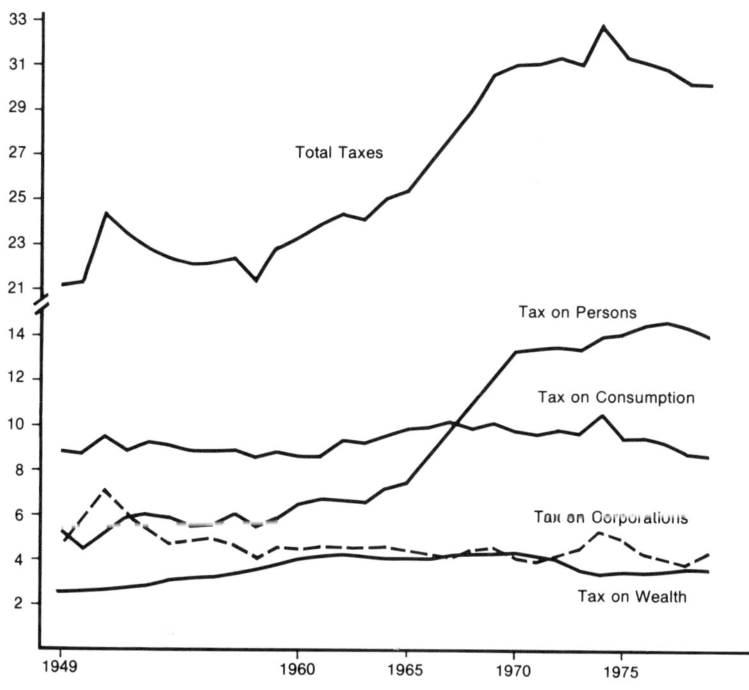

Source: R. Bird, *Financing Canadian Government: A Quantitative Overview*, Canada Tax Foundation 1979 and Dept. of Finance, *Economic Review*, 1980.

Figure 4.2 also includes several particular taxes as a per cent of GNE. This illustrates the source of the relative growth in total taxes—the taxation of persons through income and payroll taxes. The growth has been sufficiently dramatic that personal income taxes now account for 47 per cent of the total tax revenue. This is compared to 20 per cent in 1950. Both corporate and consumption taxes have declined in importance. This was quite dramatic in the case of corporate tax, which now accounts for just over 12 per cent of taxation, compared to 27 per cent in 1950.

A third measure of relative growth in various taxes is the effective rate of various taxes; that is, tax revenues as a percentage of the gross tax base. Once again, personal income taxes and payroll taxes have undergone the most dramatic growth, as Figure 4.3 clearly illustrates. Indirect taxes as a percentage of total consumer expenditure *do not* suggest a slight upward trend over time. This inference is somewhat altered if we calculate indirect taxes as a percentage of *taxable* consumer goods, especially during the period 1960–1968 when several provinces introduced or increased their retail sales taxes. The ratio of property taxes to gross rents rose rather dramatically during the period from the late 1950s to the late 1960s and then declined. This reflected, in part, the introduction of property tax credits and other policies to reduce the burden of the property tax on home owners and renters. The corporate profits tax as a percentage of profits exhibits considerable instability over time, as one would expect, and shows a slight downward trend over the 1949–1979 period.

It appears that the absolute and relative growth in the tax revenues of Canada has largely been determined by the rapid growth in taxes on personal income and wages. Both property and consumption taxes contributed to this growth trend, especially in the early 1960s, while the most rapid expansion in personal income taxes occurred in the late 1960s. The most dramatic changes have been in the composition of total taxes. Personal income taxes now dominate as a share of tax revenue with corporate and consumption taxes assuming a steadily less important role over the 1949–1979 period.

THE VALUE OF TAX EXPENDITURES OVER TIME

The tax system of Canada gives preferential treatment to persons or businesses in exchange for directing income or investments in particular directions. These provisions, labelled Tax Expenditures,* have

*Strictly speaking, the philosophy underlying this concept implies that government owns the entire national income, and that all monies which remain in the hands of the citizens, after taxes have been paid, are "tax expenditures" (money which the government could have collected in the form of taxes, but refrained from so doing)—ed.

Figure 4.3
Taxes and the Tax Base.

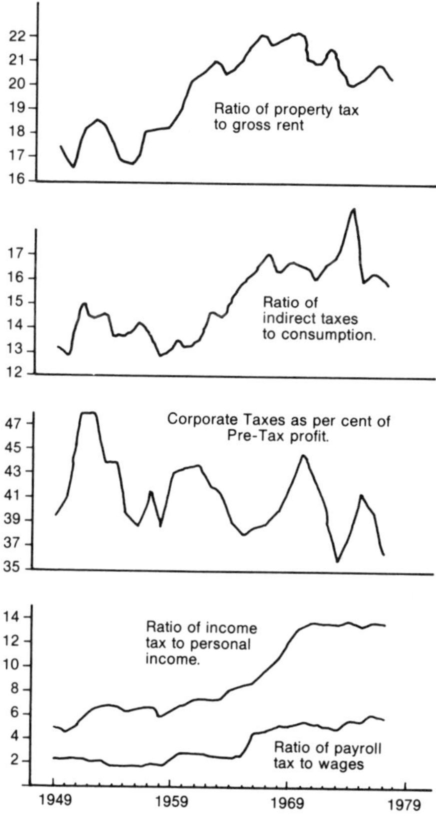

Source: Bird, op.cit., Table 13.

TABLE 4.5

Foregone Tax Revenue Due to Three Selected Personal Income Tax Expenditures* (1977)

Income Group	Tax Revenue Loss ($millions)
5,000	4.1
5,000–10,000	166.7
10,000–15,000	306.4
15,000–20,000	376.9
20,000–25,000	323.5
25,000–over	738.1
	1,915.9

* These include Registered Retirement Savings Plans, Interest Income deductions and the Registered Home Ownership Plan.

Source: Dept. of Finance, Tax Expenditure Account, Dec. 1979

important allocative and redistributive effects. They also have a significant and changing impact on total government revenue. For 1977, the tax cost or foregone revenue of three selected types of tax expenditures can be approximated by multiplying the dollar value of tax expenditure by the marginal tax rate for each income class (assuming an "average" taxpayer). The results are shown in Table 4.5.

The amount, almost $2 billion, is not insignificant! More important, however, is whether or not these tax expenditures are growing relative to income assessed. As an indication of this growth, we have calculated the value of tax expenditures associated with savings and retirement income schemes as a percentage of income for seven years over the 1950–1977 period. The results are shown in Table 4.6.

In 1950, pension fund deductions were equal to 1.2 per cent of assessed income. By 1960, a second tax expenditure, retirement savings premiums had been added. This boosted the value of deductions to 2.0 per cent of income and this increased slightly by 1965. By 1970, additional tax expenditures to encourage savings had increased the value of these deductions to 3.1 per cent of assessed income. By 1975, the use of these tax expenditures increased to 5.1 per cent. This was a 250 per cent rise over 1965 levels and more than 400 per cent over 1950.

TABLE 4.6

Claims for Three Selected Tax Expenditure Items as a Per Cent of Assessed Income 1950–1977

Assessed Income Group[a]	1950[b]	1955[b]	1960[c]	1965[c]	1970[d]	1975[e]	1977[e]
I	.5	.2	1.1	.6	1.7	5.1	5.2
II	1.2	1.1	2.1	1.6	2.9	4.0	4.0
III	1.5	1.7	2.2	2.4	3.6	4.8	4.7
IV	1.8	1.8	2.5	3.1	4.4	6.1	5.5
V	1.1	1.9	2.5	3.1	4.6	7.6	6.3
VI	.5	.8	2.1	1.5	4.1	4.3	4.0
average of all income groups	1.2	1.4	2.0	2.1	3.1	5.1	4.6

Source: Revenue Canada, *Taxation Statistics,* Annual.

Footnotes:

[a] Income groups I and VI represent, roughly, the lowest and highest 10 per cent of taxpayers. The income group II to V correspond roughly to 20 per cent of taxpayers from the second lowest to second highest income group.

[b] Pension fund contribution added.

[c] Pension fund contribution and retirement saving plan added.

[d] Canada and Quebec Pension Fund contribution added.

[e] Interest income deduction and registered home ownership plan added.

Up to 1975, the propensity to "use" these particular tax expenditures increased with income, until the upper most income groups (IV or V) was reached when the dollar limit to such tax expenditures reduced their relative value. This changed by 1975 due to the investment income deduction claimed by many retired people whose assessed income was low.

III. ALLOCATIVE AND STABILIZATION IMPACT OF TAXATION

TAXATION AND THE SUPPLY OF LABOUR

The impact of the personal income tax system on labour supply operates through two separate channels. First of all, increasing marginal tax rates or changing the average tax rate may encourage or discourage work effort. This will depend upon the relative weights of the income and substitution effects,* for those who can vary their hours of employment. This, in turn, can theoretically lead to a lower or higher cost of labour.

Higher income taxes may, alternatively, lead to increases in before-tax wages as a means of compensating for the increased tax burden (Brennan and Auld, 1968). Lower taxes could, if the process is symmetrical, lead to a reduction in wage demands. Evidence on the possibility of either phenomena in Canada is limited and the results are not conclusive.

(a) Work effort

In 1968, Professors Chatterjee and Robinson (1969) examined the effect of the progressive income tax on work effort. They used a selection of professional and non-professional occupations in the Kitchener-Waterloo area as their sample. They concluded that "... taxation influences on the aggregate supply of effort seem to be relatively negligible." Further they stated that "... one must conclude that work incentives ... are in no way significantly affected by the present personal income taxation nor are likely to be in the event of future tax changes" (*ibid.*, p. 219).

Nine years later, a similar study (Babey, *et al.*, 1978) was undertaken to determine if the progressive income tax structure had any impact on work effort among a group of academics who could alter their hours of work and earn additional income. The sample, as the authors admit, was small and not altogether representative of the labour force. Still, within their study cohort, they found some evidence that both disincentives and incentives were present. The effects, however, were weak and lead to the conclusion that "... the personal income tax had relatively little effect on the work effort of our sample ..." (*ibid.*, p. 589).

(b) Taxation and wages

There have been several studies on the impact of personal income taxes on wage change (Auld, 1974; Kotowitz, 1978; Wilson and Reid, 1979). These studies include a "tax variable" in a wage determination model, and examine the influence of such a variable on wage changes and other explanatory variables. Although the authors of these studies advise

*The income effect measures the change in the desired number of hours worked after (real) income, but not wage levels are changed. The substitution effect measures the change in the desired number of hours worked after wage levels are changed, but (real) income is also changed, so as to leave total income as it was before—ed.

caution in drawing any strong conclusion from the analyses, there is some evidence that rising taxes have accelerated the rate of change of wages.

These studies used aggregate wage data. They did not specifically link the progressive income tax structure to the income earned by a representative taxpayer. In contrast, David Wilton and the present author employed micro-wage data in an attempt to unearth any effects of the tax structure on base wage rates (Auld and Wilton, 1980).

As a starting point, we assume that workers implicitly bargain in terms of their net after-tax wage rate ($\dot{W}^N$) and that the rate of change in net after-tax wages is structurally determined by a set of variables (X). Letting A and M represent average and marginal income tax rates, then the rate of change in net after-tax wages can be expressed in the following manner:

$$(1) \qquad \dot{W}^N = \left(\frac{1-M}{1-A}\right) \dot{W}^G = f(X)$$

where $\dot{W}^G$ is the observable gross before taxes. To the extent that M exceeds A (*i.e.*, the income tax system is progressive), the after-tax change in wages will be less than the gross before-tax change in wages.

Equation (1) can be rewritten in a slightly different form which proves more convenient for statistical testing:

$$(2) \qquad \dot{W}^G \quad 1 + \delta\left[\left(\frac{A-M}{1-A}\right)\right] = f(X)$$

If δ equals unity, then equation (2) reduces to equation (1). On the other hand, if δ equals zero, then workers bargain strictly in terms of gross (not net) wages. To the extent that δ exceeds zero (in the zero-one interval), the progressive income tax is shifted forward into higher wages and rates of wage inflation.

Our resulting equations were:

$$(3) \qquad \dot{W}^G = \underset{(7.81)}{3.66} + \underset{(5.19)}{.20\ \dot{PE}} + \underset{(15.80)}{.52\ \dot{PCU}} + \underset{(4.52)}{2.12\ LM}$$

$$(4) \qquad \dot{W}^G = \underset{(8.60)}{3.51} + \underset{(4.63)}{.17\ \dot{PE}} + \underset{(11.56)}{.44\ \dot{PCU}} + \underset{(3.79)}{1.62\ LM} + \underset{(3.30)}{.80\ PROG}$$

Where $\dot{PE}$ represents price expectations, $\dot{PCU}$ a variable to capture price catch-up, LM is the regionalized help-wanted index and PROG is the tax variable. The T-scores are in brackets below the estimated coefficients.

It is our tentative conclusion that the progressivity element of the personal income tax is shifted forward onto wage rates. Whether or not the full shifting implied by this analysis holds true under all conditions will have to await further analysis. However, even partial shifting suggests that the tax structure may be contributing directly to the rate of inflation.

TAXATION AND INVESTMENT

Corporate taxation policy, designed to alter the level of investment, is normally viewed as a means of counter-cyclical fiscal policy. As far as short-term effects are concerned, this is likely to be effective only in selected industries such as residential construction. In most instances, these tax policies should be viewed as an attempt to bring about structural changes in the economy over a longer period. The efficacy of these policies is a matter of considerable debate.

Ottawa, and to a lesser extent some provincial governments, have in the past accepted the view that tax policy influences short-run investment behaviour. This attitude may be due to the influence of the Carter Commission which, in 1966 concluded,

> . . . fiscal policy can influence the level of investment . . . changes in the tax structure which change the level of gross business savings at a given level of output will probably affect the level of investment (Royal Commission on Taxation, 1966).

This conclusion was based on empirical work for the 1950–1964 period. The Report stated that changes in investment could be induced through changes in the schedule of corporate income tax rates, or allowable capital consumption allowances.

Between 1963 and 1975 there were five major corporate income tax changes designed to stimulate investment expenditure, either broadly or selectively. They were as follows:

1963:	accelerated capital cost allowance
1966:	deferred allowances
1970:	increase in capital cost base
1972/1973:	tax reduction and accelerated allowance
1975:	investment tax credit

The most recent and thorough study of the effects of these corporate tax changes on investment is by Harman and Johnson (1978). Earlier studies were done by McFetridge and May (1976) and Hyndman (1974). Because the results of the Harman and Johnson study generally confirm the earlier work, we report only on the most recent study.

The 1963 policy allowed manufacturing and processing companies with a required degree of Canadian ownership to apply a 50 per cent straight line rate of capital cost allowance on machinery and equipment during 1964 and 1965. It was later extended to 1966.

To curb investment spending in 1966, capital cost allowances on assets purchased between March 29, 1966 to October 1, 1967 were partially deferred. This reduced a number of allowances (effectively) by 50 per cent. For 1970, manufacturing firms could increase their cost base by 15 per cent for the purpose of calculating the capital cost allowance.

In 1972, it was widely believed that the slow rate of increase in capital expenditures was not just the result of short-term business cycle fluctuations but rather a long-term structural problem. To deal with this, two permanent changes to the corporate income tax legislation were made. First, fixed assets acquired in the manufacturing sector would be written off in two years. Second, corporate tax rates were cut from 49 to 40 and 25 to 20 per cent, respectively, for large and small corporations.

In 1975, a short-run change in corporate tax was introduced. The government allowed a tax credit equal to 5 per cent of expenditures on eligible assets against federal income tax. There was an upper limit on the credit for 1975 but firms could carry forward to future years, any credit above the ceiling.

Detailed econometric analysis led Harman and Johnson (1978) to conclude that, "... the effectiveness of investment incentive tax policies ... is not at all apparent" (p.704). The analysis did reveal investment effects in some cases, but with long impact lags.

Corporate tax policy appears to be ineffective as a short-run stabilization tool but may have significant effects on investment over a two or three year period. In the long run, however, investment in fixed assets will largely be determined by expectations about demand, technology, and the relative costs of labour and fixed assets.

TAXATION AND SAVINGS

One of the most intriguing macroeconomic patterns to emerge during the 1970s was the rapid rise in the household savings ratio (see Figure 4.4). There have been relatively few published analyses of this phenomenon. To date only limited attention has been paid to the role of the public sector in this growth in personal savings (Auld, 1980; Economic

Figure 4.4

S=personal savings
PDI=personal disposable income

Source: Department of Finance, *Economic Review* (Annual), Ottawa

Council of Canada, 1979, ch.2). Although there is no "hard" evidence on the effect of the tax system on the savings ratio, several tax changes were certainly conducive to the growth in savings.

1. Commencing in the early 1970s, there was a significant growth in the number of two wage-earner families. Since separate tax returns are filed by each income recipient, to the extent that the second income earner's marginal tax rate was lower than the original income earner's, the family's marginal tax rate would decline. This would raise the after-tax rate of return on savings and encourage higher savings. Alternatively, one could view the participation of the second income earner strictly in terms of a family target for savings, with high MPS for the second income earner.
2. The use of Registered Retirement Savings Plans (RRSP) was certainly encouraged by the tax system. As incomes (and marginal tax rates) increased, the tax saving resulting from such contributions

increased, especially prior to the indexation of the tax system in 1974.

3. The decision in 1974 to allow $1,000 of tax-free investment income was clearly an incentive to savings. For example, a $5,000, ninety-day certificate of deposit renewed throughout 1973 would have yielded $375 in interest. After accounting for inflation at 6.6 per cent per annum ($330) and tax on the $375 (assume a 35 per cent marginal tax rate) the after-tax real rate of return is –1.7 per cent. With no tax, the real return becomes + 1.0 per cent, a rise of 2.7 percentage points.
4. Indexation of the personal income tax system from 1974 onwards was an encouragement to household savings. Rising incomes would no longer place taxpayers in a higher tax bracket within a short period of time. A constant (or close to constant) marginal rate of taxation would contribute to increased aggregate savings as incomes rose.
5. The introduction of RHOSP (Registered Home Ownership Savings Plan) certainly led to greater savings, although if it postponed new home purchases it would affect personal savings in the form of household equity.
6. Changes in the law related to contributions made to RRSP had the effect of increasing the maximum annual family contributions over the 1974–1979 period faster than the rise in disposable income. This also was an encouragement to a higher savings ratio.

These structural changes in the tax system, combined with tax rate reductions in the mid to late 1970s, all contributed to an environment that encouraged greater personal savings. Whether they were entirely responsible for the doubling of the savings ratio is not known and remains the elusive goal of statistical research.

TAXATION AND ECONOMIC STABILIZATION

The confidence that once surrounded the use of tax policy as *the* means of keeping the economy on a non-inflationary full employment path all but disappeared during the latter half of the 1970s. The theoretical dimensions of the debate surrounding the use of policy for stabilization purposes has recently been reviewed by this author (Auld, 1979). The conclusion reached was that the harsh judgement rendered by some critics is not altogether warranted. Both the theory and empirical evidence suggest that selective tax policies may be appropriate to achieve some short-run adjustment in the economy. The type of policy and size of adjustment must be carefully chosen.

For example, the reduction in personal income taxes and sales taxes in 1974 did, according to T. Wilson and G. Jump (1975) have a significant impact on raising GNP in 1975. Gusen's study (1978) of the impact of the Ontario retail sales tax rebate on automobiles concluded that the tax rebate had a large effect on stimulating demand in the short run; too large in fact, as the substantial increase in sales during the rebate period led to a significant slowdown afterwards! In 1978, the federal and provincial governments combined in a joint fiscal policy effort (to curb cost-push inflation and expand demand). Provinces which reduced their sales taxes would be compensated by the federal government for a portion of their loss in revenue. The jury is still out as far as the effectiveness of that measure goes in reducing inflationary expectations and stimulating demand. Finally, although there were several corporate tax changes designed to stimulate investment, we have already seen that such measures had little short-run impact on the economy.

It would appear then that the effectiveness of tax policy as a short-run stabilizing tool of government was rather limited.[4] One must, however, keep in mind the fact that both monetary and expenditure policy were often at work at the same time. The influence of tax policy alone is thus not easy to discern. Compared to both the United States and Britain, additional research in this area of public policy in Canada is needed.

IV. REDISTRIBUTION AND TAX POLICY

There is no question but that tax policy and existing tax structures do alter the distribution of income. But in what way, and by how much, is income redistributed? The burden of taxation has been an issue ever since governments introduced compulsory levies in a consistent manner. In recent years, the matter has been more intently explored in terms of the redistributive implications of the total public budget. After all, a government which establishes a highly progressive tax structure in order to undertake expenditures that largely benefit the rich may be doing very little to redistribute income.

THE GENERAL INCIDENCE OF TAXATION

In spite of the increased sophistication of economic analysis, there is still considerable controversy over the incidence of taxation. Analysis by Mieszkowski (1972), Aaron (1975) and Browning (1978) has focused attention on alternative approaches to the incidence of property and retail sales tax. A constant stream of empirical studies gives us a variety of results concerning the shifting of the corporate income tax and its ultimate incidence. Finally, examination of taxation within the

TABLE 4.7

Effective Tax Rates for the Total Tax Structure Using the 'Broad Income' Concept, 1969

Tax Source	Family Money Income Class							
	Under $3,000	$3,000–$3,999	$4,000–$4,999	$5,000–$6,999	$7,000–$9,999	$10,000–$14,999	$15,000 and over	Total
Federal Taxes, Total	12.54	16.81	14.28	11.78	16.93	25.44	27.04	18.60
Personal Income Tax	.47	1.16	1.67	3.34	6.42	11.48	13.75	6.73
Corporation Income Tax	2.45	1.21	1.20	1.25	1.84	2.50	4.29	2.20
Sales Tax	2.49	2.54	2.51	2.57	3.89	5.36	4.07	3.64
Selective Excises	.79	.78	.65	1.09	1.42	1.91	1.26	1.27
Import Duties	.94	.79	.78	1.02	1.42	1.87	1.39	1.30
Estate Duties	.00	.00	.00	.00	.00	.28	.68	.16
Social Security Contributions	5.40	10.33	7.47	2.52	1.94	2.03	1.61	3.30
Provincial and Local Taxes Total	12.39	9.88	11.15	12.53	17.29	23.19	20.86	16.70
Personal Income Tax	.16	.39	.56	1.11	2.14	3.83	4.58	2.24
Corporation Income Tax	.67	.33	.33	.34	.50	.68	1.16	.60
Sales and Excises	3.89	3.77	3.59	4.55	6.63	9.11	6.51	6.04
Succession Duties	.00	.00	.00	.00	.00	.39	.95	.22
Hospital & Medical Insurance Plan	.72	.42	1.88	1.13	1.17	1.18	.60	1.04
Property Tax	4.48	2.68	2.33	2.69	3.60	4.39	3.69	3.51
Other Tax	.99	.69	.74	.79	1.30	1.83	2.17	1.33
Social Security Contributions	1.48	1.60	1.74	1.93	1.95	1.79	1.20	1.72
Total Taxes, All Levels	24.93	26.39	25.43	24.31	34.23	48.63	47.89	35.30

Source: Bardecki (1972) Columns may not add precisely due to rounding

framework of life-time earnings may appreciably alter the incidence of the personal income tax. The manner in which government expenditures affect tax progressivity is especially important in this regard.

Irwin Gillespie has studied the incidence of taxation in Canada for the last fifteen years. In his view of the burden of corporate taxation (Gillespie, 1980, p.8):

> If we as technicians are truly honest, we would admit to the layman that we do not know the incidence of the tax.

He added that "... the same goes for the property tax and sales tax" (*ibid.,*). Viewing the tax system as a whole, he said, "... it is not a straightforward matter to inform the layman as to who bears the incidence of Canadian taxes" (*ibid.,* p.12).

A study by N. Bardecki (1972) estimated the effective tax rates for all federal, provincial and local taxation in the year 1969 for seven different income groups. The results are shown in Table 4.7. Unfortunately, the upper income group was $15,000 and above. The results are thus not comparable to what we would deem high and middle income today. There is a fairly steep progression from the fourth to sixth income group which turns roughly proportional after that. The methodology was similar to that used by Gillespie in his earlier work.

The Fraser Institute published a monograph entitled *Tax Facts* (1979) in which a table was constructed to show how total tax liability changes as cash income and total income increase. The results are summarized below in Table 4.8. The method of allocating various taxes to

TABLE 4.8

Cash Income	Total Income[a]	Total Taxes as Per cent of Cash Income	Full Income
5,000	6,657	24.1	18.9
10,000	14,162	34.1	26.0
15,000	19,755	35.0	28.0
20,000	27,101	34.9	27.6
25,000	36,815	49.4	35.2
30,000	47,818	57.3	37.5
35,000	59,545	61.5	39.3
40,000	71,435	64.1	40.3

Source: *Tax Facts* (1979), The Fraser Institute, pp. 37–41.

[a]Total income is defined comprehensively and includes imputed net rent, fringe benefits, unshifted corporate profits and several other components.

income classes and the definition of income are discussed in the monograph. As in all tax incidence studies, there is room for disagreement over the appropriateness of different assumptions. The Fraser Institute results show a significant increase in the tax burden between the $20,000 and $25,000 cash income levels, and a 15 per cent rise in the effective tax rate. On a full income basis, the rise is only 7.6 percentage points. But this is still very significant. For example, as total income goes from $27,101 to $36,815, some particular taxes rise by extraordinary amounts, as indicated in Table 4.9. These results presumably stem from the assumptions about how the tax base is distributed at the various income levels. Still, it is rather surprising to see burden of property tax rises 312 per cent when full income increases by only 35 per cent; an elasticity of 8.9 is very high indeed.* This method of allocating the sales tax produces an effective tax rate (as a percentage of cash or "broad" income) that increases once we pass the $27,101 full income group, suggesting that the tax is progressive over this range. These findings are in conflict with other recent empirical work (Ruggeri, 1978). Similarly, the profits tax, again in terms of total income, is regressive up to $27,101, steeply progressive from there up to $36,815, and then mildly progressive after that. This result is also in constrast to other estimates.

The assumptions differ, the results differ and the debate continues over the incidence of the Canadian tax system.

These broader measures of incidence or the change in incidence do not indicate how particular public policies have affected the distribution of income. We turn now to a brief survey of such policies.

SPECIFIC POLICIES OF THE 1970s

(a) Tax reform of 1972

On January 1, 1972, Canadian taxpayers were faced with a new tax structure involving a new definition of taxable income, a new rate structure, new exemption levels, an averaging procedure, and partial integration of the corporate and personal income tax. The impact of this reform on the progressivity of the personal income tax has been carefully analyzed by Allan, Poddar and Le Pan (1978). They concluded that:

> the overall impact of reform was to redistribute tax liabilities towards those with incomes in excess of $10,000. Reform improved the progressivity of the personal income tax system.

---

*Elasticity $= \dfrac{\text{percentage change in property tax}}{\text{percentage change in full income}} = \dfrac{312\%}{35\%} = 8.9$ ed.

TABLE 4.9

Percentage Increase in					
Full Income	Sales Tax	Liquor, Tobacco, etc. Taxes	Auto and Fuel Tax	Property Tax	Resource Tax
36%	56%	56%	56%	312%	312%

Source: Ibid.

TABLE 4.10

Federal Tax Distribution by Income Group (1975)

Assessed Income (selective group)	Share of Assessed Income (%)	Share of Taxes by Assessed Income	
		Pre-Reform	Reform
less than 3,000	3.40	1.01	.37
3,000 - 5,000	5.75	2.93	2.65
5,000 - 7,000	8.78	6.19	5.83
7,000 - 10,000	15.38	12.99	12.45
10,000 - 15,000	26.85	25.51	25.68
15,000 - 30,000	29.11	33.58	34.49
30,000 - 50,000	5.73	8.35	8.68
50,000 and over	6.01	9.45	9.85

Source: Allan, Poddar and Le Pan (1978)

The degree of improvement can be seen in Table 4.10. Whether one would characterize these changes as substantive or meaningful is a matter of personal judgement. Khetan and Poddar in another paper (1976) examine in considerable detail the progressivity of the income tax structure in Canada up to 1975. They demonstrate that the tax changes in the budgets of 1972–1975 had a far greater impact on the progressivity of the tax system than the 1972 reform. This is confirmed in the Allan, Poddar and Le Pan study of 1978.

(b) Indexation

Indexation of the rate structure, and of personal exemptions associated with the personal income tax would, if all wages increased by the rate of inflation, virtually "freeze" the effective rates for all taxpayers. This would effectively result in a proportional tax for all. Without indexation, and given the present tax schedule, there would have been a significant narrowing of effective rates across income groups (because of the smaller tax brackets at the lower income levels). For example, an increase in taxable income from $10,000 to $11,000 raises the marginal tax rate from 33.75 to 37.80 per cent. At the $18,000 level, it takes almost a 30 per cent rise in taxable income to elicit a similar rise in the marginal rate. Indexation, during the latter 1970s, has thus prevented a reduction in the progressivity of the tax structure.

Even by 1975, the effect was noticeable. Allan *et al.*, (1978) have demonstrated that in percentage terms, the advantage of indexation in terms of tax savings went to those whose income was in the $5,000 to $10,000 range. For example, while the $5,000 to $7,000 income group accounted for 5.35 per cent of assessed income they received 8.22 per cent of the tax saving. The $20,000 to $25,000 income group (accounting for 10.2 per cent of income) received 10.3 per cent of the tax saving.[5]

(c) Corporate tax changes

Changes in the legislation affecting corporate taxes have largely favoured the resource sector, the manufacturing sector, and some financial institutions. Unfortunately, little is known about the redistributive effects implicit in these changes. If such a tax is shifted forward, then tax reductions in these sectors are equivalent to a fall in the sales tax. But this would have little effect on income distribution, since this tax is roughly proportional (Ruggeri, 1978). If we adopt the Browning (1978) approach to tax incidence, then these corporate tax changes have benefitted the higher income groups.

(d) Tax credits and income transfers

Tax credits and specific transfer payments interact with exemptions to alter tax burdens and thus affect the progressivity of the tax structure.[6] At the federal level, Canada has a combination of the child exemption, family allowance and refundable child tax credit, the latter dependent upon joint family income. In addition, there is the Old Age Security Transfer and age exemption. These programs are discussed and analyzed by Kesselman (1979). While the system does contribute to a redistribution of income, Kesselman argues that a restructuring of the system, given the same public revenue cost, could further enhance redistribution and simplify the overall system for the public and bureaucracy. The "cost" of such changes would fall mainly on those with incomes in the $15,000–$20,000 range. This could bring the equity goal of tax policy into direct conflict with the stabilization objective – if those experiencing higher taxes attempted to shift them forward by demanding higher gross wages.

There are tax credits and transfers at the provincial level as well. Wc comment on two of these only because of their importance in terms of revenue loss and high visibility.

(e) Property tax credit

The property tax credit was first introduced in Ontario. It was later adopted by several other provinces to partly offset what was generally regarded as the regressive elements of this tax. The scheme in Ontario operates in the following manner for a home owner:

$$\text{Tax Credit} = [\$180 + .10\,(\text{property tax paid})] - .01\ \text{Taxable Income}.$$

For a home owner with a $1,000 property tax bill, the credit vanishes once taxable income reaches $28,000. For renters, the taxpayer replaces property tax liability with 20 per cent of annual rent.

(f) Sales tax credit

The sales tax credit is another creature of a provincial (Ontario) government, first introduced in 1973. A taxpayer may claim 1 per cent of total personal exemptions against 1 per cent of taxable income. In this case, the point at which the credit vanishes depends upon the size of the taxpayer's exemptions, mainly a function of the number of dependants. The *combined* tax credit for a home owner is:

$$\text{Tax Credit} = [\$180 + .10\ \text{Property Tax} + .01\ \text{Personal Exemptions}] - .02\ \text{Taxable Income}.$$

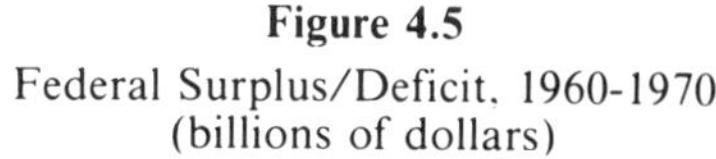

Figure 4.5
Federal Surplus/Deficit, 1960-1970
(billions of dollars)

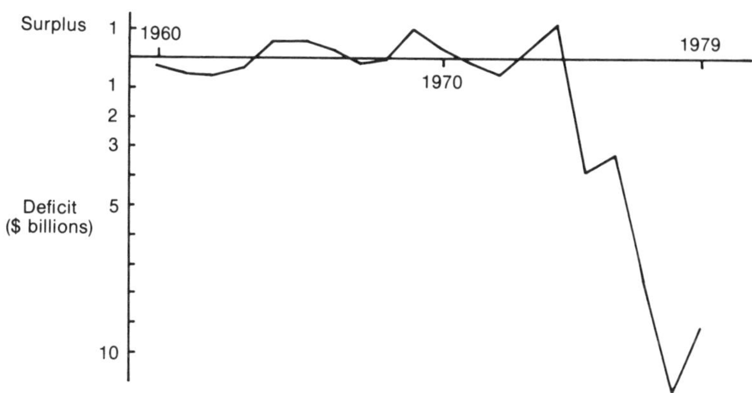

Because these tax credits decline and ultimately vanish as taxable income rises, they tend to increase the progressivity of the personal income tax. But their precise contribution towards higher progressivity rates is difficult to estimate, given the scope of current published data.

V. PUBLIC DEBT VERSUS INCREASED TAXATION

"For the moment, however, it seems safe to say that anyone worrying unduly about the growth of the public debt in Canada is for the most part wasting their time" (Bird, 1979).

A brief glance at the financial pages of most newspapers over the past two or three years would suggest that many people are wasting their time. To some individuals, a growing public debt is *the* cause of our economic maladies. In addition, the effects of inflation distort the effects of government debt (Barber, 1979). Unfortunately, it is not possible simply to set out the facts and then draw unambiguous conclusions regarding the impact of public debt growth on the economy. Our task here is thus limited to presenting some of the facts about public sector growth and to indicate where the areas of controversy exist.

As Figure 4.5 clearly shows, the size of the federal government deficit has been increasing in recent years.[7] Figure 4.6 indicates the recent

Figure 4.6

Net Debt Charges as Per Cent of GNP

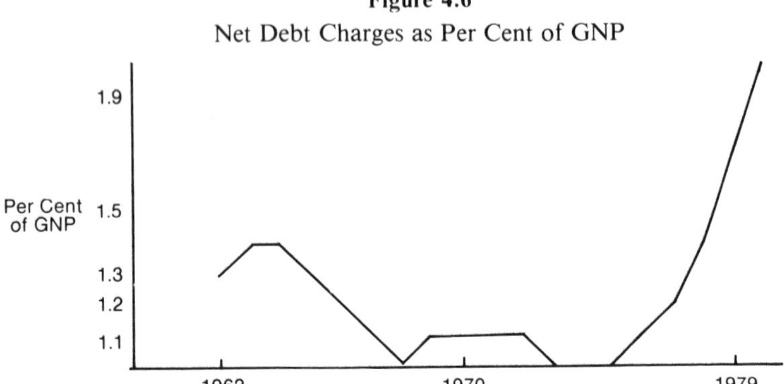

Note: The data on the deficit/surplus are on a national accounts basis. The debt charges are on a fiscal year basis

Source: Author's calculations.

demands on the federal treasury to service this increasing debt. This growth is dramatic, and the comparisons with earlier periods are a source of concern. For example, between 1960 and 1969, the average annual federal budget balance was a surplus of 61 million dollars. In the next decade, the average balance was a deficit of 3,433 million dollars!

As dramatic as these data are, the "burden" of the federal public debt has not reached heights hitherto unknown. Although net federal debt was 24.2 per cent of GNP in 1979 (up from a low of 15.0 per cent in 1975) it is still below the 33 per cent reached in 1964, and 52 per cent in 1952 (the latter year reflected accumulated war debt). In order to debate intelligently the issues surrounding the question as to the appropriate size of the public debt, three preliminary questions must be answered:

(i) why has the federal debt risen?
(ii) how has it been financed?
(iii) what are the economic consequences of the method of financing?

The increased federal deficit since 1974 is partly the unintended result of two sets of fiscal policies. For the past five years, the federal government has reduced taxes by allowing tax liabilities write-offs for savings. In addition, as we have already seen, Canada introduced, in 1974, a major change in the tax structure – indexation – which has resulted in a reduction in the growth of federal tax revenue. How much did indexation and other recent tax changes contribute to the slowdown in revenue growth?

In order to determine the revenue "loss" during the 1974–1979 period, we regressed personal income tax revenue (TPER) against national income (GNP) for the 1955–1973 period and used the estimated parameters to forecast revenue levels in the absence of these changes. The results were as follows:

$$TPER = -2.760 + \underset{(28.8)^*}{.115\,GNP} \quad \bar{R}^2 = .980$$

(*T – score in brackets)

TABLE 4.11

Year	Estimated TPER ($B)	Actual TPER ($B)
1974	14.09	13.77
1975	16.18	15.57
1976	18.99	17.77
1977	21.02	19.05
1978	23.62	20.31
1979	27.07	22.44

Data Sources: *Taxation Statistics,* Revenue Canada
Statistics Canada, *National Income and Expenditure Accounts*

This is a rather crude method. Nevertheless, it does give some idea of the effect of recent tax changes, and the magnitude of the revenue foregone.

The combination of indexation and tax cuts in the last half of the 1970s clearly contributed to the fiscal squeeze. To further exacerbate the problem, a number of cash transfers were indexed for inflation. Without very significant increases in tax rates or large reductions in spending on goods and services, a growing deficit was inevitable.

A popular impression, especially amongst conservatives, is that public sector deficits cause inflation. However popular, this view should be given little credence. If the economy is operating close to capacity, and *if* public deficits are financed by increasing government cash balance in exchange for Bank of Canada liabilities, then the inflationary consequences of deficits are fairly obvious. But they are due to the method of finance, *not* the debt itself.

To gain some insight into just how the deficit is being financed, we have calculated the distribution of the federal debt by major debt holders (Table 4.12).

Several points emerge from this table. First of all, non-resident holdings of federal debt are increasing rapidly and have reached their highest level in over 20 years. While the present generation may escape the burden of this debt, it may be a significant cost for future generations. Second, Canada Savings Bonds are falling rapidly in importance and are being replaced significantly by marketable debt held by the public. Third, and most important, the Bank of Canada's share of the debt has remained constant.

Much of this marketable debt is held by financial institutions whose ability to purchase government bonds has been enhanced by the steady rise in the overall savings ratio, since a significant portion of personal savings finds its way into financial institutions. Without the rise in savings, liquidity in these institutions would be limited.

It all fits together quite nicely. Tax policies encourage savings, and because of the nature of the incentives, revenue growth is slowed. This leads to a mounting deficit, which is financed by government borrowing from the accumulated savings pool. In a macroeconomic sense, the system is conveniently closed – increased private saving offsets public sector dissaving. There is a concern, however, about the behaviour of the government if the savings rate should significantly decline. Another concern involves the share of the debt held outside Canada. The drain on the federal treasury is no longer a small phenomenon. Richard Bird's statement about the federal debt may have been justified in terms of the data in 1977, but needs to be tempered in light of the experience from then until 1980.

VI. SUMMARY AND CONCLUSIONS

The review of the Canadian tax system in this paper and the background work for this paper lead to a conclusion that the tax system has returned to the pre-Carter Commission era. This does not mean we have reached the same tax structure as the early 1960s, nor the same level of taxation. What has occurred is that the tax system, if it can be called a system, has disintegrated into an "ad hoc" pattern, representing short-term political considerations rather than long-term economic goals.

Since the tax reform of 1971, the personal income tax has undergone more significant changes than in the previous two decades. There is no real structure to the corporate income tax, as it constantly changes from budget to budget, both at the federal and provincial levels. Indirect taxation is, with one or two exceptions, a collection of political

TABLE 4.12

Distribution of Federal Debt (Held Outside Government) 1975 to 1979 (% of Total)

Year	Bank of Canada	Chartered Banks	Public Held Marketable Debt	CSB*	Non-residents
1975	21.1	20.9	15.3	42.2	2.6
1976	20.3	20.8	18.4	40.2	4.2
1977	20.9	19.3	22.2	37.0	4.6
1978	20.1	16.4	29.6	33.6	7.7
1979	20.1	15.7	37.2	27.6	9.1

*Canada Savings Bonds
Source: *Bank of Canada Review*, Feb. 1980.

expediencies and *ad hoc* changes. Finally, although politicians constantly speak of property tax reform, there is little action except to enhance tax credits.

The changes have been coming so rapidly that to assess the redistributive or allocative effects of the entire system is almost a waste of time. The traditional criterion for a tax system, that it offer certainty, may be old-fashioned. Yet in a world of increasing uncertainty, some stability ought to be welcome.

The piecemeal approach to tax change that seems to pervade both the federal and provincial government is unhealthy. It only suggests further change down the road. The massive tax expenditures of the 1974–1980 period were surely a major contributing factor to the deficit of 1980, but it would be political suicide to scale these down to raise the rate of revenue growth. Instead, the government talks of removing indexation. The temptation to make a multitude of small changes to the system at frequent intervals is enhanced by the incredible complexity of the system.

An alternative to the present system would be to replace the present federal personal, corporate, and sales tax with a proportional tax on a broadly defined personal income tax base. The foreign disbursement of corporate profits would have to be taxed separately. But for Canadians, profits are reflected in dividends and capital gains. Eliminating the sales taxes would likely bring about a decline in the rate of inflation—which would offset the demands for higher wages from those whose tax rate would increase.

Proportionality means that tax expenditures are worth the same to all taxpayers in terms of tax saved per dollar of tax expenditure. Without a direct corporate profits tax, the problem of tax shifting would tend to disappear. Indexation of tax rate brackets would no longer be necessary, and many worrisome labour supply effects would not exist. Finally, without a progressive rate structure, the pressure for higher gross wages to offset higher marginal tax rates would be eliminated.

It would require a flat rate of 21.6 per cent of assessed personal income to generate the same revenue that the three forms of taxation generated in 1977 for the federal government. In addition to the advantages noted above, there would be a noticeable reduction in the public bureaucracy now required to administer the tax system. Finally, the accountability of Parliament to the public on the funding of public programs would be enhanced.

Is the change from a progressive to proportional tax system a reactionary reform? I think not. Progressive rates of taxation were largely a feature of wartime taxation. It was deemed improper at that time for individuals to receive very high incomes as a consequence of the war effort. But progressivity persisted, with changes, after both world wars. It was justified on the basis that an additional dollar of income to a low-income earner was of more "utility" than an additional dollar of income to a higher income earner. To my knowledge, this generalization lacks empirical validity.

To those who would argue that such a move is tantamount to a return to the "dark ages" in terms of social justice and redistribution, I would respond that this is not the case. Redistribution could still be attained by way of guaranteed minimum incomes and tax credits. In addition, and most important, proportionality would create a more simple, certain, and stable method of collecting revenues – in place of what is now a rather dismembered system.

NOTES

1. The term "own-source" is used to exclude inter-governmental transfers.
2. Approximately 72% of total resource revenue is derived from royalties. (See Statistics Canada, *Consolidated Government Finance* (1981).
3. The lower effective tax rates in 1977 compared to 1974 reflect tax reductions and both the introduction of new and greater use of existing selective deductions.
4. It should be noted that one structural change in the tax system, indexation, did affect the fiscal systems' ability to act as an automatic stabilizer. Stephenson and Grady (1977) estimated that indexation significantly reduced the elasticity of personal income tax, and therefore lowered built-in flexibility.
5. For a more detailed analysis of indexation and income redistribution, see Allan, Dodge and Poddar (1974).
6. See Kesselman (1979) for a careful analysis of some features of the tax-transfer system in Canada.
7. It must be kept in mind that because of high inflation, the real value of this debt is somewhat lower.

REFERENCES

Aaron, Henry. *Who Pays the Property Tax?,* Washington, D.C.: The Brookings Institution (1975).

Allan, J. R., D. Dodge, and S. N. Poddar. "Indexing the Personal Income Tax: A Federal Perspective," *Canadian Tax Journal,* 22:4:355–69 (1974).

Allan, J. R., S. H. Poddar, and N. D. Le Parr. "The Effects of Tax Reform and Post-Reform Changes in the Federal Personal Income Tax, 1972–75," *Canadian Tax Journal,* 26:1:1–30 (1978).

Auld, D. "The Impact of Taxes on Wages and Prices," *National Tax Journal*, March, 27:147–51 (1974).

______."Aggregate Savings and the Fiscal System: Some Preliminary Explorations," *Canadian Taxation*, 2:3:149–54 (1980).

Auld, D. and D. Wilton. "The Impact of Progressive Income Taxes on Base Wage Rates in Canada," mimeo, University of Guelph (1980).

Auld, D. "The Scope for Short Run Fiscal Stabilization Policy Within Confederation," *Fiscal Dimensions of Canadian Federalism*, R. Bird (ed.), Toronto: Canadian Tax Foundation (1980).

Babey, M. et al. "Effects of the Personal Income Tax on Work Effort: A Sample Survey," *Canadian Tax Journal*, 26:5:582–90 (1978).

Bardecki (nee Goodlet), N. *Intertemporal Comparison of Net Fiscal Incidence in Canada*, University of Guelph, M.A. Thesis (1972).

Barber, C. "Inflation Distortion and the Balanced Budget," *Challenge*, Sept.-Oct. (1979) pp. 44–47.

Bird, R. *Financing Canadian Government: A Quantitative Overview*, Toronto: Canadian Tax Foundation (1979).

Boadway, R., and H. Kitchen. *Canadian Tax Policy*, Toronto: Canadian Tax Foundation (1979).

Brennan, G., and D. Auld. "The Tax Cut as an Anti-Inflationary Measure," *Economic Record*, 44:108:520–26 (1968).

Browning, E. K. "The Burden of Taxation," *Journal of Political Economy*, 86:4:649–71 (1978).

Chatterjee, A., and J. Robinson. "Effects of Personal Income Tax on Work Effort: A Sample Survey," *Canadian Tax Journal*, 17:3:211–20 (1969).

Economic Council of Canada. *Two Cheers for the Eighties*, Ottawa (1979) Chapter 2.

Gillespie, I. "What Do We Know About Tax Incidence in Canada?" *Conference on Tax and Income Redistribution*, Osgoode Hall, Toronto (1980).

Gusen, P. *The Role of Provincial Governments in Economic Stabilization*, Ottawa: Conference Board (1978).

Harman, F. J. and J. A. Johnson. "An Examination of Government Tax Incentives for Business Investment in Canada," *Canadian Tax Journal*, 26:6:691–704 (1978).

Hyndman, R. M. "The Efficacy of Recent Corporate Income Tax Reductions for Manufacturing," *Canadian Tax Journal*, 22:1:84–97 (1974).

Kesselman, J. R. "Credits, Exemptions and Demogrants in Canadian Tax-Transfer Policy," *Canadian Tax Journal,* 27:6:653–88 (1979).

Kotowitz, Y. *The Effects of Direct Taxes on Wages,* Ottawa: Anti-Inflation Board, 1978.

Khetan, C. P., and Poddar, S. N. "Measurement of Income Tax Progression in a Growing Economy: The Canadian Experience," *Canadian Journal of Economics,* 9:4:613–29 (1976).

Mieszkowski, P. "The Property Tax: An Excise Tax or a Profits Tax," *Journal of Public Economics,* 1:1:73–96 (1972).

McFetridge, D. G. and J. D. May. "The Effects of Capital Cost Allowance Measures on Capital Accumulation in the Canadian Manufacturing Sector," *Public Finance Quarterly,* 4:3:307–22 (1976).

Pipes, S., and M. Walker. *Tax Facts,* Vancouver: The Fraser Institute (1979).

Report of the Royal Commission on Taxation. Volume 2, Ottawa (1966).

Ruggeri, G. C. "On the Regressivity of Provincial Sales Taxation in Canada," *Canadian Public Policy* 4:3:364–72 (1978).

Stephenson, D. R. and P. Grady. "Some Macroeconomic Effects of Tax Reform and Indexing," *Canadian Journal of Economics,* 10:3:378–92 (1977).

Wilson, T., and F. Reid. *Wage and Price Behaviour in Canadian Manufacturing: An Econometric Analysis,* Ottawa: Anti-Inflation Board (1979).

Wilson, R. A. and G. V. Jump. "Macro-economic Effects of Federal Fiscal Policies," *Canadian Tax Journal,* 33:1:55–64 (1975).

COMMENT

Jonathan R. Kesselman

Professor Auld has provided a useful survey of issues concerning the economic impact of the Canadian tax structure. The scope of such a survey is ambitious, perhaps overly so for anything short of a full volume. Hence, there will inevitably be questions of taste and judgement about what precise topics to include, as Auld himself would acknowledge. I shall begin my discussion with critiques of several analytical points in the paper. Then I shall note some omitted issues which I feel to be equally important in assessing the economic impact of the tax structure. In closing, I shall extend Auld's discussion of the role of political expediency and the potential of a broad-based, proportional income tax as a goal for tax reform.

CRITIQUE

I find Auld's characterization of indexing in the Canadian personal income tax since 1974 unnecessarily complex. Simply put, the personal exemptions (which might be viewed as a zero-rate bracket) and the tax-rate bracket boundaries are indexed. The refundable child tax credits (essentially a transfer program) are also indexed, but there is no indexation for the more widely applied tax reduction credits. None of the other deductions, such as the standard deduction, interest and dividend deduction, or education deduction are explicitly indexed. However, it is true that certain deductions which are tied to a percentage of earned income (employment expense and RRSP) will be implicitly indexed for individuals who have not yet reached the dollar-ceiling claim on the deduction type; but the dollar ceilings themselves are not indexed. Perhaps more important, there are no provisions in the Canadian tax for indexing the inflation component of capital-source incomes.

Auld provides estimates of the substantial revenue losses due to indexing and other tax changes for 1974–1979. Although he does grant that his estimation method is "rather crude," I would still take issue with it. First, the estimating equation should be in double-logarithmic rather than straight arithmetic form. A logarithmic form would more properly reflect an unchanging progressive tax rate schedule, whereas the arithmetic form incorrectly suggests a constant marginal-rate schedule. Second, it would be useful to separate the revenue effects of indexing from those of the other tax changes. The beginning of the 1974–1979 forecast period coincides with tax-expenditure innovations which Auld described elsewhere in his study. Tax revenues were lost due to the introduction of deductions for interest income and RHOSP contributions in 1974, deductions for dividend and pension incomes in 1975, and raising of the RRSP contribution ceilings in 1976. The associated tax expenditure estimates, such as those provided by the Department of Finance, could be subtracted from Auld's estimates to isolate the revenue effects of indexing.[1]

MACROECONOMICS

I do not agree with some of Auld's interpretations, elaborated or implicit, concerning the relations among the current deficit, the outstanding public debt, inflation, and indexation. To begin, we must recall that the public debt does not grow in real terms by the rate of the current deficit. High inflation rates are rapidly eroding the real burden of the outstanding debt. At 11 per cent annual inflation, the current federal debt of nearly $75 billion is falling in real value at a rate of $8 billion, or more than half of the apparent current deficit of around $14 billion per year.

Auld's treatment of the burden of debt service charges (Figure 4.6) is also somewhat misleading. Nominal interest paid to bondholders currently includes a large inflation premium; the other side of this premium is a steady erosion in the real burden of the outstanding bond liabilities and future interest payments. I would further resist Auld's suggestion that indexation of personal taxes or cash transfers in the 1970s is in any fundamental sense responsible for the current "fiscal squeeze."[2] Tax indexation merely keeps the real level of tax revenues constant if real income is unchanged. Similarly, indexing income transfers simply maintains their real value. Hence, given constant or rising real incomes, indexation alone cannot explain a growing real deficit. Rather, the growing level of tax expenditures and tax cuts also cited by Auld, plus real growth in various direct expenditures, must be responsible for the rapidly mounting deficits.

THE ROLE OF TAX INCENTIVES

One of the pivotal assumptions of the study is that tax incentives have been dramatically effective in raising the rate of personal savings in Canada. The savings rate of the last several years has been nearly double the 1955–1970 average rate. Auld's arguments linking tax changes of the 1970s "to an environment that encouraged greater personal savings" are certainly suggestive. Yet, until extensive evidence including careful statistical analysis is provided, I feel that the hypothesized effectiveness of tax incentives warrants a healthy dose of skepticism.

First, much of personal savings comes from households whose savings exceed the annual ceilings on permissible tax deductions; they are thus beyond the margin of the tax incentives. Second, tax-preferred savings vehicles such as the RRSP do not actually require an increase in the rate of savings out of current income. Taxpayers can derive the tax benefits merely by shifting previously acquired assets into the tax-sheltered forms. Third, innovations such as the RHOSP may potentially decrease the savings rate by causing individuals to defer the purchase of new homes. Fourth, the absence of tax indexation for capital-source incomes occurred during the 1970s inflation upsurge; this combination reduced net-of-tax real returns to many savers, often yielding negative returns.

Finally, there may be other, non-tax factors which would explain the rising savings rate from 1972 onwards. Auld has cited one such factor – the dramatic rise in the number of two-earner families occurring over this period. Another factor might be the coincidental dramatic escalation of housing prices over this period. Households meeting the higher financial burdens of new housing would have contributed toward the increased rate of personal savings.[3] Yet another explanation could be the spurious elements which can cause personal savings to be mismeasured in inflationary periods.[4]

INCOME TAXES AND PAYROLL TAXES

Last in my critique, I would question Auld's tendency to blur the distinction between personal income taxes and payroll taxes. In terms of their potential effects on the economy's structure, payroll taxes have important distinguishing properties, whether levied to finance social insurance, or for any other purpose. Auld has at one point lumped payroll taxes together with other personal taxes (Figure 4.2) and has more generally ignored these differential effects. Payroll taxes differ from income taxes in several important respects: they are levied at flat rather than progressive rates; they typically lack exemptions and other such refinements;[5] they have ceilings on the annual liability per worker; and they strike only earned income to the exclusion of capital-type incomes. These differences have commonly been cited as imparting a relatively regressive incidence to payroll taxes.

In addition to their distributional properties, payroll taxes have potentially significant effects on many aspects of the economy's structure. They may alter the demands for capital vis-a-vis labour, the relative demands for various occupational and skill classes of labour, and employer decisions regarding hiring, layoffs, and overtime work. These effects, in turn, have implications for income distribution, economic efficiency, and industrial composition. The predicted outcomes are discouragement for lower-skill and part-time employment and for labour-intensive industries. While not that much is known quantitatively about these effects, representing payroll taxes as simply another personal tax will not encourage the much-needed research. Perhaps as noteworthy as Auld's observation about the dramatic rise in Canadian payroll taxes is the fact that they still play a relatively small role in comparison with other Western economies.[6]

ADDITIONAL ISSUES

I would like to turn now to several important areas that were not treated in the study. While Professor Auld understandably had to be selective in the choice of topics to include, I would not want these additional issues to be forgotten. The Canadian tax system has at no time made formal or systematic adjustments for inflation in the measurement of capital-source incomes. With the rapid inflation of recent years, this treatment has had notable effects on the taxes borne by capital. Historical-cost based capital consumption allowances have dwindled in real value, interest incomes and interest deductions have been overstated, and capital gains have been exaggerated by measuring them in nominal rather than real terms. Even with the preferential half-taxation of capital gains, in many cases the real burden imposed on capital gains has exceeded that on earned income sources.

These inadequacies of the tax provisions have exacerbated the natural biases found in other provisions, such as the non-taxation of capital gains on owner-occupied dwelling units. Any judgement of whether capital has been under- or over-taxed in recent years would have to consider the role of inflation in the tax base, as well as the special tax provisions favouring savings.

INCOME OR EXPENDITURE TAXES

A topic of considerable current interest in the United States and Britain, at least among taxation specialists, is whether the tax system should be re-oriented from an income to an expenditures basis. This topic has not yet attracted great attention in Canada, but it nevertheless raises interesting questions. Auld shows (Figure 4.2) the steadily rising share of "taxes on persons;" this contrasts with the relatively stable share of "taxes on consumption." While "taxes on persons" includes essentially the personal income tax and various payroll taxes, it is not synonymous with a tax on income or even a tax on earned income.

As Auld discusses elsewhere, there has been a growing array of provisions in the income tax to exempt partially or to favour savings. Hence, it would be interesting to know whether Canadian taxation has actually become more consumption-base oriented, despite the growing reliance on personal income taxation. Of course, the issue of non-indexation for capital-source incomes would also interact with this assessment. To assemble some ballpark figures on this question should not be all that difficult, but this has not yet been done.

My earlier point relating to payroll taxes can be generalized to virtually all aspects of the taxation system. Namely, how have the various tax provisions affected the demands for and the supplies of all the narrowly defined factors of production—and hence their equilibrium prices and quantities? In the payroll tax context, I have mentioned some of the possible effects on labour types. There is a similarly wide range of possible effects on capital usage. In response to tax incentives, capital may be more or less labour-intensive, more or less durable, and utilized to a greater or lesser degree on a planned basis. Moreover, capital may be taxed at differential rates by industry, owing to industry-specific tax provisions. Provisions for corporate taxation and preferential treatment of small corporations in Canada have likely influenced the economy's industrial composition as well as forms of business organization and ownership.

All of these effects have further implications for the nominal income distribution, for the relative prices of final goods and services, and consequently for the resulting distribution of real welfare based on households' nominal incomes and consumption preferences. As there are hardly any studies examining these aspects of Canadian taxation, it is not surprising to find Auld silent on these matters. Nevertheless, they are of the foremost importance in assessing the tax system's economic impacts.

FUTURE RESEARCH

Auld's survey examines a wide range of studies on the allocative and distributional effects of the Canadian tax system. The estimated effects in these studies are subject to debate regarding appropriate data construction, economic modelling, and statistical techniques. Many of the estimated impacts are wide of the mark, not to mention inconsistent with estimates of other behavioural responses. Moreover, the incentive effects have direct implications for the redistributive effects—the latter being the direct tax burden on an entity plus or minus any effects via tax shifting.

It would be most useful to have a general equilibrium micro-simulation model of the Canadian economy, with a well-articulated fiscal structure, within which the disparate estimates could be evaluated more critically. Such a model has been developed for the United States economy under the auspices of the Treasury Department.[7] While there are many limitations and pitfalls to such a model, it can at least help to suggest feasible bounds for the range of tax-induced effects. Work on a Canadian model is already advanced, and further development should have high priority for future research in this area.[8]

THE POLITICAL ECONOMY OF TAXATION

Professor Auld has observed that political expediency can lead to the disintegration of the tax system's rational basis. He has argued that increasing deficiencies of the Canadian tax structure have been in large part responsible for the mounting federal deficit. While this point might be debated, the converse relation may still hold some truth. A growing federal deficit—particularly one perceived as "out of control"—renders politically expeditious the attempt to raise more revenue in indirect or hidden ways. The prospective removal of tax indexing as a revenue-raising measure is one example. Another is the shifting of much unemployment insurance financing from general revenue to payroll taxation effective mid-1980.[9] Most remarkable, payroll taxes now cover the full costs of the public employment services and job referrals. Clearly, the short-run gain of revenues in the politically least sensitive manner has been allowed to pervert desirable taxation features that have taken many years to evolve.

Perhaps as his last hope for an attractive and enduring tax structure, Professor Auld has expressed support for a broad-based, proportional income tax. I agree with his brief assessment of the potential advantages of such a system. I would simply note that the advantages are maximized when the system replaces all personal exemptions with universal credits or demogrants. Payment of the credits allows the flat-tax rate to be applied to all dollars of income, from the first to the last. This approach removes many opportunities for tax manipulation and eases withholding and filing requirements.

My own research on such a program, called a credit income tax, suggests that it could be easily administered and could also accommodate the indexation of capital-source incomes.[10] Corporate taxation would no longer be necessary except as a tax-withholding device, and the entire field of business and investment income taxation would be simplified beyond all recognition. If the credits were differentiated to provide higher support for specified categories of people, the scheme could further replace most traditional income transfer programs—without the substantial complications of a negative income tax. Canada already has an unusually good foundation for a credit income tax in the existing demogrants for children and aged persons. Despite the efficiency, equity, administrative, and compliance advantages of a credit income tax, the political obstacles to its adoption should not be underestimated. Our fate may be to endure much more deterioration of the tax structure before society is prepared for a radical change.

NOTES

1. The ideal method of simulating the revenue costs of indexing and the tax expenditure provisions—both separately and jointly—would yield still more reliable estimates. It should not prove very difficult for someone with access to a tax simulator.
2. This point is significant in view of the Liberal government's repeated suggestions preceding the 1980 budget that indexing might be abolished as one way of controlling the deficit.
3. In the national accounts, purchase of new housing structures is counted mainly as personal savings. Only the current flow of housing services, measured as the imputed net rental value for owner-occupied units, is counted as consumption.
4. See Gregory V. Jump, "Interest Rates, Inflation Expectations, and Spurious Elements in Measured Real Income and Saving," *American*

Economic Review, Vol. 70, December (1980). As Jump notes, "Rates of personal saving rose to record high levels in the mid-1970s throughout the industrialized world. With the notable exception of the United States, these high saving rates have persisted into this decade" (p. 990).

5. The Canada Pension Plan is an exception to this typical format, with its annual exemption on the worker's first $1,300 of earnings.
6. See the figures in *Revenue Statistics of OECD Member Countries, 1965–1978,* Paris: Organisation for Economic Co-operation and Development (1979). As recently as 1977, "social security contributions" in Canada were only 3.5 per cent of gross domestic product and 11.0 per cent of total taxes collected. Typical percentages for most other OECD countries were two to four times these figures.
7. An application of this model is described by Donald Fullerton, Thomas King, John Shoven, and John Whalley, "A General Equilibrium Appraisal of U.S. Corporate and Personal Tax Integration," in Robert H. Haveman and Kevin Hollenbeck, eds., *Microeconomic Simulation Models for Public Policy Analysis*, Vol. 2, New York: Academic Press (1980); also see my critique of the model and its policy application in the same volume.
8. See J. Gregory Ballentine and Wayne R. Thirsk, *The Fiscal Incidence of Some Experiments in Fiscal Federalism,* technical report of Community Services Analysis Division, CMHC, Ottawa: Supply and Services (1979).
9. A public opinion survey taken in 1975 found most people did not mind the unemployment insurance payroll tax and would even accept increased rates for increased benefit provision.
10. Jonathan R. Kesselman, "Taxpayer Behavior and the Design of a Credit Income Tax," in Irwin Garfinkel, ed., *Income-Tested Transfer Programs: The Case For and Against,* New York: Academic Press (1982).

DISCUSSION

Edited by: Walter Block

The informal discussion following the presentation of Auld's paper on Canada was spirited and wide-ranging.

Kesselman began with a critique of de-indexing the income tax. He objected to this plan on the ground that although it might be politically expedient, it was rather underhanded: "an attempt to raise more revenue in very hidden and indirect ways." He recommended a bit more forthrightness. Instead, government could "revise the rate schedules of direct and indirect taxation," or perhaps, for example, shift "the financing of the Canadian Unemployment Insurance system from general revenues to the payroll tax."

Courchene offered a modified de-indexing program, which would delete from indexation "once and for all major increases in prices" such as occurred in the cases of food and oil, but would leave in all more normal price changes.

But Clark insisted upon the retention of full indexing, on the following grounds: "One, it will lead to greater efficiency in the allocation of resources and in the long run to higher levels of real income. Secondly, full indexing acts as a break on the rate of growth of government expenditures. In the absence of such a break, governments in office are prone to be ambivalent about reducing inflation, for they are usually the chief beneficiaries of inflation both as tax collectors and as debtors. In both Denmark and the Netherlands, according to an OECD committee study published in 1976, indexation was seen as a means by which government has explicitly to justify any increase in public expenditures. Third, inflation is, I believe, the most unfair of all the forms of taxation used in modern democracy. In every income group, but especially in the lowest income groups, it hurts most those least able to protect themselves against it. Under indexing, as the same OECD study points out, 'the government undertakes a prior commitment to protect the taxpayer from the effects of inflation in relation to its income tax liability.' And fourth, inflation is a tax, but not one imposed by direct parliamentary vote. In a modern democracy, I believe that the issues of higher taxation, tax expenditures and other expenditures can in the public interest best be debated where the public and their elected representatives are made aware of the real costs of alternative opportunities. As far as direct taxation is concerned, this can best be done when individuals and businesses are taxed on their real incomes."

Kesselman resisted Courchene's suggestion of partial de-indexing as well. He saw no basis in it—apart from political expediency. Seldon, however, rejected Kesselman's alternative to de-indexing (revising rate schedules, or shifting the burden of taxes from one form to another). Said Seldon "Kesselman is mistaken in thinking that the interest of my country (Great Britain) lies in transferring taxes from earnings to spending. That is a view held by a few tax specialists, but they speak for a small number of people, mostly themselves. It's true that the Thatcher government's first budget last year did shift taxes onto income tax and onto VAT, but that was a temporary measure that did not meet with general approval. The only really important desire among the populace of the U.K. is to find means of *cutting* taxes—and not simply to shift them around."

Seldon also demurred from Auld's finding of "purposelessness" in the Canadian tax system. "I can't believe that in a country where the national and local government is extracting something like two-fifths of the national income that there are no long-term aims or objectives or principles that govern the tax structure. Although that tax system seems to be based on annual "ad hoc-ery," as it were, I can't help thinking that if the Canadian citizenry taxpayers and voters had any cognizance of what their government is up to, they must insist on some new direction or general objective with some accountability in terms of consequences. So it is possible that there are some long-term aims which possibly differ from the government's objectives or even the minister's personal opinions, but there must be an implicit, even if unconscious, long-term objective."

The next topic of conversation concerned the Canadian deficit: its significance, importance, and implications for public policy.

Daly started the ball rolling by remarking that, "the current federal deficit as a per cent of expenditure or of GNP is one of the highest of the countries represented around the table. It is roughly twice as large as the U.S. deficit." He took issue with Auld's claim that "based on the percentage distribution of holdings of federal debt by the Bank of Canada and others, there really hasn't been much contribution by the Bank of Canada to monetary expansion. I think that is a dangerously misleading way of looking at the issue. If you turned around and asked how much have the Bank of Canada's holdings of federal debt gone up, then I think you have a better way of looking at it. I didn't have the material here, but my recollection is that over the last four or five years the Bank of Canada holdings of federal debt have roughly doubled.

"This is a very significant rate of expansion. It is an important consideration given the existing cash reserve ratio of the chartered banks and the rate of increase in any of the more comprehensive measures of money supply. I think this element, the potential implications of deficits of that size to monetary expansion, is one of the underlying considerations about the degree of concern on the debt. I was surprised that it didn't get more consideration in Auld's paper."

Courchene took exception to this view, holding that, "It is quite misleading to say that a 20 per cent distribution of a given deficit that doesn't change over a period of time means that there is absolutely no change in the Bank of Canada's liabilities. On the contrary, the deficit suddenly doubles its per cent of high powered money from financing government deficits." Berndt added the point that in any treatment of government debt in a country with a federal system such as Canada's, provincial debt must also be considered.

Next, Buchanan, seconded by Walters sharply rebuked Auld, Courchene and Kesselman for their employment of the concept of "tax expenditures," (untaxed dollars, money which the citizens are allowed to keep, are a cost to government, or a "tax expenditure"). Said Buchanan: "I think early on in this discussion I should raise very, very serious objection to the use of this term 'tax expenditure.' We should know what is involved. This is a term that was invented by Stanley Surrey of Columbia University, in the mid -1960s, for the purpose of justifying an attempt to get the income tax made comprehensive in the United States. The idea that a tax expenditure is a bad thing is very clear in the Auld paper. Well, if it is a bad thing, it's because people are already locked into accepting the notion that somehow a comprehensive income tax is the ideal tax. To be quite explicit about it, this assumes that every dollar of income is somehow the government's, a very erroneous thought. Somebody ought to have raised an objection earlier to the usage of this term."

The informal discussion then shifted to the income and substitution effects, and the proper methodical treatment of taxes as a part of consumer welfare. Lindbeck held that for the analysis of resource allocation, efficiency problems, and welfare economics, only the substitution effect of tax changes, not the income effect, was of importance (apart from questions of externalities). Why? "If you reduce the income of an individual and he chooses to cut down his demand for leisure (*i.e.,* work more hours – ed.), and not only for commodities, that is not necessarily a distortion of the economy; that is his choice. There is a distortion only to the extent a substitution effect in favour of leisure occurs due to a reduction in the marginal return on effort." And further, "it is doubtful if we should talk about an income effect at all, for the economy as a whole, even in positive economics. It may not exist for the 'average citizen.' For if taxes rise from 0 per cent to 50 per cent in an economy, this does not mean that disposable income falls by half in the economy. People get the money back in the form of public spending and transfer payments. It is then rather suspect to talk about an income effect for the average citizen."

But Giersch defended the income effect: "I think that the income effect has important repercussions on the general atmosphere of the country, and thus implications for individual behaviour. There may be an enterprising atmosphere where you have these externalities on others. Let us compare the behaviour of Turkish workers in Turkey, and of Turkish workers in Germany. I find they are much more efficient in Germany because of the whole atmosphere which affects individual behaviour there. I personally think that the whole tax structure and the tax system must have an impact on the general attitude toward work, including work ethics."

Fisher also criticized Lindbeck: "Lindbeck said a moment ago that if the tax rate went up from 0 per cent to 50 per cent certain things wouldn't happen in relation to the income effect, but if we went from 0 per cent to 100 per cent, then our discretionary policies in enterprise economy would go from whatever they are to zero. Even if you dismiss that point and only go half way, then the forms of business organization which we live with would change and we would then have to discuss their relative efficiency. So, while I go some of the way with Mr. Lindbeck and his reservations about the income effect, I thought this example went very much too far in the other direction. This is true even though the income effect, I think, would be in the opposite direction from that normally assumed."

As did Block: "I should like to take issue with Professor Lindbeck's view that personal disposable income can enter the utility function in much the same way as can the expenditures governments (presumably) make on behalf of their citizens. I think there is a great difference between the money that the citizens spend for themselves and the money that the government spends on their behalf. We should not equate them. For one thing, the consumer voluntarily "plunks down his cash on the barrelhead" when he makes a purchase; in contrast, the often overburdened taxpayer is *forced* to cough up his money. For another, the economist is entitled to deduce from the accomplishment of a voluntary trade through the economic process that all parties gain at least in the *ex ante* sense; that is, buyer and seller must feel that what they give up is less valuable to them than what they receive. Otherwise one or the other would have refused to trade. But economists cannot deduce from the fact that people pay taxes that they receive products of greater value to them; for example, we cannot even know that taxpayers value, at all, the limousines etc., the government bureaucrats provide themselves with, to say nothing of all other government expenditures."

The last topic of discussion was of particular relevance for the Canadian economy—its relationship with the U.S. Walters began by registering his "surprise to see a paper on Canada which didn't recognize the obvious fact that from a European standpoint, Canada is really only equivalent to four states of the United States as far as economics is concerned. That means you've got very severe limitations. Canada is to a large extent locked into having a tax burden which can't be very different from that of the United States. Otherwise industry will flood into the United States, just as it now flows from Massachusetts to New Hampshire, and back again, in response to tax changes."

Courchene took up this theme as follows: "My vantage point at this conference is one of a person who is very, very concerned with the impact of federal systems. Here there are four papers from federal states and four from unitary states, but there is very little discussion of inter-provincial or inter-state problems. But there are a fantastic number of such difficulties in Canada, so at some point I would suggest that the group discuss some of the implications of the distinctly federal nature of the tax system, and the major distortions thereby created in Canada. For example, corporate income tax in Canada is shared between Ottawa and the provinces. However, right now we have a reasonably comparable tax base across provinces, but very, very different tax rates. We have an allocation formula such that if a corporation is located in a particular province, then it allocates its corporate profits across provinces according to half of the total payroll in that province and half of the total sales in that province. We are about to enter a situation where it's quite possible that one of the provinces is going to change its allocation. Then there will be, on the tax side, the equivalent of non-tariff barriers."

Auld dealt with this question in his summary of the informal discussants: "The question that Walters raised about the Canadian tax system being restrained by the United States is an interesting one. Right now there are provinces trying to fight this, attempting to compensate for the kind of tax changes taking place in the United States by offering tax incentives to companies in Canada to stay where they are. In a sense, there is almost a tax war going on between Ontario, for example, and some of the states south of the border which have offered significant tax advantages for locating industry there. Perhaps the question that Professor Fisher raised with regard to wages and taxes deals with the issue."

CHAPTER 5

TAXES IN THE UNITED STATES

Edgar K. Browning and William R. Johnson

The U.S. tax system and its economic effects are too complex to summarize adequately in a brief space. In what follows, we present a selective survey of the issues, focusing on what we regard as the more important topics. Section I contains a brief overview of the growth of taxes in the U.S. and of the composition of the tax system. Section II presents recent evidence on the incidence of taxes. Section III explains why international comparisons of tax systems may be highly misleading and suggests a partial remedy. Section IV emphasizes the allocative and distributive effects of taxes and Section V discusses taxes and total resource supplies.

I. OVERVIEW OF THE U.S. TAX SYSTEM

Taxes in the United States are collected by the federal government, fifty state governments, and a multitude of local governments. The magnitude of revenues collected, as well as the relative importance of different tax instruments and levels of government in the collection process, have changed greatly during this century. Table 5.1 shows the growth of total revenues relative to GNP for federal, state, and local governments. In 1902, taxes comprised only 6.2 per cent of GNP, with two-thirds of the revenues collected by state and local governments. By the 1970s taxes had risen to about 30 per cent of GNP with the federal government now responsible for two-thirds of the total. (The downturn in the ratio for 1975 does not reflect any reduction in tax rates, but was instead the result of the severe recession and the subsequent reduction in tax revenues.)

Table 5.2 indicates the relative importance of various taxes in 1975. At the federal level, the individual income tax and the social security payroll tax dominate the picture, together producing three-fourths of total federal revenues. At the state level, general sales taxes are the most important revenue source, while the property tax contributes more than four-fifths of total local government revenues.

Considering the total tax system, the U.S. relies fairly heavily on personal income taxes, with one-third of all revenues produced by these taxes. Payroll taxes rank second at 23.4 per cent and have been growing

TABLE 5.1

Tax Revenue as a Per Cent of GNP

Year	Federal	State	Local	Total
1902	2.3	0.7	3.2	6.2
1913	1.7	0.8	3.3	5.8
1922	4.6	1.4	4.2	10.2
1927	3.6	1.8	4.7	10.1
1940	5.7	4.4	4.5	14.5
1950	13.6	3.4	2.9	19.9
1960	18.2	4.5	3.8	26.1
1970	19.8	6.0	4.2	30.0
1975	17.7	6.4	4.0	28.1

Sources: U.S. Bureau of the Census, *Historical Statistics for the United States; Colonial Times to 1957,* pp. 724, 727, 729; U.S. Bureau of the Census, *Government Finances,* 1959-1960, 1969-1970, and 1974-1975.

TABLE 5.2

Tax Revenue by Source in 1975 (percentage composition)

Type of Tax	Federal	State	Local	Total
Individual Income	45.2	19.2	4.2	33.4
Corporation Income	15.0	6.7		11.0
Payroll	29.7	18.3	3.6	23.4
Sales and Excise	6.5	48.3	10.6	16.6
Property	—	1.6	81.6	12.0
Other	3.6	5.9	1.0	3.6
Total	100.0	100.0	100.0	100.0

Source: U.S. Bureau of Census, *Government Finances,* 1974-1975.

in importance in recent years. (Payroll taxes produced only 10 per cent of total revenue in 1950.) Although corporate income and property taxes together generate only 23 per cent of total revenue, this total still represents much heavier reliance on these tax sources than by most other countries. On the other hand, the U.S. tends to rely less heavily on product (sales and excise) taxes.

II. INCIDENCE OF THE TAX SYSTEM

One of the central questions pertaining to any nation's tax system concerns the way it distributes tax burdens among households. We have recently investigated this question in a study of tax incidence in the United States in 1976.[1] Before reporting the major results of that study, a few preliminary remarks are in order.

Tax incidence studies usually report their results in the form of average tax rates – the total tax burdens divided by before-tax income – for each household or income class. Although generally taken for granted, the concept of before-tax income is important to understand if the results are to be interpreted correctly. In our study, we have used a broad measure of income that includes a number of items not generally thought of as income such as imputed rents on owner-occupied housing, retained corporate earnings, etc. The result is that our aggregate measure of income is 30 per cent greater than total money income of families as generally reported. In terms of tax rates, this, of course, means that the rates may appear surprisingly low because the denominator of the tax burden ratio is larger than normally recognized.

This is familiar to all economists specializing in public finance who are well acquainted with the use of broad definitions of income like the Haig-Simons definition. One ingredient of this approach, however, deserves special mention: household before-tax income is defined to include government transfers (cash and in-kind). This is a generally accepted practice and is intuitively appealing since the receipt of welfare benefits or a social security pension is as much income to the recipient as a royalty check or a private pension. It does, however, mean that total before-tax income as defined, exceeds national income since transfers are added to income but the taxes necessary to finance them are not netted out. In addition, the very existence of transfers creates some further problems in evaluating and comparing tax incidence studies across countries, as will be emphasized in Section III.

THE CONTRIBUTION OF INCIDENCE THEORY

The calculation of the tax burdens falling on households requires the use of the results of tax incidence theory. Since elements of this theory remain controversial, the estimates must be viewed with caution. The findings presented here are based on a competitive general equilibrium analysis, assuming fixed total supplies of factors of production. The familiar results of this model can be summarized as follows: personal income taxes are borne by the taxpayers themselves; payroll taxes are borne in proportion to the covered earnings of workers; corporate and property taxes are borne in proportion to capital income from any source.

One novel, and somewhat controversial, feature of our approach is that we do not allocate sales and excise taxes in proportion to the consumption of households. While this is the commonly accepted approach, we instead assume that sales and excise taxes fall in proportion to labour and capital earnings. The basis for our procedure is a revised theoretical analysis of these taxes which takes into account the existence of transfers as an important source of income.

Excise and sales taxes are commonly believed to raise the prices of consumer goods, thereby placing a burden on households in proportion to their consumption outlays. This view is inadequate, however, because it fails to recognize that some consumption is financed by government transfers which are indexed to the price level. For example, if excise taxes raise the prices of certain goods, and therefore the overall price level, this does not place a burden on a person whose entire income is a social security pension—since the pension is increased when the price level rises. Instead, the tax burden falls on income that is not indexed to the overall price level, that is, on labour and capital income.[2] Allocating sales and excise taxes in proportion to factor earnings rather than consumption makes little difference for many households, but it does greatly change the estimated tax burden for low-income households, since transfers are very important sources of income for the lower income classes.

A PROGRESSIVE DISTRIBUTION OF TAXES

Using the incidence assumptions just discussed, Table 5.3 shows the distribution of tax burdens among income classes for 1976. For each decile of households the average tax rate is shown for the tax system as a whole as well as for the four basic groups of taxes: sales and excise taxes, payroll taxes, personal income taxes, and property and corporation income taxes. Considering the tax system as a whole, the distribution of tax burdens is sharply progressive. Taxes are 11.7 per cent of the total before-tax income of households in the lowest decile, and the average tax rate rises steadily until it reaches 38.3 per cent for the highest decile. In absolute terms, the tax burden for the average household in the lowest decile is $353 while it is $24,624 for the average household in the highest decile. Households in the top two deciles pay 57 per cent of all taxes; households in the lowest two deciles pay less than 2 per cent of all taxes. The average tax rate for all households (total taxes of $458 billion divided by total before-tax income of $1,574 billion) is 29.1 per cent.[3]

Our finding of sharp progressivity in the U.S. tax structure contrasts with most previous studies which have concluded the system was only proportional or mildly progressive.[4] The difference in results is largely

TABLE 5.3

Average Tax Rates by Income Decile (per cent)

Income Decile	Type of Tax				
	Sales and Excise	Payroll	Income	Property & Corporation Income	Combined
1	2.3	3.3	0.7	5.5	11.7
2	2.6	3.9	1.8	4.2	12.5
3	3.4	5.4	3.0	4.5	16.3
4	4.1	6.9	4.7	4.4	20.2
5	4.7	8.0	6.4	4.1	23.2
6	5.0	8.5	8.1	3.9	25.5
7	5.2	8.2	9.5	3.8	26.7
8	5.3	7.9	10.8	4.1	28.1
9	5.3	7.2	12.2	5.3	30.0
10	5.5	3.8	13.6	15.4	38.3
Top 1 per cent	5.6	1.1	12.4	28.8	47.9
All deciles	4.9	6.2	10.0	7.9	29.1

Source: Browning and Johnson, *The Distribution of the Tax Burden*, Table 6.

due to our treatment of sales and excise taxes. In earlier studies, these taxes have been allocated in proportion to consumption. Consequently they become highly regressive elements in the tax system, that tend to offset the progressivity of other taxes. As already mentioned, we believe this approach to be incorrect, and that sales and excise taxes (and any other that are believed to be "shifted to consumers") should be allocated in proportion to factor earnings. When this is done, sales and excise taxes are progressive, as shown in Table 5.3, which reinforces the progressivity of the other taxes. Any tax that falls in proportion to labour and capital earnings will necessarily be progressive with respect to total income, because transfers fall as a proportion of total income (and labour and capital income rises) as we move up the income scale.

THE SOCIAL SECURITY SYSTEM

Some further explanation for the reasons why the various categories of taxes produce the rates shown in Table 5.3 is in order. Sales and excise taxes have already been considered. The payroll tax category principally represents the federal social security payroll tax. This tax is composed of two equal levies of about 6 per cent each applied to labour earnings, one collected from the employee and one from the employer. Of course, it is generally agreed by economists that this nominal separation into employee and employer portions has no bearing on its real burden: workers bear the full burden of both parts of the tax. Thus, the tax is essentially a flat-rate tax on earnings, but it applies only up to a ceiling level of earnings, about $15,000 in 1976.

Although the social security tax is widely referred to as a regressive tax, Table 5.3 indicates that this is misleading. The tax is actually progressive up to the sixth decile, with the rate then declining slightly to the ninth decile, and then more sharply for the tenth decile. The progressivity at the lower end of the scale is due largely to the importance of government transfers as a source of income. The lowest decile receives 60 per cent of its income in the form of transfers and only 26 per cent as labour earnings – and the social security tax applies only to the labour earnings part of total income. Transfers decline and labour earnings rise as a proportion of total income as we move up the distribution, so the social security tax is a larger fraction of total income. On the other hand, the regressivity above the sixth decile is due to the ceiling on taxable earnings and the increasing importance of capital income. Together this means that taxable labour earnings decline as a share of total income. In passing, it might be noted that the ceiling on taxable earnings has recently been raised (it will be $29,700 in 1981). This will mitigate the regressivity of the tax at upper income levels and increase the progressivity of the overall tax system.

THE PERSONAL INCOME TAX

Personal income taxes are the most progressive type of tax in the U.S., with the rate rising from 0.7 per cent for the lowest decile to 13.6 per cent for the highest. The federal income tax is the major component of this category, producing 85 per cent of personal income tax revenues. It is a graduated rate levy applied to taxable income as defined in the tax laws. Because of numerous special provisions in these laws ("loopholes"), taxable income is less than one-half of the more comprehensive measure of income used in our study. Nevertheless, this tax remains highly progressive despite the "loopholes," since the estimates reported here compare actual tax liabilities with total income, not with taxable income.

The federal income tax does not apply to government transfers, so a large portion of income at the bottom is not taxed. In addition, personal exemptions and the standard deduction (zero rate bracket) exempt huge amounts of factor earnings. For example, a married couple with earnings of $5,400 in 1979 paid no federal income tax, and the comparable figure for a family of four was $8,483. These two factors together account for the very low tax rate for the lowest deciles. The progressivity through the higher deciles occurs because a larger fraction of total income is subject to tax, and it is taxed at higher rates.

CAPITAL TAXES

Corporate and property taxes are grouped together in Table 5.3 because incidence theory suggests that both impose burdens in proportion to total capital income, regardless of the source of that income. Consequently, the tax rates reflect the percentage of total income received as capital income by each income class. Since the highest decile receives a much larger share of its income as capital income, its tax rate relative to total income is correspondingly larger.

Two factors suggest the importance of interpreting the tax rate of capital taxes with caution. First, data on capital income received by households is notoriously unreliable since it is widely under-reported in surveys, or not reported at all. Although we attempt to "gross up" the reported figures to take account of accrued capital gains, imputed income of owner-occupied housing, and the like, the final results are certain to be less reliable than for either labour or transfer income. Second, the data we use pertain to a period of substantial inflation in the United States. Inflation tends to increase nominal interest rates and investment returns for well-known reasons. As a result, the data on capital income tends to overstate real capital income.

Despite these two problems, the estimates in Table 5.3 are in close agreement with the estimates of Pechman and Okner for corporate and property taxes.[5] Since the Pechman and Okner estimates refer to 1966, a year of substantially less inflation, and their data on capital income is more complete, the close agreement between the two estimates may mean that these two problems tended to offset one another in our study.

TAX IMPACT ON CAPITAL AND LABOUR

In addition to the distribution of tax burdens by income class, it is also important to consider how heavily taxes impact on capital and labour income separately. There is a growing consensus in the United States that capital income is being taxed too heavily relative to labour income, and a number of studies have pointed out that the U.S. taxes capital at a higher rate than most industrialized countries, even some with heavier overall tax burdens.

To establish the rate at which taxes fall on capital and labour income separately, it is necessary to allocate the burden of each to the type of income which generates the tax. As already pointed out, under competitive conditions, corporate and property taxes fall on capital income, while payroll taxes fall on labour income—up to the ceiling on taxable earnings. In our analysis, sales and excise taxes are equiproportionate levies on capital and labour income. Personal income taxes strike both labour and capital incomes, but because of the many special provisions in the tax law, it is not clear whether both forms of income are treated equally. In particular, there are a number of provisions designed to treat certain types of capital income preferentially. So it is probable that personal income taxes place a greater burden on labour incomes than on capital incomes. Despite this presumption, in generating our estimates, we assumed that personal income taxes fall equally on capital and labour income, since we have no evidence of how preferentially capital income in the aggregate is treated. Thus, our results may be biased to a degree.

Table 5.4 shows the calculated tax rates on labour and capital income, once again by income decile. Across all income classes, the average rate on labour income is 26.6 per cent, while it is more than twice as great, 56.1 per cent, for capital income. This disparity reflects the importance of corporate and property taxes, taxes which fall on capital income at a high rate. Thus, at least if the competitive incidence assumptions are appropriate, it appears true that the U.S. system is strongly biased against income from capital.

As mentioned earlier, these estimates fail to take into account the way inflation interacts with the tax system to change the effective tax rate on capital income. Several recent studies have found that inflation

TABLE 5.4

Tax Rates on Labour and Capital Income (per cent)

Income Decile	Average Tax Rate on Capital Income	Average Tax Rate on Labour Income
1	45.9	19.9
2	48.3	21.0
3	49.3	22.1
4	50.8	23.5
5	52.1	24.8
6	53.5	25.9
7	54.7	26.4
8	56.0	27.2
9	57.6	27.8
10	58.5	26.8
All deciles	56.1	26.6

Source: Browning and Johnson, *The Distribution of the Tax Burden*, Table 16.

tends to strongly increase the effective taxation of capital income. For example, Feldstein and Summers found that inflation-induced mismeasurement of depreciation and inventories increased the total tax paid by corporations by 50 per cent.[6] Taxation of nominal capital gains under the federal income tax also produces untoward results, with many instances of taxes being paid when there was a capital loss in real terms. While it is beyond the scope of this paper to consider this matter in detail, it seems likely that inflation has aggravated the tax system's already harsh treatment of the income from capital.

III. A NOTE ON INTERNATIONAL COMPARISONS OF TAX SYSTEMS.

Comparisons of the tax systems of different countries usually proceed by using data of the type discussed in the last two sections. For example, taxes in the U.S. are generally not considered to be particularly onerous in comparison to other countries because taxes are only 30 per cent of GNP, a relatively low figure. A more sophisticated approach not only emphasizes the overall weight of taxes, but also their breakdown by type of tax (as in Table 5.2), and possibly also the incidence of the tax system by income class (as in Table 5.3).[7] There are a number of well-known reasons why comparisons along these lines may be misleading, and in this section we add one further reason to the list.

The point can be most easily illustrated with a numerical example. Consider a society of seven persons who have earnings as listed in Table 5.5. We will specify two alternative tax systems for this society, systems which are absolutely identical in their real economic effects but which appear drastically different when compared using data of the type commonly employed.

Tax System A is a simple flat-rate tax of 50 per cent applied to earnings. The proceeds are returned to the taxpayers in the form of equal per person transfers. The results are shown in columns (2) through (5) in Table 5.5. (DY refers to disposable income, and ATR refers to average tax rate.) Note that this tax results in a highly progressive pattern of rates even though it is a flat-rate tax. Since the tax is divided by the sum of earnings and the transfer to calculate the average tax rate, this rate rises smoothly as we move up the income distribution.

Tax System B avoids the overlapping feature of System A by only collecting the net tax (or paying the net transfer) to each person. In effect, it is composed of a negative income tax with an income guarantee of $7,500, a marginal tax rate of 50 per cent, and a breakeven income of $15,000, financed by a 50 per cent tax on earnings in excess of $15,000 (the first $15,000 in earnings is exempted from taxation). The results are shown in column (6) through (9) in Table 5.5.

TABLE 5.5

Comparison of Alternative Hypothetical Tax Systems

	Tax System A				Tax System B			
(1) Earnings	(2) Tax	(3) Transfer	(4) DY	(5) ATR (2) [(1) + (3)]	(6) Tax	(7) Transfer	(8) DY	(9) ATR (6) [(1) + (7)]
$ 2,000	$ 1,000	$ 7,500	$ 8,500	10.5%	$ -0-	$ 6,500	$ 8,500	0.0%
5,000	2,500	7,500	10,000	20.0	-0-	5,000	10,000	0.0
10,000	5,000	7,500	12,500	28.6	-0-	2,500	12,500	0.0
15,000	7,500	7,500	15,000	33.3	-0-	-0-	15,000	0.0
20,000	10,000	7,500	17,500	36.4	2,500	-0-	17,500	12.5
25,000	12,500	7,500	20,000	38.5	5,000	-0-	20,000	20.0
28,000	14,000	7,500	21,500	39.4	6,500	-0-	21,500	23.2
$105,000	$52,500	$52,500	$105,000	av = 29.5	$14,000	$14,000	$105,000	av = 8.0

Source: Hypothetical example.

A CONTRAST?

These two tax systems produce identical effects. Each person's disposable income is the same under either system, and each person confronts a 50 per cent marginal tax rate under either system. Yet these two tax systems would appear to be drastically different if the conventional comparisons are made. Under System A, for example, taxes are 50 per cent of GNP (total earnings), while taxes are only 13.3 per cent of GNP under System B. Tax burdens by income class also apparently vary widely, as a comparison of columns (5) and (9) shows.

What this simple example demonstrates is that conventional descriptive data on tax systems are potentially highly misleading. The factors that determine the real economic impact of a tax system on income distribution is how the net tax (the difference between taxes paid and transfers received) varies by income level. Unfortunately, the usual summary data provide no clue to this aspect of the tax system, as our example shows.

Although this example illustrates that the usual data may be misleading when used to make international comparisons, it does not imply that this is actually the case. Nor are we in a position to demonstrate that the point made here is of practical importance. There are some features of the U.S. system, however, that suggest it is more like System B than are several other countries with higher aggregate tax-to-GNP ratios.

For example, the U.S. relies relatively heavily on capital taxes and rather lightly on product taxes in comparison with other countries. Since capital taxes are more progressive than product taxes, on this count the U.S. should have higher marginal tax rates relative to average tax rates than other countries. In addition, the U.S. relies heavily on income-tested transfer programs. These operate like the negative income tax in System B and impose high marginal tax rates on low-income families.

Consider, for example, that the U.S. subsidizes medical care primarily for low-income families through Medicare and Medicaid, thereby restricting medical transfers to the lower end of the income scale, just as transfers are so restricted under our hypothetical Tax System B. By contrast, many countries have more widespread medical subsidies that benefit all income levels, just as transfers are widely distributed under Tax System A.

MARGINAL TAX RATES

We do not want to push this point too far since our knowledge of the tax systems of other countries is too limited for us to draw any sweeping conclusions. It is important to consider further, however, how tax systems can be described so as to facilitate comparisons and avoid the problems illustrated in our example. One way which appears attractive, though probably by no means the only way, is to focus on the level of effective marginal tax rates. Note that in our example the effective marginal tax rate is 50 per cent for every person under both tax systems. Focusing on the marginal tax rate suggests that the two tax systems are identical, which is in fact the case.

We suggest, therefore, that it may be worthwhile to consider effective marginal tax rates for purposes of comparing tax systems. (Marginal tax rates are also important for investigating the economic effects of any given tax system.) Table 5.6 shows our estimates of marginal tax rates by income deciles for the U.S. Our method of estimating these rates was to relate average before-tax, before-transfer (BTBT) income for each income class to its average disposable income (after-tax, after-transfer, or ATAT) and then to use the change in moving from one income class to another to calculate the marginal tax rate for that interval.[8] Table 5.6 also shows the separate contribution of transfers as well as taxes to the effective marginal rates. At low-income levels, the implicit marginal tax rates of transfer programs are more important than the rates implied by taxes.

Marginal tax rates are typically a good deal higher than the average rates reported in Table 5.3. At the bottom of the income distribution, marginal tax rates are slightly above 60 per cent, for approximately the lowest third of all households, while they are 46 per cent for the interval from the ninth to the tenth decile. Apparently, marginal tax rates are close to or above 50 per cent for about half of all households. It may also be interesting to calculate a single marginal rate to represent some sort of average for all households. One way to do this is by noting that while average household earnings rise by $61,015 in moving from the lowest to the highest income class, disposable income rises by only $33,247. This ratio implies an "average" marginal rate of 45.5 per cent over the entire interval. Since the average tax rate for the nation as a whole is about 30 per cent, it appears that the typical marginal tax rate is about 50 per cent greater than the average rate.

One word of warning: if marginal tax rates are compared for different societies, it is important that they be estimated in a consistent way and related to a uniform measure of income. The rates reported here are related to a broad measure of income, as discussed earlier. It would be a mistake to compare them to the nominal marginal rates specified in various tax laws. For example, in the U.S. the federal income tax applies marginal rates of 14 to 70 per cent to taxable income. Since taxable income is only half of total real income, however, the effective marginal rates of this tax would be (roughly

TABLE 5.6

Marginal Tax Rates

Decile	Average Amounts (dollars)				Marginal Tax Rate (per cent)		
	BTBT Income	Transfer	Tax	ATAT Income	Transfer System	Tax System	Effective Combined Rate
1 – 2	903	5,292	366	5,842			
3	4,963	3,859	1,478	7,351	35.3	27.4	62.9
4	8,725	2,525	2,433	8,817	35.5	25.4	61.0
5	11,996	1,897	3,389	10,504	19.2	29.2	48.4
6	16,091	1,582	4,671	13,003	7.7	31.3	39.0
7	19,413	1,268	5,730	14,953	9.4	31.9	41.3
8	23,901	1,282	7,273	17,909	- 0.3	34.4	34.1
9	30,729	1,268	9,759	22,239	0.2	36.4	36.6
10	61,918	1,726	22,724	39,089	- 1.5	47.4	46.0

Source: Browning and Johnson, *The Distribution of the Tax Burden*, Table 17.

speaking) only half the statutory rates. A detailed empirical study is necessary to produce estimates of effective rates such as those reported in Table 5.6.

IV. TAXES AND THE DISTRIBUTION OF INCOME

Perhaps the issue that attracts more attention than any other with regard to taxes is the way they affect the distribution of income. Of course, taxes operate to reduce the level of disposable income, but the relative distribution of the reduced total can also be significantly altered. A proportional tax leaves the relative distribution unchanged: each income class receives the same share of total income after taxes as it did before taxes. Any progressive tax leads to a more equal distribution of after-tax income.

There are several ways to measure the effect of taxes in the distribution of income. Perhaps the simplest is to calculate how it affects the shares of income accruing to different income classes. Using our estimates of the incidence of the U.S. tax system by income class, we find that the lowest 20 per cent of households (the lowest quintile) receives 4.7 per cent of total before-tax income, but 5.7 per cent of total after-tax income. The progressivity of the system thus adds one percentage point (amounting to about $11 billion in 1976) to the share of the lowest quintile. At the other extreme, the share of the highest quintile drops from 46.9 per cent to 42.6 per cent, a loss of about $45 billion. To put these figures in perspective, recall that total taxes in 1976 were $458.6 billion.[9]

Viewed in this way, it may appear that the U.S. tax system is not very redistributive. This is misleading, however, since it ignores the role of the other side of the government budget, principally transfer programs, in redistributing income. In the United States, government transfers have a greater effect on income distribution than the taxes that finance them, so an emphasis on the tax side of the budget obscures the reality. This is especially true for lower income classes, where transfers are a large component of income. For example, the lowest decile receives government transfers that are five times as large as the total tax burden it bears: taxes are relatively unimportant. In our view, any appraisal of the redistributive effect of a tax system is seriously incomplete and potentially misleading unless transfers are simultaneously considered.

THE EVIDENCE

Table 5.7 presents evidence on the distribution of taxes and transfers by income quintiles in 1976.[10] Households are assigned to quintiles

TABLE 5.7

U.S. Taxes, Transfers, and Income by Income Class ($ in billions)[1]

Lowest to Highest Income Groups in Quintiles	Before-tax, Before-transfer Income	Cash Transfers	In-kind Transfers	Taxes	After-tax, After-transfer Income	% Share of Income: Before-tax, Before-transfer	% Share of Income: After-tax, After-transfer
First	5.7	60.4	21.6	3.2	84.4	0.4	7.8
Second	99.0	38.9	10.2	28.0	120.1	7.4	11.0
Third	209.4	23.2	4.2	59.2	176.8	15.6	16.2
Fourth	321.8	17.1	2.3	96.2	245.1	24.0	22.5
Fifth	704.8	19.8	2.5	264.6	462.4	52.6	42.5

[1] Households ranked by before-tax, before-transfer household income.

Source: Edgar K. Browning and William R. Johnson, "Taxes, Transfers, and Income Inequality," Table 7-4, in Gary M. Walton (ed.), *Regulatory Change in an Atmosphere of Crisis* (New York: Academic Press, 1979).

based on their before-tax, before-transfer incomes (*i.e.*, factor earnings): the significance of this will be apparent in a moment. Note that the bottom quintile receives an estimated $82.0 billion in cash and in-kind transfers and paid a total of $3.2 billion in taxes, for a net transfer in its favour of $78.8 billion. The lowest two quintiles together received a net transfer of about $100 billion. The top quintile paid taxes of $264.6 billion and received only $22.3 billion in transfers. The last two columns show the effects on the relative distribution. Before taxes and transfers, the income of the top quintile was 131 times as great as the bottom quintile, while after taxes and transfers, the top quintile has only 5.4 times as much.

These figures suggest that the overall fiscal system, taxes as well as transfers, accomplish a massive redistribution of income. Two points, however, should be mentioned in this connection. First, not all benefits from government expenditures are allocated in Table 5.7. Cash and in-kind transfers amounting to $200 billion are included, but since government spent about $500 billion in total, not all benefits are accounted for, and it is not clear how their inclusion would modify the picture. (Not very much, we suspect.)

Second, the estimates are based on the implicit assumption that household earnings are unaffected by taxes and transfers. This may well be untrue. For example, it is possible that the earnings of the lowest quintile (only $350 per household per year) would have been higher in the absence of the disincentive effects of the system. In other words, taxes and transfers may make the *realized* before-tax distribution of earnings more unequal. If so, the differences between the before and after-tax and transfer distributions overstates the equalizing effect of government on the distribution of income.

ONE MORE PROVISO

There is at least one other difficulty in measuring the redistributive impact of a fiscal system. This concerns how households are ranked by assigning them to income classes. In Table 5.7 households were ranked on the basis of their before-tax, before-transfer income. Table 5.8 presents the same information but now with households ranked on the basis of their before-tax, after-transfer income. (This is the more common ranking since most statistics include transfers as income and then rank on the basis of income inclusive of transfers.) It is important to understand that Table 5.8 differs from Table 5.7 only in the method of ranking: each household's taxes and transfers are the same in both tables.

It is apparent from comparing Table 5.8 with Table 5.7 that simply changing the ranking method significantly alters the apparent out-

TABLE 5.8

U.S. Taxes, Transfers, and Income by Income Class: Alternative Ranking ($ in billions)[1]

Lowest to Highest Income Groups in Quintiles	Before-tax, Before-transfer Income	Cash Transfers	In-kind Transfers	Taxes	After-tax, After-transfer Income	% Share of income Before-tax, Before-transfer	% Share of income After-tax, After-transfer
First	24.6	29.2	11.8	6.8	58.8	1.8	5.4
Second	101.1	38.5	13.8	27.1	126.3	7.5	11.6
Third	201.8	30.8	6.6	57.5	181.7	15.0	16.7
Fourth	317.1	28.1	4.2	95.6	253.8	23.6	23.3
Fifth	696.6	33.0	4.0	265.1	468.5	51.9	43.0

[1] Households ranked by before-tax-after-transfer household income.

Source: Edgar K. Browning and William R. Johnson, "Taxes, Transfers, and Income Inequality," Table 7-5, in Gary M. Walton (ed.), *Regulatory Change in an Atmosphere of Crisis* (New York: Academic Press, 1979).

come. The lowest quintile in Table 5.8 receives a net transfer of $34.2 billion – while the lowest quintile in Table 5.7 received a net transfer of $78.8 billion. In general, Table 5.8 suggests that the fiscal system is less redistributive than is implied by the figures in Table 5.7. This illustrates how seemingly unimportant differences in the way data are organized and presented can materially affect the results.

Despite these problems, it is clear that the U.S. fiscal system is quite redistributive – when both taxes and transfers are considered. This discussion, however, does suggest how difficult it is to make meaningful international comparisons. Not only is the measurement of redistribution sensitive to a number of not so obvious problems, but there are also difficulties in obtaining comparable data. For example, in our own case we were able to obtain data on the distribution of in-kind transfers, but in many cases such data are not readily available. The central point is, however, that only by considering taxes and transfers jointly is a true picture of the redistributive impact of a country's fiscal system likely to emerge.

V. TAXES AND TOTAL RESOURCE SUPPLIES

Taxes can affect the allocation of resources in two different ways. They can alter the composition of total output, and they can alter the quantity of total output. Most taxes will have effects that fall into both categories. The corporation income tax, for instance, affects the composition of output by inducing a flow of capital from the heavily taxed corporate sector into the lightly taxed non-corporate sector. But it may also affect total output by depressing the net rate of return and discouraging saving. In this section we will concentrate on the effect of taxes on total output through their effects on the total supply of resources, because the breadth and importance of the policy implications of this issue.

The extent to which taxes affect the supplies of labour and saving has important implications. The distributional effects of taxes depend on whether labour and capital supply are responsive to taxes: recall that our tax incidence analysis is based on the assumption that the total quantities of labour and capital are unaffected by the tax system. If that assumption is incorrect, then some commonly accepted conclusions, such as the notion that income taxes are not shifted, are incorrect. Perhaps more importantly, if taxes reduce resource supplies, total output falls, and the well being of the public suffers. Another issue of importance in the United States currently is whether tax rate reductions might generate such an increase in output that tax revenues would not decline. This ultimately depends on how much labour and saving respond to changes in the tax rates applied to these activities.

These issues highlight the importance of determining how the tax system affects resource supplies. According to economic theory, however, even the direction of effect is uncertain. Consider a tax on labour income. Such a tax reduces the net rate of pay received, but a reduction in the net rate of pay affects labour supply through substitution and income effects that are in opposing directions, so the direction of the net effect is theoretically indeterminate. A similar analysis applies to capital taxes that reduce the net return on saving. Thus, although it is possible that taxes reduce labour supply and saving, this is not a matter that can be predicted unequivocally by economic theory. Empirical evidence is necessary to determine the direction and magnitude of the effect of taxes on resource supplies.[11]

TAXES AND LABOUR EFFORT

For a long time, probably until the 1970s, the mainstream view was that taxes in the United States had a zero effect on total resource supplies. This view was not based on any sophisticated empirical studies—there were none until recently—but instead probably reflected the fact that the average work week in manufacturing and the national saving rates were approximately constant during the post-war period, despite a 50 per cent increase in the national average rate of taxation. While interpreting these facts to mean that taxes have no effect would constitute the *post hoc* logical fallacy, these historical data make it hard to believe that taxes have a large depressing effect on resource supplies.

Recently, however, even the constancy of these data has been cast in doubt. Drawing on several pieces of evidence, Alan Blinder has conjectured that the typical lifetime labour supply of workers has declined 16 per cent in the post-war period.[12] It also seems clear that net saving is not so stable as once thought. This underscores the importance of a more careful investigation of the relationship between resource supplies and taxation.

In surveying the current state of the empirical evidence on the subject, we are fortunate in being able to rely on recently published articles devoted to this topic. Harvey Rosen summarizes the empirical evidence on labour supply with two propositions.[13] First, for prime age males, the substitution effect of changes in the net wage upon hours of work is generally found to be small and often statistically insignificant. Second, the labour supply of married women is quite sensitive to changes in the net wage rate, with an elasticity higher than 1.0 found in some studies. Taking these two together, and recognizing that married women constitute about one-fourth of the labour force, it seems likely that a weighted average value for the labour supply elasticity of 0.2 is plausible, even if the elasticity is zero for prime age males. Moreover, as Rosen emphasizes, labour supply can be varied in ways other than hours of work (such as changing the retirement age), and these have not been adequately investigated. Thus, the relevant measure of the elasticity of labour supply may well exceed 0.2.

THE ELASTICITIES

Turning to the effect of taxes on saving, Boskin and Shoven conclude their survey of the literature by noting that "... [these findings] clearly suggest that heavy taxation of capital income substantially curtails private saving by reducing the real net rate of return..."[14] Boskin's own preferred estimate of the elasticity of saving with respect to the rate of return is 0.4. On the other hand, Blinder observes that "... other investigators have obtained negligible interest elasticities of saving. No one at this time can confidently claim that a strong saving response to higher interest rates is well established."[15]

Given the proclivities of conservatives to detect high elasticities and of liberals to unearth low elasticities, it is apparent that not too much confidence can be placed on precise estimates of these elasticities. Granted this, however, the evidence indicates that elasticities in the 0.2 to 0.5 range are plausible. Let us consider briefly some of the implications of elasticities of these magnitudes. If we assume an elasticity of saving and labour supply of 0.3, and combine this figure with our estimate of an "average" marginal tax rate of 45 per cent, we can conclude that total resource supplies have been reduced by about 13 per cent by the tax system. This would imply an annual loss in GNP of about $300 billion per year at current prices.

SIGNIFICANT LOSSES

A loss of $300 billion in GNP is not a net loss to society, since people gain leisure and present consumption when labour supply and saving are reduced. Browning attempted to estimate the net welfare loss from labour income taxes for 1974.[16] Assuming a labour supply elasticity of 0.2 he found the welfare loss to be $13 billion—a loss that would be at least $20 billion by 1980. Boskin assumed an interest elasticity of saving of 0.4 and estimated the welfare loss from taxes on capital income to be $60 billion.[17] Thus, an annual welfare loss from reduced resource supplies of $80 billion is implied. Boskin's finding of a very large loss from capital taxation (especially in comparison to the revenue yield from capital taxes) lends credence to the view that capital income is too heavily taxed in the U.S. Of course, these estimates are no better than the assumed elasticities on which they are based.

Elasticities in this range are also relevant in assessing whether a general reduction in tax rates would sufficiently stimulate economic activity so tax revenues would not fall. As it turns out, these values imply that tax revenues would fall sharply if tax rates were cut. For revenues to remain unchanged by a tax rate reduction, the elasticity of resource supply would have to be at least 1.5 – far beyond anything suggested by the available evidence. Elasticities in the 0.2 to 0.5 range also imply that tax rates in the U.S. are well below levels that would maximize total revenues.

If total resource supplies are as responsive as elasticities of 0.2 to 0.5 suggest, then the detrimental effect of the tax system on total output is clearly significant. Nor should it be forgotten that taxes result in resource misallocation of other types also. While we cannot be overly confident of any of the exact elasticities cited here, they suggest that the time is past when concern over the impact of taxes on labour supply and saving could be cavalierly dismissed.

NOTES

1. Edgar K. Browning and William R. Johnson, *The Distribution of the Tax Burden,* Washington, D.C.: American Enterprise Institute, (1979).
2. For a more detailed discussion of the theoretical basis for allocating sales and excise taxes in proportion to factor earnings, see Browning and Johnson, *op. cit.,* especially Chapter 2 and the Appendix.
3. See Note 1 above, Tables 7, 10 and 11.
4. See, in particular, Joseph A. Pechman and Benjamin A. Okner, *Who Bears the Tax Burden?,* Washington, D.C.: The Brookings Institution (1974); and Richard A. Musgrave, Karl E. Case, and Herman Leonard, "The Distribution of Fiscal Burdens and Benefits," *Public Fianance Quarterly,* II (July 1974), 259–311.
5. The comparable results in the Pechman and Okner study are reported in Table 4–9 (Variant lc) of their study.
6. Martin Feldstein and Lawrence Summers, "Inflation and the Taxation of Capital Income in the Corporate Sector," NBER Working Paper No. 312 (1979).
7. A typical comparative analysis is Richard A. Musgrave and Peggy B. Musgrave, *Public Finance in Theory and Practice*, Third Edition, New York: McGraw-Hill, (1980), Chapter 15.
8. There are some problems in using this procedure to estimate marginal tax rates. We are currently experimenting with other approaches, but the results do not differ significantly.
9. See Note 1 above, Table 9.
10. There are some small differences in the data used for Tables 5.7–5.8 and Tables 5.3–5.4. Tables 5.7 and 5.8 were completed before imputed income from owner-occupied housing was added to the data base.

11. For some purposes it is only necessary to use the substitution effect of taxes, and this always results in diminished resource supplies. This is the case in estimating welfare costs when compensated supply curves (containing substitution effects only) are the appropriate relationship to use.
12. Alan S. Blinder, "The Level and Distribution of Economic Well-Being," forthcoming in Martin Feldstein (ed.), *The American Economy in Transition,* Chicago: University of Chicago Press (1980).
13. Harvey S. Rosen, "What Is Labor Supply and Do Taxes Affect It?, *American Economic Review,* May (1980) 171–176.
14. Michael J. Boskin and John B. Shoven, "Issues in the Taxation of Capital Income in the United States," *American Economic Review,* May (1980) 169.
15. Alan S. Blinder, "Discussion," *American Economic Review,* May (1980) 190.
16. Edgar K. Browning, "The Marginal Cost of Public Funds," *Journal of Political Economy,* April (1976) 283–298.
17. Michael J. Boskin, "Taxation, Saving, and the Rate of Interest," *Journal of Political Economy,* April (1978) S2–S27.

COMMENT: Incidence of Taxation in the U.S.

Edgar L. Feige

The Browning-Johnson (BJ) paper presents an overview of U.S. taxes and their composition, evidence on the incidence of taxation, difficulties encountered in international comparisons of tax systems, and a discussion of the allocative and distributive effects of taxes.

Their brief overview of the growth of taxes and their warnings concerning the hazards of casual comparisons of diverse tax systems are quite straightforward and require no additional comments.

PROVOCATIVE AND CONTROVERSIAL FINDINGS

But the sections dealing with the incidence and allocative and distributive effects of the tax system raise the most interesting questions, and report results that are both provocative and highly controversial. Browning and Johnson have utilized some important ideas that deserve serious attention, yet, I have strong reservations about the specific manner in which they arrived at their striking and apparently novel findings. For, as I shall attempt to show, their empirical findings depend very heavily on assumptions that may be unwarranted, and their empirical methods display a questionable pattern of what appear to be selective adjustments. This leads inextricably to their two major conclusions—namely, "sharp progressivity in the U.S. tax structure" and "that the U.S. system is strongly biased against income from capital."

BJ's finding of sharp progressivity in the U.S. tax structure contrasts markedly with previous studies of tax incidence. Whereas other studies reveal that "the burden of taxes... is almost exactly proportional for most of the population" (Minarik, 1979),[1] BJ present estimates suggesting an average tax rate for the lowest income decile of 11.7 per cent, as compared with 38.3 per cent average tax rate for the highest income decile. These results stand in contrast to the findings of the Pechman-Okner study which, for 1966, estimated an average tax rate for the lowest decile of 27.5 per cent and a tax rate for the highest decile of 25.9 per cent under "conventional" incidence assumptions.[2] (See Table 5.9, Col. 2 and 3). How are we to reconcile such dramatically different findings? The key lies in the definition of income used for each income class and in the particular set of incidence assumptions employed by the authors. Given the novelty of the BJ conclusions, I had hoped to find in their paper more careful documentation, and I would have welcomed a sensitivity analysis revealing precisely the reasonable range of tax incidence results stemming from alternative incidence assumptions

TABLE 5.9

Comparison of Incidence Results
Effective Average Tax Rates (Federal State and Local)
by Income Decile

	Pechman - Okner[a]	Pechman - Okner[a]	Browning-Johnson[b]
Decile	Varient 1c	Varient 3b	
	1	2	3
1	16.8	27.5	11.7
2	18.9	24.8	12.5
3	21.7	26.0	16.3
4	22.6	25.9	20.2
5	22.8	25.8	23.2
6	22.7	25.6	25.5
7	22.7	25.5	26.7
8	23.1	25.5	28.1
9	23.3	25.1	30.0
10	30.1	25.9	38.3
All Deciles	25.2	25.9	29.1

[a] Pechman, J.A. and Okner, B.A. *Who Bears the Tax Burden?*, The Brookings Institution, p. 38.

[b] Browning, E.K., and Johnson, W.R. "Taxes in the United States," Conference Paper.

and alternative definitions of income. Unfortunately, such an analysis is lacking, and in its absence, we can only generally point out the likely implications of each of BJ's methodological innovations.

THE DEFINITION OF INCOME

The first major conceptual innovation in the BJ approach to the incidence problem concerns their adoption of the familiar Haig-Simons definition of income. The Haig-Simons definition is "the money value of the net accretion to one's economic power between two points in time." Operationally, therefore, it is the sum of the market value of rights exercised in consumption, and the change in the value of the store of property rights, between the beginning and the end of the period in question. I am in full sympathy with the notion that incidence should be defined in terms of this broad income concept. Yet, BJ tell us only that "we have used a broad measure of income that includes a number of items not generally thought of as income such as imputed rents on owner-occupied housing, retained corporate earnings, etc."

My concern with their results stems in large part from their lack of specificity in clarifying precisely what is meant by that enigmatic and all important "ETC." As we shall see, the incidence results depend critically on just which incomes are included in the Haig-Simons definition, and the issue of how different income sources are likely to be distributed by income class.

The tax incidence game is inherently quite simple. Proportional tax burdens are the more likely outcome when the incomes of the lower deciles are understated and the incomes of the upper deciles are overstated. Conversely, progressivity is the likely outcome when lower decile incomes are inflated while upper decile incomes are systematically understated. Since I have, unfortunately, not had access to the BJ cited study, *The Distribution of the Tax Burden,*[3] I can only guess from the information reported in the present paper that they have used the Haig-Simons definition in such a way as to give the appearance of strong progressivity, when perhaps the reality conforms to the earlier studies' findings of a proportional tax burden.

AN UNREPRESENTATIVE TIME PERIOD

In the correct spirit of the Haig-Simons definition, BJ include transfer payments as part of before-tax income; and since transfers fall disproportionately on low-income recipients, this inclusion swells their income and reduces their effective tax rate. Unfortunately, the incidence results reported in their Table 5.3 do not reveal to the reader the date for which the relevant data were collected, yet their Table 5.2 suggests that the period in question was 1974–1975. Since these years represented the worst depression in U.S. history since the 1930s, it is also, not surprisingly, a period in which transfer payments were abnormally high. I would have wished the authors to provide us with some further information indicating the degree to which their surprising results are affected by this particular choice of time period. Surely, a more representative year might have been selected for comparison.

UNDERESTIMATING THE INCOME OF THE RICH

Having thus swelled the incomes of the lower deciles, how has the broad Haig-Simons definition of income been applied to upper deciles? Do BJ include in their "etc.," the value of gifts and bequests, for example, which Haig-Simons include as income and which fall disproportionately on upper income groups? And does their "etc.," include, as it should, imputations for the increase in the value of existing assets such as stamps, antiques, gold, jewelry, and other real assets whose values have sky-rocketed? Does their upper income definition include estimates of consumption services provided by business for its employees, particularly top management? This latter figure alone was estimated by Eisner[4] to amount to almost 14 billion dollars in 1976. In short, have BJ used the Haig-Simons definition selectively, or have they applied it fully and uniformly?

My fear is that they have omitted from their "broad" concept of income a huge amount of imputed income that would reasonably be expected to be allocatable to the rich. If this is so, they have selectively bloated the incomes of the poor and thus lowered their estimated average tax rates and, conversely, they have then understated the incomes of the rich, thus overstating their estimated tax rates.

The combined effect of such income adjustments is, of course, to induce the appearance of progressivity, when none may exist. We can only guess at the approximate size of the incomes that BJ have not included in their broad concept. They state that their imputations expand adjusted gross income by some 30 per cent, indicating imputations of an order of magnitude of perhaps $300 billion in 1976. Eisner,[5] who has recently developed and estimated a total incomes system of accounts (TISA) that extends the conventional national income accounting system, has produced estimates of income some $1,200 billion greater than BEA estimates for 1976. It appears that the BJ "broad" income concept may capture but a fraction of total income, and their incidence findings may be heavily affected by this fact.

UNCONVENTIONAL INCIDENCE ASSUMPTIONS

The second major source of the BJ progressivity findings results directly from their unconventional incidence assumptions, which, as shown in Table 5.10 below, depart from those used in other incidence studies.[6] Here again, I would have welcomed a sensitivity analysis, which would have revealed to the reader just how much of a difference their particular departures from conventional incidence assumptions make to the final result.

Table 5.10 reveals that BJ have changed the normal incidence assumptions in such a manner that a major share of the tax burdens usually assumed to fall on consumers now falls directly on capital income, with the obvious result of making the tax incidence appear much more progressive. Yet how reasonable are these assumptions? No rationale is provided for the shift from the standard assumptions concerning the corporate income tax, the payroll tax, and the property tax burden, nor are we told how significantly this change in assumptions affects the final outcome. Yet a comparison of the consequences of these different assumptions is revealed by the Pechman-Okner exercise (Columns 1 and 2).

The Pechman-Okner Varient lc differs from Varient 3b on the basis of different allocations of the burdens of the corporate, payroll, and property taxes. Varient lc (Column 1, Table 5.10) represents incidence assumptions which are closer to those of Browning and Johnson with respect to these taxes, whereas Varient 3b employs "conventional" assumptions of the type suggested by Musgrave. Varient lc reveals more overall progressivity than 3b, but both suggest essentially proportional taxation from the 3rd to the 9th decile compared with BJ's sharp progression 16.3 per cent–30.0 for the same range of income.

SALES AND EXCISE TAX

BJ do feel compelled to justify their assumption concerning sales and excise taxes, which, in this analysis, falls heavily on capital income, rather than on consumption. I find their rationale very difficult to take seriously. We are told that, since social security payments are indexed to the price level, the sales and excise taxes should fall on unindexed income, which they identify with labour and capital income. Since transfers make up such a large fraction of the income of the poor, this effect appears to change their results significantly.

I agree with their general analytic point: that the burden should be apportioned to those whose incomes are not appropriately indexed nor responsive to inflation. Yet to claim that such unindexed income corresponds to "labour and capital income" is a *non sequitur*. Clearly, a good portion of labour income is implicitly and explicitly indexed and we can be sure that such indexing typically accrues to the benefit of higher-paid workers, executives and professionals. Medical incomes, for example, have risen far in excess of the price level, and this is true in general for upper income earners.

TABLE 5.10

Comparison of Incidence Assumptions

Tax	Musgrave[a]	Pechman - Okner[b] Varient 1c	Pechman - Okner[b] Varient 3b	Browning-Johnson[c]
	ASSUMED BURDEN			
	1	2	3	4
Personal Income Tax	Taxpayer	Taxpayer	Taxpayer	Taxpayer
Payroll Taxes	Consumers + Employees	Employees	½ Employees ½ Consumption	Employees
Corporate Taxes	½ Consumption ½ Capital Income	½ Dividends ½ Property Income	½ Consumption ½ Property Income	Capital Income from any source
Property Taxes	Homeowners, Tenants, Consumption + Capital Income	Property Income	Landowners + Consumption	Capital Income from any source
Sales and Excise Tax	Consumption	Consumption	Consumption	Proportion of labour and capital earnings

[a] Musgrave, R.A. and Musgrave P.B., *Public Finance in Theory and Practice,* McGraw Hill Book Corp. 3rd ed. page 268.
[b] Pechman, J.A. and Okner, B.A. *Who Bears the Tax Burden?*, The Brookings Institution, p. 38.
[c] Browning E.K., and Johnson, W.R. "Taxes in the United States," Conference Paper.

What is more, capital earnings are, of course, implicitly indexed, particularly when we consider the Haig-Simons definition of income. Inflation is reflected in the rise in the price of existing assets; and furthermore, if we are to employ competitive assumptions, then why not assume that capital income reflected in nominal interest rates already includes a premium for expected inflation à la Fisher?[7]

In short, it seems that if BJ were to carry their own insight to its logical conclusion, they would assign the burden of sales and excise taxes specifically to earners of unindexed income—and my guess is that this burden falls disproportionately on the lower income groups. The standard assumption, while conceptually less sophisticated than BJ's assumption, is therefore practically closer to the spirit of their analytic approach than is their own empirical application.

It appears that the BJ treatment of sales and excise taxes is crucial to their findings and their approach has been strongly criticized by Smeeding who argues that the "alleged progressivity of sales taxes is the result of conceptual and arithmetic errors."[8] Smeeding takes account of the effect of higher taxes on consumer prices; differences in consumption patterns by income group; and differential indexing of transfers and factor incomes, and argues persuasively, that an analysis which ignores these effects will produce results which "are not very useful and must be rejected."

A PROGRESSIVITY BIAS

BJ recognize the unreliability of their own estimates of capital income, yet their conclusion that the "final results (for capital income) are certain to be less reliable than for either labour or transfer income" should be stated correctly—that is, capital income is much more likely than either labour or transfer income to be understated. And this despite their attempts to "gross up" capital income, thus imparting to their estimates a much greater illusion of progressivity than is likely to exist in fact.

BJ also make the argument that data on capital income tend to overstate real capital income. Certainly, inflation will lead to the overstatement of *any* real income, if nominal measures are used. But since their entire analysis is carried forward in nominal terms, I fail to understand why they cite the effect of inflation exclusively on real capital incomes.

Their entire analysis depends upon the assumption of competitive conditions with fixed total supplies of factors of production. Yet, given what we know of the relative mobility of capital, particularly to flee the country (an option not easily available to labour), can we really take seriously an entire line of reasoning that ignores the consequences of capital's inherent international mobility?

In estimating their tax treatment of capital, they also ignore the preferential treatment given to physical capital. Should they not take account of interest deductions, or accelerated depreciation or depletion allowances, or untaxed gains on existing assets? These are huge preferences. To tell the reader simply that the "results may be biased to a degree" is to avoid the issue. If we are to know how to evaluate these controversial findings, we must know to what degree they are biased.

In short, I see the BJ exercise as making use of every possible assumption to give the impression of a highly progressive tax system, when indeed the system may very well be proportional, as earlier studies have claimed. I find that since many of their assumptions are controversial and that even their own insightful concepts are applied in a less than even-handed manner, the resulting findings must be viewed with some scepticism. I would therefore underline each of their own cautionary statements, so that no one is left with a strong, unqualified impression of a steeply progressive incidence system in the U.S.

DISTRIBUTIVE AND ALLOCATIVE EFFECTS

The second section of interest deals with the distributive and allocative effects of the tax system, and this section appears marred by several of the same difficulties as were found in the section on incidence. BJ correctly point out that the distributive effects of the taxation system should be viewed in light of the distributive consequences of the expenditure side of the budget. Once again, their analysis pays great attention to direct transfer programs, which increase the redistributive effects they apparently seek to find. Yet, by their own admission, they simply ignore the remaining $300 billion of government expenditures, which they claim would not modify the distributive picture very much. In fact, there exists evidence to suggest that the benefits from national defense, education, central administration, international affairs, transportation, agriculture, and natural resource expenditures tend to accrue more importantly to the higher decile groups. To simply ignore these effects without detailed analysis of the type devoted to transfer payments gives this reader the impression of an uneven-handed treatment of the issue.

BJ's discussion of the effect of taxes on resource supplies is of special interest to me, since it is my contention that the tax system does indeed provide massive incentives for resources to shift from the observed sector of the economy to the unobserved sector. It is interesting to note that BJ's calculation of the annual loss of GNP of $300 billion (an estimate derived solely from the assumed elasticities of savings and labour supply and the estimated "average" marginal tax rate) is certainly in the ball park with independent estimates of the magnitude of the monetary unobserved sector. Yet, if this amount is not lost output but simply unobserved output, it does not necessarily represent a direct welfare loss.

In summary, the BJ analysis reveals as much about our state of ignorance over incidence, distribution, and allocation effects of the tax system as it does about our state of knowledge. Since all estimates of this kind are likely to be subject to significant margins of error, only a serious sensitivity analysis will inform us about the degree of robustness of the substantive results to alternative specifying assumptions. BJ's analysis has helpfully broadened the domain of interesting assumptions to worry about, but I fear they have left us with an impression of a sharply progressive tax structure that is simply not warranted by their analysis. What they have demonstrated is that virtually any substantive result can be gleaned from the available data base with a judicious choice of specifying assumptions. Obviously, what we require are direct tests of some of the crucial assumptions, and this issue of independent testing has unfortunately not been addressed.

NOTES

1. Minarik, J. "What Has Happened to the Middle Class Tax Burden?" Washington, D.C.: The Brookings Institution, (1979) p. 5.
2. Pechman, J.A. and Okner, B.A. *Who Bears the Tax Burden?,* Washington, D.C.: The Brookings Institution (1974).
3. Browning, E.K. and Johnson, W.R. *The Distribution of the Tax Burden*, Washington, D.C.: American Enterprise Institute (1979).
4. Eisner, R. "Total Income, Total Investment and Growth," American Economics Association, Atlanta, December 29 (1979).
5. Op. cit.
6. Musgrave, R.A. and Musgrave, P.M. *Public Finance in Theory and Practice,* Third Edition, New York: McGraw Hill, (1980).
7. Fisher, I. *The Theory of Interest,* Kelley (1930).
8. Smeeding, T. "Are Sales Taxes Progressive?" Institute for Research on Poverty, Madison: University of Wisconsin June (1979).

REPLY

Edgar K. Browning and William R. Johnson

Professor Feige devotes nearly all his comments to the section that examines the incidence of the U.S. tax system. He finds our incidence assumptions "poorly grounded in theory" and our concepts "applied in a systematically biased manner." He even suggests that we have "[made] use of every possible assumption to give the impression of a highly progressive tax system." These are strong criticisms, and we are delighted to have the opportunity to respond.

In the first paragraph of the section in question, we state that we are "reporting the major results" of our study of tax incidence in the U.S. in 1976 and cite our monograph that was published in 1979.[1] Feige admits that he has not read the monograph. Had he done so, he would have found many of his objections answered. We find it surprising that he is willing to launch a stream of rather severe criticism, without first making an attempt to see if we hadn't considered some of the obvious points he raises. It should be clear that all of the supporting detail in a major tax incidence study cannot be covered in one section of a short paper.

Feige has two major criticisms: that we have estimated and/or defined household income in a way that biases the results; and that our theory is questionable. We shall consider each criticism in turn, but for a fuller treatment we invite the reader (and Professor Feige) to consult our monograph.

MEASURING HOUSEHOLD INCOME

Feige's major concerns about our measurement of household income are that we have systematically omitted large amounts of income, that these omissions were deliberately designed to understate the income of the wealthy, and that such understatement makes the tax system look more progressive than it really is. He is wrong on all three counts.

First, while it is true that we did not include imputed income of jewellery, stamps, etc., or consumption services provided by businesses for their employees, neither does any other major tax incidence study, for fairly obvious reasons. We have used an income measure which is broader than any other study with the possible exception of the Brookings (Pechman-Okner[2]) studies which use their MERGE file. We do include one source of income, in-kind transfers, which Pechman and Okner do not. In comparison to other studies, then, we have used a very broad definition of income.

As for the second charge, that we deliberately rigged our income measure to "bloat" the incomes of the poor and understate the incomes of the rich, we can only say that, if that were our goal, we certainly wasted many tedious manhours imputing unrealized capital gains on corporate equities and estimating the rental income of owner-occupied housing.

Finally, even if upper incomes are significantly understated in our data, (and we do not believe they are, certainly in comparison with other studies), Feige is wrong when he claims that any understatement would make the tax system appear more progressive than it actually is.

At least this is true if we (and others) have missed some capital income in the top decile. Under competitive assumptions (more on this later), this omission would mean we also understated the corporate and property taxes for the top decile. Since the rate of tax on capital income is higher than our 38.3 per cent average rate for the highest decile, this will raise the combined average tax rate for the decile. It would also lower the average tax rate on lower deciles, since it would reduce the share of corporate and property taxes they bear. So Feige has it backwards: if he is correct and we have failed to include some capital income at the top of the income distribution, we have *understated* the progressivity of the tax system.

If Feige is suggesting that the omitted income is largely the kind that escapes taxation (corporate perquisites and the like), we plead guilty along with every other user of reliable income data. However, if an attempt were made to estimate all the untaxed sources of income, we suspect that the inclusion of the biggest of these sources, namely leisure time, would push the system to even greater progressivity.

MEASURING CAPITAL INCOME

Feige is puzzled by our statement that capital income tends to be overstated in inflationary times. In fact, he claims that inflation will lead to the "overstatement of any real income if nominal measures are used." This is doubly false. Labour income is not overstated: if prices and labour earnings are 10 per cent higher this year, then the nominal money earnings are the real earnings *relative to prices prevailing in the period being studied.*

This, however, is not true of capital income. For example, if an investor receives $100 in interest income which contains an inflation premium, it does not mean that the recipient can purchase $100 in goods at prevailing prices without depleting his real net worth. This is because the principal is eroded by inflation. It is only the interest income—exclusive of the inflation premium—that (ideally) should be included. One would have thought this to be well known. For it has been discussed widely in connection with the defects of income taxes on nominal interest income in inflationary times.

Feige thinks we chose a year of deep depression that biased upwards the income of the poor through expanded transfers. This is not true; we based our estimate on data from 1976. Feige chides us for not revealing the time period our estimates pertain to. The first paragraph of the section in question clearly states that the study was of tax burdens in *1976*. Admittedly, we did not include the year in the title of Table 5.3, and if this misled anyone, we apologize.

SIMILARITY TO OTHER STUDIES

It is possible to give some direct evidence that should lay to rest Feige's misgivings about our measurement of income—at least in comparison to other studies. Table 5.11 compares, for every tax except sales and excise taxes, our estimates with those reported in the Pechman-Okner study. The incidence assumptions used are the same, except that Pechman-Okner allocate half of the corporate income tax to dividends and half to capital income. (This difference has a trivial quantitative impact.)

It should be clear that if we were manipulating the income measure, this would show up in the pattern of rates for all taxes since all tax rates are reported as a per cent of the same income. Yet, as Table 5.11 shows, our estimates are quite close to Pechman-Okner's. (The small differences that exist are due in part to the different time periods studied—1976 in our study and 1966 in Pechman-Okner's—and in part to different data bases.) Indeed, the degree of progressivity, as indicated by the ratio of the combined tax rate for the top decile to the rate for the bottom decile, is actually slightly *greater* in the Pechman-Okner study. (For us, 32.8/9.5 = 3.45; for Pechman-Okner, 26.8/7.5 = 3.57). This comparison demonstrates quite clearly that we have not manipulated the definition of income in a biased way, at least in comparison to what has generally been regarded as the major study of tax incidence in the United States.

INCIDENCE ASSUMPTIONS ARE QUITE LEGITIMATE

Now we may turn to Feige's second area of criticism: our use of different incidence assumptions. To begin with he has a table purporting to show that our assumptions "depart quite radically from those used in other incidence studies." He states that the "standard assumption" for the corporate tax is half on dividends and half on consumers, and for the property tax is "consumers of housing." We find this remarkable, since he gives no source for these "standard assumptions," and as far as we know, they are not the standard assumptions. He also states that we give "no rationale whatsoever" for using the assumption that these taxes fall on capital income from any source.

As stated, we were using the results of "competitive general equilibrium tax analysis" and thought that adequate explanation. We apparently should have referred specifically to the development of the Harberger model[3] since the early 1960s, and its application to the property tax by Mieszkowski[4] in the early 1970s. These models, which are now widely accepted by tax specialists, imply the incidence pattern we use. (Indeed, several studies[5] suggest that this assumption would be

TABLE 5.11

Comparison of Tax Incidence Studies
(Average Tax Rates in Percentages)

	Payroll		Income		Property and Corporate Income		Combined	
Income Decile	B-J	P-O	B-J	P-O	B-J	P-O	B-J	P-O
1	3.3	2.6	0.7	1.1	5.5	3.8	9.5	7.5
2	3.9	3.8	1.8	2.3	4.2	4.7	9.9	10.8
3	5.4	5.4	3.0	4.4	4.5	4.8	12.9	14.2
4	6.9	6.1	4.7	5.4	4.4	4.0	16.0	15.5
5	8.0	6.3	6.4	6.3	4.1	3.5	18.5	16.3
6	8.5	6.2	8.1	7.0	3.9	3.1	20.5	16.3
7	8.2	5.8	9.5	7.5	3.8	3.3	21.5	16.6
8	7.9	5.4	10.8	8.3	4.1	3.6	22.8	17.3
9	7.2	4.8	12.2	8.8	5.3	4.4	24.7	18.0
10	3.8	2.2	13.6	11.4	15.4	13.2	32.8	26.8
All deciles	6.2	4.4	10.0	8.5	7.9	6.9	24.1	19.8

Sources: E.K. Browning and W.R. Johnson, *The Distribution of the Tax Burden,* Table 6; J.A. Pechman and B.A. Okner, *Who Bears the Tax Burden?* (The Brookings Institution, 1974), Table 4-9.

appropriate under non-competitive conditions.) Since these developments in the tax incidence field are so well known, we did not think it necessary to give a "rationale" for drawing on the results of modern tax incidence analysis.

A DEPARTURE

The only place where our incidence assumptions depart from previously accepted treatment is in the case of sales and excise taxes. We allocate these taxes in proportion to factor earnings (*i.e.*, labour plus capital income), while previous studies allocate them to consumption. This means we find a moderately progressive pattern for these taxes instead of a highly regressive one. It is this change in procedure that largely accounts for the difference in findings between our study and others. We explicitly stated this in our paper, yet Feige apparently did not believe us and spent most of his time searching for other culprits. As we have seen, all the other "defects" Feige unearths are red herrings. When he finally addresses the sales and excise tax issue, he devotes only one paragraph to it, and then misinterprets our position at that. For example, he seems to think that the fact that labour and capital incomes rise with prices during an inflation (*i.e.*, are "indexed") is relevant. It is not. What we are concerned with is the possible one-shot rise in prices following an excise or sales tax, and in that case there is no tendency for labour and capital income to rise (if they did, where would the tax revenue come from?).

Our explanation and defense of our treatment of sales and excise taxes occupies a large portion of our tax incidence monograph (see especially Chapter 3 and the Appendix). We cannot adequately summarize it here, but we hope that anyone seriously interested in this question will consult that work.

Only one other point raised by Feige seems worth mentioning. At a few places, he wishes we had tested the robustness of our findings with a sensitivity analysis using different incidence assumptions. We have done so in our monograph. Our results stand up well.

Overall, this exchange with Professor Feige seems to stem from our attempt to summarize the results of a lengthy and detailed monograph in a short paper. Obviously, we could not go into great detail here given the space limitations. If our summary leaves out some crucial issues, we apologize to the readers. We sympathize with the handicap Feige encountered being out of the country and thus unable to acquire the monograph. We think, however, Professor Feige could have been a bit more hesitant in making sweeping criticisms of results developed in a study he has not read. We feel his criticisms are either wrong, or apply with equal force to numerous other tax incidence studies.

The *one* controversial innovation in our study is the treatment of sales and excise taxes. We hope that fair-minded readers, even those who are not entirely persuaded by our arguments, will at least acknowledge our approach as a plausible alternative to conventional tax incidence analysis.

NOTES

1. Edgar K. Browning and William R. Johnson, *The Distribution of the Tax Burden,* Washington, D.C.: American Enterprise Institute (1979).
2. J.A. Pechman and B.A. Okner, *Who Bears the Tax Burden*?, Washington, D.C.: The Brookings Institution (1974).
3. Arnold C. Harberger, "The Incidence of the Corporation Income Tax," *Journal of Political Economy,* LXXI June (1962) 215–40.
4. Peter M. Mieszkowski, "The Property Tax: An Excise or a Profit Tax?" *Journal of Public Economics,* I April (1972) 73–96.
5. Harberger op. cit., and Henry J. Aaron, *Who Pays the Property Tax?* Washington, D.C.: The Brookings Institution (1975).

DISCUSSION

Edited by: Walter Block

As the discussion which followed the Browning and Johnson paper was relatively brief, and highly focused, it is repeated here in its entirety, without further editorial comment.

Malcolm Fisher: "If there is a generalized set of numbers used in a model along with various tax incidence assumptions, only one set can be consistent with what generated that data. The rest must be wrong. If there is a tolerance in the system of alternatives, then there is a "smudge" situation, where the data is undiscriminating. Certainly in the Australian context, and perhaps more generally, there is an attempt to make a whole lot of assumptions and to let the data speak for itself. But unless there are clear cut independent checks, not much is accomplished, because only one set of numbers can be consistent.

"For example, consider whether the corporate income tax is borne by shareholders in some sense or passed on to consumers in the form of price increases. Some researchers feed in these alternative assumptions and hope that the numbers will show something for the same set of published data. But only one set of assumptions can be consistent. Unless there is some independent way of discriminating, no inroads will be made. If both alternatives seem to gel in some overall sense, then the data is itself not disclosing what the incidence is."

Assar Lindbeck: "The issue of shifting and incidence is of course one of the most difficult problems in economics. Principally, I guess one can do two things. First is to say, 'let's make the best possible assumptions about how the taxes are shifted forward on price and backward on the wage rates.' But we must admit that nobody has been able to do that in a really convincing way.

"In the paper under discussion, this is accomplished very practically by the escalator clause. I think that Professor Feige is right; it is extremely arbitrary to assume that only one specific group in society is able to shift consumer taxes by raising their factor incomes. Why only people living on transfer payments? Why neglect the possibilities that other groups might be able to do the same thing? That is really too arbitrary to be accepted. What can be done instead? One less ambitious method would be to say 'let's admit that with the present state of knowledge, we don't know how the tax is shifted.' Then we can accept a very partial study which looks at *the direct impact* on the various income groups *assuming* that factor incomes are given for everybody. But this is only an attempt to measure the immediate impact on the various income groups.

"How should that be done? Well, traditionally, economists have assumed that consumption should be used as a base for such a study; *i.e.,* that it must be assumed that the incidence falls in proportion to consumption. That means that the tax looks regressive: low-income people are consuming a larger share of their income than those of higher income. But I think the basic flaw in that approach is that if there is a proportional consumer tax on everything, the real value of saving is also reduced, not only the real value of consumption.

"So I would rather argue that a completely homogeneous consumption tax falls on *all* consumer groups, proportionally, and hence influences real income by the same proportion in all income groups. It is really a proportional tax. It reduces the real value of the part of income that is saved in the same way as the real income for the part that is consumed is decreased.

"Now we know that most consumer taxes are not homogeneous. Rather, they are selective. We must therefore look at how consumption is allocated in different income brackets and derive different price indices for every income group. We must then deflate the income in every decile by a *specific* price index. That's the way I would try to approach it. So I think the authors of this study are correct when they criticize the conventional literature for allocating consumer tax in proportion to consumption. But I think they are really wrong in the way they do it themselves."

Jonathan Kesselman: "Professors Browning and Johnson argued

that the groups receiving transfer payments are fully protected through indexation. Professor Feige has properly argued that other groups may also have some sort of partial indexation of their incomes for the direct and indirect effects of increased taxes. However, I think that we might also question the extent to which recipients of transfer payments are effectively indexed. If we go back several years in the U.S. Social Security program, payments were not formally indexed because congressmen liked the power to legislate, on a discretionary basis, periodic rate increases. Still, there is always a possibility of discretionary increases in transfer payment levels above and beyond the rate of inflation. Indexation simply reduces the frequency and magnitude of these discretionary increases in transfer payment levels. Given this possibility then, even indexation of transfer payments does not necessarily protect these groups totally to the extent that is argued by Browning and Johnson. If society adopts a higher aggregate tax burden, it is not implausible that the poor will be called on to make their contribution, too, through smaller increases in their real levels of transfer payments. We should also not dismiss the possibility that, in a period of negative real growth, recipients of transfer payments will be faced with real decreases. Current discussion of reducing Social Security indexation in the United States points out the realism of this possibility. In short, the Browning-Johnson assumption appears highly suspect."

James Buchanan: "Perhaps I shouldn't make this comment but I'm going to anyway. I think that we have all been sitting around here under a set of illusions. The whole discussion has been under a set of illusions.

"Now, if we're honest with ourselves, we all know from those studies that the United States tax system was not progressive. We know why those studies were made. They were made at the Brookings Institution; they were made with Brookings innovations. And we know that the ideological thrust of the whole set of those Brookings studies was to show that the United States' tax system is genuinely proportional not progressive. The intention, unconscious or not, was to argue that we should therefore increase the progressivity of the American structure; that we should tax the rich and give the money to the poor. We know that to be the fact.

"Therefore I applaud the Browning-Johnson thrust. It comes in and says, 'Look, if you slightly modify their methodology, even on their own terms, their results don't hold.' You can argue that maybe Browning and Johnson had an ideological thrust too. But at least in an adversary type proceeding, it's good to have something on the other side that meets them on their own grounds. And I think this is to be applauded.

"If you are really going to talk about tax burden, let's forget about all these kinds of studies—they don't mean anything. Let me quote something that I learned from Armen Alchian twenty years ago, 'The real burden of taxes is not measured by these kinds of studies at all, the real burden of taxes can be found in the structure of marginal taxes. All you need to do is look at the marginal rates and that's where the burden is. If you talk about distribution of burden you don't need to go through all this.'"

Edgar Feige: "Would you accept a quote from Milton Friedman which I think is very relevant here? Milton and Franco Modigliani were in an argument at Northwestern University, and Franco accused Milton of obtaining certain empirical results because obviously he was motivated to get those results. Milton rightly answered, 'I'm here to engage in economic analysis not psychoanalysis.' I just can't accept that position as a defensible one. What you're saying is that we are a bunch of biased academics."

James Buchanan: "You're saying we like to remain under these illusions."

Edgar Feige: "I'm saying that if they are illusions, we ought to follow a certain set of principles. And if those principles are violated by fudging economic analysis, then I think we have a duty to say so. But I don't think we can impute to results, motives that are substantiated by faults in the analysis."

James Buchanan: "I will agree with you when you show me a Brookings study that shows that the United States' system is very progressive and, therefore, we need to cut back the rate of progression. Once you show me that, I will completely throw in the towel."

CHAPTER 6

TAXATION IN THE UNITED KINGDOM

Arthur Seldon

I. THE MAIN FEATURES OF THE TAX STRUCTURE

GENERAL DESCRIPTION

The principal forms of taxation are shown in percentages in Table 6.1. The progressiveness of the income tax, which supplies 40 per cent of central government revenue is shown in Table 6.2 and of capital taxes in Table 6.3. Tax revenues as percentages of GDP are shown in Table 6.4, and average household income and national insurance taxes are shown with the main items of expenditure in Table 6.5.

Since the Finance Act of 1977, the allowances against taxable income have been indexed. The 1980 Budget indexed investment income where the investment income surcharge became payable. The corporation income tax is not indexed.

The rate of income tax required to raise the revenue yield by the present progressive income tax would be 15 per cent, if calculated mechanically on initial impact. Since the change would influence output and GDP, the ultimate incidence proportional tax would be lower. (Taxable income in 1978 was £125 billion, and income tax revenue was £19 billion.)

Tax transfers are used extensively if measured *gross* as as percentage of income but the *net* effect is relatively small. Regulation is not used extensively as a substitute for taxes.

Tax exemptions, remissions and reliefs ("expenditures") are of many kinds and have significant effects on the degree of progressiveness of the income taxes and probably on the expenditures.

The revenues form the main taxes as percentages of total tax revenue since 1938–1939 are shown in Table 6.6 and as percentages of GNP since 1946–1947 in Table 6.7. Although the weight of capital taxes has fallen since the war, the effective progressivity has increased because of the change from estate duty to capital transfer tax. It is the combination of very high marginal tax rates with potent anti-tax-avoidance measures that makes the system damaging.

TABLE 6.1

Tax Sources of Central Government Revenue 1978-1979

Tax Source	%
Income Tax	40.88
VAT	15.94
Corporation Tax	9.27
National Insurance surcharge*	5.91
Oil duty	5.83
Tobacco duty	5.14
Liquor duty	4.77
Petroleum Revenue Tax	2.88
EEC duties and levies	2.34
Capital Taxes	1.67
Car Tax	1.26
Stamp duties	1.22
Betting and gaming	0.80
Development land tax	0.05
Other excise duties	0.02

Source: Inland Revenue

* A tax imposed through the National Insurance (NI) system. NI contributions are excluded as insurance premiums although they are also better treated as a form of tax (and are so usually regarded, even in some official statistics).

TABLE 6.2

Progressiveness of Income Tax 1979-1980

£	%
0 - 11,250	30
11,251 - 13,250	40
13,251 - 16,750	45
16,751 - 22,250	50
22,251 - 27,750	55
Over 27,750	60

Source: Inland Revenue

TABLE 6.3

Progressiveness of Capital Transfer Tax at Death 1979-1980

£'000	%
0 - 50	—
50 - 60	30
60 - 70	35
70 - 90	40
90 - 110	45
110 - 130	50
130 - 160	55
160 - 510	60
510 - 1010	65
1010 - 2010	70
Over 2010	75

Source: Inland Revenue

TABLE 6.4

Taxes as Percentages of GDP 1978

	%
Local Taxes (Rates)*	4.01
National Insurance	6.39
Central government taxes on income and expenditure	15.72
Capital Taxes	0.63
Other central government taxes	12.34
TOTAL	38.46

*Local "rates" are not separately identified. Because income and expenditure figures relate to different periods a surplus of recorded income over recorded expenditure cannot be construed as saving.

Source: Inland Revenue

TABLE 6.5

Expenditure of the Average Family, 1978

	Income, Taxes, Expenditure	£
Income	Average Weekly Household	106.13
Taxes	Income Tax payments less refunds	15.13
	National Insurance contributions	3.57
Expenditure	Housing	11.87
	Fuel Light Power	4.76
	Food	19.31
	Alcoholic Drink	3.92
	Tobacco	2.72
	Clothing Footwear	6.78
	Durable Household Goods	5.66
	Other goods	5.99
	Transport and vehicles	10.90
	Services	7.66
	Miscellaneous	0.69

Source: Family Expenditure Survey.

"Deferred taxation" by accumulation of government borrowing through the budget deficit is shown in Table 6.8. The national debt as a percentage of GDP was 52 per cent in 1979 and has not changed much in the last few years.

IMPACT OF THE TAX SYSTEM

It is difficult to assemble convincing evidence of the effects on labour supply, saving, and investment. There is a general disposition to doubt the disincentive effects of high marginal tax rates, mainly on the ground that the income effects (which increase effort, etc.) neutralize the price effects (substitution between work and leisure) which reduce effort, etc.). It is difficult to establish the effects empirically one way or the other. We are left (as hypotheses) with only the practical judgements of noted economists. I offer the judgement of Lord Robbins:

> I suppose that all but the completely unworldly would agree that a marginal rate of 100 percent would have some adverse effects on the disposition to work or save of most ordinary people. Why then assume that the rates which actually prevail in the United Kingdom in the present day should not operate in the same way? Is it really to be supposed that the disincentive is absent until one reaches 99.9 percent and then suddenly becomes complete.[1]

TABLE 6.6

Individual Tax Revenues as a Percentage of Total Taxes

	Income and Surtax	Corp. Tax etc.	Capital Taxes	PRT*	Customs & Excise	SET*	Stamp Duties and Misc.
1938/39	44.5	2.5	8.6	—	38	—	6.4
1940/47	39.0	16.1	4.7	—	37.4	—	7.8
1960/61	45.7	4.6	4.1	—	41.8	—	3.8
1970/71	42.4	11.0	3.5	—	33.4	5.8	3.9
1979/80	40.2	9.9	1.6	1.5	37.3	—	9.4

* PRT — Petroleum Revenue Tax
* SET — Selective Employment Tax

Source: Inland Revenue

TABLE 6.7

Tax Revenue as a Percentage of GNP

	Income and Surtax	Corp. Tax etc.	Capital Taxes	PRT*	Customs & Excise	SET*	Stamp Duties and Misc.
1946/47	14.9	5.8	1.7	—	13.4	—	1.0
1960/61	11.6	1.2	1.0	—	10.6	—	1.0
1970/71	13.8	3.6	1.1	—	10.8	1.9	1.3
1979/80	12.4	3.1	0.5	0.5	11.5	—	2.9

* PRT — Petroleum Revenue Tax
* SET — Selective Employment Tax

Source: Inland Revenue

TABLE 6.8

Budget Deficit as a Percentage of GDP

Year	%
1963	3.13
1966	2.91
1969	- 1.13
1972	3.69
1975	11.24
1976	8.20
1977	4.82
1978	5.90
1979	7.93

Source: Inland Revenue

There may be some poetic justice in the larger scope for tax avoidance and evasion by the self-employed in small firms. These people have probably suffered more in the post-war period by the tendency of British government (of both parties) to heed the more highly organized interests of big business or the trade unions. That small firms have survived on a larger scale in other countries suggests that their demise in the U.K. is not necessarily the result of diseconomies of scale.

Evidence that high marginal tax rates do not reduce work-performance may be accepted too readily. If accurate, it remains to be explained why cost-conscious firms in competitive markets, especially overseas, incur large costs in untaxed (or less-taxed) "perks," if not to retain or attract employees disgruntled by highly taxed earnings. The inference is that without "perks" high marginal tax rates would reduce work-performance. That non-taxed or lower-taxed elements are twice (or more) as large in the U.K. as in France or Germany is further circumstantial evidence.

The distortion introduced by badly designed taxation is illustrated by the U.K. corporate taxes which have led firms to retain profits as the main source of risk capital. There can be little doubt that this distortion accounts for the survival of firms by ploughing back to escape the judgement of the capital market.

II. THE IRRELEVANCE OF INTERNATIONAL COMPARISON

Are British taxes too high or too low?

A common judgement has been reached by diverse international authorities. Mr. Pechman,[2] for example, has said: "The aggregate tax burden in the United Kingdom, when compared with that in other developed countries, does not seem excessive." This view is congenial to economists and politicians temperamentally or doctrinally inclined to high government expenditure, and therefore to high taxation. It has re-appeared fitfully in the reports of the British National Institute of Economic and Social Research. In a comparison of social security in Britain and other countries, its *Economic Review*[3] concluded from a scrutiny of statistics for twelve countries, eight in Europe and the U.S.A., Canada, Australia and New Zealand, that expenditure on the British National Health Service "compared favourably" with expenditure on medical care in the other countries, but that state pensions were "much less adequate." The Intelligence Unit of the London *Economist*,[4] which has not always stoutly resisted fashion in economic thinking, calculated in a review of social security financing and benefits in the Common Market, that the U.K. spent less in taxes on social security than Luxembourg, France, Germany, the Netherlands, Belgium, and Italy, but more on medical care.

The most distinguished exponent of this view has been a British economist who has defended British Labour economic policy as Ambassador to the U.S.A. Now at the Brookings Institution, Mr. Peter Jay, then Economic Correspondent of the London *Times*, drew on OECD, Japanese and U.S.A. statistics[5] to demolish "the myth" that Britain "was the most highly taxed country in the world" or that its "government current expenditure takes too large a slice of the national cake." He maintained that the international comparisons "completely fail to corroborate the view that U.K. government expenditure and taxation are out of line with those in other developed countries." Moreover, he found that taxation as a percentage of GNP was lower and rising more slowly in Britain than in most other countries. Therefore, "the obvious scope for raising extra revenue appears *by international standards*" (my emphasis) to be in social security contributions (since they formed a lower percentage of total tax revenue in the U.K. than in the U.S.A., France, West Germany, the Netherlands and Sweden) and in purchase tax (lower than in the last four).

GOVERNMENT CALCULATIONS

Not surprisingly, the British bureaucracy has weighed in with its own calculations. Its latest compilations for nineteen OECD countries[6] show again the familiar finding that the U.K. is by no means at or near the top of the international league table for taxation, with or without social security contributions, as a percentage of GNP (or as measured in most other ways). (See Tables 6.9, 6.10 and 6.11.) And, although the bureaucrats are too polite or tactful to emphasize the alleged lesson for

TABLE 6.9

Taxes (Including Social Security Contributions)
as % of GNP, OECD, 1970 and 1976
(Ranked by Order 1976)

	1970	1976
Sweden	46	58
Norway	48	55
Denmark	48	53
Netherlands	44	51
Finland	37	46
Belgium	39	45
France	41	44
West Germany	39	44
UNITED KINGDOM	43	40
Canada	37	37
Italy	33	36
Australia	29	34
USA	33	33
Switzerland	25	32
Greece	28	30
Spain	19	23
Japan	22	22

Source: *Economic Trends*, HMSO, December, 1978.

policy—that since British taxes are "too low" they could be raised (even) higher, it is there for all except the blind—or the right-wing Thatcherite or Reaganite reactionary—to read.[7]

I must confess I find all these statistical pyrotechnics unconvincing. My instinctive response is to echo the Americanism, "So what?" How dependable or significant are these *international* comparisons for *national* tax policy? What have *macro* average or total statistics to do with *micro* economic individual decisions to work less or more?, save more or less?, invest less or more?, at home or overseas?, invest or disinvest?, take more or fewer risks?, remain at home or emigrate?, pay taxes and sink the family firm or escape taxes and live in sin?, help others to escape taxes or lose friends?, pay all taxes or take your "fair" share of avoidance and evasion?, beat the taxman or join the tax-rebels?

TABLE 6.10

Sources of Taxes
Family Income, Firms, Expenditure, 1976
(Ranked by Order of Taxes on Family Income)

	Family Income	Firms	Expenditure
Denmark	56	4	39
Finland	45	5	34
Australia	45	12	41
Sweden	44	3	30
UNITED KINGDOM	39	5	36
Canada	35	14	40
USA	33	13	29
Belgium	32	7	29
West Germany	29	4	31
Netherlands	28	7	25
Japan	25	19	31
Italy	20	5	32
France	15	7	37
Spain	10	12	32
Greece	—	—	54
Norway	—	—	38
Switzerland	—	—	21

Source: *Economic Trends,* HMSO, December, 1978.

What conclusion is to be drawn for British taxes from the implication that other countries have even higher taxes? Must we maintain that the percentage of British taxes—a mere 40 per cent in 1976 including social security contributions—should be raised to the 58 per cent of Sweden? If not, what conclusions are intended for the British reader?

CAVEATS

The British bureaucrats soberly list the cautions in using the 1970–1976 statistics, "... there is no single precise definition of the term 'taxes and social security contributions.'" "... the comparisons should be regarded as giving only a broad indication etc. etc. ... " But these qualifications throw doubt on the significance of the calculations per se. Yet in their accompanying commentary the British bureaucrats, fallible

TABLE 6.11

Taxes as % of Total Personal Income 1976

	Including Employers' Contributions	Excluding Employers' Contributions
Netherlands	31	24
Finland	30	27
Belgium	25	19
UNITED KINGDOM	24	20
France	23	12
USA	20	16
Italy	20	9
Canada	19	16
Australia	16	16
Spain	14	5

Source: *Economic Trends,* HMSO, December, 1978.

like the rest of us, forget their cautions and introduce a spurious precision.

My reservations are more deep-seated than can be read into the bureaucrats' cautions. And they are more severe than those of Professor Richard Bird,[8] with whom I wholly agree that "none of these comparisons can lend much weight to any policy recommendations, one way or the other." (Although I cannot share his apparent acceptance of the Canadian Department of Finance view[9] that international comparisons "provide a perspective in which to evaluate specific concerns arising from analysis of individual circumstances" on the ground that tax policy must be judged by its effects on economic policy as a whole which may differ from the sum of the effects on individuals.)

UNRELIABLE STATISTICS

I suggest that international tax comparisons are often too precarious to deserve the respect of economists; that they have been used to support pre-judgements about the desirability of raising tax revenue to finance extensions of government. Most fundamentally, that policy in general cannot be judged apart from the effects on individuals. If high taxes depress individual output, the nation cannot gain.

Mr. Jay said that OECD had an expert staff of economists from several countries with access *to governments.* And there's the rub. The

OECD is supplied with its figures by "national statistical offices." I vividly recall the unsuppressed mirth (which almost had him rolling around on the floor) of the Chinese Director-General of Medical Services in a market oasis of Asia whom I had asked to comment on the comparative national expenditures on a medical service reported in a WHO report. Oh, yes; he loyally supplied the figures requested by WHO. But they were largely guesswork. And, he suspected, so were some others. So he tore them up. They were no use to him. And I doubt if they are to anyone else — except to certain bureaucrats with an ax to grind.

The late Professor Warren Nutter used OECD data (in comparing growth of government)[10] because national governments report national accounts based on standardized concepts. This is the most that can be claimed. The question is whether the national figures are good enough, whether national accuracy in compilation is sufficiently similar. On that, there is uncertainty and there must be room for doubt. Apart from discontinuity in some national series and incomparability between national series, the implicit assumption of accuracy and integrity in national computation and reporting is far from self-evident.

I regard all official government statistics as suspect; guilty until proven innocent; and I know no method of vindicating a whole bureaucracy. As a lowly military statistical bureaucrat in the British War Office and its extension in the field, I hoped my figures (reinforcements required by convoy from the U.K. to keep the first Army in Africa and Italy up to strength) were never responsible for avoidable casualties or deaths. Even with computer accuracy in the 1980s, why should we suppose politicians are seekers after truth or bureacrats public benefactors?

We need more realism about the political process and more common sense about the motivations — or temptations of bureacrats. Are they never pressed by harassed politicians to re-define the composition or re-time the publication of official statistics if great issues of state are at stake?

THE TAX PRICE INDEX

To avoid impugning the many men and women of integrity in public life and the bureaucracies, I consider the opposite circumstance, in which expediency is served rather than thwarted by accuracy in tax statistics. The British government's efforts to reduce taxes is obstructed by the statistical accident that direct taxes are not treated as prices for the Retail Prices Index. A switch from direct taxes to charges in paying for government services would thus appear to raise "the cost of living" to which the wages and salaries of many in the labour force are informally linked.[11] The new government has rightly introduced, since August 1979, the Tax and Price Index. It is accused of "cooking the books" by trade union leaders whose collective bargaining is hamstrung by having to relate wage claims to more accurate rather than to unrealistic or meaningless statistics.

In any event, if there are differences in tax "levels," revenue, or value, it does not follow that they should be (or can be) removed. There may be good reasons for them in social and cultural reactions to government tax policy. Germany raises a higher percentage of GNP in taxes to finance state pensions; it does not follow that Britain is spending "too little" and should raise taxes to pay higher state pensions. The main explanation is that occupational pensions in the market have spread much further in Britain because Bismarck in 1889 nationalized German pensions (for cynical political reasons). In contrast the 1908 and 1925 state pension reforms in Britain had not spread far enough by the war to stop the post-war development of private occupational pensions.[12]

MARKET ALTERNATIVES

As countries become wealthier, it is argued, they "can afford" to spend more on social, public, government, welfare services. But this is a *non sequitur*. As countries grow richer, *so do their populaces*, so individuals can pay for more welfare services in the market. Government can then gracefully withdraw, leaving the public with lower taxes, more money in their pockets, more choice in spending it on the products of competing suppliers, and therefore higher total utility from their expenditures.

Not least, it is surprising that economists lean on macro-statistics of *averages*. These are irrelevant for the micro-decisions of individuals taken at the *margin* of (small) changes in income and leisure. Have economists at the National Institute for Economic and Social Research (NIESR), at the British Embassy, the *Economist* or at Brookings dismissed the marginal revolution of Jevons, Menger, and Walras? If we may regard taxes as a more disagreeable method of paying for "public" services than prices — since a tax is a *deduction* from income and a price is a *disposal* of income — we may formulate an Irrational Tax-Pain or Head-Banging Hypothesis for the "raise taxes" brigade. To show the British employee that on average his Swedish counterpart passively yields more of his income in taxes is hardly likely to induce him to rejoice at the prospect of yielding still more. If taxes are disliked and regarded as painful (as they increasingly are in Britain), why should the British taxpayer accept additional pain because the average Swede or Dane is suffering even more? If the lunatic bangs his head against the wall because it is pleasant when he stops, does the "raise taxes" school want the British taxpayer to bang his head harder because the relief is all the more?

In the realm of public finance where individuals add up to form total policy, it does not help a British government to know that other governments ruling people with different histories, attitudes, habits, distribution of income and socio-economic structures, have been able to persuade them to yield more of their income to the state. There is no sign at all that British taxpayers will voluntarily yield a higher proportion of rising incomes for what the political advertisers call "social wages." The stronger likelihood is that they will want to keep a higher proportion for private expenditure, as the British in every social class indicate they want to do, and are trying to do—illegally if driven by government and the law. Far more important for the individual earner and taxpayer than *international* comparisons are the *internal* comparisons he makes over time as his personal taxes are changed from year to year. These influence his decisions to work and earn less or more, and his ability to buy in the market better education, medical care or other services than the state tries (but fails) to supply equally for all out of taxation.

III. TAXPAYER "AVOISION"

Whatever the outcome of the debate among economists on the relevance of international comparison, the British taxpayer has shown increasingly that he does not care a fig for such esoteric exchanges, still less for the even worse plight of taxpayers in some other countries. A distinguished Swedish economist has described his highly taxed countrymen as "a nation of cheats." The British are historically a law-abiding people, but if democratic government requires the consent of the governed, British politicians, including some of the new British Cabinet, have misjudged the readiness of the British to absorb continually rising taxation without demur. If not "a nation of cheats," the British must now be described as "a nation of tax-resisters."

A knowledge of British history should have warned of the dangers of excessive taxtion. In 1381 Wat Tyler led the Peasants' Revolt against taxation from the County of Kent. In 1688 the Glorious Revolution was a bloodless but decisive reaction against the divine right of the Stuart monarchy *inter alia* to tax. In 1776 the British in the American colonies declared their independence from their home country and its insensitive taxes.

In the 1800s taxes were generally low. But 1980 has seen a new revolt that has taken a new and potentially demoralizing form. Growing amounts of taxation have been required since the 1939–1945 war to finance the losses of inefficient nationalized industry. The undisciplined (because largely price-less) "free" services of the welfare state, and more lately the inflated activities of local government, have also caused tax levels to rise.

TAX "AVOISION"

These phenomena have led from the legally proper (although frowned on) tax avoidance and the legally improper and condemned tax evasion to a mixture of the two that threatens to undermine the observance of the law as the essential ingredient in the consent of the governed. The combination which I have dubbed "tax avoision,"[13] is tax-rejection that develops from avoidance to evasion and ends in a mixture that in the taxpayer's mind is regarded as moral—though illegal.

Rising taxation induces a search for new methods of tax avoidance—the rearrangement of taxable activities of working or spending, buying or selling, saving or investing, to minimize taxes. Familiarity with new methods of tax avoidance induces sailing near the wind of tax evasion—the understatement of earnings and/or the over-statement of the costs incurred in acquiring them. The pressure to minimize taxes and maximize net earnings induces a struggle to maintain family finances and firms' profitability. It brings increasing resentment against the tax bureaucracy and the politicians and government that underly them.

The distinction between illegality and immorality becomes blurred. The apogee is reached when tax yields can no longer be further raised by variations in taxes, tax bases, or tax rates. It would appear that this high point has been reached in Britain.

THE UNDERGROUND ECONOMY

As usual, private enterprise pioneered for officialdom and government to follow. The extent of the growing "black," "hidden," or "underground" economy may well be a measure of tax avoision—cash payments leave less distinct trails for tax departments to follow. In 1976 the Institute of Economic Affairs asked its field research advisers to help measure the extent of tax evasion. Since it was unlikely that people who *received* cash would be reliable witnesses, it was decided to investigate a sample of people who *paid* in cash for services other than customary shopping. A pilot sample of 712, 512 men and 200 women, were questioned in October 1976. Broadly the findings revealed that cash was paid by 55 per cent of the sample in all socio-economic groups (70 per cent ABCD1, 44 per cent 2DE) for a wide range of personal and domestic services from the most common to the least:

window cleaning	painting/decorating
carpet laying	plumbing
electrical	gardening
carpentry/woodwork	chauffering
car maintenance	home help
baby-sitting	typing/secretarial
medical/dental	coaching
accounting	architectural

The recipients were thus also representative of all socio-economic groups – white collar and blue collar.

Apart from the statistical findings on payment by cash, the survey revealed a surprisingly high degree of tolerance of illegality in tax evasion and a reluctance to condemn the non-disclosure of earnings. Fifty-one per cent thought they should not declare earnings from such services against 36 per cent who thought they should; 60 per cent against 31 per cent approved of payment by cash rather than by cheque; 69 per cent against 23 per cent thought they should not have to pay tax on their earnings "in their own time." These replies indicate the widespread prevalence of tax "avoision:" the refusal to condemn the illegal as immoral.

Attitudes on the taxation of "perks" and payments in kind were similarly revealing. Only 31 per cent thought radios in cars used for business should be taxed. Twenty-four per cent paid cash for spare time jobs, 21 per cent received free travel or other employment "perks," 13 per cent supplied food for overtime work, 13 per cent made telephone calls to home from places of work, 9 per cent reported proceeds from the sale of goods made in spare time, and only 8 per cent reported "gifts" made in payment for services.

BARTER

Apart from payments in cash and kind, tax is avoided also by barter. My favourite example is of the dental surgeon "paid" by an architect with plans for an extension to his home. Such episodic evidence requires verification by continued sample surveys, but they indicate both the changing attitude to illegality and the apparently insuperable task of tracing and preventing its devices.

Official cognizance is fairly recent. In 1979, the then Chairman of the Inland Revenue, Sir William Pile, suggested in evidence to the House of Commons Expenditure Committee that tax was evaded on some 7½ per cent of the GNP, or around £10 million. This amounted to some £800 per average family of two parents and two children. Since tax evasion is no doubt unevenly distributed, the average is libellous of some British families and too complimentary about others.

An earlier Chairman of the Inland Revenue, Sir Norman Price, was less statistical but more censorious. In evidence to a 1978 session of the committee he said: "I think avoidance (sic) has become a national habit. Even if rates of tax were reduced quite considerably it would still go on."

It seems that not only taxpayers, but also the Inland Revenue is confusing the legal with the moral, but with less excuse. Since tax avoidance is not illegal, it is not strictly the business of the Inland Revenue to censure it. Sir Norman then became even more analytical but more tortuous; when asked by an MP who is now a Treasury Minister how he defined "avoidance" he replied, ". . . the re-arranging of one's affairs in an artificial manner. . . for reasons only of avoiding tax." But this distortion of what would otherwise be the pattern of economic activity and use of resources is really a condemnation of the tax system, not of the taxpayer.

In 1976 an Inland Revenue spokesman replied to a question on the disincentive effect of taxes from a committee enquiring into local government finances, "We cannot tell how much tax is evaded – one cannot know the unknowable – but there are signs that evasion (sic) has reached a point that is very serious indeed...."

BIASED STATISTICS

By 1980 the Central Statistical Office (CSO) for the first time announced that "Reports and anecdotal evidence from this country and others suggest that tax evasion and other fraudulent behaviour have reached epidemic proportions," and set out to examine[14] whether "unreported economic activities have impaired the credibility of official statistics." It asked, "Have statistics of economic activities been corrupted here (in Britain)?" Since payment was made not only in cash but also by exchange of goods and services or by using undisclosed bank accounts, there were legal as well as illegal untaxed transactions. The CSO report defined "the hidden economy" as "the economic activity generating factor incomes (wages, salaries, gross trading profits from producing goods and services) which cannot be estimated from the regular statistical sources used to compile the income measure of GDP." The CSO described these incomes as "concealed."

The CSO thought that "since it is not (yet?) illegal for the receiver of the service to pay cash, for example to window cleaners and house repairers... (these payments) would not normally be concealed ... especially since the sums involved may often be small."[15] The CSO therefore regarded the *expenditure* estimate of GDP (derived from answers to sample surveys) as an "unbiased" estimate of the value of all transactions.

But the *income* measure of GDP, derived largely from the Inland Revenue, probably fell "short of true income levels especially for . . . the self-employed." This under-reporting of income was confirmed by comparison with the expenditure measure of GDP. Current national accounts estimates of tax-evaded income are based on the gap between the income and the expenditure measures. The gap was approximately 0.2 per cent of GDP in 1960, 1 per cent in 1963, and 2.2 per cent in 1971, and rose to 4 per cent in 1974, but then evidently dipped to around 3.3 per cent in 1978. The rise from 1960 to 1974 is plausible. The (recorded) dip to 1978 is implausible. I conclude that the gap is defective as a measure of unrecorded and untaxed economic activity.

To this gap are added concealed expenditure, such as on "the informal sale of fruit by the side of country roads" or of "home-made wines to friends and neighbours," or of "clothing produced and sold informally by outworkers ("a loss of data which may be exacerbated if the cloth itself is pilfered"). Also included is concealed income in kind, such as use of office telephones.

A FALSE DISTINCTION

The CSO then attempts an intriguing and straight-faced, if somewhat hilarious classification of personal gains based on whether or not they are part of the hidden economy. Working for no pay (housework, do-it-yourself, gardening, charity work, car-sharing) is in the household not the hidden economy. These are not part of the hidden economy because they are outside "the boundary of production." But this is mistaken. These activities are part of the national output, income and wealth, even if unpaid and therefore untaxed. Working for money fully declared to the Inland Revenue is "the formal economy" not regarded by the CSO as part of the hidden economy. But five more categories of "personal gain" are so regarded:

1. expense account living with tax advantage, such as "5-star accommodation when conducting important business abroad on behalf of employer;"
2. fringe benefits whose market value exceeds their taxed value;
3. illegal under-reporting of earnings from a second job, or from self-employment; undeclared earnings such as tips; or when supposedly "unemployed" or "sick;" company tax evasion; "some" undeclared barter transactions;
4. frauds in the formal economy, such as office pilfering, fiddling by employees, employment of employees "off-the-books," shoplifting;
5. undeclared earnings from crime such as drug-trafficking or from immorality such as prostitution.

If, says the CSO, perfect information on 1 to 5 were available "at a low cost" these items could all be included in an estimate of national economic welfare. But the value of tax-dodging non-market transactions cannot easily be measured, and they are therefore excluded from national accounts measures of economic activity (except for owner-occupied and rent-free homes for which a national rent is calculated). Nevertheless—in this view, some assessment of such hidden (and untaxed) transactions, such as the increase in self-service in cars and washing machines or supermarkets, could be attempted. (With how large an army of tax-detectives? Would it not be simpler to appoint a tax officer in each street, block or family?)

But "a judgement must be taken on the extent to which criminal and 'immoral' activities" should be included. The difficulties of measurement and the "incongruity" of regarding an increase in crime as an increase in economic activity suggest to the CSO that it would be "problematical" to include crime in the national accounts definition of the hidden economy, so estimates of value added by crime "should await better data."

THE FIDDLE

The CSO report is not wholly statistical. On expense "fiddling" it claims "anecdotal evidence" showing that the self-employed (and others) sometimes receive tax relief for expenses more properly regarded as entirely consumer expenditure. And it warns that this tendency, which cannot also be checked by tax inspectors who have no time to dispute small tax claims, would "depress" the estimates of GDP.

Little misses CSO scrutiny. An employee who travels second class but who claims first class fares, or who entertains needlessly or lavishly, and thereby enjoys income but evades tax on it, is adding to the hidden economy. No doubt all employees could be required to demand rail, bus and coach tickets, receipts from taxi-drivers, cloakroom attendants, newspaper sellers and tip-recipients. No doubt the national accounts could be made to record a more complete estimate of the GDP. But the time and paper required to complete the records would itself reduce the GDP. Not every minute form of tax evasion in every form of unrecorded activity and earning is worth tracking down in order to complete the national accounts.

MEASURING TAX EVASION

The CSO offers estimates of tax evasion—Table 6.12, which suggests a large expansion among the self-employed and an even more rapid expansion (though much smaller in absolute value) among wage- and salary-earners.

TABLE 6.12

Tax Evasion by Category of Earnings
1972, 1975, 1978

	1972		1975		1978	
	£m	% of Total	£m	% of Total	£m	% of Total
Self-employment income	410	8.0	1,720	19.0	2,760	21.0
Wages and salaries	100	0.3	320	0.5	850	1.0
Company profits	25	0.3	25	0.2	25	0.1
TOTAL	540	1.0	2,070	2.2	3,640	2.6
GDP (at factor cost) bn.	55		193		141	

Source: C.S.O., *Economic Trends,* January, 1980.

Methods of measurement are various. First, cash held by the public has been regarded as a measure of the trend in tax-evading cash payments. In 1979 adults were estimated to hold on average £200. In view of the increase in payments by cheque and credit cards, notes and coin in circulation have fallen less than might have been expected proportionately to M3 (from 20 per cent in the middle 1960s to 15 per cent in 1978) and the GDP (from 7.5 per cent to 5.5 per cent) in these years. Moreover, higher denomination notes in circulation have increased faster than inflation. (£10 and £20 notes rose from a quarter to a half of the value of notes in circulation from 1976 to 1979; and a £50 note is expected for the first time in 1980. Some wage agreements provide for £10 notes in pay packets.

The 1978 national accounts allowed 2½ per cent for tax-evaded income – a small allowance for payments in kind, almost certainly too small. The official view, that the growth in the hidden economy in the last 20 years has not been spectacular, is thus probably wrong. The 1980 national accounts will attempt to allow for more elements of this hidden economy, especially payments in kind. Since these are even less detectable than payments in cash, the official statisticians are likely to incur a higher marginal cost of search than they will achieve in marginal revenue by statistical comprehensiveness.

Non-compliance in Britain has grown, is growing, and will probably not stop growing, even if taxation is reduced, as the Thatcher government has promised. It is a habit-forming practice with a ratchet effect. Two conflicting judgements – one of a tax-gatherer, the other of a former tax-gatherer and more lately a Cabinet Minister – may be better guides to trends in the 1980s than official or academic statistical forecasts or projections. The General Secretary of the Inland Revenue Staff Federation (the tax-gatherers' trade union) has said defiantly of the tax dodgers:

> ... whatever is the measured tax bill from each and every one of us will need to be paid.... We (tax-collectors) must will ourselves to face a deal more hissing.[16]

The former General Secretary of the Federation, a Minister under Harold Wilson, and former Chairman of the Parliamentary Labour Party, retorted more realistically and soberly:

> It is unthinkable that the disciplines and fiscal exactions and enforcements... can be pushed to still further limits of official powers and penalties. There now exists a precarious balance between bureaucracy and the public.[17]

IV. THE RELEVANCE OF PUBLIC GOODS

Economists who describe the taxation of the U.K. as "not excessive" imply that the system will not have a disproportionately adverse effect on output in the U.K. They may also imply that, since taxation appears to have been absorbed into the "chemistry" of the body economic, a restriction in taxation would be undesirable or at least not advantageous. I suggest that for a democratic society, which the U.K. tenuously remains (although not for long if the state does not reduce its "take" of national income), a more fundamental criterion is whether British taxation is higher than it must be or than the British people would prefer it to be.

It is therefore important to examine how much of British taxation is unavoidable. That is, how much of it is necessary to finance the public goods that government must provide out of taxation – since they could not be purchased on the market – or to redistribute income. The extent of public goods in the British "public" (more accurately "government") sector is briefly reviewed in this section, the extent of redistribution in VI.

To calculate the proportion of British government expenditure – national and local-made on public goods, we must consider the following categorizations:

1. public goods proper. These have inseparable benefits for which charging is technically impracticable or feasible but uneconomic;
2. public goods with some separable benefits for which charging is practicable and economic;

3. services yielding wholly or largely separable benefits for which charging is practicable and economic;
4. transfer payments and other cash disbursements, including interest on the National Debt.

This classification is a rough one. Most (if not all) government expenditure is on services—such as education and medical care – that distribute external benefits to third parties. It is argued that they should therefore be provided by government and/or financed by taxation. But this proposition is debatable, since there are few private activities that do not at all affect third parties. If externalities were the sole criterion, all goods and services would be provided by government (or at least subsidized or taxed to stimulate or discourage their production.) We must also keep in mind the classical advantages of consumer choice between decentralized competitive private suppliers, vis-a-vis government—bureaucratic sloth and inefficiency.[18] The question thus becomes one of weighing off the advantages of government enterprise in dealing with externalities, as against the advantages in efficiency of the market sector.

Without agreement on the optimum margin of substitution, my classification will perhaps differ from that of others. But, it cannot be argued that all activities of British government, national, or local, are for the production of public goods, and that the externalities argument always and ever outweighs the efficiency argument. It will then presumably be conceded that at least some of the taxation raised to finance current government production may be dispensable. (I abstract from government borrowing and money-printing.)

FIRST APPROXIMATION

The first approximation is shown in Table 6.13. "Environmental services" (Group II) imply a public good characteristic, but include services that are chargeable. "Community services" (Group I) are similarly ambiguous. Research councils may provide public goods or private benefits. And the hilariously dubbed "personal social services" (since they cannot be both exclusive and share) are personal, not social: residential care, day nurseries, home helps, meals on wheels (Group III). These separable *personal* services are wrongly described as "social" because they are lazily thought of as ingredients of a welfare state.

Group I, the public goods proper, are presumably indisputable. Even here, some analysts have argued that the products of research, flood protection, even justice,[19] are separable and chargeable in the market. The Northern Ireland item conceals a large element of personal services. Still, for any estimate I count only 5 per cent as chargeable – £763 million.

Group II comprises largely common services, but with a sizeable (and perhaps growing) element of personal services that could be priced – not least police and fire services, and certainly roads,[20] in which Britain is backward in pricing by tolls. Here I count 10 per cent as chargeable – £553 million.

A CLEAR CASE

Group III provides the clearest, although perhaps for Messrs. Jay, Pechman, *et al.*, the most disputable, identification of services that modern government in an advanced industrialized society need not finance by taxes. It is here that the British taxpayer can most plausibly argue he would do a better job of shopping and choosing than politicians and bureaucrats do for him.

A chunk of the education bill might be interpreted as a public good for its "melting pot" externality in creating a common culture. But even that is a tenuous proposition. A common culture may be more securely based on a tolerance of differences than an intolerant *Gleichschaltung*. It requires an inordinate stretch of the imagination to claim heavily subsidized "further education" classes in basket-weaving for free-riding middle-aged, middle-income matrons as a public good without which British society would disintegrate.

Certainly a large part of the health bill is spent on public health environmental and preventive services. But this is not so for the larger part spent on hospitalization of the elderly and even the mentally ill. They could be provided for in the market. This is true for the middle-aged and younger short-term chronic sick as well. Surely, no tax revenue is essential for housing, where the market, although partly destroyed by government, could quickly recover. And the same holds for retirement pensions, and for the bulk of the other items in this Group. I therefore estimate 75 per cent of the total as *not* necessarily financed by taxation – £34.8 billion.

All of Group IV is left in the public goods sector, just for the sake of argument – and in order to bend over backwards not to bias the case in favour of the market. That leaves over £36 billion out of £67 billion spent on goods and services that need *not* be financed by taxes. This is way over half of the total.

Moreover, since we cannot, sadly, assume that government is conducted with optimum efficiency and economy, we may lop off a cautious 30 per cent from the remainder (£31 billion) for a range of bureaucratic offences from Niscanen's budget inflation through ineffi-

TABLE 6.13

How British Government Spends Its Taxpayers' Money, 1979-1980

		£ Million	% of Total Govt. Expenditure (£80 b.)	% of GNP (£140 b.)
GROUP I	PUBLIC GOODS PROPER WITH INSEPARABLE BENEFITS			
	Defence	7,723		
	Overseas aid	1,226		
	EEC (etc.)	919		
	Drainage, flood protection	211		
	Administration of justice	242		
	Prisons, etc.	362		
	Civil defence	31		
	"Community services"	47		
	Research councils	308		
	Parliament, tax collections, surveys	1,014		
	Civil service offices and pensions	1,047		
	Northern Ireland	2,136		
		15,266	19	11
GROUP II	PUBLIC GOODS WITH PARTLY SEPARABLE BENEFITS			
	Environmental services (other than local)	461		
	Roads and transport	3,073		
	Police	1,447		
	Fire	346		
		5,327	6	4

TABLE 6.13 (continued)

GROUP III	MAINLY OR WHOLLY SEPARABLE BENEFITS			
	Education	8,939		
	Health	7,688		
	Housing	5,373		
	Pensions (retirement)	8,804		
	Other social security (including administration)	10,086		
	Employment training and trade	1,212		
	Water	589		
	Local environmental services (parks, refuse collection, recreation, theatres, etc.)	2,012		
	Arts and libraries	408		
	Personal social services	1,380		
		46,491	58	33
GROUP IV	CASH DISBURSEMENTS (SUBSIDIES, GRANTS, PENSIONS, ETC.)			
	Agriculture	944		
	Regional aid, industrial subsidies	1,008		
	Scientific and technological "Assistance"	282		
	Aerospace, shipbuilding, steel	202		
	Nationalized industries — subsidies	266		
	Nationalized industries — lending	1,900		
	Interest on National Debt	9,000		
		13,602	17	10
	TOTAL GOVERNMENT EXPENDITURE	80,686	100	58

ciency[21] to ordinary everyday common corruption. This comes to £10 billion—leaving £21 billion (out of £81 billion total government expenditure, barely over a quarter) to be financed by unavoidable taxation. Thus less than a third of government expenditure on goods and services is seen to be justified.

LOCAL GOVERNMENT EXPENDITURE

The extent to which British government non-public goods and services are over-financed by taxation is seen in Table 6.14. Local government services have been divided into two categories. The first is "rate fund services" and these are run as "social" services. They are financed largely by the local (property) tax called "the rates." The second category is "trading services," ostensibly run as commercial ventures, they are financed largely by charging a fee. Housing, however, has been regarded as neither, a good example of (unintentional) official humour. The 1976–1977 figures in Table 6.2 show education, personal social services, administration of justice, transport, environment services as rate-financed.

Interest is shown both excluded from and included in the expenditure figures. Interest on and serving of debt is a poor measure of the (opportunity) cost of the capital in current use, because the debt was incurred at varying times and interest rates. The expenditure figures shown are thus (sometimes severely) under-stated. The income from charges, fees, fares, rents, and other prices appear in some few cases to exceed the expenditure. This might suggest that local governments were using their monopoly powers to mulct the consumer. When interest is included, the calculations show more nearly the proportion of current outgoings covered by current income. Even here the high proportions for the final category of "trading services" seem unreasonable; they are much higher than in 1974 and there has been no marked rise in charges to explain the general rise.

The proportion of expenditure covered by pricing indicates the short-fall required to be financed by taxation (national as well as local); rates provide only 33 per cent to 40 per cent of local expenditure. Observation indicates that many services are needlessly financed by taxes. On what economic grounds do taxpayers subsidize, for example, 30 per cent of car parking, 90 per cent of refuse collection and 50 per cent of housing costs.

The tax-revolt sparked off in California may reflect anger at the precipitate rise in the property tax. As well, it indicates the long-standing elemental preference of taxpayers for more money to spend on themselves rather than to give over these funds, in the form of taxes, to be spent by government. In Britain it also reflects the increasing dissatisfaction with falling standards in government education and medical care and other personal services. These are not public goods, but government continues to provide and finance them out of tax revenues. Government either cannot or will not return the provision of these services to the market.

If government were instituted *de novo* in Britain (or the U.S.A. or Canada or elsewhere) in 1980, it would begin and end with the provision of public goods. It would be laughed out of court if it pretended to supply schools, or hospitals, or homes, or mechanisms for saving, or water or car parking or libraries or abattoirs or allotments—or any of the 101 other barnacles that have grown fast to the ship of state. British taxation is increasingly seen by taxpayers as too high for the services that government must perform. Adam Smith knew broadly what these were in 1776. Keynes largely reproduced his criterion and formula in 1926. What they said is good enough for the British taxpayer in 1980.

V. REDISTRIBUTION

The second major justification for (possibly "high") taxation is to redistribute income either outside the market by providing free or subsidized goods and/or services or in the market by providing purchasing power.

In Britain, both are done. The question is how much taxation is worth raising for how much redistribution at the margin? The disincentives and other defects of high marginal tax rates might be worth risking for the advantages of a less unequal distribution of income.

COALS TO NEWCASTLE

I calculated an approximation of the proportions of taxes returned in benefits to the households from which they came (1976 data). The results are shown in Table 6.15. The tax figures covered rather over half of the then £41.6 billion of government expenditure, and the benefits accounted for rather under two-fifths.

The table shows the average tax by retirement status, and numbers of adults and children, households and the value of the benefits "returned" to them. The totals for all households indicate that rather under half of the taxes were returned to the households where they originated. This proportion would of course be changed if all taxes and benefits could have been traced to individual households. Corporation and capital taxes could not be allocated, though this amounted to about 30 per cent of all tax revenue. A further 13 per cent of government expenditure was covered by rents, interest or other trading income. The rest, 15 per cent, was accounted for by what is tendentiously called the "public sector borrowing requirement." This implies that *all*

TABLE 6.14

Local Public Goods-Cum-Private Benefits — Payment by Taxes and Pricing 1976-77

Service	Expenditures (a) Excluding Debt Charges	Expenditures (b) Including Debt Charges	Fees, Charges, etc.	£ m Charges as % of Expenditures (a)	£ m Charges as % of Expenditures (b)
A EDUCATION					
Schools					
Administration and Inspection	234.5	234.6	1.5	0.6	1.6
Nursery education	23.8	25.6	0.1	0.4	0.4
Primary education	1508.4	1641.9	9.7	0.6	0.6
Secondary education	1909.8	2118.9	29.1	1.5	1.4
Special education	261.4	280.4	20.8	8.0	7.4
Further education					
Polytechnical	249.3	277.6	39.1	15.7	14.1
Agricultural colleges and institutes	16.3	18.1	5.1	31.3	28.2
Other major establishments	677.5	734.0	116.8	17.2	15.9
Evening institutes	45.5	46.2	9.5	20.9	20.6
Other	375.4	375.5	40.7	10.8	10.8
Other education					
Child guidance and other health services	10.5	10.7	0.1	1.0	0.9
Facilities for recreation and social and physical training					
Youth service	47.6	53.0	1.8	3.8	3.4
Adult recreation and other services	21.3	23.0	2.5	11.4	10.9
Other educational services (including research)	8.2	8.5	1.8	22.0	21.2
School meals, milk and other refreshments	545.7	560.0	140.3	25.7	25.1

B PERSONAL SOCIAL SERVICES					
Field Work					
Social Work — staff and related expenses	113.032	113.036	1.034	0.9	0.9
Administration	42.852	43.309	0.178	0.4	0.4
Residential Care					
Local authority community homes	129.996	139.694	20.828	16.0	14.9
Controlled community homes	21.748	22.43	8.094	37.2	36.1
Other children's homes	26.500	26.506	0.324	1.2	1.2
Homes for the elderly	266.118	295.105	99.527	37.4	33.7
Homes for the younger physically handicapped, blind and deaf	16.895	18.088	4.358	25.8	24.1
Homes for the mentally handicapped	29.854	34.638	7.441	24.9	21.5
Homes for the mentally ill	6.870	7.818	2.144	31.2	27.4
Mother and baby homes	0.923	0.946	0.085	9.2	9.0
Temporary accommodation	2.685	2.878	0.578	21.5	20.1
Other accommodation	0.498	0.524	0.156	31.3	29.8
Administration	54.791	55.095	2.931	5.4	5.3
Support Services					
Day Care					
Day Nurseries and pre-school play groups	35.266	37.482	2.546	7.2	6.8
Other day care for children	2.208	2.314	0.185	8.4	8.0
Day centres and clubs for the elderly	14.816	16.272	2.167	14.6	13.3
Day centres for younger physically handicapped, blind and deaf	11.545	13.299	0.997	8.6	7.5
Adult training centres and centres for the mentally handicapped	38.161	13.506	5.167	13.5	11.9
Day centres and clubs for the mentally ill	2.709	3.217	0.240	9.2	7.5
Day centres and clubs for multi-purpose	5.326	6.453	0.622	11.7	9.6
Community Care					
Home helps and laundry	116.588	116.616	5.505	4.7	4.7

TABLE 6.14 (continued)

Local Public Goods-Cum-Private Benefits — Payment by Taxes and Pricing 1976-77

£ m

Service	Expenditures (a) Excluding Debt Charges	Expenditures (b) Including Debt Charges	Fees, Charges, etc.	Charges as % of Expenditures (a)	Charges as % of Expenditures (b)
Boarded Out					
Children's Care	20.979	20.981	1.283	6.1	6.1
Others	0.167	0.167	0.077	46.1	46.1
Preventive and supportive services (families)	4.533	4.580	0.289	6.4	6.3
Meals in the home	16.212	16.383	4.225	26.1	25.7
Other community care services	29.331	29.693	2.749	9.4	9.3
Miscellaneous support services	6.275	6.401	1.119	17.8	17.4
Administration	44.759	44.976	1.117	2.5	2.5
Research and Development	1.686	1.896	0.009	0.5	0.5
Administration	3.432	3.439	0.019	0.6	0.6
C ADMINISTRATION OF JUSTICE					
Magistrates courts, etc.	107.033	115.249	5.437	5.1	4.7
D LOCAL TRANSPORT					
Highways	447.789	551.875	64.810	15.1	11.7
Public lighting	69.124	75.525	1.503	2.2	2.0
Parking	38.225	60.627	42.507	111.2	70.1

F LOCAL ENVIRONMENTAL SERVICES					
Refuse Collection	241.613	245.118	17.003	7.0	6.9
Refuse Disposal	67.171	81.613	9.297	13.8	11.4
Recreation, parks and baths	347.314	405.634	100.071	28.8	24.7
Environmental Health	161.981	167.79	20.253	12.5	12.1
Consumer Protection	24.868	25.211	7.875	31.7	31.2
Town and Country Planning	179.086	244.615	44.298	24.7	18.1
Agriculture and Fisheries	53.354	60.047	8.763	16.4	14.6
Cemeteries and crematoria	33.085	35.214	13.769	41.6	39.1
G HOUSING REVENUE ACCOUNT					
Housing	696.937	2,113.476	1,021.171	146.5	48.3
H TRADING SERVICES AND CORPORATION ESTATES					
Passenger Transport	85.438	88.612	81.276	95.1	91.7
Civic Halls and Theatres	32.787	39.905	17.312	52.8	43.4
Fishing Harbours	0.576	0.722	0.650	112.8	90.0
Ports and Piers	20.637	23.762	23.152	112.2	97.4
Civic Restaurants	6.588	6.616	6.596	100.1	99.7
Markets	22.208	29.008	31.744	142.9	109.4
Slaughterhouses	6.967	8.867	6.357	91.2	71.7
Aerodomes	25.412	31.928	26.645	104.9	83.5
Industrial Estates	3.719	17.758	15.561	418.4	87.6
District Heating Schemes	0.881	1.024	0.965	109.5	94.2
Other Trading Services	72.515	82.338	73.457	101.3	89.2
Corporation Estates	17.983	35.402	34.080	189.5	96.3
Toll Bridges	5.396	11.979	10.395	192.6	86.7

Source: *Local Government Financial Statistics*, 1976/77, HMSO, 1978.

TABLE 6.15

Abortive Taxation or Coals to Newcastle
A First Approximation by Averages for Groups of Households, 1974

Households		Original Income (£)	Average for Each Group of Households: Taxes Paid	Benefits Received	Taxes Returned in Benefits		Total Taxes	
Composition	Number		£	£	£	%	Paid	Returned
1 adult (retired)	579	under 381	125	781	125	100	72,375	72,375
	46	381 - 556	183	633	183	100	8,418	8,418
	38	557 - 815	286	631	286	100	10,868	10,868
	27	816 - 1,193	424	553	424	100	11,448	11,448
	20	1,194 - 1,748	542	635	542	100	10,840	10,840
	14	749 - 2,560	781	578	578	74	10,934	8,092
2 adults (retired)	340	under 381	225	1,241	225	100	76,500	76,500
	73	301 - 556	242	1,090	242	100	17,868	17,686
	56	557 - 815	370	1,045	370	100	20,720	20,720
	46	818 - 1,193	493	1,034	493	100	22,678	22,678
	31	1,194 - 1,748	661	1,024	661	100	20,491	20,491
	30	1,749 - 2,560	793	872	793	100	23,790	23,790
	18	2,561 - 3,749	1,293	928	928	72	23,274	16,704
1 adult (not retired)	69	under 381	155	969	155	100	10,695	10,695
	19	381 - 556	223	650	223	100	4,237	4,237
	43	557 - 815	310	561	310	100	13,330	13,330
	63	816 - 1,193	400	413	400	100	25,200	25,200
	107	1,194 - 1,748	605	290	290	48	64,735	31,030
	118	1,749 - 2,560	863	147	147	17	101,834	17,346
	63	2,561 - 3,749	1,146	130	130	11	72,198	8,190
	29	3,750 - 5,489	1,747	79	79	4.5	50,663	2,291
	12	5,490 +	3,116	95	95	3.0	37,392	1,140

TABLE 6.15 (continued)

2 adults (not retired)	27	under 381	309	1,105	309	100	8,343	8,343
	18	381 - 556	290	1,171	290	100	5,220	5,220
	42	557 - 815	310	983	310	100	13,020	13,020
	57	816 - 1,193	429	906	429	100	24,453	24,453
	138	1,194 - 1,748	583	551	551	95	80,454	76,038
	318	1,749 - 2,560	837	378	378	45	266,166	120,204
	445	2,561 - 3,749	1,184	292	292	25	526,880	129,940
	339	3,750 - 5,489	1,647	197	197	12	568,333	66,783
	120	5,490 +	2,789	197	197	7	334,680	23,640
3 adults	10	under 381	407	1,631	407	100	4,070	4,070
	19	1,446 - 1,748	716	1,104	716	100	13,604	13,604
	61	1,749 - 2,560	1,820	2,149	1,820	100	111,020	111,020
	141	2,561 - 3,749	2,503	1,306	1,306	52	352,923	184,146
	166	3,750 - 5,489	3,544	969	969	27	588,304	160,854
	83	5,490 +	2,761	421	421	15	229,163	34,943
3 adults 1 child	18	2,116 - 2,560	841	1,012	841	100	15,138	15,138
	54	2,561 - 3,749	2,259	1,791	1,791	79	121,986	96,714
	69	3,750 - 5,489	3,188	1,744	1,744	55	219,972	120,336
	36	5,490 +	2,677	876	876	33	96,372	31,536
3 adults 2 children	41	2,561 - 3,749	2,085	2,663	2,085	100	85,485	85,485
	41	3,750 - 5,489	3,134	2,259	2,259	72	128,494	92,619
	16	5,490 +	2,308	1,122	1,122	49	36,928	17,952
2 adults 1 child	11	816 - 1,193	332	1,000	332	100	3,652	3,652
	45	1,194 - 1,748	561	631	561	100	25,245	25,245
	177	1,749 - 2,560	784	461	461	59	138,768	81,597
	221	2,561 - 3,749	1,112	438	436	39	245,752	96,356
	114	3,750 - 5,489	1,550	388	388	25	176,700	44,232
	26	5,490 +	3,330	322	322	10	86,580	8,372

TABLE 6.15 (continued)

Abortive Taxation or Coals to Newcastle
A First Approximation by Averages for Groups of Households, 1974

Households		Original Income (£)	Average for Each Group of Households				Total Taxes	
			Taxes Paid	Benefits Received	Taxes Returned in Benefits			
Composition	Number		£	£	£	%	Paid	Returned
2 adults 2 children	49	1,194 - 1,748	540	871	540	100	26,460	25,460
	194	1,749 - 2,560	773	657	657	85	149,962	127,458
	320	2,561 - 3,749	1,071	641	641	60	342,720	206,120
	173	3,750 - 5,489	1,475	652	652	44	255,175	112,796
	51	5,490 +	2,403	646	646	27	122,553	32,946
2 adults 3 children	12	under 381	430	2,320	430	100	5,160	5,160
	21	1,194 - 1,748	465	1,201	465	100	9,765	9,765
	63	1,749 - 2,560	746	983	746	100	46,998	46,998
	128	2,561 - 3,749	1,060	1,002	1,002	95	135,680	128,256
	70	3,750 - 5,489	1,406	1,009	1,009	72	98,420	70,630
	34	5,490 +	2,499	853	853	34	84,966	29,002
2 adults 4 children	17	1,194 - 1,748	453	1,593	453	100	7,701	7,701
	26	1,749 - 2,560	663	1,459	663	100	17,238	17,238
	31	2,561 - 3,749	1,035	1,379	1,035	100	32,085	32,085
	26	3,750 - 5,489	1,406	1,313	1,313	93	36,556	34,138
	10	5,490 +	2,493	1,253	1,253	50	24,930	12,530

Source: *Charge*, Maurice Temple Smith (London), 1977.

government expenditure is imperative; and that government is "required" to borrow the balance it cannot finance by taxes or trading income.

The benefits that could not be allocated revealed the questionable activities of government. There is no dispute that public goods cannot be allocated – defence, tax collection, etc. The other excluded items are more debatable: regional and industrial aid, investment grants, research and roads. These were excluded, said the government statisticians, because their effects on individual households could not be estimated. Environmental and protective services (parks, etc.) were also excluded. So was capital expenditure on the social services and public corporations. Many of these items could have been allocated if they had been priced. And even the items allocated (education, medical care, etc.) represented apportionment of costs (inputs) which can be very different from the subjective valuations of consumers (outputs).

ABORTIVE TAXATION

This estimate is the nearest approximation to the proportion of taxes that has no redistributive effect – since it is returned to its sources. Analysis of groups of households by income indicates how far tax and benefits cancel out.

On this showing, at least half of British taxation for that purpose is unneccessary to redistribute income. Whatever the proportion of this unnecessary or "abortive" taxation, the question is how the optimal degree of redistribution can best be ensured. This cannot be accomplished by raising a very much larger total of taxation than required, for that also entails the financial and other costs of administrative effort. As well, it involves bureaucratic ballast, probable disincentives, tax "avoision" and its muting of the respect for law, the tension between taxpayers and tax-collectors, the expansion of government into personal services, the weakening of the family, the loss of human resources by emigration, the monopoly control of welfare and other services, the discouragement to innovation, and the strengthening of syndicalist trade unionism. In addition, it creates inequity for lower-income families by making them do battle with higher income counterparts for access benefits in kind (not least education and medical care).

VI. THE EFFICIENCY OF TAX PRICES

What type of taxes are the most efficient method of paying for non-public goods – as measured by the subjective judgements of the public? Since 1963 the Institute of Economic Affairs in London has mounted four field studies (1963, 1965, 1970, 1978) of preferences between taxes and prices in payment for education and medical care. (These are the two main benefits-in-kind now financed almost wholly by taxation.) The device of the voucher was adapted to create a hypothetical demand curve based on two prices. The question was, how far would the public take up an education or health voucher (and even add to it) so as to pay for a choice of schooling or medical service in the market.

The surveys began with working male heads of households as the family decision makers concerning education and medical care. Following criticism from the late R.H.S. Crossman in 1963 that the omission of women and pensioners had biased the response, and by Riker[22] that women make most budget decisions on health and education, women were introduced as a pilot check in 1970, and in full sample in 1978.[23]

The survey methods used were, in my judgement, a working "substitute for the market." Riker further objected that the micro-economic questions might not yield a demand curve because the respondents' replies stated, "how men believe they ought to act for their families, not how they do act." But this was a recognized and unavoidable limitation. The surveys claim only to have uncovered hypothetical demand.

POLITICALLY IMPOSSIBLE?

These surveys were a response to objections by academics and politicians. They claimed to know the state of British public opinion sufficiently to declare that reform of the structure or financing of the British welfare state, especially state education and the National Health Service (NHS), was "politically impossible." But this is a political hypothesis not an axiom. (The surveys are reported in *Overruled on Welfare.)*[24]

In the course of the investigations the studies uncovered massive ignorance of the tax-price of state service.[25] The ignorance continues. The only light in this darkness in Britain was displayed among the 4–5 per cent who paid in the market for the largely private benefit of education and the 3–4 per cent who paid, through insurance, for the non-public good of personal medical care.

These researches revealed as misleading the intermittent opinion polls that had recorded (since 1948) 80–90 per cent approval of tax-financing in the welfare state, with around 85 per cent for the NHS. The most recent of these surveys, where the price option was strictly ignored in late 1978, showed 84 per cent "satisfaction." But the IEA surveys, which included price as a variable led Professor Mark Blaug to remark, "Economists will recognize immediately that the inquiry in effect elicited information about the slope of the demand schedule. . . ."[26]

VOUCHERS

The device of the voucher can be seen as a method of refunding taxes with which taxpayers can pay for their own education and medical care in the market. The education voucher was calculated as one-third and two-thirds of the tax-cost of (secondary day) state education. The health voucher was calculated as one-half and two-thirds of the current cost of insuring in the market for the insurable range of personal health services (that is, excluding the public goods of environmental and preventive services and chronic geriatric/psychiatric services). Two voucher values indicated that the results were logically consistent with the laws of demand: the higher-valued vouchers, requiring less topping up, that is, representing a lower net price, evoked a higher demand. This was measured by the percentage of the samples that indicated acceptance in lieu of "free" state education and the "free" personal services of the NHS.

In education there was a simple choice between state and private education. In medical care the choice is complicated by the ability to use both systems in series or in parallel.

Three conclusions may be drawn from these findings:

1. The public approval of tax-financing of welfare (education and medical care) relative to private alternatives in the market was lower than indicated by mainstream opinion polls.
2. It was not "politically impossible" in 1978 (though it *may* have been in 1963) to reform the tax-financing of welfare. In any event, the judgement of politicians on "political impossibility" is strategic: they have an incentive to claim knowledge of public opinion to consolidate their power and obstruct any reform that threatens it. David Hume, we may recall, said "every man ought to be supposed a knave, and to have no other end than private interest."
3. The divergence between the findings of price-less and price field research indicates the great degree to which British government has frustrated and suppressed public preferences. By insisting on tax-financing for health and education, "representative" government in Britain has become unrepresentative.

IN CASH OR IN KIND?

There is another implication of these studies. Tax-financing for benefits in kind, such as education and medical care, is inegalitarian, since it is less difficult to correct differences in money income than in the power or influence that decides access to services in kind. As Professor Buchanan argued:

> The evidence seems to indicate that general redistribution of purchasing power... is not widely desired. Instead members of the public want... relief for specific spending patterns.
>
> I advance the refutable hypothesis that distribution in kind is the predictable outcome of the political process.[27]

The British public also wants to help the poor because they are poor, as well as because their visible poverty is embarrassing. Compassion may therefore demand such a high price that it may have to yield, at the margin, to the requirement of liberty. And the taxpayer may *not* prefer benefits in kind, which destroy the market, to transfer payments, which bolster it.

The priced research dispels a paradox in public attitudes to paying taxes that perplexes politicians and non-politicians alike.

Lord Diamond, a former Treasury Minister, wrote:

> Public services have not been thrust on an unwilling public; they have been increasing demanded by an articulate one.
>
> One must not confuse the age-old unpopularity of the tax-gatherer with the popularity of the services provided 'free' out of taxes so gathered.[28]

This confusion was accepted by a New Zealand enquiry as a profound insight; it thought Lord Diamond provided:

> a useful perspective against which to examine the trends... in public expenditure from 22–23 per cent of GDP in the 1950s and 1960s to 34 per cent in 1979....[29]

The non-economist does not easily grasp that the "demand" for a product in the market cannot be conceived independently of its price. The notion of elasticity in the longer run is, unfortunately, foreign to him. This makes it all the more difficult for the lay person to conceive of the tax-price of a public good. But this is entirely understandable. Although he may on reflection recall that products in the market have prices, he knows that public goods (or at least public services whether collective public goods or separable private benefits) often have no prices because they are supplied "free." The Friedmans have said:

> No one can dispute two superficially contradictory phenomena: widespread dissatisfaction with the results of (the) explosion in welfare activities, continued pressure for further expansion.[30]

The cause of the confusion and the contradiction is the absence of price in the supply of government services, whether public goods or not. Priced surveys, such as undertaken by the IEA, remove this confusion by restoring the missing link. If the public were asked:

> Are you in favour of paying more in taxes for more/better state welfare at a price? (better still—at a low price, a medium price, a high price; best of all—if your income were to rise by, say, £500)?
>
> and
>
> Are you in favour of lower taxes if you had to pay for education, medical care (etc.) by fees, charges, or insurance premiums?

there would be no confusion or contradiction.

So far the theorems ingeniously devised by public choice theorists for revealing preferences in public goods—by insurance, by taxes, by veto or other means—are too complicated to be incorporated into field research. An imperfect method such as these priced alternatives may at least yield practicable results.

VII. THE SOCIAL WELFARE FICTION

Economists have long tried to devise a social welfare function that would assimilate individual preferences and so make credible the task of social/central planners. Since Professor Kenneth Arrow's discovery that the social welfare function is "impossible," says Professor Buchanan:

> The formal collective or social choice theorists, shocked by the...impossibility theorem, have continued to try to examine the restrictions on individual preferences that might be required to generate consistent social orderings.[31]

These restrictions can be regarded as justifying taxation to enable government to provide services that taxpayers would accept only reluctantly, or not at all, in return for their taxes.

How would a sample of Britons act as Chancellors of their own Exchequers in *spending* their taxes? By asking this, we can discover how representative contemporary British governments (but not the present one, since it inherited a legacy it will take at least a decade to modify) have been in spending the people's taxes, or, contrarily, how far they were frustrating the individual preferences of the taxpayers. We shall discuss individual preferences under four headings: government (expenditure) as a whole, state education, the National Health Service, and then local government.

CENTRAL GOVERNMENT

Before asking the respondents how they would like their taxes spent[32] my first step was to discover whether they *knew* how their taxes were being spent by government. The degree of civic ignorance uncovered should humble economists who talk of "tax-prices" as analogues of market-prices. While consumers know the latter vividly since they pay them daily in the market, they are in almost complete ignorance concerning the former.

Government expenditure was represented by three substantially public goods: defence, roads, unemployment benefits, and by four substantially personal benefits: education, health, housing, and retirement pensions.

The extent of public knowledge of tax spending is shown in Table 6.16 column 1, together with the estimated expenditure on each of the seven items out of each £100 spent on all seven. The public was, even on average, far out on most items. And even where the average was near the estimate, the reason would appear to be chance, and the cancellation of error, rather than knowledge. The full extent of public ignorance and civic illiteracy is indicated in the range of "guesses." We

TABLE 6.16

Knowledge of Tax Expenditure, U.K. 1978

	Latest Estimate of Expenditure (£ Out of £100 on All Seven)	Average 'Guess'	Range % Giving 'Guess'				
			£1-10	£11-20	£21-30	£30 +	Don't Know
	£	£	%	%	%	%	%
Education	24	17	33	40	17	5	5
Retirement pensions	22	11	62	28	4	1	5
Defence	18	16	44	29	17	5	5
Health	17	16	33	44	14	4	5
Housing	15	12	57	32	5	1	5
Roads	2	9	72	20	2	1	5
Unemployment (benefits)	2	20	31	31	20	13	5

Note: The replies were groups of £10; smaller groups would have made clearer the nearness or remoteness of the guesses. 5% were sufficiently certain of their uncertainty to reply 'don't know.' The remaining 95% responded to the invitation to 'guess.'

Source: Public opinion poll conducted by author.

must sadly conclude that, on this evidence, the British have little idea how their taxes are really spent.

The respondents were then told the true figures and asked how they would *like* their taxes spent. Did they want them spent differently, more on some services and less on others? It was hoped to avoid priceless "Diamond" replies by building into the questions awareness of the *cost* to the individual taxpayer of requiring government to spend more on some services. They were therefore promptly asked the *source* of the additional spending:

i) by transfer from other services on which less would be spent, or
ii) by paying higher taxes.

Conversely, those opting for less spending on some services were asked whether they wanted the taxes:

i) moved to other services, or
ii) returned to them.

It was thus hoped to make each respondent think of spending his taxes *micro*-economically on services supplied by government in the same way as in spending his "take-home" pay on services in the market.

INDIVIDUAL WELFARE

It was thought the responses would show how far "individual welfare functions" would be found to differ from, or were dispersed around, the social welfare function implied in current government decisions. How much agreement among citizens is required to authorize "representative" government in spending taxes? Unanimity? A simple majority? Two-thirds? Three-quarters? Nine-tenths? Presumably little agreement would have to suffice for spending taxes on public goods, since the alternative was no supply at all. But a high degree of agreement would be desirable for spending taxes on separable benefits that could be obtained in the market. Otherwise, there would be frustration or suppression of preferences, (as there is).

The results are revealing. The first finding was that 70 per cent thought *more* tax revenue should be spent on one or other of the seven government services and *less* spent on the others: only 30 per cent were satisfied by the generalized ranking in the social welfare function. This proportion was fairly general in all the sub-groups. It may be that this consistency is itself significant.

The sub-analysis by service is shown in Table 6.17. The highest proportion (34 per cent) predictably wanted more spent on health

TABLE 6.17

Individual Preferences in Tax Expenditure, U.K. 1978

At the Expense of Less on ↓ / Spend More on →	Defence	Education	Health	Roads	Housing	Unemployment Benefit	Retirement
	177 (9%)	246 (12%)	675 (34%)	415 (21%)	179 (9%)	80 (4%)	158 (8%)*
	%	%	%	%	%	%	%
Defence	—	60	56	54	66	52	53
Education	30	—	1	23	12	25	18
Health	12	4	—	5	4	4	3
Roads	8	4	2	—	2	2	6
Housing	42	17	18	2	—	12	21
Unemployment	24	14	13	12	5	—	20
Retirement	25	11	15	11	15	20	—
Don't know	1	2	1	2	1	—	—

*These figures represent the number of respondents and proportion of total sample asking for more to be spent in each category.

Note: Each vertical column adds to more than 100% as many respondents suggested switching tax money from more than one source.

Source: Public opinion poll conducted by author.

services, and most of them (56 per cent) would take the money from defence. The next highest proportion (21 per cent) wanted more spent on roads (not, as might be thought, on education – only 12 per cent), and again most of them would transfer the money from defence. But only 9 per cent wanted more spent on defence, and most of them (40 per cent) would transfer the money from housing.

Whether these preferences are judged wise or unwise, short-sighted or long-sighted, they seem clearly different from the "political priorities" evidently embodied in government use of taxes or the implicit social welfare function on which it is conceptually based.

UNDERSPENDING ON PUBLIC GOODS?

There is a significant difference in the attitude toward spending taxes on public goods and on personal benefits. This may be seen from the contrast between the low vote for additional tax spending on defence and the high vote for additional tax expenditure on health. The benefits of defence are remote, contingent or intangible, of health services more immediate and personal. That more individuals would spend more of their taxes than does government on health than on defence suggests they see the NHS as a personal, not (though much of it is) as a public, good. Hence the tendency that might otherwise emerge to underspend on defence (and other public goods) and to overspend on health (and other personal benefits).

Were these answers "sincere?" They would not appear to have been "strategic." The only practicable ways to test their utility as a guide to policy are:

i) more extensive sample surveying,
ii) referenda on single (public) goods,
iii) placing the remaining (non-public) services on the market, as in the "Enterprise Zones" conceived by the British Chancellor of the Exchequer in which government restrictions on entrepreneurship, mobility, etc. would be minimized.

So far these are "yes" and "no" responses. A degree of sophistication was introduced by asking respondents to say *how much* (in £ sterling) they would transfer between government services. Consumers commonly make these marginal adjustments in everyday price-expenditures on purchases in the market. They should, therefore, be capable of making them in adjusting tax-expenditures.

The value responses varied widely. Among the private benefits, the largest addition, £3.42, was "voted" to be added to the £17 spent on health services. This was an increase of some 20 per cent, and not much difference was found in the sub-groups. Among the public goods the

TABLE 6.18

Knowledge of Tax Expenditure on Education — Average Guesses, 1978

	Average 'Guesses'	Recent Estimates
	£	£
Nursery	14	6
Primary	24	31
Secondary	34	50
Higher	28	13

Source: Public opinion poll conducted by author.

largest addition was for £2.05 on roads, a doubling of the current expenditure, with some differences in the sub-groups.

STATE EDUCATION

Here preferences were elicited between the four main sub-divisions: nursery, primary, secondary, and higher. Again, knowledge of tax expenditure by the state was sparse. The wide dispersion of guesses is shown in Tables 6.18 and 6.19. Only the average ranking indicates some impression of the correct broad order of magnitude, but beyond that there is evidently a vast ocean of ignorance.

If the populace is uninformed about the expenditure of its taxes by its representatives in an indirect parliamentary franchise, how can it be asked to approve proposed changes in policy? What are the "representatives" in representative democracy representing? There would appear to be scope for massive misdirection of tax funds by massive compounding of taxpayers' ignorance by politicians' ignorance.

To replace public ignorance with knowledge, the respondents were then told the estimated expenditures on each of the four sub-divisions and, as before, asked for preferences. Table 6.20 shows that most—26 per cent—thought more should be spent on nursery education—mainly at the expense of secondary education. The 16 per cent who wanted more spent on higher education also wanted less spent on secondary education, which seems out of favour generally (perhaps because of complaints about the inability of job-hunting school-leavers to read or write, truancy, indiscipline—even arson!). In all, 55 per cent (including double mentions) wanted expenditure shifted between the four sub-divisions.

TABLE 6.19

Knowledge of Tax Expenditure on Education — Range of Guesses

	Average 'Guess'	% 'Guessing'						
		£1-£10	£11-£20	£21-£30	£31-£40	£41-£50	£51 +	Don't Know/ Not Stated
	£	%	%	%	%	%	%	%
Nursery	14	50	36	7	2	1	*	4
Primary	24	5	40	43	6	1	*	4
Secondary	34	1	10	36	32	14	2	4
Higher	28	5	24	37	20	8	1	4

*less than 0.5%.

Source: Public opinion poll conducted by author.

TABLE 6.20

Public Preferences in Tax Expenditures on Education

At the Expense of Less on ↓ / Spend More On →	Nursery	Primary	Secondary	Higher
	26%	10%	3%	16%
	%	%	%	%
Nursery	—	13	43	14
Primary	16	—	20	38
Secondary	70	62	—	64
Higher	23	24	47	—
Don't know	2	3	3	3

*These figures represent the number of respondents and proportion of total sample asking for more to be spent in each category.

Note: Most columns add to more than 100% vertically because some respondents suggested taking money from more than one source. Since some also suggested adding money to more than one division, the proportion wanting more funds added to the four is less than the sum of the percentages shown against each horizontally (55%).

Source: Public opinion poll conducted by author.

Again the "Yes-No" replies were refined by evaluation. The largest groups of switchers (to nursery schools) would also switch most money—£5, or almost doubling the amount, now £6 per £100. And the smallest group of switchers (to secondary education) would switch least—£0.5 to the current £50. The responses to the stark question, "Would you personally pay more in taxes... (to enable more to be spent on nursery, etc. education)?" were intriguing. They revealed the effect on "demand" (for more expenditure) of knowledge of the "price" (in taxes). Less than half (45 per cent) of those who said more should be spent on one or other of the four education divisions said they would pay higher taxes. 28 per cent "did not know." If these were split between Yes and No, the 45 per cent willing to pay higher taxes would rise to 59 per cent and the 26 per cent not willing would rise to 41 per cent. This response was fairly stable by sex, age, and political sympathy.

Since 48 per cent of the respondents wanted more spent on one or other sub-division, and 45 per cent of them (or 59 per cent) said they would pay higher taxes, only 22 per cent (or 26 per cent) of the respondent sample would pay higher taxes to spend on state education. Since

TABLE 6.21

Knowledge of Tax Expenditure on Medical Care, Average Guesses, U.K. 1978

	Survey Replies (Averages)	Recent Estimates
	£	£
Hospitals	36	64
Local (family) doctors	21	14
Prescriptions	21	11
Public health	22	11

Source: Public opinion poll conducted by author.

British governments—until the present one—have been spending more year by year, they were reflecting only a small minority of public opinion. So much for the social welfare function.

MEDICAL CARE

These results follow those on education and can be summarized in tabular form.

Tables 6.21 and 6.22 show how far off were the expenditure estimates on the four branches of the NHS—family doctors, prescriptions, hospital and local government (mainly public goods, preventive and environmental). Again, there was extensive ignorance.

Table 6.23 shows the preferred re-arrangement of tax-expenditure. In all, 35 per cent wanted more spent on one or other branch at the expense of one or other of the others. On the whole, prescriptions came off worst (perhaps because of the continual criticism of wasted drugs).

Predictably the largest additions were for the vivid or immediate personal services of hospitals and family doctors, though the more remote public health was, surprisingly, just as important. There were suggestive differences in the sub-groups; for example, the higher-income groups wanted more spent on family doctors than did the lower-income groups, but the latter would spend more on hospitals.

Are people willing to pay higher taxes for a better NHS? That is the question that has dogged the public debate on medical care in Britain. In view of the alleged mass approval (80—85 per cent) of the NHS, it might be expected that the British would overwhelmingly pay higher taxes to improve it. Unless this conclusion follows in practice, the

TABLE 6.22

Knowledge of Tax Expenditure on Medical Care — Range of Guesses

	Average 'Guess'	% 'Guessing'								
		£1-10	£11-20	£21-30	£31-40	£41-50	£51-60	£61-70	£70 +	D/k
	£	%	%	%	%	%	%	%	%	%
Hospitals	36	5	14	24	24	20	7	2	1	3
Local (family) doctors	21	17	42	29	5	2	1	*	—	3
Prescriptions	21	24	36	22	9	3	1	*	*	4
Public health	22	23	33	25	10	4	1	—	*	4

*less than 0.5%.

Source: Public opinion poll conducted by author.

TABLE 6.23

Public Preferences in Tax Expenditure on Medicine

At the Expense of Less on ↓ / Spend More on →	Hospitals	Local (Family) Doctors	Prescriptions	Public Health
	13%	12%	2%	13%*
	%	%	%	%
Hospitals	—	30	38	36
Local (family) doctors	24	—	31	26
Prescriptions	48	52	—	42
Public health	26	27	13	—
Don't know	4	2	18	4

*As for Table 6.20 above.

Note: Most columns add to more than 100% vertically because some respondents suggested taking money from more than one source. Since some also suggested adding funds to more than one component, the proportion wanting more funds added to all the four is less than the sum of the percentages shown against each horizontally (40%).

Source: Public opinion poll conducted by author.

expression of "approval" is meaningless. Yet only 37 per cent of the respondents (35 per cent) who wanted more spent on one or other NHS branch were prepared to pay higher taxes (Table 6.24). That is, *only 13 per cent* of the total sample were prepared to pay higher taxes for better state medical care. This is the hard core of the 80–85 per cent "approvers" of the NHS who are prepared to *pay* for what they "approve:" the measure of effective demand. To the extent that the sample is representative, the nation decided seven to one (87 per cent to 13 per cent) *against* the view that the NHS should be improved or enlarged by more tax revenue. Either many Britons think the causes of its failing lie elsewhere than in too little tax-financing, or they prefer to use their money on other goods or services in any case.

Labour supporters are supposed to be especially persuaded of the advantages of the NHS. 35 per cent of them said they wanted more spent on one or other of the four branches; 44 per cent of them said they would pay higher taxes; therefore the proportion of all Labour sympathizers who would pay higher taxes for a better NHS was 16 per cent. Hardly a demonstration of mass support. (In the face of such truly underwhelming support, how can the British government justify this implicit social welfare function?)

TABLE 6.24

Public Readiness to Pay More in Taxes for the NHS

	Total	Sex		Age		Occupational Group		Political Sympathy	
		Men	Women	16-34	35+	ABC1	C2DE	Con.	Lab.
	%	%	%	%	%	%	%	%	%
Yes	37	36	40	35	39	37	38	35	44
No	60	61	57	61	58	59	60	62	52
Don't know	3	3	4	3	3	4	3	3	4

Source: Public opinion poll conducted by author.

The disinclination to pay higher taxes even for the NHS was shown when the whole sample was asked where else money for the NHS should be derived: 29 per cent said lotteries, 14 per cent social security, 10 per cent from civil service economies, 6 per cent by cutting out waste, 4 per cent from defence and overseas expenditure, 3 per cent from road tax, 2 per cent from a gambling/betting tax.

The remaining source is direct pricing: charges, fees, etc., for family doctors, prescriptions and hospitals. Table 6.25 shows the extent of knowledge of current costs. The averages were near the estimates for the first two categories, although the dispersions were wide. Even the average "guess" for hospitals was far too low; and two-thirds of the sample guessed lower than the low average. Only 7 per cent of the total sample guessed about right; but they may have been truly "guessing."

TABLE 6.25

Knowledge of Tax-Prices in State Medicine, U.K. 1978

Service	Unit Costs	Average Guess	Recent Estimate
		£	£
Family doctors	per visit	6.50	4.00
Prescriptions	per prescription	1.51	1.50
Hospitals	weekly	101.30	250.00

Source: Public opinion poll conducted by author.

The charge for family doctors (for whom there is now no charge) was put on average at £2.90 (against the average "guess" of £6.50); for each prescription at 0.57p (against the then charge of 20p); and for hospitals (for which there is no charge) at nearly £37.

LOCAL GOVERNMENT

Finally, four services about which there was recent public debate were chosen to represent local government services: one public good: the police; and three personal services: libraries, school meals, and sports facilities.

To my knowledge, the British have never been asked—by any government or social studies—whether they would like *less* spent on local government services. Table 6.26 shows the ready response (only one *person* in the whole sample said "don't know"): 38 per cent said expenditure should be reduced.

Next, what should be done with the tax revenue saved—increase expenditure on other local services or reduce local taxes? This is another question never asked before by British government or social scientists, to my knowledge. Table 6.27 shows the rather surprising response: 62 per cent in favour of re-allocating tax revenue, 34 per cent in favour of reducing taxes. Some of the sub-group differences are predictable, others are unexpected—for example, the lower-income groups were more in favour of tax reduction than were the higher-income groups.

"Votes" for increases in tax expenditure are shown in Table 6.28. Not surprisingly, the largest vote was for more taxes to be spent on the police. But only 21 per cent would pay higher taxes to supply the funds; most of the rest wanted the increase to be found by reductions elsewhere (Table 6.29).

VIII. TAX "EXPENDITURES"

Personal "tax expenditures" were severely condemned by the late Professor R.M. Titmuss and his two main collaborators, Professor Brian Abel-Smith and Peter Townsend, for much the same reasons as those outlined by Professor Maslove and by Professor J.R. Kesselman. They dilute the degree of progressiveness of the taxes, they favour the rich, or the canny who take advantage of them, and they make average tax rates higher than they could otherwise be (Professor Kesselman estimates by over 20 per cent in 1973).

The first criticism—dilution of progressivity—is self-evident but tautologous, and perhaps in a sense question-begging. If taxes on in-

TABLE 6.26

Public Preferences in Local Tax Expenditure

Percentage Wishing Less Spent on:	Total	Sex		Age		Occupational Group		Political Sympathy	
		Men	Women	16-34	35+	ABC1	C2DE	Con.	Lab.
	%	%	%	%	%	%	%	%	%
Libraries	18	20	17	16	20	14	22	16	23
School meals	12	13	12	10	14	19	8	17	8
Sports	4	4	4	2	5	4	4	5	3
Police	4	4	3	6	2	3	4	2	4
None	65	63	68	69	63	65	65	66	66

Source: Public opinion poll conducted by author.

TABLE 6.27

Public Preferences in Re-allocating or Reducing Rates/Taxes as a Result of Lower Expenditure

Preference	Total	Men	Women	Age		Occupational Group		Political Sympathy	
				16-34	35+	ABC1	C2DE	Con.	Lab.
	%	%	%	%	%	%	%	%	%
Reduction	34	33	36	30	37	29	38	35	31
Re-allocation	62	62	61	67	58	65	80	61	65
Other answers	2	3	2	1	1	4	1	2	3
Don't know	2	2	3	3	2	4	1	3	2

Source: Public opinion poll conducted by author.

TABLE 6.28

Public Preferences in Re-allocating Rates and Taxes on Local Government Services

Percentage Wishing More Spent on:	Total	Sex		Age		Occupational Group		Political Sympathy	
		Men	Women	16-34	35+	ABC1	C2DE	Con.	Lab.
	%	%	%	%	%	%	%	%	%
Libraries	6	8	3	6	5	9	4	5	5
School meals	14	14	13	16	13	9	17	11	17
Sports	33	34	31	39	28	32	33	29	36
Police	37	40	33	34	39	40	35	42	37
None	26	23	30	23	28	27	26	27	23

Source: Public opinion poll conducted by author.

TABLE 6.29

Public Preferences in Re-allocating or Increasing Rates/Taxes as a Result of Higher Expenditure

	Total	Sex		Age		Occupational Group		Political Sympathy	
		Men	Women	16-34	35+	ABC1	C2DE	Con.	Lab.
Re-allocation	%	%	%	%	%	%	%	%	%
(less elsewhere)	71	69	73	73	69	70	71	71	87
Higher rates/ taxes	21	22	19	18	22	20	21	21	26
Other answers	6	7	4	5	6	6	6	7	6
Don't know	4	4	5	5	4	5	4	4	3

Source: Public opinion poll conducted by author.

come are "progressive," it follows logically that rebates or exemptions are regressive. People who pay lower marginal tax rates receive smaller rebates; if they pay no taxes, they receive no rebates. Is that inequity? To other such complainants Churchill retorted: "What a pity. They will just have to go on not paying taxes." The "fault" lies with the politicians who created the progressivity, though there is an opportunity here to reduce differences in income.

This view also takes it as self-evident that progressivity is necessarily desirable at the current gradient. But progressivity is a weapon that the majority can use to excess in voting to increase the gradient imposed on the rich minority. Moreover, it does not discriminate between the *sources* of high incomes. It could impoverish the non-rich if it debilitates the high achievers. Even the relatively poor may suffer if equalization reduces national income, or its growth. Where there are no winners, all may be losers.

Hayek has argued for proportionality to remove the incentive of the majority to mis-use power. Hugh Dalton, argued for redistribution from rich to poor in order to equate the marginal utility of income. But this was undermined by Lionel Robbins' demonstration of the non-comparability of utility between persons.

The ability to take advantage of tax "expenditures" varies with individuals according to income and occupation, as Professor Maslove rightly demonstrates. His solution was to reduce tax allowances and exemptions by requiring publicity to increase their political unpopularity and cost. This might reduce their use as vote-winners, but does not remove their source. Whatever is done to vary the allowances, refunds and exemptions, some people will "inequitably" find ways of taking more advantage of them than others. And the rising cost of the fiscal bureaucracy in detecting and dealing with inequities would be hidden. The more certain solution is to reduce the taxation that makes allowances, refunds and exemptions politically profitable.

In the meantime, the regressiveness in tax rebates could be mitigated by reducing the progressivity of the tax structure as a whole. U.K. taxes are broadly proportional for a wide range of income, except at the extremes. Tax refunds could be made proportional or even progressive if they were broadened. This could take the form of vouchers (rather than rebates) for education fees, medical insurance, housing costs (for tenancy or purchase), pension premiums or indeed for many other purchases which were considered necessary for civilized living. The value of the voucher, now being studied in several countries, could be distributed either proportionately or regressively, by being taxed as income.

This at least would be a less objectionable way to encourage the production and consumption of merit goods. Most Western democracies may have to do this in order to offset the under-consumption that would otherwise follow from up to a century of "free" provision by government, and until taxes are reduced sufficiently for individuals to buy them on the open market.

IX. CONCLUSIONS

The experience of the U.K. tax system indicates that economists should broaden their analysis of taxation from technical/economic to include politico-economic aspects as well. This requires more systematic checking of laboratory hypotheses by field studies. On the assumption of a general acceptance of the proposition of taxpayer sovereignty, the conclusions for policy will not remain unaffected.

Such a view suggests a fundamental change in the approach to the evaluation and efficiency of taxes. Instead of asking what reconstruction or re-arrangement of taxes would best raise a given total revenue, we should concern ourselves with the purposes for which tax revenue is required. We could then consider the taxes best designed to finance these expenditures.

Mr. Pechman's[33] main proposal is to broaden the British tax base by removing the provisions that erode it. The revenue so saved, he recommends, should be used to reduce the tax rates, especially for employees taxed at "very high" marginal rates. Dr. King also emphasizes the broadening of the tax base as more important than "marginal" changes in tax rates and wishes to see a progressive personal expenditure tax.

I would welcome a broadening in the tax base so that all who benefit from public goods contribute to their costs. But for the rest, the tax base could be narrowed to yield the revenue required to redistribute income from the rich to the poor. And the transfers should take the form of reverse taxes and vouchers rather than benefits in kind. That is what the British people would prefer—if they but understood the higher costs of benefits in kind, of larger bureaucracies, of restricted choices, of the loss of the advantages of competition and in taxes, because of the relative inefficiency of government production.

The British are gradually coming to understand that most of their taxation—perhaps two-thirds—is unnecessary. The present government (or a third of the Cabinet) has, roughly speaking, accepted that insight. If the public prevails, economists will no longer be asked to advise on the most revenue-efficient tax structure. For that will yield a revenue far larger than required for public goods or legitimate redistribution.

In any event, economists will become increasingly impotent when taxpayers are no longer at the mercy of government and its bureaucracy. Even now, while representative assemblies respond to the loudest voices rather than to the best arguments, many people are using their "exits" by voting with their feet. The movement from the North

Eastern U.S.A. to the South or the West has come after years of emigration from highly taxed Britain. This will be paralleled by an exodus from the domains of British local authorities. For they are run as communes by local politicians who are building palaces for public officials, while rate-payers make do with nineteenth century factories and office blocks.

Economists will go unheeded if their analyses and advice lose sight of the developing market alternative to taxes, and of the trends which indicate that the movement in the next decades will be away from big government and high taxes.

NOTES

1. *Political Economy Past and Present*, New York: Macmillan (1976) p. 116.
2. "Taxation," *ibid.*, p. 206.
3. August, 1965.
4. May, 1967.
5. May 18 and 19, 1967.
6. "International comparisons of taxes and social security contributions 1970–1976," *Economic Trends*, London: Her Majesty's Stationery Office, December (1978)
7. In the name of the long-suffering British taypayer, the vested interest of the bureaucracy in high taxation as the source of their life-tenure pay and life-escalated pensions should be noted.
8. "Some International Perspectives," *The Tax Systems of Canada and the United States, (Ottawa 1978).*
9. *The Tax Systems of Canada and the United States, ibid.*
10. *Growth of Government in the West*, Washington, D.C.: American Enterprise Institute (1978).
11. "Informally" in the sense that they use the Index as a lever in annual pay bargaining.
12. Surprisingly, Professor Bird repeats from another source, Professor Alain Enthoven, a view common among more uncritical observers of state services that "one of the main *advantages* of public provision of health care...appears to be cost control." If the purpose is consumer satisfaction rather than cost minimization, this view is not convincing. Public provision typically offers lower quality (waiting, queuing, little or no choice, etc.). Some evidence for the U.K. is assembled by Professor Cotton Lindsay in *National Health Issues: The British Experience,* Roche Laboratories, U.S.A. (1980). Government uses its monopoly to drive costs down too far – beyond consumer preference.
13. *Tax Avoision*, Readings 22, London: IEA (1979).
14. "A Glimpse of the Hidden Economy in the National Accounts," *Economic Trends* January (1980).
15. The IEA survey suggests that the CSO is probably wrong.
16. Anthony Christopher, "The Law is the Law is the Law," *Tax Avoision,* Readings 22, London: IEA (1979).

17. Lord Houghton of Sowerby, "The Futility of Taxation by Menaces," *ibid.*
18. The question thus becomes one of weighing off the advantages of government enterprise in dealing with externalities as against the advantages in efficiency of the market sector.
19. David Friedman, *The Machinery of Freedom: Guide to a Radical Capitalism,* New York: Harper and Row (1973) especially Chapters 29, 34; Murray Rothbard, *For a New Liberty*, New York: Macmillan (1973).
20. Gabriel Roth, *Paying for Roads*, Middlesex, England: Penguin Books (1967); Walter Block, "Free Market Transportation: Denationalizing the Roads," *The Journal of Libertarian Studies,* III:2 (1979).
21. David Friedman's suggestion (*The Machinery of Freedom: Guide to a Radical Capitalism*) that government is twice as costly as the market may not be far out; a British firm is training office staff at a half to a third of government Colleges of Further Education.
22. Public Choice, Virginia Polytechnic Institute and State University (1972).
23. This made little difference, however, thus torpedoing the hypothesis that women were more market-conscious and would want individual choice in welfare more than men.
24. R. Harris & A. Seldon, IEA (1979); it relates full details of samples, sampling techniques, the range of accuracy and error of the results, and other methodological information.
25. See J.M. Buchanan, *Public Finance in Democratic Process.* University of North Carolina Press (1969).
26. *Education: A Framework for Choice*, London: IEA (1967).
27. *Economica* (1968).
28. Baron John Diamond, *Public Expenditure in Practice,* London: Allen and Unwin (1975).
29. *The Welfare State? Social Policy in the 1980s*, New Zealand Planning Council (1979).
30. Milton and Rose Friedman, *Free to Choose* New York: Harcourt, Brace Jovanovich (1980).
31. *The Economics of Politics*, Readings 18, London: IEA (1978).
32. A significant sidelight on the sociology of taxation is that the field study adviser removed this phrasing from the questionnaire as "a leading question many would think biased."
33. I hope my references are interpreted as recognition of Mr. Pechman's study of British taxation as the most recent and authoritative.

COMMENT

Sir Alan Walters

Arthur Seldon's central theme is that in Britain taxes are too high and should be diminished. My first reaction is to oppose the thesis: taxes in Britain are too low, not too high! They are too low to finance the truly massive volume of expenditure by the public sector.

Instead of tax finance, the treasury resorts to increasing the domestic money supply at a rate of 13–15 per cent—at least six times as fast as the trend growth rate of real output (less than 2 per cent), and to the pre-emption of a large fraction of investible funds through substantial sales of gilt-edged securities to the non-bank private sector. The rapid growth of the money supply sustains a chronic inflation; and the government absorption of a large fraction of investible funds starves the private sector and so stifles enterprise and growth.

Considering the size of public expenditure as given, I would argue that the amount of it that is tax-financed should be even higher. Inflation-finance, which has been pursued since the famous "go-for-growth" policy of the Heath Government in 1971, has produced the most capricious and damaging form of inflation tax. This erodes our wealth and institutions and leads to further dirigiste policies. Far better the explicit levy of the fisc than the implicit tax on our money.

Of course I am sure Arthur Seldon agrees with this! The state is providing many services—which are not public goods—which would be better financed by charges rather than taxes. The public would then be induced to demand only those services that they are willing to pay for. But it *is* important to make it perfectly clear that the real problem is the *level and growth of government spending*. The pattern in Britain has been that governments, identifying new "problems" to be solved, increase spending but, understandably, are reluctant to increase taxes. Indeed until recent years the macroeconometric models of the economy published by prestigious institutes such as the National Institute of Economics and Social Research, routinely advised increases in public spending as a solution for unemployment and low growth. The whole ethos of the 1964 Labour Plan and of the Heath fiasco of 1971–1973 was that increased public spending would launch Britain into a virtuous circle of inflation-free high growth. However, since the public spending was financed largely by increases in the money supply the net result was eventually slower growth and inflation.

INFLATIONARY POLICY

As the inflation got under way and, as capital fled the country, attempts were made to reduce the deficit. Much as governments may try, however, they usually fail to make any substantial dent in public spending. The bureaucrats are enormously powerful and very skilled in defending their interests—the first things to go are school children's meals and old-age welfare services, rather than the staff of the bloated bureaus. If a government insists on cuts, the bureaucracy will make sure they are visible and painful to the electorate—the better to demonstrate the evils of cutting "social spending." Thus "public expenditure is sacrosanct" and the only way to bring equilibrium back to the public accounts is therefore to increase taxes. So runs the conventional wisdom. This ratchet effect has ensured an unprecedented peacetime growth of the public sector.

As Arthur Seldon has shown, it is very likely that this growth of the public sector was not desired by the electorate. (Although I must confess that I have some doubts about the answers to the hypothetical questions used in opinion surveys: what one can say, however, is that Seldon's questions were less hypothetical than those which he criticizes!) Latter day Keynesians allied with a burgeoning bureaucracy have rationalized and promoted this public sprawl.

Whether the present burden of the public sector is too large, however, cannot be measured simply by the fraction of resources acquired for the state either by taxation or inflation. The burden is more appropriately measured by the *marginal* rather than the average rates of taxation. Nominally, Britain has steeply progressive rates of income from property. But from so-called "unearned income" on nominal assets one can easily see that income taxes approximate to a capital tax. With inflation at an average of 22 per cent since 1974, an average rate of return of 16 per cent on a bond would mean a negative interest rate of about 6 per cent before tax. But since the recipient will pay income tax at at least an average of 60 per cent marginal rate, this means that instead of enjoying an income of 16 per cent, he will suffer a net expropriation of almost 16 per cent of his assets each year.

Of course, the savers saw that in principle they could escape this expropriation by investing in houses (or antiques); but *everyone* saw this. The price of houses escalated at such a rapid rate that the cash payments required for down payments and to service mortgages became the effective limiting factor. (This "forced saving" may also explain why there was a phenomenally large *increase,* not decrease, in the saving ratio in the last half of the 1970s from about 8 per cent to 13 per cent.)

HIGH MARGINAL TAX RATES

Income from work was also taxed at the highest marginal rates. As Alan Prest[1] pointed out, these marginal rates often exceed 100 per cent for those on welfare at the threshold of labour. But of course the poor *can* work their way up to a marginal rate of 35 per cent. For those who paid 83 per cent at the top of the range, there was no escape except by stopping work or evasion.[2] But I suspect that much of the dissatisfaction with the tax system arises from these high marginal rates which start at 35 per cent (in 1979)—as distinct from 5 per cent in France and 7.8 per cent in Canada—and take 35 pence of every additional nominal pound from a very large number of relatively impoverished wage earners.

Furthermore, the income tax threshold has gone down as inexorably as the price level has gone up; by the late 1970s the income tax threshold for a married couple was about 30 per cent of the average wage of manual workers.[3] I entirely agree with Seldon's view that, notwithstanding the absence of "hard" econometric evidence to show that these marginal rates cause large distortions and waste, there is no doubt that they do! There is much other evidence to show that.[4]

All this is quite depressing—for Britain began this century with a tax system that was widely and justly admired. It did not attempt massively to redistribute income and wealth, but nor did it inhibit enterprise and effort. Since World War II, however, there has been a continuing thrust both to increase the spending of the state and to finance that spending by soaking the rich. Redistributive measures, applied sometimes vindictively and often without understanding the effects, are responsible for much of the mess of the British tax system, and particularly the income tax.

In many ways this is a pity. Henry Simons[5] argued that the single income tax system broadly based and at low rates was the best way of financing the state. But Britain is so far from this ideal and loaded with such a high level of public spending that it seems unreachable. Certainly it would be foolhardy to anticipate that much can now be done to improve radically the income tax system in the United Kingdom. Promises of reform are merely the litter of party platforms.

CUTTING OUT THE FAT

As a final comment, let me return to the categories of public expenditure with a view to discovering prime candidates for the axe. Seldon's classification of the non-public sector is a useful one, but it does not identify those items which have grown explosively and have the potential for vast future calls on the treasury. In the 1970s these have been subsidies either to publicly-owned or pseudo-private industry. The most obvious examples are British Steel (BSC) with a current annual deficit of at least £400 mn, British Rail (some £800 mn), and so on. Attempts to control these have been fitful and ineffective.

and promotes the collusion of the interest groups concerned. Remorseless wage claims and substantial featherbedding are characteristic of such subsidized activities. Restrictions on competitors is also an attractive way to both government and BSC and BR; they do not need to be financed. Although the costs are just as large, or even larger, they are not at all obvious. The subsidy buys inefficiency rather than lower prices. For these reasons such subsidies should be regarded as first to go.

There are many examples of governments which have successfully dealt with such problems. In Chile, for example, the State Railway had a deficit in 1971 of $124 million (1976 United States dollars) but by 1980 the deficit has almost disappeared. The labour force was whittled down from a maximum of 40,000 to 12,000. This testifies to what can be achieved when, as in Chile, the government loan guarantee was withdrawn. Hence I agree with Arthur Seldon that "privatization" should be the main way in which the tax burden can be reduced. But I would urge that such reforms will be effective *only* if a policy of competition and free entry be pursued as a parallel measure.

NOTES

1. Alan Prest, "Social Benefits and Tax Rates," IEA Research Monograph No. 22, 1970 and Ralph Howell, "Why Work?" London, Centre for Policy Studies, 1981.
2. In 1976 Britain had the highest marginal tax rate on earned income, except for Egypt and Algeria (Hansard, June 14, 1976, Written Answers *358).
3. Against the stern advice of the Treasury, in 1976 Britain took a timorous step towards indexing the tax brackets with the Rooker-Wise rule. This provided for an escalation of the tax threshold; but that is as far as the government would allow.
4. C.V. Brown and E. Levin, "The Effects of Income Taxation on Overtime: The Results of a National Survey," *Economics Journal,* Vol. 84 December (1974).
5. Henry Simons, *Economic Policy for a Free Society*, Chicago: University of Chicago Press (1948).

REPLY

Arthur Seldon

My paper argued that British taxes are unnecessarily high; that in order to finance the services that government must provide (public goods), only a third of current government expenditure is required; and that taxes are not the most efficient way to finance non-public goods. This is a judgement about the long-term structure and size of British government and holds true whatever the current state of Keynesian or Friedmanite macroeconomic management, monetary and fiscal, for the control of inflation and unemployment.

Professor Walters does not basically dissent from this view. His main response is that, *given the existing quantum of services,* taxes are too low for effective macroeconomic management. This shifts the ground of the argument to current policy, and raises major issues in the debate on "supply-side economics" and the synchronizing (and volume) of reductions in government expenditure and taxing. Here, I proposed a radical reconstruction of government financing from taxes to charging—where practicable for non-public goods. That puts my position somewhere between the supply-side economists who would risk reducing taxes before cutting expenditure in order to galvanize supply, and the macro-managers who would cut expenditure before taxes in order to discipline demand.

I could therefore not agree with Professor Walters that the (only) alternative to lower taxation is "inflation-finance." It is disappointing that market-minded economists, of whom Professor Walters is an outstanding British "model," neglect the power of the market instrument of pricing. Prices serve both as an alternative source of income and as a discipline on demand for government services now supplied "free," or subsidized in Britain. On both counts the net budget deficit that requires taxation or money-creation is reduced. The former by increasing revenue, the latter by reducing expenditure.

TAXING AND PRICING

Market-minded economists would accept Professor Walter's preference for the explicit levy of taxes over the implicit tax of inflation. But we should carry this logic further. A tax is not readily identified by the taxpayer, since it is a macro-sum paid for a bewilderingly wide assortment of services—in kind and cash—that are not priced separately. Few, if any, taxpayers in Britain know the tax-price of a week in a state hospital, a year in a state school, removing 1,000 tons of sewage or a wasp's nest. The reason why taxpayers do not resent taxes more angrily is that they cannot relate them to individual services. Only micro-pricing would enable them to do that. It is the explicit levy *par excellence.*

In the short run charging a price may be too slow to replace the revenue lost by tax cuts (if they do not quickly galvanize production and the tax base). But the plight of the British economy is the outcome of concentration on the short run to the complete neglect of the long-term reform of the structure of government, the unremitting expansion which has intensified the difficulties of coping with the short run.

Skillful — or merely lucky — tacking to changing winds and current has kept the ship afloat. But it has relentlessly approached the port which the passengers fear: progressive state control of their daily lives. Successive expansion by conservative and labour governments of the nationalized industries, public corporations, welfare services and local authorities' activities has removed more and more economic life from the market where costs are disciplined, however imperfectly, by demand in competition. This has made government helpless in resisting the inflation of expenditure financed by taxation and/or money creation.

The short-term mastery of inflation is frustrated by the long-run neglect of government obesity. British government, even under Mrs. Thatcher, is an irresponsible, profligate, spendthrift employer that finances unearned increases in wages, salaries, pensions, fringe benefits, *et al.*, by money it does not possess and cannot raise by the honest method of taxation. So it borrows or counterfeits money, and creates the very inflation it cannot master. Inflation is not fomented by private entrepreneurs in a competitive market. They cannot tax or print money in order to pay higher wages or other costs. They cannot pass these on to captive consumers. Inflation is created, tolerated and fuelled at No. 10 Downing Street, the residence of the Prime Minister. The buck must stop on her desk and nowhere else.

So far, she has failed to cut down the comically-described "public" (or rather "anti-public" sector). Instead, these items have been lavished with bounties that require further taxation or borrowing — bringing inflation in their wake. And for what? In order to mine coal that builds coal mountains, produce steel that industry does not want to pay for, run railways without (enough) passengers, make motor cars that consumers refuse to buy, build hospitals with maintenance staffs but no patients because there is no money for doctors or nurses, run swollen local authority services stuffed with self-perpetuating bureaucrats and "jobs-for-the-boys."

All these and more are not excuses for failing to reduce taxation, or even to raise it, as the March 1979 conservative budget did. Rather, they are further failures of government in tolerating a comic-opera economy in which the leader of the miners' trade union can say it must sell every ounce of coal they dig out, without being locked up as a lunatic.

LITTLE SUPPORT FOR GOVERNMENTAL EXPENDITURES

Professor Walters emphasizes the amount and growth of government spending. However, we should rather focus on the way it is *financed*. I would object less to a larger volume of government spending financed by pricing, than to a smaller volume financed by taxing, borrowing or printing money. The objection to the larger volume is *political*, not economic; *i.e.*, government would be less likely to discipline its expenditure by demand based on pricing once it is established.

But in Britain the growth was not a response to public demand for more government services and a readiness to pay for them by taxes. I am myself in no doubt, based on IEA surveys over 15 years, that referenda which clearly put the choice between more government spending and lower taxes would reveal a profound public desire for the latter. This would bring about numerous accompanying benefits—efficiency, equity, choice, restoration of the bonds of family, reduced tax avoidance and evasion—of the marketplace. (Hypothetical questions, unfortunately, are the best that can be devised, given the present state of the art in Britain. But their findings can be confirmed or confounded by sceptics—so long as their investigations incorporate *price*, the missing link in other British surveys. These have, for example, asked preferences between the National Health Service and Medicine in Yugoslavia or other outlandish places!)

The strategy of higher taxes to obviate even more government borrowing or printing may in any event founder on the rock of public resistance. Tax "avoision" takes progressively more ingenious forms, and the tax-evader is always a lap or two ahead of the tax-gatherer. Professor Edgar Feige's estimate of 27 per cent of national income for the "unobserved economy" in the U.S.A. would probably be exceeded for the U.K. In the Report for the year ended March 31, 1980, the British Board of Inland Revenue belatedly recognizes the undeniable in a chapter headed, "The Black Economy." It proudly points to the first Report in 1806 which said: "the... exemption... on... income under £60 a year... has been introductive of the greatest frauds upon the Public. (Note how bureaucrats have long hoped to present themselves as defenders of the people, not—perish the thought—as attacking an honest citizenry)... persons living... in apparent affluence (note the contemporary Galbraithian influence) have returned their income under £60, although their annual expenditure has been treble that sum...."

THE HIDDEN ECONOMY STRIKES AGAIN

But it is doubtful if any pig farmer in 1806 charged gold-plated bathroom taps as pig pens. At least one did in 1979–1980, which leads the Inland Revenue Board to declare solemnly that the tax inspector may have to make enquiries about "the taxpayer's private as well as business affairs." Pitt's original income tax, only 8 years old in 1806, was resented as "inquisitorial." Will the inspector stop in the bathroom when it is *en suite* with a bedroom? The gift of a prize bull to a company chairman was recorded as a business expense, not as a taxable benefit.

More solemnly, proceeds the Report, there may be some "receiving unemployment or sickness benefit while engaged in an undisclosed business or employment." You can say that again, Mr. Tax-Gatherer. Some of Britain's 2.5 million *unemployed* have never worked harder in their lives. The most common categories are in plumbing, decorating, car repairing, barmen or petrol pump attendants. Losses of revenue affect not only income tax, but also National Insurance contributions (and the surcharge), corporation tax, VAT. A finger is also wagged at tax *avoiders* who, although within the law, "exploit... artificial arrangements" to deprive the Inland Revenue of mònies "the Finance Acts were intended to secure." So taxpayers are to read the minds of the law makers.

The Board has not raised its estimate in 1977 that undeclared incomes were around 7½ per cent of GDP. It reports a U.S.A. Internal Revenue Service tax audit for a sample of 50,000 taxpayers which also indicates around 6 per cent to 8 per cent of tax evasion. It refers to Feige's estimate of 27 per cent (without naming him) but adds "there is no consensus among economists." The evidence shows, however, that both the extent and the rate of growth are severely under-stated.

The Board's main intellectual failing is that it does not understand supply and demand. The higher taxation is raised, the more benefits there will be from evading taxation, the more taxation will be evaded. This is the most profound argument against taxation as a weapon against inflation.

Professor Gunnar Myrdal has described his Swedish countrymen as "a nation of cheats." But he has not felt in any way responsible for driving them to this sorry state by advocating the social democratic welfare state that required high taxation to finance it. As a long-standing critic of the British welfare state, I have a clear conscience, but no gratification, in reporting that in Britain all, or most, taxpayers are cheats, but some are cheating more than others. And I don't think they will willingly pay higher taxes, even to ward off inflation, because no taxpayer can know that others are reducing their evasion equally. Now, a law that enforced equality in tax evasion is the end logic of taxation raised to finance unnecessary government expenditure.

DISCUSSION

Edited by: Walter Block

The relation of an onerous tax system and the rise of the hidden economy was once again a topic of interest.

Smith began with a caution: cash payments are not a reliable, and certainly not a necessary, indication of tax avoidance for many items are traditionally paid in this manner. "I have experience in property management in apartments, and no matter how logical it would be for tenants to pay rents by cheque, you find that about 20 per cent persist in paying by cash. There's no particular reason. I cannot figure out why. They just prefer to do it that way.

"This is a large payment, it's regular, and tenants know it must be paid in advance. It could be paid on different days so they don't have to worry about not having the bank balances in the bank on a given day when payment might be due. It's not small, it's not uncertain. There are a whole variety of reasons why you would think that no one would pay in cash. The incentive, especially on the landlord's side is always to get the payment by cheque. For then there are no possible fallouts of theft, or various other risks.

"Notwithstanding that, returns are still largely paid in cash. That being the case, it should not be so surprising then, that a large number of items show up as payments in cash. The mere fact that there are cash payments cannot be interpreted as an attempt to avoid tax or to avoid reporting. There may be some of that, to be sure. But I don't think that cash payments at all indicate the magnitude of tax avoidance, or even indicate the source of the pressures for cash payments."

And Lindbeck chimed in with support for Smith's view, pointing out that one can scarcely deduce from the fact that babysitters are not paid by cheque or credit card, that there is a vast tax avoidance plot afoot.

In Seldon's view, however, cash payments have become ever so much more prevalent, spreading to areas where they were never traditional. "Some years ago, I sold a car, a second hand car, for around a thousand pounds. Normally I would have expected a cheque because my purchaser, the man who was going to buy the car, was my local garage owner. All his transactions would normally have been conducted by cheque. But instead he handed me a thousand pounds of greasy bank notes, pounds, single pounds. Now that is one small example which is becoming exceedingly common. You can't imagine just how widespread is this practice."

This position was taken up by Feige, who supported Seldon's finding of ever increasing tax evasion levels. But there was one puzzle. The

British Central Statistical Office (CSO) had reported a steadily increasing index of tax evasion from 0.2 per cent of GDP in 1960 to 4 per cent in 1974, and then, inexplicably a *fall* to 3.3 per cent in 1978. Seldon had dismissed this finding as implausible, and the CSO as unreliable. But there was a story behind this decline. Said Feige: "I was in London a month before that report was issued at the central bank, and after a lot of finagling, received a preliminary copy. It has a chart in it which I looked at very carefully, and that chart had a 1978 figure of 5.5 per cent. A month later, when the report came out this figure was published as you correctly reported it, 3.3 per cent. That disturbed me greatly. I called the CSO and I said, 'What happened? That's not the chart you had in your original paper.' They gave me the most ridiculous story that they had somehow uncovered a 10 billion error somewhere that totally revised the figure. I ask you—two weeks before publication?

"So, I want to suggest that your notion that that dip was implausible was in fact an accurate one. But not because the method was wrong. I really think there was incredible political fudging on that report. If you check it out with CSO, I'd be interested to find out what excuse you get for that change between the initial draft and the second one."

Next, the discussion turned to Seldon's advocacy of pricing government services, rather than financing them through the tax system (and then giving them away for "free"). Fisher supported this initiative, urging a tack from taxing to pricing on the grounds of "greater efficiency" and reducing the role of government to "manageable proportions."

Walters, however, criticized the Seldon proposals for not going far enough. Pricing government services may be an improvement, "But I would go much further. I say it is best to *privatize*, and to get the government out of it completely. What I don't go along with is a fee paying system and a continuance of government monopoly. The critical thing seems to me to be to open enterprise opportunities up to the private sector."

Spindler, too, took this "hard nosed" approach. "I would like to raise a question of whether you've actually gone far enough when you allow that public goods are properly provided for by government. I think the economic case for market failure of provision of goods applies symmetrically to government failure in the provision of public goods. This would be a failure of anyone short of God, or a similar omniscient and omnipotent entity to provide public goods optimally. But to the extent that there is any case at all for government provision of services, these ought to be provided for under the principles of benefit taxation," said Spindler. "Instead there was an implicit acceptance of an equalitarian ability-to-pay approach to the revenue side of the budget while the benefit approach was applied to the expenditure side. This seems inconsistent to me.

"I think that the budget constraint requires a similar rationale for both sides of the budget. That is, if we are going to use the benefit principle to justify providing public goods through the public sector, then these goods should be financed by taxes that conform to the benefit principle rather than the ability-to-pay principle."

Block agreed that it would be ideal if all goods and services were provided by the marketplace, but saw an additional implication for tax policy, should government attempt to provide services on a pricing basis: not benefit taxation, but regressive taxation. "I would point to the price system as analogous to a regressive, not a proportional or progressive taxation system.

"Unfortunately the very word 'regressive' has negative connotations. It seems to imply 'bad' or 'backward looking' or what have you. But if we had even a proportional, let alone a progressive price system, this would mean absolute income equality! If the rich man had to pay proportionally more than the poor man for a watch, or for shoes, or for socks, or food, he would end up with an identical income, in real terms, as the poor man. Even if he were twice as rich, he would end up no better off in terms of consumer welfare.

"Certainly the price system which applies to all private goods, is a very regressive system – in comparison to taxes. I think it's time we try to inject some positive regard for the regressive system in taxes. That is, if we must have taxes at all, and cannot substitute prices for them."

As against this, Lindbeck defended redistributionist policies, which could not be accomplished with regressive taxation. "People are certainly not born with equal opportunities in society. Rather, they are born with very different opportunities. I think it is not at all ridiculous to try to modify the outcome of economic competition when you start with a rather unequal distribution of entitlements at birth." Giersch felt, however, that "equity" and "equality" did not necessarily mean the same thing.

Seldon welcomed the call to go beyond pricing government services towards complete privatization. He insisted, however, that although privatization may be the ultimate goal, pricing was a necessary "stage one." Stage one, moreover, will tend to bring about the more radical proposals, which can be considered as "stage two or stage three."

CHAPTER 7

THE SWEDISH TAX SYSTEM—WHAT CAN WE LEARN FROM IT?

Charles Stuart

Among western countries, Sweden is generally regarded as having come the furthest toward developing a welfare state. The efficiency of the Swedish system in protecting citizens against the randomness of nature and in promoting economic equality has provided progressives in many other countries with a model to be emulated and has been a source of pride to the Swedes themselves. At the same time, the system is of necessity fed with tax revenues collected from the populace. Thus in leading the way with the welfare state, Sweden has also led the way with taxes. Since many other countries are moving down paths similar to the one Sweden has followed, a study of the Swedish experience should be of particular importance to researchers elsewhere.

While it is always possible to find somebody who will complain about any tax, it is probably fair to say that the general feeling among Swedes, until recently, has been that the tax system needed periodic fine-tuning—but was basically sound. Today, some years into the experiment, Swedes are starting to notice a number of longer-term disincentive effects of high taxes and are slowly beginning to question the soundness of the system itself. It is certainly the case that the Swedish economy has had its share of difficulties in the 1970s, and that little improvement is expected in the early 1980s. However, there is as yet little consensus as to what extent (or in some quarters whether) these difficulties are tax-related.

In this paper, I will examine the make-up and effects of the Swedish tax system. A coarse description of my picture of the subject is: (a) Swedish tax rates are very high; (b) increased taxation has come about largely via increases in "hidden" taxes; (c) the high, observed rates of taxation have significant long-term *socio-economic* effects. Note that for the short run, there is little evidence that increased taxation has significant distortionary effects. In the short run, therefore, I would term both the increases in taxation as well as the distortionary costs of taxation as hidden. A final component of the picture: (d) there is little reason to believe that taxes will be reduced in the near future.

I. A DESCRIPTION OF THE SWEDISH TAX SYSTEM

AN OVERVIEW OF THE TAX RULES

Personal income in Sweden is subject both to a progressive national income tax, and to a proportional local income tax. The national tax reaches a maximal marginal rate of 58 per cent for income exceeding 162,000 kronor; the local rate varies somewhat, but averages 29 per cent.[1] The national tax schedule – but not the standard deduction – is indexed to follow the CPI. Aside from the standard deduction of 4,500 kronor, deductions to income for tax purposes are allowed for costs of earning income (including travel to work) and for all interest payments. Joint returns have not been allowed during the 1970s; all income earners must file separately.

Payroll taxes are imposed on employers. These are extracted at a constant rate of 35.2 per cent on each krona of income paid to employees, as long as total income is less than 111,750 kronor (as of March 1980 – this figure was indexed to the CPI). Above 111,750 kronor, the payroll tax rate is 23.2 per cent. It should be noted that the payroll tax is used to finance, among other things, sick pay and pension payments, and that these benefits increase somewhat as a function of income and hence of payroll taxes paid. Regarding the whole payroll tax as a tax on labour supply may thus be unwarranted.[2]

There is a general value-added tax of 21.63 per cent on most commodities. The VAT is somewhat lower for building structures. Indirect taxes on liquor and tobacco, and energy (mainly gasoline and heating oils) are also substantial. For recent years, non-VAT indirect taxes have been 40–50 per cent of total indirect taxes.

The taxation of capital is more complicated.[3] There are wealth, gift, and inheritance taxes, but these result in almost negligible tax revenues. More important is the direct taxation and capital gains treatment of stocks, bonds, bankholdings, own companies, houses, consumer durables, and pension funds.

Dividends from stocks, bonds, and bank accounts are treated as personal income, although there is an 800 krona deduction (1,600 for couples) for such capital income. This treatment taxes both the real and inflation-compensation returns from these forms of capital. Income extracted from small (non-stock) companies is treated as wage income. Imputed income from housing is calculated as 3 per cent of the assessed value, or roughly 1.8 per cent of the market value, of the structure. (Actually, imputed income is progressive, varying between 3 and 10 per cent. However, the minimum rate is applied to most houses.) This imputed income is then included in taxable personal income. There is no tax on consumer durables. All (nominal) interest payments are deductible from personal income as these are regarded as costs of obtaining income. For instance, interest payments on housing loans are treated as a cost of generating income from housing.

The treatment of pension plans is slightly more complicated. Whereas other forms of capital must be purchased by individuals net of tax income, pension contributions are deducted from gross income in deriving taxable income. However, payments from pension plans, which include principal plus interest, are taxed as personal income. If we view the tax rate on capital investments as the rate on an after-(income) tax krona placed in a given investment, this rate will generally be close to zero for pension contributions, since the income tax paid on returns from a plan is balanced by a deduction for contributions. (These two effects will exactly balance if an individual's internal rate of discount equals the real return on contributions, and if the marginal tax rate on personal income is the same during the years of contribution and of withdrawal.)

Forty per cent of nominal long run (exceeding two years) capital gains from the sale of stocks are treated as taxable income. Capital gains from the sale of houses are taxable as income; however, such gains are calculated on a real basis – the purchase price of the house is indexed to the present by application of the CPI. Capital gains on own-occupied housing is deferred if a new home is purchased. Other forms of capital, including bonds, art, and consumer durables, are not subject to capital gains taxes if owned for more than five years.

The corporate tax rate on profits in Sweden is 55 per cent. However, special regulations often permit profits to be retained in firms, where depreciation rules are quite generous. The result is that the corporate income tax can be deferred, in effect providing the firm with an advantageous, zero-interest loan until profits are paid out. In addition, the "Annell Law" – which took effect in 1963 and was designed to stimulate corporate equity finance – permits dividend payments of up to 5 per cent of a stock's issue value to be exempted from the 55 per cent corporate tax during the first 15 years following the issue of the stock.

MARGINAL RATES OF TAXATION

In Table 7.1, I present estimates of effective marginal tax rates for the "average" Swede for a number of economic activities. A more detailed description of how these rates are derived is presented in Appendix I. The personal income tax rate is useful as a benchmark – not only as the other rates are calculated using the 60 per cent figure but also as this figure bears on the after-tax value of various deductions. The 60 per

TABLE 7.1

Effective Marginal Tax Rates
on Various Economic Activities

	Activity	Rate
1.	Personal Income Tax (national and local)	60%
2.	Supply of labour	81%
3.	Real return on owner-occupied housing	36%
4.	Real return on consumer durables	0
5.	Real return on new stock, dividend paid today	264%
6.	Real return on new stock, profits retained 10 years and extracted as capital gain	57%
7.	Real return on new stock, 5% dividend paid today, rest deferred 10 years and extracted as capital gains	213%
8.	Real return on bonds	233%
9.	Real return on savings in banks	233%
10.	Real return on investment in non-stock company	195%

Note: For activities 3-10, it is assumed that the real return is 3% and that inflation is 8%. Throughout, it is assumed that the marginal tax rate on personal income was 60%. For details, see appendix I.

cent figure should however be regarded as several per cent below the true effective rate on personal income, since increased income often leads to reduced transfers from the government sector.

The other figures indicate the magnitudes of taxation on labour and capital. Several points deserve mention as regards the taxation of capital. First, the rates given are rates on the real return. These are in several cases greater than 100 per cent due to the fact that not only the real portion, but also the inflation component of returns to capital, are subject to taxation. Thus, the effective rate of taxation increases with the rate of inflation but decreases with the real rate of return.

The method of calculating these rates was conservative—the rates given are lower bounds for the true rates (see Appendix I). This is especially the case with the 57 per cent rate derived for new stock issues for profits which are retained 10 years and then extracted as a capital gain. There is one problem with such a deferred dividend scheme. The mathematics of the Swedish tax system dictate that it is always better to defer dividends since this reduces the effective tax rate. At the same time, an infinite deferral of dividends makes investment unattractive. For this reason, the 213 per cent rate on new stock with some deferral is probably the most realistic effective rate on new stock issues (given the assumed real return and inflation rate).

The figures in Table 7.1 do not reflect the fact that many investments are financed with loans, which improve their after-tax profitabilities. Loans for housing are relatively easy to obtain, for instance, and funds obtained for such purposes are often diverted to investment in consumer durables. An investment which is 75 per cent loan-financed at an 11 per cent rate of interest yields a deduction with an after-tax value of (.75) (11) (.6) = 5.0 per cent. This is equivalent to a −167 per cent tax rate on a 3 per cent real return. The net tax rates on the real returns for owner-occupied housing and consumer durables, when 75 per cent loan-financed, are thus −131 per cent and −167 per cent respectively.

These estimates point to effective differentials between rates of taxation on housing and consumer durables ("personal durables") on the one hand, and investments in "corporate durables" (to use John Whalley's dichotomization) on the other, of more than 300 per cent. The extreme nature of these differentials, and of the economy's adjustment to them, is easily seen. For instance, an abolition of the taxation of capital income as personal income would lead to an *increase* in the government's total tax take. Why? Because interest and other deductions due to the taxation of capital income are so large. In 1978, these deductions amounted to roughly 12 billion kronor, while income from capital was only 5.5 billion kronor.[4]

DISTRIBUTION

The high marginal tax rates displayed in Table 7.1 indicate a highly progressive tax system. The redistributional effects of the system have been studied by Franzén, Lövgren, and Rosenberg (1976) along lines developed by Gillespie (1965).[5] The conclusion is that the combined effect of taxes and government expenditures redistributes strongly from high to low incomes. A summary of their results is presented in Table 7.2. This conclusion is buttressed by recent work of Lindbeck (1980), who shows that the distribution of *per capita* disposable income is very even indeed.

It is hardly surprising that the calculated redistributive effects of government should be this large. The distributional aspects of different governmental actions are usually given a strong weight in public policy discussions.

TAXES IN THE POST-WAR PERIOD

Table 7.3 contains a summary of the behaviour of various tax aggregates in the post-war period. Analysis of the raw data in the table indicates that the total tax take more than doubled as a percentage of GNP over the period considered, increasing from 20.9 per cent in 1950 to

TABLE 7.2

Redistributive Effects of Government, 1970
Final Consumption as a Per Cent of Before-Tax Income

	Income, 1000 Kronor					
Civil Status	0-10	10-25	25-40	40-60	60-100	100-
Single, no children:						
case A	270	107	78	64	57	45
case B	220	101	81	71	66	57
Single, with children:						
case A	801	188	136	105	82	64
case B	731	182	139	112	92	76
Married:						
case A	497	173	109	89	77	62
case B	455	167	113	96	87	73

Note: Final consumption is disposable income plus the value of public consumption and investment expenditures. Under case A, these expenditures are allocated on an equal basis to all households; under case B, the allocation to households is as a proportion of household income. Before tax income is net of deductions.

Source: Franzén, Löfgren, and Rosenberg (1975).

53.0 per cent in 1977. This amounts to an increase of 1.19 percentage points per year. Breaking down the total tax increase into its major components, we see that the personal income tax revenues have increased an average of 0.45 percentage points yearly, while revenues from payroll and value-added taxes have increased by 0.58 and 0.26 percentage points respectively per year. (The other components have all decreased slightly as a proportion of GNP.) Since the personal income tax is progressive, while payroll and value-added taxes are proportional, it appears there has been a shift from relatively more to less progressive forms of taxation. This trend has been most pronounced in recent years. One reason, revealed by Table 7.3, is that while increases in personal income tax revenues as a per cent of GNP have been fairly even over the period in question, the proportional payroll and value-added taxes have increased most sharply during the 1970s. In addition, the personal income tax itself contains a progressive national component and a proportional local levy. From 1950 to 1965, the local portion of personal income tax revenues was roughly 50 per cent. Since then, this portion has increased, with local taxes accounting for 63 per cent of personal income tax revenues as of 1977.

TABLE 7.3

Swedish Taxes in Relation to GNP, 1950-1977 (Million Kronor)

Type	1950	1955	1960	1965	1970	1975	1977 (est)
I. INCOME TAXES	4,289	8,672	13,570	26,926	49,501	101,912	139,817
Personal Income Tax	3,170	6,420	9,177	18,064	31,842	60,959	77,490
Corporate Income Tax (Swedish Corporations)	925	1,549	1,513	2,105	2,600	4,763	5,290
Payroll Tax	140	558	2,655	6,414	14,605	35,216	56,155
Other	54	145	225	343	454	974	882
II. OTHER DIRECT TAXES[a]	277	370	544	836	1,123	1,681	2,123
III. INDIRECT TAXES	2,147	3,626	6,594	11,891	17,831	30,985	43,539
VAT[b]	—	—	1,074	4,147	7,109	15,806	24,500
Other	2,147	3,626	5,520	7,744	10,722	15,179	19,039
IV. TOTAL TAXES	6,713	12,668	20,708	39,653	68,455	134,578	185,479
V. GNP	32,120	50,876	72,153	113,294	170,711	286,947	349,960
VI. CPI (1950 = 100)	100	132	157	188	234	344	422

Notes: [a] Main components are wealth, gift, lottery, and stamp taxes.
[b] Before 1969, figures refer to general sales tax.

Source: SOU 1977:91.

One possible explanation for the shift to less progressive forms of taxation is that without it, marginal tax rates on labour supply for high income households would approach or exceed 100 per cent. (Note that marginal rates on labour supply seem to be roughly constant across income-earners at an 80 per cent level.) As we will see below, such a situation is likely to cause severe disincentive effects among such households.

"HIDDEN" TAX INCREASES

It is often said that indirect taxes are hidden and that direct taxes are not hidden, in the sense that taxpayers are likely to be less conscious of the former than of the latter. A notion such as taxpayer awareness of taxes, or of tax increases, is potentially useful. But the simple dichotomization into direct versus indirect taxes hides part of the usefulness of the hidden-tax concept. In particular, I would broaden the concept of hidden taxation to include the following:

(a) Increases in direct taxation caused by the combined effects of progressive tax schedules and inflation. Such tax increases are hidden in two senses. First, no politician need vote for higher taxes. Second (in the short run at least) taxpayers may have trouble distinguishing real from nominal magnitudes, and may thus fail to realize that inflation has increased their real tax rates.

(b) Payroll taxes, especially when these are not reported to employees as taxes on gross-income. This is the case in Sweden, where payroll taxes are assessed on employers as a per cent of the wage received by employees. Employee's pay-checks do not report the true total gross wage; the reported gross wage is the true gross wage net of payroll taxes. In addition, the Swedish term for payroll taxes translates most exactly as "employer fees," a term which also tends to hide from employees the fact that their labour is subject to a tax.

(c) Taxation of cash holdings due to inflation. Once again, the government's budget benefits from the use of the printing press, but no politician need vote for higher taxes.

(d) Deficit finance. An excess of current expenditures over current revenues creates a latent tax debt. The correct measure of the yearly amount of deficit finance is the increase in the national debt, less any rise in the amount of capital owned by the government. Deficit finance has become increasingly important in Sweden in the last 5 years. The budget deficit has grown from roughly 10 billion kronor during the mid-1970s to 55 billion kronor for 1980/81. Much of the increase is due to a deficit on current, non-capital expenses.

(e) Increases in the taxation of capital due to inflation, and the nominal-return basis for much capital taxation.
(f) Extra-normal profits of government monopolies. Tobacco, alcohol, and airplane tickets are sold by government monopolies in Sweden at prices which are clearly in excess of the prices charged for similar goods and services under more competitive circumstances elsewhere in the world.

In Table 7.4, I have calculated the magnitudes of several (but not all) items on this list of hidden taxes. The size of various yearly hidden tax increases since 1950 is compared to the size of total tax increases. I would draw the following conclusions:

- Increases in hidden taxes constitute the major portion of total tax increases, although this proportion may be falling slightly.
- The use of deficit financing has, up to 1977, been slight. Indeed, for most of the period 1950–1970, government capital accumulation exceeded increases in the public debt, so a net budget surplus was earned. (However, there is reason to believe that this situation has been dramatically reversed since 1977.)
- The inflationary tax on cash balances has produced significant additional revenues in the last decade, although these have not been as great as tax increases due to non-indexation of the personal income tax schedules. The combined effects of inflation indicate that inflation has been a powerful tool of taxation. (Note that the two inflation taxes considered in the table do not provide a complete accounting of how inflation increases government tax revenues since effects on capital taxation, as well as on the real returns to existing government bonds, are not included.)
- Hidden tax increases have increased secularly as a proportion of total tax increases. This has occurred to the point that non-hidden taxes actually declined while total taxes rose for the last period considered. Since total tax increases per year have risen in real terms over the entire period, one is left with a picture of pressure on the politicians from both sides. On the one hand, taxes are apparently quite unpopular, but on the other, spending is equally popular. I suspect, however, that such a high ratio of hidden to total tax increases is indicative of a situation which is not an equilibrium; hidden taxes become unhidden with time, and if this causes a reduction in total taxes, then spending must also fall. However, there is little evidence of such an adjustment at this date—one need only witness the current budget deficits (and roughly constant tax rates) to see this.

TABLE 7.4

Hidden Tax Increases, 1950-1977 (Millions of 1950 Kronor)

Types of tax increase	1950-1955	1955-1960	1960-1965	1965-1970	1970-1977
A. Total yearly increase in taxes according to budget	577	719	1,580	1,632	2,100
B. Yearly deficit financing of central government	- 367	95	- 1,076	- 236	124
C. Inflationary tax on cash balances per year	223	142	160	214	580
D. Yearly increase in personal income tax revenues due to combined effects of inflation and progressivity	133	111	167	305	808
E. Yearly increase in payroll tax revenues	57	254	344	566	1,009
F. Yearly increase in indirect tax revenues	120	291	425	259	385
G. Total yearly increase in taxation (A + B + C)	433	956	664	1,610	2,804
H. Total yearly increase in hidden taxation (B + C + D + E + F)	166	893	20	1,108	2,905
I. Hidden tax increases as per cent of total tax increases (100xH/G)	38.3%	93.4%	3.0%	68.8%	103.6%

Note: Much of the data is from Table 7.3. Deficit financing is the change in the (real) national debt (source: Riksgaldskontoret, 1978) less real central-government capital investments (source: national accounts, various years). The tax on cash balances is the yearly change in the CPI times the average real money supply (currently) over the period (source: Sveriges Riksbank, 1978). Taxes due to non-indexation are the yearly rate of inflation, times the elasticity of taxation minus one (i.e., times 0.6 — see Jakobsson and Normann, 1974, p. 160) times the average real level of personal income taxes over the period.

II. IMPACT OF THE TAX SYSTEM ON LABOUR SUPPLY

With current levels of marginal taxes on labour supply at the 80 per cent level, it would be surprising if there were no labour supply effects. However, there has been little consensus among economists as to the disincentive effects of such high taxes on labour. Two arguments have been common. First, it has been pointed out that labour supply elasticities are typically quite small and that income effects may dominate.[6] Under such circumstances, taxation which reduces the net of tax wage should have only small disincentive effects. The second argument, which is also an appeal to empirical observation, is that despite the high rate of taxation on labour supply, people still generally work a 40-hour week, and that aggregate hours worked have fallen off only slightly in recent years.

My own work on labour supply using a general equilibrium framework suggests that these two arguments are seriously flawed, and that the distortionary effects of Sweden's 80 per cent tax on labour supply may be surprisingly strong. Since these two arguments are likely to be invoked for analysis of taxes in other countries, I will discuss them both.

There is a problem with the argument that the income effects of a tax increase may outweigh the substitution effects. It fails to take account of the fact that increases in taxes cause equilibrium increases in government spending.[7] To the extent that this government spending provides taxpayers with goods and services which 1) would otherwise have been purchased with after-tax income, or 2) are close substitutes for goods and services purchased with after-tax income, an additional income effect will exist. Here, taxpayers will gain real income from government expenditures, and will thus reduce the quantity of labour supplied. These conditions are met, for example, if the extra government spending takes the form of cash transfers to individuals, or of subsidies in kind for goods such as medical care, child-care, etc., which would otherwise have been obtained with after-tax income.

THE GEOMETRY

The forces at work are illustrated in Figure 7.1 where the effects of a small tax increase on a single taxpayer are considered. It is assumed that the tax increase depresses the net wage in equilibrium, thus rotating the budget line inward. This change in the net wage suffices to move the taxpayer from an initial equilibrium at A to point B, where more labour is supplied (*i.e.*, the taxpayer's labour supply curve is backward bending here).

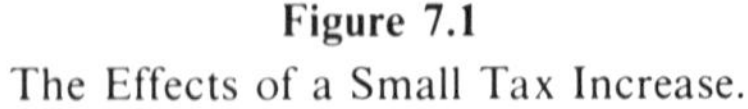

Figure 7.1
The Effects of a Small Tax Increase.

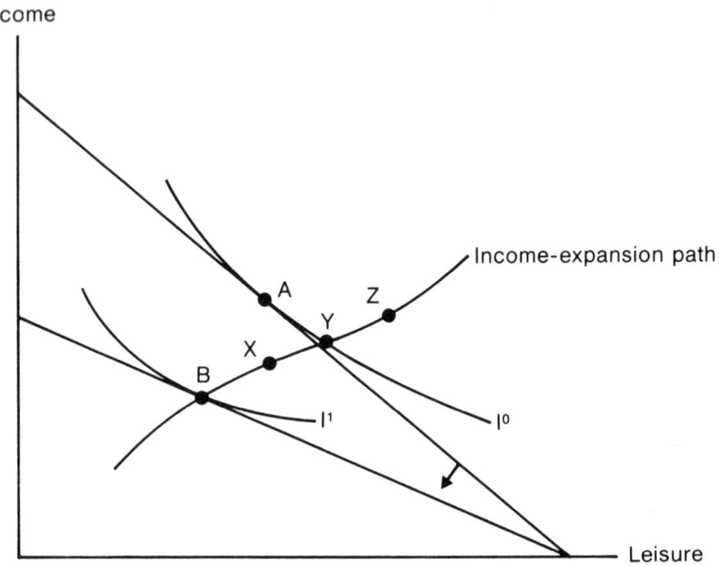

Source: Hansson and Stuart (1980). (For a more precise and accessible treatment, see Hansson, Ingemar, and Charles Stuart. "Taxation, Government Spending, and Labour Supply: A Diagrammatic Exposition," *Economic Inquiry,* 21:584-587 (1983).)

However, point B is not an economy-wide equilibrium since government tax revenues must be greater at B than at A. Government spending must thus increase somewhat. Assume for simplicity that this additional government spending provides a perfect substitute for after-tax income. Its effect is then to move the taxpayer to the northeast along his income-expansion path, until a new equilibrium is finally attained at a point such as X, Y, or Z.

We thus see that there are two income effects relevant to a tax increase; first, the effect caused by increased taxes, and second, the effect caused by the general equilibrium requirement that the government balance its budget. The net effect of these two effects depends on the level of transfers the individual obtains and on the slope of the supply curve for labour.

Since we are interested primarily in aggregate effects, let us consider the "average" taxpayer. Assume that t* is the socially optimal rate of taxation, in the sense that t* maximizes the average taxpayer's utility. We then have three possible situations:

1. The initial tax rate is t*. In this case, the taxpayer's final utility is unchanged by the (small) tax increase, so point Y is the final equilibrium. The two income effects thus exactly balance, and the only effect of the tax increase is a pure (compensated) decline in the quantity of labour supplied. The case where the initial tax rate is t* was originally analyzed by Scitovsky in 1951 (pp. 90–92).
2. The initial tax rate is below t*. Here, the tax increase raises final utility, so the final equilibrium is at Z. The expenditure income effect outweighs the taxation income effect, so the substitution effect is strengthened by the net income effect.
3. The initial tax rate is above t*. The tax increase lowers final utility, yielding a final equilibrium at X. The net effect can be either an increase or a decrease in the quantity of labour supplied depending on the magnitude of the income effect of taxation and of the real income decline.

The conclusion is thus that even if an aggregate labour supply function is backward bending, a tax increase can be expected to cause an equilibrium increase in labour supply only if welfare (real income) declines sufficiently due to increased taxation. Indeed, perhaps the best *naive* treatment of the labour supply response to taxation is that this response is governed by the substitution effect alone.

INSTITUTIONAL INERTIA

The argument that the labour supply effects of high marginal taxes must be small since no significant decline in total reported hours worked has been observed is also subject to difficulties. The problem is that social norms and institutional structure act as a brake on the instantaneous adjustment of labour supply. To illustrate this point, I will summarize the simulation study in Stuart (1981). The results of this study indicate that the probable equilibrium effects of recent tax increases on labour supply in Sweden are quite a bit larger than what has been revealed by measured yearly hours worked. A full labour supply adjustment, if it is large, would require a major shift in norms and institutions which could come about only after a relatively long period of adjustment.[8]

The starting point for the analysis in Stuart (1981) is a dichotomization of the economy into a taxed and an untaxed sector. A single representative household is endowed with a fixed quantity of labour which is then allocated to these sectors so as to maximize a (Cobb-

Douglas) utility function. Labour allocated to the taxed sector receives a taxed wage which is then used to purchase output from the taxed sector. Government tax revenues are returned to the household on a lump-sum basis and are also assumed to be used to purchase output from the taxed sector. Labour allocated to the untaxed sector is inserted into a (Cobb-Douglas) production function and yields output directly. It is the quantities of the outputs of the two sectors which are arguments in the utility function. The taxed sector is also represented with a Cobb-Douglas production function. Taking the output of this sector as numeraire, it is assumed that the taxed sector is competitive in the sense that the (gross) wage equals the marginal product of labour in that sector.

The taxed sector in the model corresponds roughly to the portion of the Swedish economy which is covered in the standard national income accounts. The untaxed sector is far more variegated. Its major components are home production, black market activities and simple barter subject to covert tax evasion, and labour which is compensated with untaxed fringe benefits. In addition, leisure is untaxed and may be included in the untaxed sector by suitable parameterization of the model. Indeed, when one begins to consider the sorts of activities for labour which are untaxed, it becomes apparent just how much escapes taxation.

For instance, Swedish workers who work overtime are often reimbursed not with some multiple of their normal hourly wage, but instead via compensatory time-off, which is untaxed. Likewise, allowing employees to make private phone calls on the job, to visit doctors and dentists, to take long coffee-breaks, or perform their jobs at a more leisurely but less productive pace all are untaxed. These activities seem to have increased in recent years, although accurate statistical measurement of such trends has not to my knowledge been made. It is obvious, however, that to the extent that "on the job leisure" has increased, the reported statistics on hours worked may be seriously misleading.

THE TAX MODEL

In order for the model to be used as a basis for simulations, it was necessary to set parameter values in the production functions and the utility function, as well as to specify the household's total endowment of labour. The method for this parameterization was to pick a given year (1969) as a base year and to assume that the economy was in equilibrium during that year.

The taxed sector production function was easily parameterized using national income account data on GNP and compensations to labour. A more difficult task was to estimate the value of output and labour inputs of the untaxed sector during 1969, in order to parameterize that sector's production function. There are two sources of difficulty. First, there is no direct reporting of many of the activities included in this sector. Second, the sector includes such vastly different activities that aggregation might be a problem.

The method for judging the size of the untaxed sector in 1969 was to only include activities that could be measured with reasonable certainty. Specifically, an estimate of the value of home production was calculated for 1969. This was used as a proxy for the size of the untaxed sector. By leaving out many (most?) other untaxed uses of labour, the productivity of labour in untaxed uses was underestimated. This imparts a conservative bias to the results; that is, the results tend to give a lower bound for the true effects on labour allocation of a change in the tax rate.

Due to uncertainty as to the correct parameterization of the model, a number of alternative parameterizations were simulated. These allowed for the inclusion of leisure in the untaxed sector, and the assumption that the Swedish economy was subject to an adjustment lag. If so, 1969 observations of economic activity represented an equilibrium with respect to 1964's (lower) marginal tax rate, etc. The effect of these alternative assumptions was generally to increase the reaction of labour to tax increases. However, sensitivity of the results was not particularly great.

When the model was parameterized, simulations were run by taking the marginal tax rate as exogenously determined and by calculating the equilibrium allocation of labour to the two sectors. By applying the historical relationship between the marginal and average tax rates, it was then possible to estimate, for different levels of the marginal tax, the level of tax revenues received by the government in equilibrium.

THE EMPIRICAL RESULTS

A summary of the results for the preferred parameterization of the model is presented in Table 7.5. For this parameterization, total tax revenues reached a maximum at a 73 per cent marginal rate—roughly 7 per cent less than the rate as of 1980. During the year chosen to parameterize the model (1969), the marginal tax rate was 65.5 per cent. Presumably, the model is most accurate for predicting the effects of tax changes which do not change the economy too much. For this reason, I have reported the effects of a 1 percentage-point increase in the tax rate from initial levels of 50 per cent, 65 per cent and 80 per cent, the latter being the 1980 rate.

Two aspects of the results in Table 7.5 stand out. The first is that a 1

TABLE 7.5

Effects of 1%-Point Increases in the Marginal Tax-Rate

Marginal Tax	%Δ Taxed Labour	%Δ Untaxed Labour	Ratio, Taxed to Untaxed Labour
80	- 3.24	+ 1.83	1.73
65	- 1.46	+ 1.46	1.01
50	- 0.83	+ 1.19	0.69

Note: Percentage changes are calculated as the effects of tax increases from 80 to 81%, from 65 to 66%, and from 50 to 51%.

Source: Stuart (1981).

percentage-point increase in the tax rate has increasing effects as a function of the initial value of the tax rate. The reason for this pattern is that households are influenced not by the portion of the wage that goes to the government, but rather by the portion which is retained. That is, households weigh the value of extra untaxed production against the after-tax wage. As the tax rate rises by 1 per cent-point increments, the amount retained by households declines, and does so at an increasing rate. For instance, a 1 per cent tax increase from 50 to 51 per cent represents a 2 per cent decline in marginal retentions at a constant wage (i.e., in one minus the tax rate), while a similar tax increase from 80 to 81 per cent results in a 5 per cent decline in retentions. The effect on households is thus greater at greater initial tax rates. The implication of this tendency is that countries with low taxes are less likely to undergo undesirable distortions in the face of raising taxes than are countries with high taxes.

The second aspect of the results is that the effects of recent tax increases on the equilibrium allocation of labour are, according to the calculations, surprisingly large. This is highlighted by considering the fact that tax increases over the past decade, which have moved the Swedish economy from a 65.5 per cent to an 80 per cent marginal rate on labour, should have changed the ratio of untaxed to taxed labour from 1.01 to 1.73. Thus, if a 40 hour week (in the taxed sector) was an equilibrium as of 1969, a 29.5 hour week would be an equilibrium given today's tax rate. (Logic: recall that the total amount of labour is constant – in this case it is 80.40 (= 40x(1.0 + 1.1) hours/week. Thus L_t + L_u = 80.40 and L_t/L_u = 1.73 implies L_t = 29.5.)

The gross statistics on aggregate hours worked do reveal a decline in recent years, but the decline is nowhere near the magnitude predicted to occur in equilibrium by the model. There are a number of possible explanations. First, there might be something fundamentally wrong with the model. However, the model does do a fairly good job of predicting the trend in taxed-sector employment during the 1960s, and predicts the development of GNP (= taxed sector output) during both the 1960s and 1970s (see Stuart, 1981, pp. 1032–34). A second possibility is that female employment has increased for non-tax-related reasons and that this has merely clouded the time-series on hours worked. A third possible explanation is that the Swedish economy has not yet attained a new equilibrium. If this is the case—or as well if a new equilibrium has been attained but the reported statistics on hours worked are for some reason unreliable—then there should be other signs of an adjustment to the 80 per cent tax rate.

THE BLACK MARKET

There are a number of such signs. However, many of them are not to be found in official statistics, presumably since governments tend not to tax activities that they find hard to measure. First, there is tax-evasion. A recent public opinion poll[9] concluded that roughly 730,000 Swedes supplied services without receipt in order to evade taxes in 1979, while 990,000 Swedes purchased services in the same manner. Sweden's total population was roughly 8 million in 1980. These figures should be interpreted as a lower bound on the true extent of tax evasion since many of those involved in this practice are likely to deny illegal activity when polled. Unfortunately, no such poll was conducted in earlier years, so it is difficult to know with certainty whether receipt-free trade has increased. The general feeling, which is to some extent buttressed by the lack of earlier studies, is that there has been a significant increase.

There are a number of occupations which are regarded as particularly susceptible to tax-evasion. These include private child-care (where evasion seems to be the rule rather than the exception), auto-repairs, and building and related services. A study by Kjell Olsson of Svenska Byggnadsentreprenörsföreningen (a branch organization for building entrepreneurs) is suggestive as to the trend.[10] Olsson compared the value of output in the building industry with the volume of labour employed in the industry. Since productivity per worker has been unchanged in recent years, any excess of growth of output over growth of reported employment can be interpreted as due to unreported labour. Olsson estimated that untaxed reimbursement of labour in the building industry increased from roughly 2 per cent of industry sales in 1972 to 11 per cent of sales as of 1977.

A second sign that a long-term adjustment of labour supply is taking

TABLE 7.6

Percentage Distribution of Women's Desired Hours of Work Outside the Home

Number of Hours Desired	0	1-9	10-15	16-19	20-34	35-
Per Cent of all Women	8	3	5	22	47	15

Note: Figures are based on 1976 observations.

Source: Hultåker and Trost (1979, p. 19).

place is a desire for a shorter work-week. This desire is most clear among women, which may in part be due to the fact that women are less subject than men to a social norm dictating full-time (40 hours/week) work. A poll of 7,500 Swedish women by Hultåker and Trost in 1979[11] revealed a median desire to work something like 20–30 hours/week outside the home. The distribution of responses to the question "How many hours would you wish to work outside the home if you could choose yourself?" is displayed in Table 7.6. Even these figures are liable to overstate women's desires to work, as Hultåker and Trost point out, since some respondents who had no work but wished to work might actually have done so only if offered a job with sufficient pay, if child-care could be arranged, etc.

It is not only among women that desires for a shorter work-week have been expressed. A poll conducted by the university-graduates labour union asked: "Do you wish to work less?" (see *SACO–SR tidning*, March 5, 1978). The percentage of men who responded affirmatively increased from 14 per cent in 1975 to 27 per cent in 1978. In addition, 60 per cent of all members surveyed stated a preference for a shorter work-week instead of increased pay. These numbers contain a suggestion that the expression of a desire to work part-time depends on the way the question is posed: fewer expressed a desire to work part-time when they thought they would be doing it alone than when they thought that the general work-week would decline. If this is so, it indicates that the presence of norms, in this case to work full-time, can slow the response of labour to increased taxes.

INSTITUTIONAL IMPEDIMENTS TO CHANGE

Institutions can also slow the adjustment process. One such institution is Sweden's legislated 40 hour work-week. It is of interest that all of the major political parties in Sweden except the conservatives (with 20 per cent of the vote) are in favour of a 30 hour work-week. (The conservatives feel the matter should be left to union-management negotiations.) Such a change would, according to the calculations presented above, just about exactly restore equilibrium. The question is, why is a 30 hour work-week not legislated? There are (at least) two possible reasons. One is that the parties believe that such an adjustment would result in a social loss – it would permit the full distortionary effects of today's tax rates to make themselves felt. The second reason, which is related, is that the parties realize that a 30 hour work-week would diminish government tax revenues and cause problems for the regime in power. At any rate, the desirability of a 30 hour work-week is, for the moment, simply accepted, while its enactment is put off as "too costly."

Legislation or none, there is still a sizable trickle of workers who have shifted from full- to part-time employment. Over the period 1975–1979, the number of part-time employees increased by 251,000, which was about 6 per cent of the work force as of 1979.[12] During that time, the number of full-time employees fell by 142,000. Over the four-year period, a total of roughly 3.4 per cent of the labour force thus appears to have moved from full- to part-time (reported) employment.[13]

There are many other signs of an equilibrating adjustment in labour supply in Sweden. Unfortunately, the "evidence" at this stage is largely anecdotal. While the obvious caveat on the rigorousness of anecdotal evidence must apply, increases in untaxed fringe benefits and decreases in work intensity have most certainly occurred. As regards the latter, it may be that a shift to a 30 hour work-week would partially reduce the desire for on-the-job leisure.

Another recent trend which likely derives from the high tax rates on labour is a reduction in motivation to move to jobs with a greater wage. (Neither physical nor psychic moving costs are deductible from income.) This is liable to have had an effect on the choice between working and early retirement. Indeed, many older workers who lose their jobs exercise an option to retire early with only slightly reduced net-of-tax benefits.

I would conclude the following from the Swedish experience with high taxation of labour. First, high taxes do influence labour supply decisions. Second, however, the effect of tax increases is not simply an instantaneous adjustment of number of hours worked. Instead of a single effect there are a large number of long-term changes in tax ethics, attitudes toward work and home production, work intensity, etc. Some of these effects manifest themselves quickly, but others may take years or even decades to become part of economic life. The textbook picture of capital as variable only with time and labour as instantaneously variable does not apply when taxes on labour increase greatly. Labour supply decisions are part of the social fabric and are subject to considerable social inertia.

III. OTHER CONSEQUENCES OF HIGH TAXES

SAVINGS AND INVESTMENT DECISIONS

I know of no studies specifically aimed at analyzing how savings and investment decisions have been influenced by taxes on capital. However, the basic forces and effects are fairly clear. From Table 7.1, we see that a tremendous bias exists in the capital market. Housing and consumer durables are subject to far more favourable tax treatments than are investments in corporate capital. The result has been a booming housing market during the 1970s and little private investment in the corporate sector.

New stock issues have been particularly hard hit. During 1978, new stock issues where 832 million kronor, a figure which is small compared to the 19,295 million kronor of funds obtained by firms in the capital market during the same year.[16] Most of the externally financed corporate investment which takes place is instead loan-financed by government and privately administered pension funds. It is unclear what the net effects of this system are. Given that the government attempts to maintain corporate financing via pension investments, it may well be that no net decline in corporate investment has occurred.[17] A suspicion, however, is that such government investments may be directed more to politically advantageous projects than to those projects which yield the greatest returns.

PERVASIVE EFFECTS

A complete catalogue of the effects of taxation would be an arduous task—the effects are so pervasive. I will give three examples to illustrate this pervasiveness. First, the service sector in Sweden is quite a bit different than in many low-tax countries. Purchased services which an individual can perform himself—such as bagging groceries or filling a gas tank—are rare or non-existant. Other services, when they require taxed labour, are also restricted. For instance, gas stations close early; as long as a customer only needs gas, this presents no problem as gasoline dispensing machines exist at many stations. (I have yet to see an oil dispensing machine.) Services provided by industries where tax-evasion is common have a different problem; it can be difficult to purchase the services legally. Indeed, some branch organizations (notably in the painting industry) have expressed a fear that "honest" companies will be driven out of business entirely in the next decade.

A second area where taxation has had an effect is higher education. Clearly, progressive taxation makes higher education unattractive since this raises yearly income, but reduces the number of active years in the labour market. Despite zero tuition, cash subsidies to students, and advantageous study loans for essentially all students, few continue on to graduate studies, and indeed few attempt to study advanced undergraduate courses in more difficult subjects.

A final example of the effects of high taxation is interesting as it illustrates how extreme the result of a tax expenditure can be when marginal rates are high. Expenses for travel to work in Sweden are deductible. This counteracts the tendency of people to not live too far from work, and does so in a surprisingly strong way. For instance, yearly deductions of 10,000 kronor for travel to work are not uncommon. At a 60 per cent marginal tax rate, such a deduction is worth 6,000 kronor per year. If this is discounted at a 10 per cent rate of interest as a perpetuity, the stream of future deductions has a present value of 60,000 kronor. (Such amounts are presumably capitalized into the value of outlying housing.)

GROWTH AND DEVELOPMENT

In Stuart (1981), I considered the effects of increasing taxes on labour on the Swedish growth rate. That analysis is easily summarized. The effect of a 1 percentage-point increase in the marginal tax rate, starting at an initial level between 65 per cent and 80 per cent, is an equilibrium reduction in taxed sector employment sufficient to reduce taxed sector output by roughly 1.5 per cent. Over the period from 1961–1979, taxes increased from 65 per cent to 80 per cent, which is a 1.5 per cent yearly increase. In equilibrium, we would thus expect something like a 2.25 per cent yearly decline in taxed sector output. Of course, there is normally an "exogenous" growth in output due to technological advance, the growth of capital, etc. However, from the early 1960s to the late 1970s, the growth rate of GNP has declined from 4.4 per cent to 1.4 per cent yearly. This suggests that recent tax increases might explain 75 per cent (2.25/3) of the decline in the growth rate. However, if the Swedish economy is not yet in a new equilibrium, this 75 per cent figure is too high. (On the other hand, due to the use of conservative assumptions, the 75 per cent figure could be an underestimate.)

There may well also be negative influences on growth due to the taxation of capital, or due to other tax effects. However, we cannot be sure whether such negative influences actually exist (or are empirically significant) before we go through the possible sources of the growth rate decline and investigate them separately.

Lest the negative influences of taxation on growth receive too much attention here, it should be pointed out that tax increases which have caused large growth rates for the untaxed sector may cause us to overestimate the net decline in the growth rate. Quite simply, most of the untaxed sector does not get included in the national account statistics, so a disproportionate growth in this sector will not have the same effect on the statistics as it does on utility.

IV. CONCLUSION

As a foreigner living in Sweden, I have found a study of the Swedish tax system to be interesting indeed. Although I have been accused of being pessimistic by nature, I believe I am witnessing a country which has gone too far in one direction and which will have great trouble correcting its course. With a 1980 budget deficit of more than 10 per cent of GNP (the figure has increased while I have been writing this paper!) and with further adjustments toward decreased employment of taxed labour likely, it is hard to be optimistic. Further, there seems to be little solid desire by politicians to actually reduce taxes—the short-term effects of such a painful reduction would be a decline in tax revenues. Perhaps the situation would be better if there were fewer political parties and/or a longer electoral period. (Parliamentary elections are held a minimum of every third year.)

I see no signs of a taxpayer movement to reduce taxes. Many people are employed by the government or receive significant subsidies, and these would surely be against a reduction in the size of government. But more important, a shake-up of the present system would have both positive and negative effects on nearly all, and I suspect that the degree of risk-aversion among the populace is sufficient to rule out a mass desire to rock the boat.

It is not surprising to me that a country could increase taxes beyond the point of maximum tax revenues. The reason is that the negative effects of such tax increases are felt only in the long-term, and thus could not have been particularly visible to either the decision makers or the populace at the time of the increases. The current situation thus appears to be the result of two (short run) invisibilities: first, there is the invisibility of the negative long-term effects of high taxes, and second, there is the invisibility (hiddenness) of many of the tax increases themselves.

One final impression of the Swedish tax and subsidy system concerns welfare. It certainly appears that this system has had a considerable impact in redistributing wealth from rich to poor. However, as a practical matter, it appears that the costs of bringing about this redistribution have been increased significantly by a failure to carefully identify who is actually poor. Poverty is generally defined in terms of this year's reported income, a procedure which unavoidably makes it attractive to report low incomes. I would argue that the present system, to a great extent, taxes the middle classes and gives to the middle classes. An example: what is the marginal tax rate on labour income of a head of family making 120,000 kronor per year, with four children, and with a wife who doesn't work? Answer: 100 per cent. Reason: the high level of subsistence income for such a family. That is, any income increases (up to 120,000 kronor per year) merely result in reductions in transfers designed to prevent citizens from not subsisting. While this example is a bit of a quirk, there are others which are not. They include the interest rate deduction to homeowners, low deductibles for sick pay, and outright subsidies (instead of loans) to parents. The list could be made much longer.

APPENDIX I
DETAILS OF ESTIMATES OF EFFECTIVE MARGINAL TAX RATES

The personal income tax rate (1) is simply the effective rate on state and local tax from the standard tax tables. IUI (1977, p. 81) presents a figure for the average (over the taxpaying population) marginal rate for 1971 and 1974; these rates were 52.2 per cent and 56.7 per cent respectively. Jakobsson and Normann (1974) present comparable figures for earlier years. The tax table was indexed in 1978. This should have caused the rate of increase in taxes to decline. The trend seems to have been slightly more than a 1 per cent per year increase, hence the (approximate) figure of 60 per cent for 1980.

The method for calculating the rate on labour supply (2) is in Stuart (1981). The 81 per cent figure includes state and local income, payroll, and indirect taxes, in addition to a correction for the effect of income-based transfers.

Gunnar DuRietz has calculated (unpublished) effective rates on labour supply for 1980 on a disaggregated basis including the taxes listed above and applying the actual rules for transfer payments. DuRietz's figures are several per cent too low due to the fact that they are based on an assumed 10.26 per cent VAT, instead of the 21.63 per cent VAT actually in effect on most goods. These calculations indicate 1) that the 81 per cent figure appears to be a good estimate of the average Swede's marginal rate on labour supply, and 2) that the range of marginal rates for various family types is quite small. Several examples (the rate is on the first income given):

Single person, no children, income of 75,000 kr — 79% rate
Single person, one child, income of 55,000 kr — 86% rate
Couple, no children, incomes of 30,000 kr and 30,000 kr — 64% rate
Couple, no children, incomes of 85,000 kr and 0 kr — 84% rate
Couple, two children, incomes of 45,000 kr and 30,000 kr — 81% rate
Couple, two children, incomes of 90,000 kr and 30,000 kr — 86% rate
Couple, three children, incomes of 95,000 kr and 50,000 kr — 89% rate
Couple, three children, incomes of 55,000 kr and 90,000 kr — 73% rate

Rates on each of the forms of capital investment (3–10) assume a 3 per cent real rate of return and an 8 per cent rate of inflation. In addition, it is assumed that the table marginal rate on income, 60 per cent applies. It might be noted that application of the unmodified table rate neglects marginal effects resulting from losses of income-based transfers due to higher personal income. The use of the 60 per cent figure thus results in estimates of capital taxation which are too low.

The rate on owner-occupied housing (3) assumes that a krona invested in housing gives a krona of market value, of which 1.8 per cent is taxed at a 60 per cent marginal rate each year. This gives 1.08 per cent of market value in taxes, while 3 per cent of market value is real return, for a tax rate of 1.08/3 = .36.

New stock yields a nominal return of 11 per cent. If all this is paid out as dividends (case 5), 5 per cent will not be subject to the corporate tax due to the Annell Law. The remaining 6 per cent is taxed at the 55 per cent corporate rate, causing taxes of 3.3 per cent. This leaves 7.7 per cent as income, taxed at the 60 per cent personal rate, so total taxes are 3.3% + (7.7%) (.60) = 7.92%. The real return is 3 per cent, so the tax rate is 7.92/3 = 2.64.

If the return on stocks is extracted as a capital gain after 10 years of deferred taxes in the firm, no corporate tax is paid (case 6). In most cases, complete avoidance of the corporate tax will not be possible, so the calculated rate given in Table 7.1 is a lower bound. At any rate, a krona invested in this way grows to $e^{1.1}$ = 3.00 kr of which 40 per cent is treated as personal income and taxed at a 60 per cent rate, for taxes after 10 years of .481. This reduces the 3.00 kr recovery to 2.52 kr, which has a present value of $2.52e^{-.8}$ = 1.13 kr. Thus 1 kr grows to 1.13 kr after 10 years, a real net return of 1.3 per cent yearly. Taxation thus reduces the real return from 3 per cent to 1.3 per cent, implying a tax rate of 1.7/3.0 = .567.

Case 7 is a mixture of cases 5 and 6, where 5 per cent of the 11 per cent return is paid as a corporate-tax-free dividend. This engenders taxes of 3 per cent at a 60 per cent rate. The remaining 6 per cent of the return is taxed at a 56.7 per cent rate, so total taxes are 3 per cent + (6%) (.567), which when divided by the 3 per cent real return gives a tax rate of 2.13.

Bonds and bank savings are assumed to be subject to a full 60 per cent marginal rate. The return is $e^{.11} - 1$ after one year, whence taxes are .070, for a rate of .070/.030 = 2.33.

The return on a non-stock company is calculated under the assumption that income taxes on profits can be deferred for 5 years by retaining profits in the firm, where they earn income. The nominal return on a krona placed in the firm for 5 years at 11 per cent is thus $e^{.55} - 1$ = .733, which is subject to a 60 per cent marginal income tax, yielding .293 after tax. This is equivalent to a nominal, after tax yearly return of .051 (5.1%). The tax rate is thus (.11 – .051)/.03 = 1.95.

NOTES

1. In recent years, the krona has fluctuated between 4 kr/$ (US) and 5 kr/$.
2. The most thorough analysis of the relationship between payments to the pension system and compensations is contained in Kruse and Ståhlberg (1977).
3. A description of the rules for capital taxation and of the effects of inflation on capital taxation is contained in Hansson (1978).
4. Riksrevisionsverket (1978).
5. A critique of the methodology of Franzén, Lövgren, and Rosenberg is contained in Lindgren and Söderström (1979).
6. Preliminary work on econometric estimation of a labour supply function for Sweden has been carried out by Axelsson, Jacobsson, and Löfgren (1979).
7. Much of the material on this point is drawn from Hansson and Stuart (1980).
8. To the extent that this picture is correct, one might wonder whether traditional econometric measurements of labour supply are very accurate, but this is a more complicated matter.
9. See Arbetet, January 8 (1980).
10. See Hantverk och industri, III, February 28 (1980).
11. See Hultåker and Trost (1979).
12. Ekonomidepartementet och Konjunkturinstitutet, January (1980) p. 95.
13. This 3.4 per cent figure may underestimate the true shift since 1979 was a business cycle peak while 1975 was not. The general demand for labour should therefore have been (temporarily) greater in 1979.
14. Ekonomidepartementet och Konjunkturinstitutet, January (1980).
15. Ståhlberg (1980) has analyzed the effects of the system and concluded that it has caused a significant reduction in private saving.

REFERENCES

Axelsson, Roger, Roger Jacobsson, and K-G Löfgren. "On the Determinants of Labor Supply in Sweden," working paper, University of Umeå, December (1979).

Ekonomidepartementet and Konjunkturinstitutet. *Konjunkturlaget,* Stockholm, January (1980).

Frazén, Thomas, Kerstin Lövgren, and Irma Rosenberg. *Skatters och offentliga utgifters effekter på inkomstfördelningen,* Stockholm (1975).

Gillespie, Irwin, "Effect of Public Expenditures on the Distribution of Income," *Essays in Fiscal Federalism,* Washington, D.C.: The Brookings Institution (1965).

Hansson, Ingemar. "Skattesystemet, inflationen och investeringarna," *Ekonomisk Debatt,* 4:213–23 (1978).

Hansson, Ingemar, and Charles Stuart. "General Equilibrium Effects of Taxation on Labor Supply," working paper, University of Lund (1980).

Hantverk och Industri, No. 3 February 28 (1980).

Hultåker, Örjan, and Jan Trost. *Hemmafruar och arbetsmarknad,* Uppsala University (1979).

Industriens Utredningsinstitut. *IUI:s Långtidsbedömning 1976 (bilagor),* Stockholm: Almqvist & Wiksell (1977).

Jakobsson, Ulf and Göran Normann. *Inkomstbeskattningen i den ekonomiska politiken,* Uppsala: Almqvist & Wiksell (1974).

Kruse, Agneta and A-C Ståhlberg, *Effekter av ATP—en samhällsekonomisk studie,* Lund Economic Studies (1977).

Lindbeck, Assar. "Comment," Chapter 7 of this volume.

Lindgren, Björn and Lars Söderström. "Om den offentliga budgetpolitikens betydelse för inkomstfördelningen," working paper 1979:56, Department of Economics, University of Lund.

Riksgäldkontoret. *Årsbok, 1977/78,* Stockholm (1978).

Riksrevisionsverket, *Statens Finanser,* Stockholm (1978).

SACO-SR tidning, No. 4, March 5 (1979).

Scitovsky, Tibor. *Welfare and Competition: The Economics of a Fully Employed Economy,* Chicago: Irwin (1951).

Statens offentliga utredningar (SOU), Översyn av skattesystemet, SOU 1977:91, Stockholm.

Stuart, Charles. "Swedish Tax Rates, Labor Supply, and Tax Revenues," *Journal of Political Economics* 89:1020–38 (1981).

Ståhlberg, A-C. "Effects of the Swedish Supplementary Pension System on Personal and Aggregate Household Saving," *Scandinavian Journal of Economics* 82:1:25–44 (1980).

Sveriges Riksbank, Statistisk Årsbok, Stockholm (1978).

COMMENT

Assar Lindbeck

I think that Professor Stuart has written an interesting paper. It consists of three parts. First is a description of the Swedish tax system, second a theoretical discussion of income and substitution effects, and third an attempt to find some empirical evidence of these incentive effects in Sweden. I shall comment on each.

The first part, the description, is basically a correct formulation of the Swedish situation. One oversight, though, is that there have been some changes in recent years which are not included in the paper. These concern basic deductions for household taxation and dividend payments. As well, there is an important omission. The paper ignores the investment fund program which is really a 100 per cent accelerated appreciation system. But basically, Professor Stuart does give a correct picture of the main features of the Swedish tax system.

Nevertheless, it is always possible to add additional information. Of particular interest are the enormous differences in the distribution of factor incomes compared to disposable incomes. I will return to that issue.

CAPITAL TAXATION

What else is missing from Stuart's paper? I think it would have been useful to give more information about the taxation of capital. This refers to his empirical studies, too, because they include some rather strong effects. Most countries combine inflation and a nominalistic tax system for assets, which yields quite a remarkable effect on the market for assets. This concerns not only saving, but the allocation decisions of saving and investments as well.

We can make headway by focusing on the required rate of return on savings which will maintain capital values constant. (Let us assume marginal tax rates of 80 per cent, a 10 per cent inflation, and a 2 per cent wealth tax, which are all normal in Sweden.) The results are truly staggering – 60 per cent interest is needed for bank savings which yield only 8 per cent or 9 per cent. Shares of stock require 37 per cent and apartment houses 30 per cent. For art and antiques only 10 per cent is needed because there is no tax at all on these items. Consequently, a rate of return just equal to the rate of inflation is all that is needed in order to break even. As Stuart has shown, the system thus siphons away savings from productive investment, from savings in banks and shares, and diverts it to private consumption and investment in durable consumer goods. It is quite conceivable that these effects on the allocation of savings have quite as strong an effect in the long run as do the disincentive effects on labour.

My point is that more emphasis is needed on taxation of capital in combination with inflation. I think it is the combination with inflation that has a really serious effect on incentives in many countries. Without inflation, the results of high capital taxes wouldn't be so serious. Suppose that interest rates were the only cost of houses! If the marginal tax rate approaches 100 per cent, housing prices become infinite because there would be no capital costs at all for the consumer! Moreover, when interest rates are deductible at 80 per cent marginal tax rates, it's extremely cheap to buy durable consumer goods. This means that when government raises interest in order to pursue economic policy, households are not very responsive. Instead the effects are mainly concentrated in the corporate sector and on investment. In order to have some kind of effect on consumer behaviour, it is then necessary for government to interfere with the credit market with rationing of various kinds.

THE BUDGET DEFICIT

Stuart's classification with regard to hidden taxes is well taken. However, he exaggerates somewhat when talking about the budget deficit. The budget deficit is reported in a very arbitrary way. It was about fifty-billion kronor in 1979. However, there was a surplus of fifteen-billion on the social security funds, but this was arbitrarily cut out of the budget. Moreover, ten-billion kronor of the expenditures are not ordinary expenditures, but rather lending to private firms. These could as well have been financed by government credit institutes issuing their own bonds, rather than through government. Ten plus fifteen makes twenty-five so we can cut the budget deficit in half by these bookkeeping adjustments.

A further point – the Arabs have really placed a tax of 3 or 4 per cent on Swedish GNP by raising prices on imported oil. In effect, Swedish consumers have been taxed by the Arabs. At the same time, household saving has been maintained. It is only natural that Sweden would have a government deficit when the Arabs are pursuing a fiscal policy for us.

The second part of Stuart's paper is a theoretical discussion of income and substitution effects. The main point made here is that it's really very unsatisfactory to analyze *ceteris paribus* changes in taxes without assuming corresponding changes in expenditures, which often wipe out the initial income effects. If anyone is interested in these points they can look at seminar paper number 198 of the Institute for International Economic Studies. There, I have tried to analyze this problem in a comprehensive way. I looked at various types of expenditures financed by taxes: income dependent transfers, income non-dependent transfers, subsidies of private goods, the provision of non-collective public goods, and the provision of public goods. The income and substitution effects of taxes are then analyzed simultaneously with income and substitution effects of public spending.

DISINCENTIVE EFFECTS?

Finally, in the empirical part of the paper there is an econometric model with a Cobb-Douglas production function for the tax and the non-tax sectors. This is a very brave analysis, and in a way, a kind of pioneering work. I think, however, that we have to be very cautious about the conclusions. This is an experiment and I am quite convinced that by changing the assumptions about the elasticities, he could have generated rather different results. Stuart believes he can explain half of the decline in the growth rate in Sweden in the late 1970s by these disincentive effects. However, there are other economists who believe that the same phenomenon can be explained by the wage explosion in the middle of the 1970s. Because of this Sweden was priced out of world markets. We lost market shares and experienced production and productivity losses.

Other economists point out that we pursued a very restrictive demand management policy which created slack in the whole economy in the 1970s. This is also a good explanation, albeit an alternative one, of why the growth rate was cut in half. So, we have three good explanations of why the growth rate was cut by 50 per cent in the 1970s. This reminds me of the problem faced by Feige when he tried to explain the fall in registered productivity on the basis of the black market sector. I'm sure that some economists could also explain this by other factors. I'm thus a little skeptical there as well.

According to Stuart's model, people should really have cut down their labour supply from 40 to 30 hours per week. Of course, no such thing has occurred. So he has to speculate that it takes a long time until that happens. That may be, but it's always a little bit disturbing when, after five years, people still have not adjusted to what the model predicts. We must start to think of how long a lag we are willing to allow before we start to question the assumptions of the model.

In spite of these points, I think Stuart's study is a very worthwhile one. By expanding the model, by making it more satisfactory in many respects, we might be able to obtain more reliable results. We have to recognize also that Stuart explains the 50 per cent cut in the GNP growth rate by just looking at the disincentive effects *on work*, without any consideration of disincentive effects on investment decisions. If those effects could be added, then the Swedish growth rate might be cut by 100 per cent. But reliable studies of the U.S. suggest that disincentive effects are greater on the saving and investment side than in the labour market. Then, if we add some other effects, maybe we can explain 200 per cent of the fall of the growth rate by disincentive effects. But then one really has to begin wondering if the model is correctly specified.

Figure 7.2

Average annual factor income per household, disposable income per household and per capita disposable income per household in Sweden 1977.

Decile groups ordered by factor income per household.

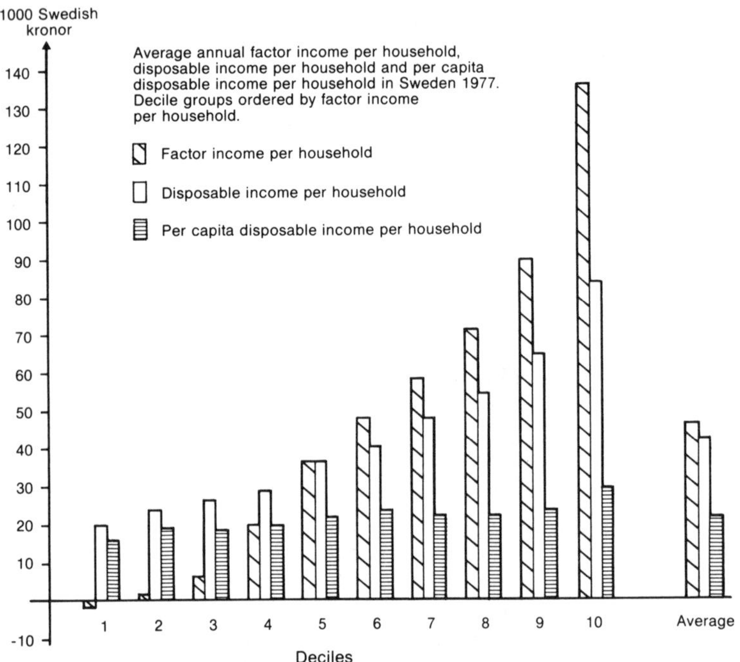

Source: Statistics from National Central Bureau of Statistics: Income Distribution Survey in 1977 (taxation statistics and other public registers for a sample of 9,454 households).

Having considered the Stuart paper in some detail, I should now like to extend my remarks by discussing the Swedish economy more generally. In an advanced welfare state like Sweden, the wedge between factor income and disposable income is nowadays so wide that the distribution of the former is a *very* poor indicator of the distribution of the latter. It is an even poorer indicator of the distribution of *per capita* disposable income and hence, presumably, also of the distribution of economic welfare. The purpose of this Comment is to show just *how* poor these indicators are, and *why*.

THE STATISTICAL PICTURE

Figure 7.2 which, like most other figures in this Comment, is based on data from taxation statistics, shows average incomes of various deciles ordered by factor incomes. The purpose of the figure is to illustrate how the dispersion of incomes of various factor income groups shrinks when we move from factor income per household to disposable income of households, and finally to per capita disposable income of households of the various factor income groups (deciles).

As is seen from the figure, the ratio between the factor incomes of the tenth and the second deciles is approximately 135 to one, whereas the ratio between the disposable incomes of the same factor income deciles is about 3.5 to one, and the corresponding ratio for per capita disposable income approximately 1.5 to one. Another way of characterizing the same statistics is to note that while for the tenth decile disposable income and per capita disposable income are 61 and 21 per cent, respectively, of factor income, the corresponding percentage figures for the second decile are 2,280 and 1,816. Most observers of this figure would perhaps agree that if the statistics were correct it would not make much difference for the income standard, on the average, whether an individual lives in a household in the tenth or in the first factor income decile, in spite of the great differences in average factor income between the deciles. Of course, there may still be considerable differences in (recorded) per capita disposable income between *individual households* in the population as a whole. For instance, a small family at the top of the tenth factor income decile will of course have a much higher per capita disposable income than a large family at the bottom of the first decile.

The observation that *per capita* disposable income is so much more evenly distributed than *total* disposable household income reflects, of course, the fact that the number of family members rises with factor incomes. Figure 7.3 indicates that this variation in the number of family members between various deciles depends more on differences in the number of adults than on the number of children. For we can see from the figure that by dividing by the number of adults rather than by the number of children (with the alternative weights of 0.5 and 1.0, respectively), the difference in per capita disposable income between the various factor income deciles is reduced. The chief reason seems to be that people in the lowest three factor income deciles mainly consist of old people (pensioners), students, or people doing their military service—with only one or perhaps two persons per household.[1] These groups of people have, of course, very low factor incomes and they live largely on transfers; this will be shown more explicitly in Figures 7.7 and 7.8.

Figure 7.3

Average annual factor income per household, disposable income per household and per capita disposable income in Sweden 1977. Decile groups ordered by factor income per household. The horizontal lines through the histograms indicate the mean income.

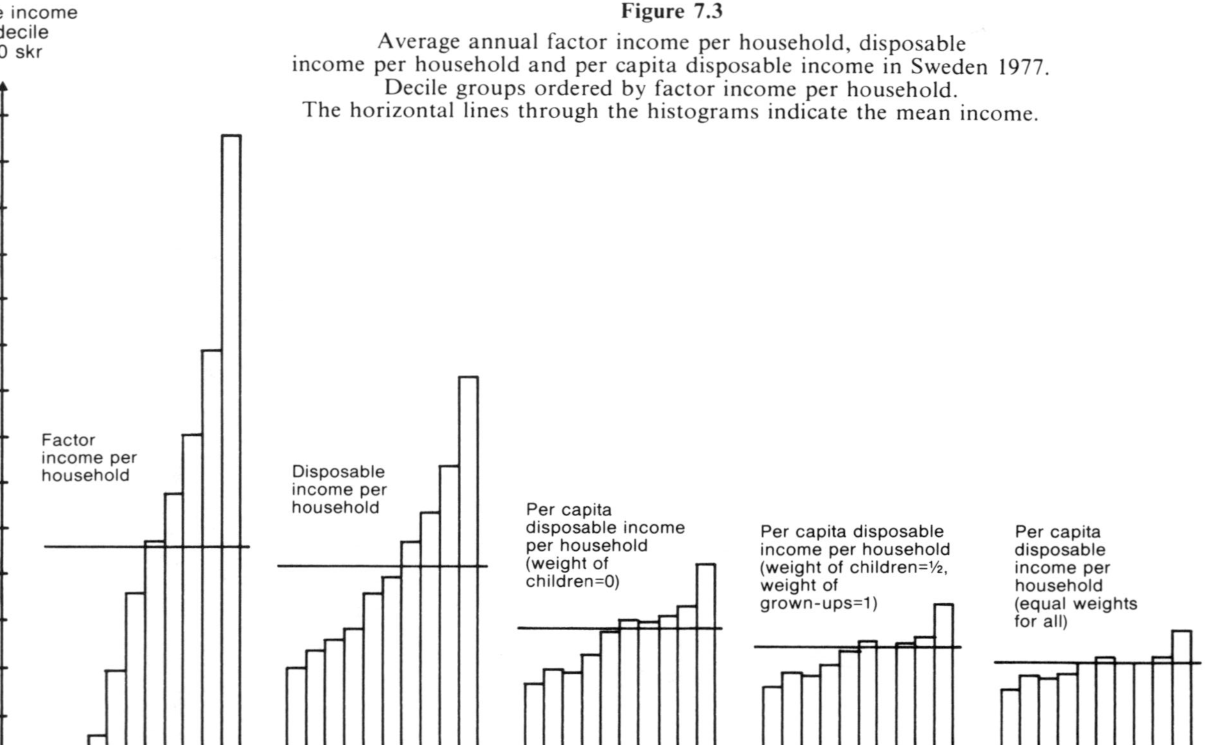

Source: See Figure 7.2

Figure 7.4
Average annual factor income per household, disposable income per household and per capita disposable income per household in Sweden 1977. Percentile groups ordered by each concept of income.

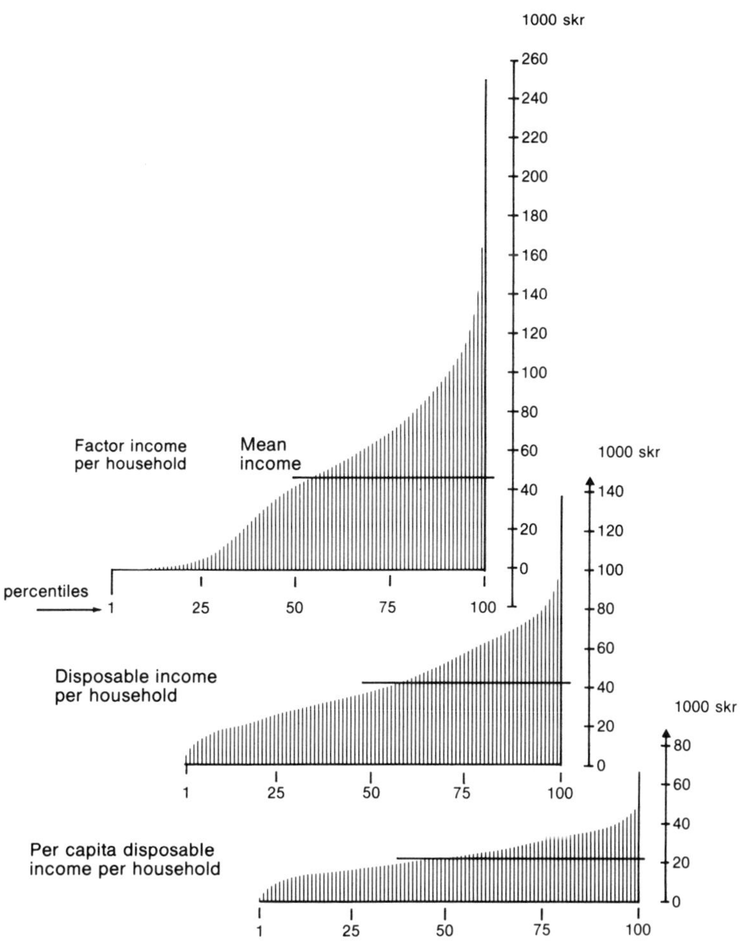

Source: See Figure 7.2

FAMILY SIZE

That family size rises systematically by factor income is probably not entirely an exogenous phenomenon from the point of view of income redistribution policy. The buildup of ambitious systems of income transfers and public services to old people, as well as subsidies for students, has made it easier for both these groups to establish their own small households. In contrast, a few decades ago these groups of people lived more frequently with their children and parents, respectively.

Another illustration of the three different types of distribution is given in Figure 7.4, where the statistics are organized on percentiles rather than deciles. Moreover, the percentiles are ordered for *each* income concept that is depicted in the various sub-figures—factor income in the upper sub-figure, disposable income in the middle, and per capita disposable income in the bottom sub-figure. The figure shows how the "profiles" of the distributions are squeezed drastically—with a regression towards the mean—when we move from the distribution of factor incomes to the distribution of disposable incomes and finally to the distribution of per capita disposable income.

Jan Pen[2]—in a brilliant chapter called "A Parade of Dwarfs (and a Few Giants)"—asked us to visualize the distribution of incomes in society as a parade of people, where each individual was assigned a "height" proportional to the size of his income rather than to his tallness in centimeters. Figure 7.4 may be regarded as a simplified version of Pen's imaginary parade of people. According to Swedish taxation statistics, we are all dwarfs nowadays when measured by the per capita disposable income of our household. It can also be seen from the figure that whereas the ratio between the factor incomes of the 100th and the 10th percentiles is approximately 250 to one, the corresponding ratio for disposable income is 7 to one, and for per capita disposable income 6.5 to one.

For completeness, let us also illustrate the various distributions by conventional Lorenz curves, as depicted in Figure 7.5. In addition to the Gini coefficient (G), the figure also denotes the so-called "maximum equalization coefficient" (E), which tells us how large a fraction of the total income sum that has to be redistributed from people above the median income to people below the median to give everybody the same income. (A reason for the rather "high" Gini coefficient, 0.501, for the distribution of factor incomes is, of course, that zero and negative incomes are included in the statistics, which is often not the case in statistics on distributions.)

In Figures 7.4 and 7.5 the "shift" from disposable income to per capita disposable income seems to equalize the distribution less than did the same kind of shift in the context of Figures 7.2 and 7.3. The rea-

Figure 7.5
Lorenz curves for factor income, disposable income and disposable income per capita of households in Sweden 1977.

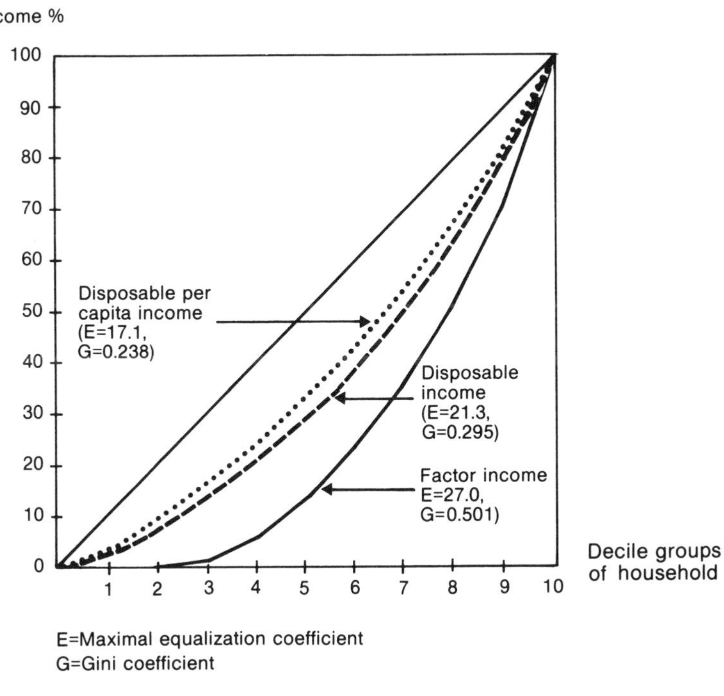

Source: See Figure 7.2

son is, of course, that whereas in Figures 7.2 and 7.3 we compare incomes of people in given *factor income deciles*, we compare different *types* of distribution in Figures 7.4 and 7.5—the factor income distribution, the distribution of disposable income, and the distribution of per capita disposable income. When in Figures 7.4 and 7.5 we shift from the distribution of total disposable income to the distribution of per capita disposable income, not only are some inequalities "removed," but new ones "emerge" when families with many members are pushed down into lower deciles, while families with few members are pulled up to higher deciles.

The importance of the choice of income concept for the distribution of income is iliustrated in a different "dimension" in Figure 7.6. It shows the consequences of shifting from *annual* gross income to dis-

Figure 7.6
Income dispersion with alternative definitions of income (1971).

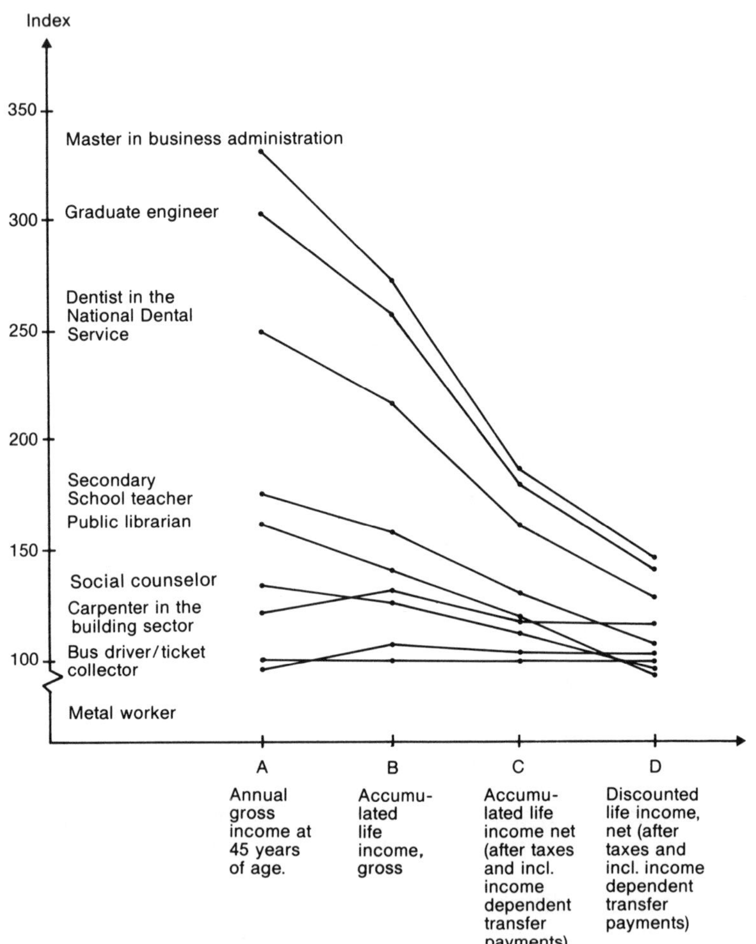

Source: SACO (Organization of Swedish Academic Employees), Stockholm.

counted *life* disposable income for some selected socioeconomic groups. For instance, while the ratio of the income of a Master of Business Economics and a low-level white collar worker (illustrated here as a bus driver or ticket collector) is 3.3 to one, when income is measured as annual gross income (at 45 years of age), the corresponding ratio is less than 2 if instead we look at accumulated disposable life income. If life income is discounted by an interest rate of 5 per cent (which in this case operates like a "real" interest rate) the ratio falls to about 1.5 to one.

It was suggested above that the differences between the distribution of factor income and disposable income may be further clarified by looking explicitly at *the sources* of the incomes in various income deciles. Figures 7.7 and 7.8 are constructed for that purpose. Figure 7.7 illustrates how large a fraction of disposable income in the various *factor income groups* (deciles) that is obtained from different sources. The three lowest deciles obviously live mainly on transfer payments, while wages and salaries play an insignificant role for them. However, from about decile number four and upwards, wages and salaries dominate completely as a source of disposable income; they amount to between 80 and 160 per cent of disposable income. (The reason why wages and salaries in the highest deciles are much larger than disposable income is, of course, that taxes – in the figure included in the concept "transfers paid" – are much larger than transfers received.) It is also of interest to note that capital income (consisting of "entrepreneural income" and "property income") constitutes a very small fraction of disposable income in all decile groups; it would be small even if we assume that in the statistics it is underestimated by, say, a factor of two or three.

In Figure 7.8, by contrast, the deciles are ordered by *per capita disposable income*, rather than by factor income. According to the figure, wages and salaries constitute some 90 to 150 per cent of disposable income for *all* (per capita disposable) income groups. It is also of interest to note that transfers received are some 20–40 per cent of disposable income in nearly all decile groups; they are, perhaps somewhat surprisingly, as high as 15 per cent for the highest decile. Capital income, again, is a very small fraction of disposable income in each decile group.

The most interesting feature of Figures 7.7 and 7.8 is perhaps that if we define poverty as low disposable per capita income, "poor people" get their income mainly from wages and salaries (Figure 7.8). They must, in fact, usually be "ordinary" wage and salary earners with many family members. On the other hand, people living on transfer payments, such as pensioners, do not *in general* seem to be particularly

Figure 7.7

Sources of incomes in Sweden 1972. Decile groups of households ordered by factor income per household. Disposable income = 100.

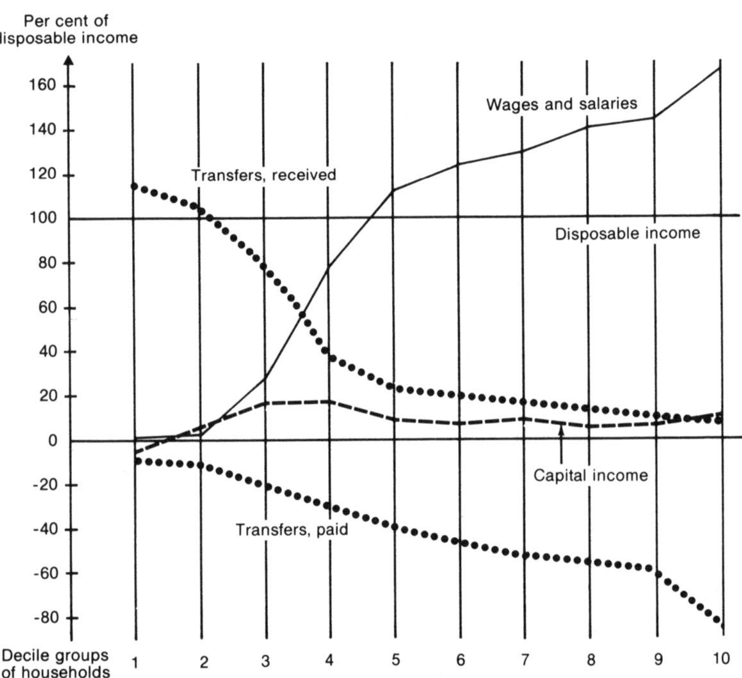

Note: Contributions to social security schemes etc. are not included in wages and salaries. Capital income = dividends, interests etc.; it also includes net operating surplus of entrepreneurs.

Source: National Central Bureau of Statistics: Swedish Survey on Relative Income Differences 1972.

poor by this definition of poverty; pensioners seem to be spread out over most decile groups when income is ordered according to disposable per capita income.[3] In other words, it is extremely important when we talk about "poverty" to decide whether we mean factor income or disposable per capita income; obviously the second concept must be the more relevant one.

Figure 7.8

Sources of Incomes in Sweden 1972.
Decile groups of households ordered by per capita disposable income. Disposable income = 100.

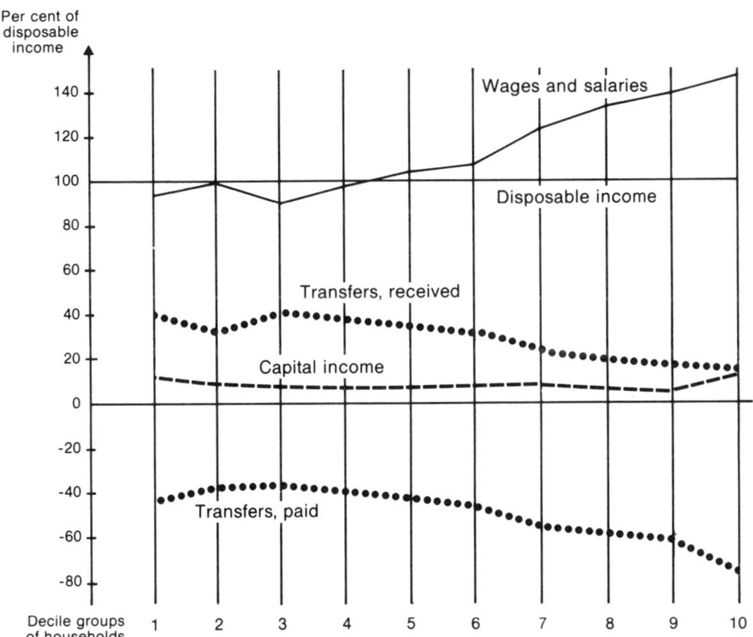

Note: See Figure 7.7
Source: See Figure 7.7

MARGINAL RATES AND ELASTICITIES

Of course, these wide wedges between factor incomes and disposable incomes imply very high marginal tax and transfer rates. The rates created by the Swedish tax/transfer system are illustrated in Figure 7.9, constructed by Irène Andersson; it depicts the marginal tax/transfer rates, defined as the sum of explicit marginal income tax rate *and* the implicit tax rate of the most important income-dependent transfers, namely rent subsidies and subsidized day nursery fees. The figure refers to married people or couples living together, both partners gainfully employed, with two children under sixteen years of age. The solid line depicts the marginal tax/transfer rates when income increases by 1,000

Figure 7.9

Calculated marginal effects of increased taxes, increased day nursery fees, and reduced rent allowance for married people/couples living together; both gainfully employed, with 2 children under 16 years of age.

Marginal effect in percentage, with an increased income of Skr 1,000 (A) and Skr 5,000 (B) respectively.

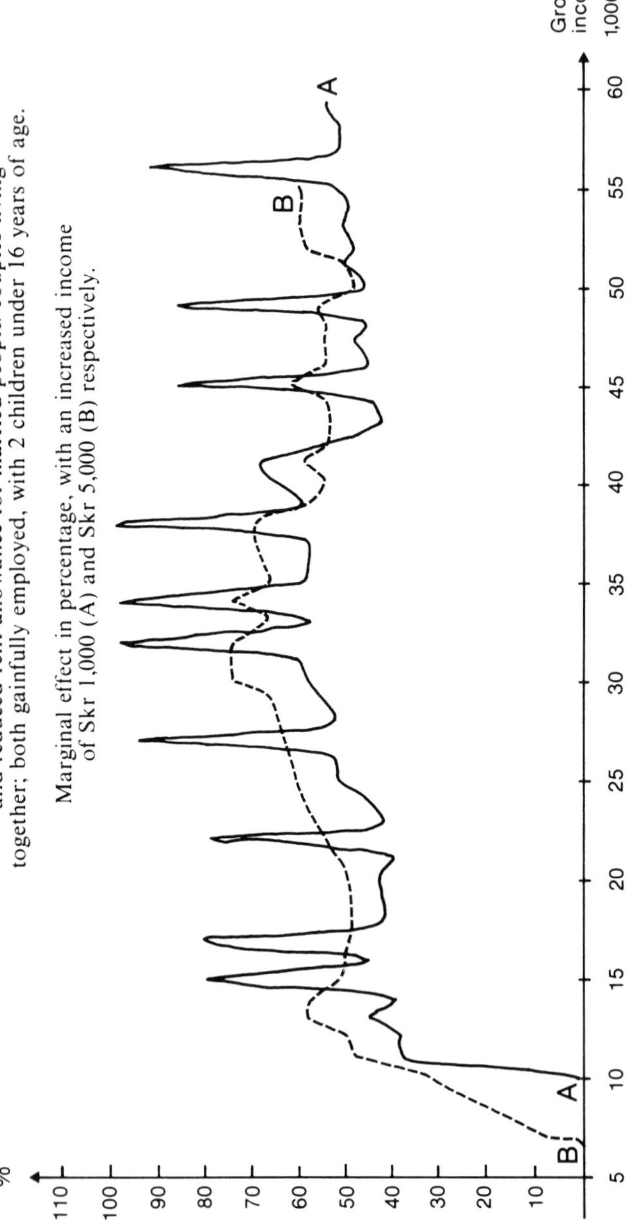

Source: Calculations by I. Andersson on the basis of existing rules of the tax and benefit system.

kronor (approx. $250). The reason for the steep peaks here and there is simply that the tax and transfer functions are discontinuous, with discrete jumps in the marginal tax rates and discrete reductions in transfer payments when income reaches certain levels. The broken line depicts the marginal rates when income increases by 5,000 (approx. $1,250); in this case the path of the marginal rates is evened out considerably.

The most interesting aspect of the figure is, perhaps, that the marginal rates are rather constant, regardless of gross income, from about 15,000 kronor and upwards. (To get 1980 income figures, the statistics in the chart should be multiplied by approximately a factor of 2.) In fact, most people depicted in the figure seem to have marginal rates of between 60 and 70 per cent in the case of large income changes (5,000 kronor). The marginal rates converged higher up (at about 200,000 kronor) to about 78 per cent.

A welfare state system like the Swedish one not only implies that it is difficult for the individual to change his disposable income much by his own effort, it also means that it is difficult for labour unions to influence the living standard of their members by way of bargaining over wage rates. This is illustrated in Figure 7.10, which is constructed by Lars Matthiessen. The figure should be read as follows. The horizontal axis depicts gross taxable income. The vertical axis on the left depicts the elasticity of disposable income with respect to gross taxable income; in other words, the figures on that axis tell us by how many per cent disposable income rises when gross taxable income goes up by one per cent. Let us look, for instance, at the curve depicted by A, which is the elasticities for a married taxpayer who is the only income earner of a family with one child; (however, the same curve is relevant also for a single taxpayer with one child). Up to about 40,000 kronor (the figures refer to 1973 and should be multiplied by a factor of about two to correspond to income levels of 1980) the elasticity is usually below 0.5, and for income earners with gross taxable incomes of between 20,000 and 40,000 the elasticity was even lower *and falling by income*. The reason is, of course, that the income-dependent transfers were gradually removed in this interval. After passing an income of about 40,000 kronor, the elasticity suddenly jumps up, however, because people at that income level have already lost most of their income-dependent transfers. After that point, when only small sums of income-dependent transfers are left, there is less fluctuation in the elasticity when income rises.

On the vertical axis to the right, the scale is reduced by an assumed rate of inflation of 4.5 per cent, and the remaining figure is multiplied by ten. Thus the axis tells us by how many per cent real disposable income increases due to a *ten per cent* increase in (nominal) gross taxable incomes when the rate of inflation is (as low as) 4.5 per cent. For the

Figure 7.10
Tax transfer system elasticities 1973.

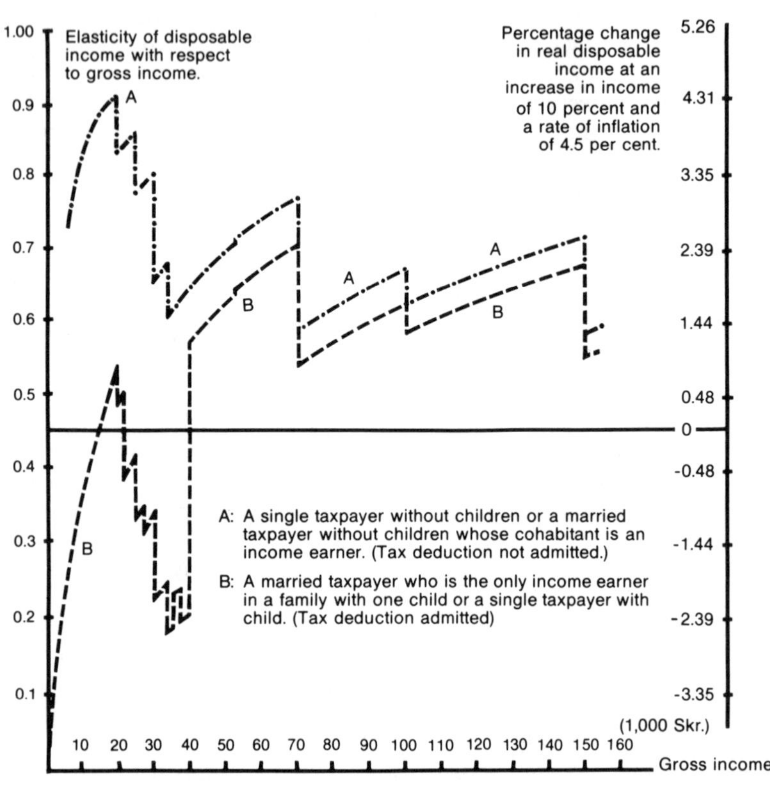

Source: L. Matthiessen. "A study in fiscal theory and policy," mimeo, the Economic Research Institute at the Stockholm School of Economics, 1973.

married taxpayer just mentioned (curve A) there will in fact be a *loss* in real disposable income (with some exceptions), if gross taxable income is less than 40,000 kronor (which was a rather "normal" income in 1973 for a full-time employee). If income is higher he will experience a modest increase in real disposable income (of between one and three per cent) when gross taxable income goes up by 10 per cent (at a rate of inflation of 4.5). The reader can himself approximately visualize the consequences of higher inflation by deducting higher rates of inflation from the figures on the vertical axis.

The wedges between factor incomes and disposable incomes which are illustrated in Figures 7.2–7.10 would have been even wider, and the marginal tax/transfer rates even higher if payroll taxes (of some 30 per cent of the wage bill) and indirect taxes (of some 20 per cent of private consumption) had been added, as then factor income (as measured by the costs for firms) would have to be blown up by some 30 per cent and disposable income would have to be reduced by some 20 per cent. Then the marginal tax/transfer rates would have to be raised by about 20 percentage points; they would then reach levels of about 80–90 per cent for most people who are depicted in Figure 7.9 (when income rises by 5,000 kronor). However, in some cases, particularly for the sick insurance and pension systems, there are elements of an actuarial connection between the fees on the wage bill and the benefits, which means that these fees cannot fully be regarded as taxes, and hence as *wedges* between factor income and disposable income; they function partly as *prices* for such insurance.

SOME MODIFICATIONS OF THE PICTURE

As the figures in the charts above are largely based on taxation statistics, they exclude some incomes that, from an analytical point of view, should have been included. Some of the most important omissions are: 1) several types of capital gains and losses due to inflation and/or relative price changes for assets; 2) legal tax avoidance; 3) barter, do-it-yourself work, and incomes connected with economic crimes, including cheating with taxes and benefits from the government; and 4) public consumption. Unfortunately we know very little about the way in which the inclusion of items like these, taken all together, would change the picture given by Figures 7.2–7.10. I will therefore restrict myself to a few simple reflections on each of these four omissions.

1. The prices of shares, bonds, and often also apartment houses in most years during the 1970s have not risen relative to the general price level; in fact for the period as a whole they have fallen considerably. The dominating *capital gains*, in real terms, in Sweden have instead accrued to people with negative net financial claims and for homeowners, particularly when the mortgages are high, as the interest rates do not seem to adjust fully to inflation; unfortunately, quantitative calculations are difficult to make, as those would require assumptions on what the interest rates would have been without the rise in inflation. However, schematic calculations indicate that during the mid-1970s the real value of the stock of existing owner-occupied houses typically increased annually by some 5 per cent of total disposable private income,[4] at the same time as the real value of mortgage debt fell.

A schematic example illustrates the potential importance of such redistribution. For instance, if inflation goes up from 4 to 10 per cent, as it did during the 1970s, a debtor with a loan of 200,000 Swedish kronor gains some 6,000 kronor per year (tax free) if the interest rate adjusts by *half* of the increased rate of inflation. For a family with a rather "normal" disposable income of say 40,000 kronor, this means an addition to disposable income of 15 per cent, which, as we have seen, is rather difficult to achieve through increased work effort in a highly progressive income tax system. Figures like these should be compared with *consciously* policy-determined redistribution among individuals, by way of hotly debated tax reforms, of perhaps a few hundred or one or two thousand kronor at the most.

As the useful calculations of the quantitative importance of *the redistributional consequences* of inflation hardly exist, and perhaps even cannot be made in a non-controversial way, we have to restrict ourselves to the observation that the composition of assets in different income brackets *suggests* that the middle-income and modestly high brackets probably have gained somewhat on inflation at the expense of the low *and* the very high income groups.[5]

2. The extent of *legal tax avoidance* is quite unknown, though it probably plays a rather important role in all factor income deciles. Perhaps we may hypothesize that do-it-yourself work and barter (formally perhaps illegal but in practice legal) play a relatively less important role, and that "tax motivated" asset transactions play a relatively more important role, in the very highest factor income deciles. The latter part of the hypothesis is illustrated by information on deductions for tax purposes (so called "tax expenditures") of deficits on capital holdings (Figure 7.11). The number of people with deficits increases rapidly by gross income – from about 5 per cent of the taxpayers in the lowest three deciles to 30–50 per cent of the taxpayers above the seventh decile. While the mean deficit is rather small, relative to mean income of the income class, in most income classes, they are above 20 per cent of mean income of the very lowest and of the very highest income classes. The frequency of deficits on real estate (due to interest on mortgage) increases too by income, except for the *very* highest income classes; however, the mean deficit is rather similar in all income classes as a ratio of mean income of each income class, except in the *very* lowest one where the ratio is no less than 4.45 – for the very tiny fraction of people with deficits in that income class (Figure 7.12).[6]
3. Incomes from *economic crimes*, including cheating with taxes and public benefits, do not much influence the *difference* between factor incomes and disposable income in each given factor income group.

Figure 7.11

Deficit on capital income in Sweden 1977 according to taxation statistics.

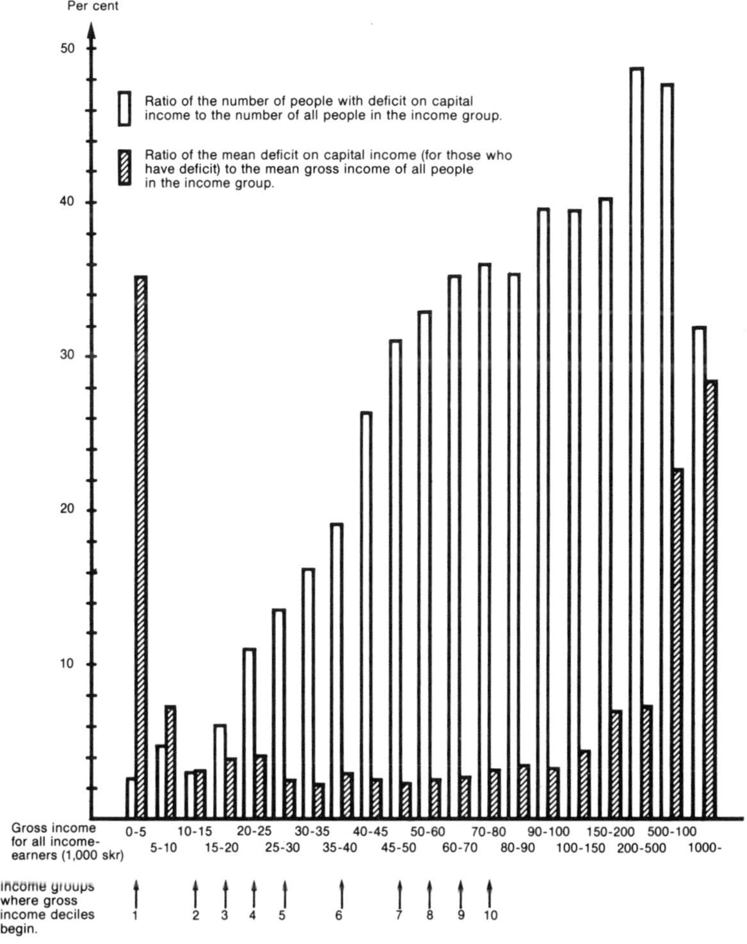

Note: "Deficit on capital income" consists of net income, when negative, from bank accounts, bonds, shares etc. and interest on debt. It does not include imputed income from owner-occupied houses or interest payment on mortgages. "Gross income" includes all kinds of incomes and taxable transfers; deficit on capital income is not deducted when gross income is calculated.

Source: National Central Bureau of Statistics: Sample survey of income tax returns for individuals. Stockholm 1979.

Figure 7.12

Deficit on income from real estate, excluding farm property in Sweden 1977 according to taxation statistics.

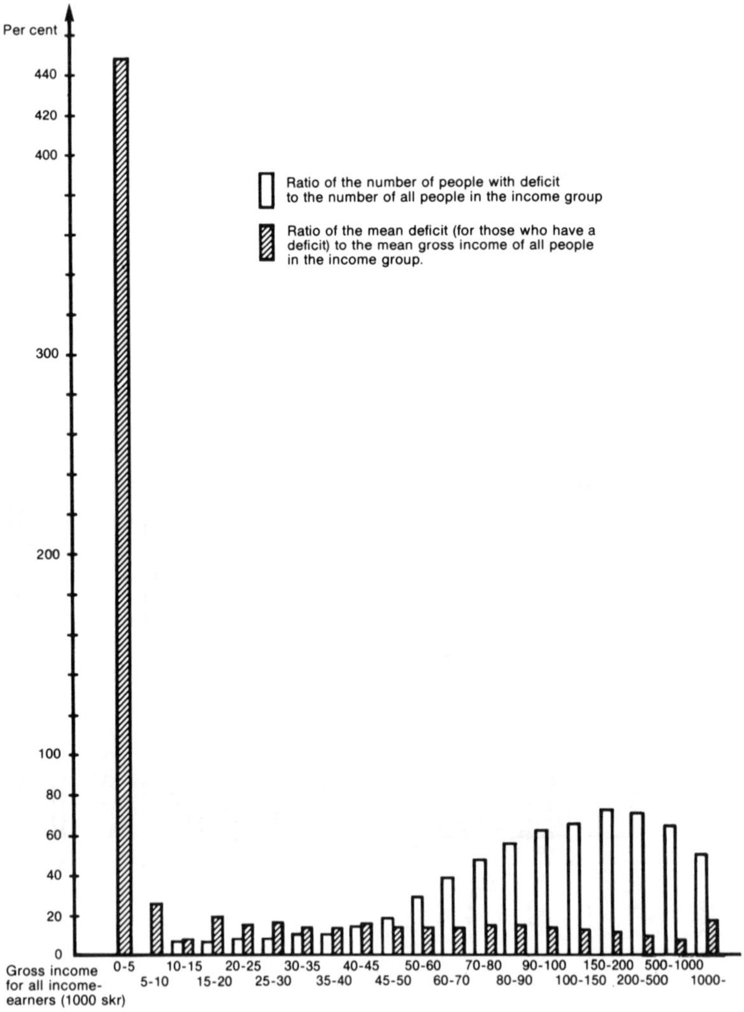

Note: Real estate, excluding farm property, is owner-occupied houses and dwelling houses etc. The total amount of the deficit comes mainly from the first category (93 per cent). See also the note on Figure 7.11.

Source: See Figure 7.11

However, we cannot of course rule out the possibility that the levels of *both* factor incomes *and* disposable incomes would both have to be adjusted in quite different proportions in different factor (and disposable) income deciles; unfortunately we do not know in which deciles the adjustments would have to be large and small, respectively. An indication that adjustments like these may not be trivial is given by rough estimates that incomes of these types may account for some 10 per cent of national income,[7] and that according to opinion polls, every fifth Swede has declared that he (she) has paid "black money" and that every seventh person has received "black money."[8] (Such figures do not include *barter* and *do-it-yourself work*.)

4. Though research attempts have been made in various countries to pin down the distribution of *public consumption* among income classes, the results are not very reliable. For instance, to find out the distribution of collective consumption is generally regarded as quite hopeless. Moreover, the distribution of public expenditures on education becomes rather different if they are allocated on the basis of lifetime income and not, as is usual in existing studies, yearly income, and if education expenditures are allocated to the parents rather than, as in most studies, to the school attendants themselves. Similarly, if public services for the elderly are allocated not to the elderly themselves but rather to their children, the size distribution of disposable incomes and economic welfare would be somewhat different. (The rationale for such an alternative allocation of calculated benefits is of course that the children, without such public expenditures, would have to spend more for the care of their parents, and/or would inherit less from them.)

However, for what it is worth, a quite competent study for Sweden,[9] along rather traditional lines, suggests that the lowest deciles gained some 30–300 per cent of their disposable income (depending on type of family), and that the highest deciles lost some 10–30 per cent (of their disposable income) relative to a hypothetical proportional distribution of public consumption. Table 7.7, copied from Franzén *et al.*, gives some information on the composition of this redistribution (for married couples).

To summarize, I am afraid that the only honest conclusion about the net consequences for the size distribution of "income" of neglecting capital gains, legal tax avoidance, tax and benefit cheating, and other economic crimes, and public consumption is that we know too little to make useful statements about it—for Sweden, as well as for other countries. We can be rather sure, however, that certain *socioeconomic groups* have considerably higher "incomes" than is indicated by the

TABLE 7.7

Change in Real Income in Per Cent of Total Net Factor Income When Government Expenditures on Goods and Services Are Replaced by Proportional Government Expenditures, 1970

Married Couples

Government Expenditures	Total Net Factor Income Class (Sw. Kr.) 0-9 999	10 000-24 999	25 000-39 999	40 000-59 999	60 000-99 999	100 000-	Total
Education							
Students 7-19 years old	-15.8	-12.1	-3.8	-0.8	1.0	4.3	-2.5
Students over 19	-19.7	1.1	1.8	2.0	2.2	2.2	1.7
Health	-190.4	-12.0	4.5	7.2	8.2	8.9	2.5
Day nurseries and day care at home for families with children	-1.2	-0.3	-0.1	0.4	-0.7	0.0	-0.1
Other child and youth care	-0.7	-0.4	-0.2	0.0	0.1	0.3	-0.1
Welfare services and care of the aged	-30.5	-5.4	1.4	2.0	2.0	2.0	0.6
Recreation and cultural services	-1.0	0.0	-0.1	0.0	0.1	0.3	0.0
Labour and manpower	-5.2	-1.9	0.3	0.4	0.5	0.6	0.1
Streets and highways	-3.6	-1.7	-0.6	0.0	0.5	1.0	-0.3
Industries							
Agriculture	-0.7	-0.4	-0.1	0.0	0.1	0.1	0.0
Other industries	-1.7	-0.5	0.0	0.1	0.3	0.4	0.0
General expenditures							
Assumption a	-42.1	-5.2	3.5	6.8	9.3	11.5	4.7
Assumption b	0.0	0.0	0.0	0.0	0.0	0.0	0.0
Total							
Assumption a	-312.6	-38.8	6.6	18.6	23.9	32.1	6.6
Assumption b	-270.5	-33.6	3.1	11.8	14.6	20.6	1.9

Assumption a: Collective goods allocated by same amount to everybody.
Assumption b: Collective goods allocated in proportion to net factor income.

Source: Franzén et al., (1975).

official statistics on disposable income. Some of the most obvious examples are craftsmen, professionals and small entrepreneurs engaged in barter and in the sale of services directly to households; owners of owner-occupied houses, particularly if they have large mortgages; parents who have been able to put their children in public day care centres (hence obtaining subsidies of some 30,000 kronor per year – tax free); "dishonest" people, engaged in economic crimes of various types like cheating with taxes and benefits, forgery, theft, drug peddling, prostitution, etc.; asset holders (legally) exploiting the possibilities of the tax system, for instance by way of high debt to finance the holdings of low-tax assets like lottery bonds, durable consumer goods, art, etc., in particular if the prices of these rise more rapidly than inflation in general.

FINAL COMMENT

The figures presented here strongly suggest that official information about the distribution of factor incomes is really quite *useless* as an indicator of the distribution of the command over economic resources or welfare – even if the statistics are completely reliable. We do not really know *how much* better the statistics on the distribution of (per capita) disposable income are in view of various statistical deficiencies. It is conceivable that a "high-tax society" moves us to a situation where officially recorded income statistics in fact hide very large individual income differences, and that the "true" income differences in that type of society depend less on productive contributions than on degrees of honesty and on the ability to avoid taxes, as well as on disparities in the return on dishonesty in different professions.

This Comment has *not* dealt with the consequences for the *performance* of the Swedish economy of the wide wedges between factor income and disposable income. However, perhaps we dare say that the Swedish experience suggests that it is possible to drive very wide wedges between factor incomes and disposable incomes without any *apparent breakdown* of the national economy – at least within, say, a decade or so. However, even if there is no "breakdown" within a few decades, it is of course likely that substantial disincentive effects, and hence economic inefficiencies, would arise – in particular perhaps in a long-run perspective such as several decades or even generations.[10]

NOTES

1. Pensions are concentrated to the three (or possibly four) lowest deciles, and the government loans to students to the lowest five deciles of the factor income distribution.

2. Jan Pen (1971).
3. When ordering deciles by disposable income, pensions are rather evenly spread over all the deciles, with an emphasis on the deciles one to eight. Government lending to students is also spread quite evenly, though with some emphasis on the deciles one to seven.
4. Sandelin and Södersten
5. The reason is that owner-occupied houses and debt play a somewhat more important role in the portfolios of middle-income and moderately high factor income brackets than in low-income brackets (where a large share of the portfolios is kept in bank deposits) and in the very high income brackets (where a larger share of the portfolios is kept in bonds, shares and apartment houses; Näslund (1977).
6. While the deficit on capital (Figure 7.11) is about 2 billion kronor, it is about 9 billion kronor on real estate.
7. Veckans Affärer (1979).
8. SIFO-study (1980).
9. Franzén et al., (1975).
10. For some preliminary attempts to pin down conceivable disincentive effects on work effort, see Lindbeck (1980) and Stuart (1980). For some estimates of the distortions of the returns on savings and investment, see Johnsson (1978), Hansson (1978) and Lodin (1978).

REFERENCES

Franzén, T., K. Lövgren and I. Rosenberg. "Redistributional Effects of Taxes and Public Expenditures in Sweden," *Swedish Journal of Economics* 77:1:31–35 (1975).

Hansson, I. "Skattesystemet, Inflationen och Investeringarna," *Ekonomisk Debatt,* No. 4 (1978).

Johansson, S. E. *Bilaga Till Kapitalmarknadsutredningen,* SOU 78:13, Stockholm: Ekonomidepartementet (1978).

Lindbeck, A. "Work Disincentives in the Welfare State," Lecture at Annual Meeting of the Austrian Economic Association, October 2 (1980).

Lodin, S. O. "Vårt Överansträngda Skattesystem," *Svensk Skattetidning,* No. 2–3 (1978).

Näslund, B. "Vem Förlorar på Inflationen?," *Ekonomisk Debatt,* No. 2, (1977).

Penn, J. *"A Parade of Dwarfs (and a Few Giants), "Income Distribution,* London: Penguin Press (1971).

Sandelin, B. and B. Södersten. *Betalt För Att Bo,* Stockholm: Raben & Sjögren (1978).

Stuart, C. This volume, Chapter 7.

DISCUSSION

Edited by: Walter Block

The analysis elicited from the Swedish presentation was very wide ranging. However, it is possible to discern four separate threads of thought.

The first dealt with savings, and the major participants were Professors Alchian, Lindbeck, and Giersch.

Armen Alchian: "What I find of great interest is the analysis of how far the price of an asset must fall for it to earn, say, 2 per cent, if the price level goes from 0 to 8 per cent per year. In other words, all those asset prices (except for the savings) are going to fall in price. These stock prices indicate almost a fall of 50 per cent, to about half their former level.

"It would be interesting to test that. One could try to obtain data on the Swedish stock market as a function of the rate of inflation and see if this is consistent with the hypothesis. What is puzzling to me is the savings rate. The savings account cannot be capitalized, so who in the world is putting money into Swedish savings accounts? Is it only bank trust accounts which are legally permitted to do that?"

Assar Lindbeck: "The amazing thing is that up until the early 1960s the savings ratio per household was about 7 per cent, according to national accounts. Then the Swedish government introduced a comprehensive pension system in the early 1960s, and we found that the savings ratio per household fell to 3 per cent by the end of the 1960s. We said that this must be because the government had taken over savings for the individual. But then the savings ratio reached 9 per cent in 1973, and has stayed there. However, I have heard that our statisticians are going to reduce the rate by re-definition of household saving. Professor Stuart mentioned some budget studies according to which expenditures would be higher than disposable income. But that does not fit the national account because, according to it, the savings ratio is certainly positive, even after the expected re-definition of the statistics. No, people do not patronize the banks so much. The big increase in savings is mainly in the form of owner-occupied houses, and, to some extent, also through collective bargaining agreements. There have also been some insurance systems created by agreements between employers and employees, and that explains much of the increase in savings."

Armen Alchian: "If I were an old person and had a savings account I would say, 'Take it out and put it in stocks.' I would then receive the normal rate of return on stocks because it has already been capitalized downwards. Although I've taken my licking once, I don't properly anticipate my losses through inflation. But given that the Swedish inflation rate is now 8 per cent, and the savings account will never be adjusted because you can't adjust the kronor account down, I would advise leaving the kronor account. A person would be better off withdrawing his money, and buying stocks with it. The only exception would be for banks who are under the trust laws. They are permitted to put money into trust accounts that earn practically nothing. They're safe. All you have to worry about is the nominal value. Why anybody, old or young, would keep a savings account there is a mystery. But the world is full of mysteries."

Herbert Giersch: "I wanted to ask a question about international capital flows. Professor Lindbeck said that it is not possible for foreigners to buy Swedish stocks, but Swedish firms can borrow abroad, and that should be able to keep the investment rate fairly high, despite a slowing down of the savings rate. Secondly, how much capital flight must there be, to call this an aspect of the underground economy? "

Assar Lindbeck: "The rate of return for firms is so low that firms don't want to invest in Sweden. So, Swedish multinational firms are mainly making their investments abroad, on their subsidiaries."

Armen Alchian: "Can they make their investment on personal services? I would think with the tax on so-called non-human assets in Sweden's corporate structure, there would be a tendency for Swedish firms to be specialized in insurance and other kinds of activities which require human skills and practically no physical capital."

Assar Lindbeck: "Yes, there is a very big development in that direction, but there is also a movement toward investing abroad in the subsidiaries, because most large Swedish firms are multinational."

The second strand concerned hidden taxation. The main protagonists were Professors Stuart, Buchanan, Alchian, Walters, and Dr. Walker.

James Buchanan: "I just wanted to ask Professor Stuart a couple of questions about his hidden tax table. It seems to me that if you count in the size of the budget deficit in that table, and then add, also, the inflation tax, that unless you are assuming that none of the deficit is monetized, you are double counting.

"The second point is related to that. Professor Stuart includes the inflation tax on cash balances in his hidden tax table. I want to find out, what did he assume about the structure of banking in that sense. It's a tax unless the banking system is assumed to be completely competitive. But it isn't. On the contrary, banks get a good part of that unless they pass it back to depositors. How did you calculate that figure for the inflation tax on cash, and didn't you double count with the deficit?"

Charles Stuart: "The inflation tax on cash balances equals the rate of inflation times the average real money supply over the period."

James Buchanan: "But part of that money supply is deposit money. That's the point."

Armen Alchian: "You see, that's the tax on the stockholder."

Charles Stuart. "I believe that I looked at bills when I did it."

James Buchanan: "So, it was just currency. That answers the question."

Armen Alchian: "Will you state the double counting issue again?"

James Buchanan: "Professor Stuart adds in as hidden taxes the size of the deficit, and he also adds in the inflation tax on cash. If part of the deficit is monetized, he is double counting. Implicitly, he must be assuming that none of it is monetized then."

Michael Walker: "The present value of the deficit, deferred taxes – what is the present value of deferred taxes in the form of, say, government bonds? The answer is the value of the deficit. It doesn't have to be monetized."

James Buchanan: "That's exactly my point. The present value of future taxes would be the full size of the deficit. But that would be assuming that it is the present value of future taxes. If any of it is monetized now, that would be in the inflation tax."

Alan Walters: "I find I disagree with the technical point raised by Professor Buchanan. It all depends on how you count signuerage. If signuerage is a tax, and I submit it is, then let's consider the following: zero inflation, just signuerage issue, which is then increased with the deficit. Thus we have a pure deficit, a pure signuerage deficit. Then, that surely is counted completely as part of the tax. But under Buchanan's system, it wouldn't be."

Attention then turned to Assar Lindbeck's assertion that the oil price rise was, in effect, an example of the Arabs raising taxes on the Swedes:

Zane Spindler: "I just wanted to raise a question with respect to Professor Lindbeck's assertion that the Arabs are doing the taxing for the Swedish government and therefore we don't have to worry about the deficit. I don't have any problem with considering OPEC as a government organization and their price increases as being equivalent to a tax . . ."

Armen Alchian: "Would you state the proposition again?"

Zane Spindler: "It seemed to me that Professor Lindbeck said that the deficit wasn't as much of a problem because the Arabs had increased these tax revenues that were balancing that."

Armen Alchian: "Can I ask why would the Arab tax apply to any deficit at all?"

Zane Spindler: "That's the question that I was raising. For it seems to me that, while it can be considered to be a tax of some sort, it's a tax which increases imports and reduces the net surplus; or increases the deficit and therefore reduces the ability to finance the deficit domestically."

James Buchanan: "That tax is like a storm."

Assar Lindbeck: "What happened is that purchasing power of

Swedish consumers is reduced by the Arab oil price increase. Of course that is a cost for the country. But to the extent that the Arab world is not able to absorb all their increased revenues, the rest of the world posts a deficit against the Arab countries. In the meantime, we borrow."

Zane Spindler: "You mean they re-invest it in Sweden."

Assar Lindbeck: "In the whole of the area and indirectly in Sweden because they re-invest in New York and London, and Swedish firms borrow money there."

Armen Alchian: "It's a balance of payment deficit."

Herbert Giersch: "I just wanted to object to the analogy of considering any deterioration of your terms of trade as a tax of foreigners on your domestic national product income. If we do that and consider it as a depressing influence, then we will always end up with expansionary fiscal policy to match that. This is not what I consider to be the market system's reaction to changes in relative prices. It may have an impact on international accounts, and what we observe now is that some of the countries who formerly had a surplus on current account now have a deficit on current account. And that's fine, because I think that this is equivalent to a new division of labour.

"The Arabs save and some countries invest, and my country (Germany) is now in a deficit on current account. Some people say that we live beyond our means. I reply to that and say we invest beyond our savings rate. It's a fine division of labour that the Arabs save and we invest."

Armen Alchian: "Of course, and then we expropriate them after twenty years."

The last topic of discussion contrasted the importance of inflation, with that of marginal rates of taxation, for public policy analysis.

Herbert Grubel started off as follows: "Could I ask a question on a very fundamental consideration? When we look at different countries, there are all kinds of different levels of marginal and average tax rates, and presumably Sweden was at the rate which the United States is now, ten or fifteen years ago. Suddenly the United States is finding that the Laffer curve is an important thing. Why didn't the same problem occur in Sweden fifteen years ago? Why did this phenomenon suddenly occur in the 1970s in many different countries? I wonder whether we are not going after the wrong thing, because what seems to be the common problem in all countries represented here in the late 1970s is the accelerating rate of inflation. That is what has caused people to become so terribly unhappy, not the different levels or the marginal rates of taxation. I wonder how you would react to this."

Assar Lindbeck: "I think this is a very important comment, because we have a nominalistic tax system, constructed for a world with a stable price level, and you get completely incredible results if you incorporate a 10 per cent, 15 per cent or 20 per cent inflation into such a system regardless of whether the tax model tax rate is 60 per cent or 80 per cent. So, I think Professor Grubel is quite right. If you make calculations of the distortions at zero inflation and 15 per cent inflation, you will get much greater differences than if you compared two countries with 60 per cent or 80 per cent model tax rates at a constant price level."

Armen Alchian: "It's the real versus the nominal tax that people are aware of."

Herbert Grubel: "I think the intellectual tendency on the subject is to blame the levels and the marginal tax rates, when it is really inflation that causes the distortion. Consider again that table on the negative rate of return on investment. We see this everywhere and it has gone on for a long time now. That, I think, is what we should be worrying about."

Herbert Giersch: "We ought to consider the combination of the tax system, inflation, and higher tax rates as compared to the 1960s plus a higher inflation rate. That creates a real problem, particularly the taxation of phantom profits."

Armen Alchian: "You've got to admit that the politicians are very clever for having invested in inflation. I wish we could do as well."

Hans-Georg Petersen: "I only add that increasing inflation diminishes money illusion and the tax illusion; tax awareness is increasing during inflation. Then we get the result that people are more aware of hidden and open tax increases."

Herbert Grubel: "What is the cost of inflation? I think there are just still too many intellectuals who feel that there is no cost to inflation at all, that all we have to do is index it. And I think this is just one instance of the kinds of things that have been neglected. So many people get rich as a result of wealth transfers, as a result of inflation. That is responsible for many of the attitudes that you have reported, I think, of people saying, 'Damn it, I'm being cheated by the system, now I'm going to start cheating as well.'"

Armen Alchian: "If you want a bigger government, there is nothing wrong with inflation. It's a damn good system for taxation."

As usual, we allow the paper-giver to have the last word. And Charles Stuart began by replying to the last comment: "I think, with regard to the Laffer curve, it's important, at least initially, to separate effects on labour and effects on taxation of labour and taxation of capital. With marginal tax rates for an average citizen of something like 80 per cent, it would be surprising if you didn't get disincentive effects, pretty serious disincentive effects, for working in the taxed portion of the economy. So, Laffer-type effects are very likely to occur.

"Before we analyze it in a country like Sweden, I'm not so sure that they're likely to occur in the United States. It may be the case that

Americans are basically less law abiding than Swedes are, but that puts us out on thin ice. I'm not sure the Laffer curve is as important for the United States for labour as it is for a country like Sweden.

"As far as capital is concerned, I think it is liable to be important too. I think it is analytically correct to look at how the rate of inflation influences the marginal tax rate on different sorts of capital investment. We have had a regime of a 10 per cent rate of inflation over a long period of time, and a tax system which is based on nominal taxation of capital. We should then calculate the effective marginal tax rate on capital. That might be 100 per cent for a specific sort of capital, and we should then expect, for that sort of capital, fairly serious misallocation effects. Whether we want to call that a Laffer effect or just a distortion or what title we want to put on it, I think, is a matter of preference. The Laffer curve to me, intuitively, seems more in place as regards labour than capital, just as a terminology, but that is arbitrary.

"As regards Assar Lindbeck's comments, I am very interested in this matter of taxation of labour and capital. I have a suspicion, and it's just a suspicion at this stage and it might not be correct, regarding taxation of labour. I feel that labour is much more sensitive to taxation than is capital. That is to say, for a given marginal tax rate, you'll find a bigger disincentive effect, or distortion, if you raised the tax rate on labour by 1 per cent than if you raised it on capital by 1 per cent. The reason I suspect this is that labour can quit, capital is locked into companies. Once people have made an investment in a company, it's locked in, and if you put a high rate of taxation on removing the funds from the company, people will tend to leave the money in the company anyway. That company may grow, but there will be a reduction in the number of such new companies. So, I think that taxation on capital is liable to have a different kind of effect in the economy than a tax on labour. Labour is just liable to drive people out of the taxed sector, whereas capital has a harder time moving. That, again is just a suspicion.

"I would like to answer two points upon which I was mildly criticized. One was the business of the budget deficit. For this year it is roughly 50 billion kroner, roughly 10 per cent of the GNP. I don't remember my exact formulation, but when I counted the yearly *deficit financing*, I did not just look at the budget deficit. The budget deficit I take to be merely suggestive, because there are a lot of adjustments to it which one would make. Certainly one would want to, ideally, make the adjustment which Lindbeck suggested: to also count pension contributions. This would, therefore, reduce the budget deficits because the government receives substantial funds in the form of pension contributions.

"At the same time, the pension system has future obligations. So if we are going to really do the bookkeeping correctly, we should also take account of them. Whether the 50 billion figure would stand or not after we go through the whole host of bookkeeping corrections is another question. My suspicion is that it would be lower. When I went through and calculated this deficit financing of the central government, I got negative figures for most of the period 1950 to 1970. Then I calculated deficit financing, not just looking at the budget deficit. So I suspect that this 50 billion figure is an overestimate. At the same time I think that the big increase is very suggestive that there is a problem there.

"The second point was this business of the lag for reaching equilibrium and the decrease in the growth rate that would be explained. I think I was pretty careful to mention that the growth rate reduction would be explained only if we assumed that a full equilibrium adjustment had occurred. It seems likely that quite a bit less than a full equilibrium adjustment has actually occurred. I would not want to be held to saying that half or three-quarters of the reduction of the Swedish growth rate depends on increases in taxes. I think that there is probably some effect, but it's pretty clear that the adjustment has not been complete.

"Also on this business of the lag – I suspect that this lag is a very long one. The crucial parameter in the model that I have referred to turns out to be the elasticity of substitution between the product of the taxed and untaxed sectors. A rough equivalent of that parameter is estimated by Wales and Woodland using cross section data. Cross section data should tell us what is going to happen in the long run, but I suspect that that long run is very long indeed.

"I don't think that five years is really sufficient for a complete adjustment. We should be very careful to try to take account of what is going to happen five or ten years down the road, in order to judge the effects of taxes on society. We should not simply say, 'Well, that's so far down the road that we will exclude it.' And while Professor Lindbeck did not put it that way, he didn't say quite that strongly that the effects way down the road are not important, I think it's very important, nonetheless, to really look at the long run."

CHAPTER 8

THE IMPACT OF THE TAX SYSTEM – FEDERAL REPUBLIC OF GERMANY

By Hans-Georg Petersen

I. INTRODUCTION

Since the strong decline of GNP growth rates in many countries in the mid-1970s, discussion of the influence of taxation on economic activities has been intensified. Often the increase of the public sector is cited as one important growth-retarding factor. The growth of the public sector is expressed on the revenue side of the budget as an increasing average tax rate.[1] Many people consider that the average tax rate has reached or already exceeds the tax burden limit.[2]

In this paper the attempt will be made to survey recent discussions of the impact of taxation on economic activities in the Federal Republic of Germany.[3] Part II deals with the influence of taxation on the supply of effort: on incentives to work as well as incentives to save and to invest. In Part III we try to shed light on the correlation between taxation and growth and in Part IV the redistribution effects of the German tax system are discussed. In Part V the impact of inflation on the tax system is analysed and Part VI tries to answer the question of which maximum average as well as maximum marginal tax rate would be appropriate. As well, some brief remarks about the implications for future tax policies are made.

II. THE IMPACT OF TAXATION ON THE SUPPLY OF EFFORT

Many attempts have been made in the literature to evaluate the limits of taxation by its effects on the supply of effort. The discussions of the micro-effects of taxation on the work supply (incentives to work)[4] as well as the capital formation (incentives to save and to invest) have not led to unequivocal results. Whether income effects or substitution effects dominate has remained theoretically and empirically an unsolved problem.

Recently some attempts have been made to estimate the disincentive effects by using macro-data and regression analysis.[5] The data and the methods used are imperfect; the interpretations of the results are rather speculative and give no evidence for causal relationships; but at least some interesting trends can be seen.

IMPACT OF TAXATION ON THE SUPPLY OF WORK

There are only a few empirical studies on the impact of taxation on the supply of work in Germany.[6] This is not very surprising because during the first two decades after World War II only high earnings were covered by income tax. This changed markedly in the late 1960s and 1970s: the growth process in Germany was accompanied by secular inflation of varying intensity, but income tax rates and the exemption regulation remained constant in the decade 1965 to 1975. The tax on wages became the one with the highest revenue of all single taxes. Today people with relatively low earnings must pay income taxes, however in the lower income brackets, tax is sharply graduated.[7]

A first comprehensive attempt to evaluate the incentive effects of taxation was made by Koch (1978). Because econometric models did not lead to unequivocal results, and experiments in the social sciences are not usual in Germany, he used the method of field interviews, which naturally has its own problems.[8] He interviewed two groups of income tax payers: salary earners on the one hand (foremen and craftsmen in manufacturing plants in Schleswig-Holstein) and the self-employed on the other hand (general medical practitioners, veterinarians, dental surgeons, architects, lawyers, and tax consultants in Schleswig-Holstein).

The interview question which is pertinent here is: "if the government were to increase income taxes by 10 per cent (100 per cent),[9] how would you react?" It is obvious (see Table 8.1) that in the latter case the reactions of the taxpayers are stronger. Category (1) describes the income effect, Category (2) the substitution effect. With one exception (10 per cent, Foreman, 1974) the income effect is larger than the substitution effect. If one uses household rather than individual income, categories (1) plus (4) comprise the income effect, thus rendering the differences between income and substitution effects even greater. Category (3) represents those salary earners who will compensate for the higher tax burden by working in their leisure time, in many cases earning non-taxed income. If we add (2) + (5), we have an estimate of those who might be willing to work in the underground economy (barter economy), engaging either in illicit (non-taxed) or do-it-yourself work.

Table 8.2 indicates the responses of self-employed persons, who have higher pre-tax incomes than the salary earners of Table 8.1. The income effect (1) is relatively small compared to Table 8.1, with the ex-

TABLE 8.1

Reactions of Foremen and Craftsmen to an Income Tax Increase According to Interviews Taken in 1972/73 and 1974 (Per Cent of Sample Size)

	How would you react to an income tax increase of 10 per cent of the average tax rate?						100 per cent of the average tax rate?					
	Total		Foremen		Craftsmen		Total		Foremen		Craftsmen	
	1972/73	1974	1972/73	1974	1972/73	1974	1972/73	1974	1972/73	1974	1972/73	1974
1. I would work more hours (overtime).	14.2	8.9	15.8	6.8	13.4	10.1	28.1	25.5	28.8	25.0	27.6	25.8
2. I would work fewer hours.	3.6	4.9	5.8	6.8	2.4	3.7	5.2	10.0	5.8	15.9	4.9	6.5
3. I would continue working the same number of hours in my present firm, but would try to earn additional income during my leisure time (on weekends).	17.4	13.2	23.0	18.9	14.2	9.7	22.9	23.5	24.0	31.8	21.9	18.4
4. My spouse would earn additional income.	2.1	2.6	2.9	4.5	1.6	1.4	10.9	11.2	12.3	12.1	10.2	10.6
5. I would continue working the same number of hours.	72.4	74.2	66.9	70.5	75.6	76.5	42.1	38.7	40.3	31.8	43.1	42.9
6. Other answers.	4.5	6.1	3.5	5.3	4.9	6.5	11.2	8.3	11.7	6.8	10.9	7.2
Total (a)	114.2	109.9	117.9	112.8	112.1	107.9	120.4	117.2	122.9	123.4	118.6	113.4
Sample size	385	349	139	132	246	217	385	349	139	132	246	217

(a) Multiple answers possible.
Source: Koch (1978, Tables 4.2.50, 4.2.51).

TABLE 8.2

Reactions of Self-employed Persons to a 10 Per Cent Income Tax Increase According to Interviews Taken in 1974 (Per Cent of Sample Size)

Answer	General Practitioners	Veterinarians	Dental Surgeons	Architects	Lawyers	Tax Consultants
1. I would work more hours	2.1	2.1	3.2	9.9	5.8	3.0
2. I would work fewer hours	25.1	14.4	41.8	23.6	14.8	11.2
3. The tax increase would have no impact on my working hours	61.3	53.1	39.6	40.3	60.5	53.2
4. I would be content with a lower net income	5.4	2.6	5.3	4.3	5.4	5.2
5. I would try to take better advantage of legal tax concessions	46.7	39.7	44.4	47.2	40.4	10.0
6. I would try to reduce my tax burden by additional depreciations	15.1	14.4	15.9	26.6	17.0	3.0
7. Other answers	44.9	63.4	51.8	29.6	48.9	40.9
Total[a]	200.6	189.7	202.0	181.5	192.8	126.5
Sample Size	390	194	791	233	223	269

[a] Multiple answers possible.

Source: Koch (1978, Table 4.2.48).

ception of the architects, who have the lowest incomes of the self-employed. The substitution effect (2) on the other hand is relatively high compared to Table 8.1 (especially for the dental surgeons who have the highest pre-tax incomes of the self-employed); and in all cases the substitution effect is larger than the income effect. The self-employed have —unlike the salary earners—further possibilities to react to tax increases. Avoiding taxes by better utilizing existing tax concessions and additional depreciations plays—as categories (5) and (6) demonstrate —an important role.[10] The distinction between business and personal expenditures is hard to make especially for the self-employed. We may surmise, then, that some "illicit consumption" is involved in category (6).

INCOME AND SUBSTITUTION EFFECTS

Tables 8.1 and 8.2 give some evidence that income and substitution effects are dependent on the level of individual earnings and on the level of the income taxation. It is likely at relatively low levels of each that the income effect is larger than the substitution effect. As they increase, —especially given a progressive income tax—the substitution effect becomes more and more important and finally dominates the income effect (see Beenstock, 1979, p. 10).

Table 8.3 shows the tax rates at which the self-employed will change their supply of effort; these have been called "critical tax rates."[11] The interviews ask only for the critical average tax rates;[12] the marginal tax rates have been calculated from the German income tax regulations for 1965. In the cases where the supply of effort has not yet been affected by income taxation (60.3 per cent of the general practitioners, 58.2 per cent of the veterinarians, etc.) the critical tax rates are higher than the effective tax rates respectively (see line (1)). In the cases where supply of effort has been affected by income taxation the critical tax rates are lower than the effective tax rates (with the exception of the lawyers[13]) (see line (3)). In the other cases the critical tax rate has just been reached. The results demonstrate that, especially with regard to the marginal tax rate, the critical values are nearly reached in the cases where supply of effort has not yet been affected, whereas the differences between critical and effective values with regard to the average tax rates are considerably higher. Compared to the first group, in the second group—where the critical tax rates are just attained—and in the third group—where the critical tax rates already affected the supply of effort—the effective tax rates are higher. The strongest reactions to be observed are those of the dental surgeons, who have the highest pre-tax incomes; more than 50 per cent will reduce or already have reduced their supply of effort. On the other hand the third group demonstrates

TABLE 8.3

Critical Tax Rates and Supply of Effort for the Self-employed (Per Cent)

Effective and Critical Tax Rates		General Practitioners	Veterinarians	Dental Surgeons	Architects	Lawyers	Tax Consultants
1. Supply of effort not yet affected by income taxation	effective average rate	39.6	28.2	39.1	26.5	30.5	28.1
	effective marginal rate	50.3	41.4	49.9	39.7	43.4	41.2
	critical average rate	49.9	38.0	51.5	39.2	45.0	45.6
	critical marginal rate	53.0	49.5	53.0	49.9	53.0	53.0
	(in per cent of the sample)	(60.3)	(58.2)	(38.8)	(57.5)	(59.6)	(70.6)
2. The attained effective tax rates represent the critical tax rates	average rate	41.3	31.1	44.1	30.3	35.8	31.1
	marginal rate	51.5	43.9	53.0	43.2	48.1	43.9
	(in per cent of the sample)	(26.9)	(26.3)	(43.7)	(30.0)	(30.5)	(21.2)
3. Supply of effort already affected by income taxation	effective average rate	42.9	32.7	42.1	41.6	33.9	42.3
	effective marginal rate	53.0	45.4	51.8	51.6	46.5	51.9
	critical average rate	36.4	28.0	37.4	33.6	35.3	37.0
	critical marginal rate	48.5	41.1	49.1	46.1	47.7	48.9
	(in per cent of the sample)	(7.2)	(5.7)	(10.7)	(7.3)	(3.6)	(4.1)
Sample size		390	194	791	233	223	269

Marginal tax rates calculated from the German income tax regulations for 1965.

Source: Koch (1978, Tables 4.3.3 and 4.3.5).

that although the critical tax rates have been surpassed, they nevertheless have continued to work. One can assume that this group would have increased work effort, if income tax rates had been lower. But some uncertainty about their real reactions affecting the supply of effort still remains, especially when considering the potentially strategic character of the answers.

Apart from this problem it is very interesting to compare the critical tax rates of the self-employed with the effective burdens of wage taxes and social insurance contributions on salary earners.[14] Table 8.4 shows the effective average and marginal rates of wage taxes and of social insurance contributions for the gross wages of public employees[15] in the Federal Republic of Germany in January 1979 for the entire public service employees (BAT) wage scale. The wage scale of public service employees has been chosen because it includes the normal range of salaries[16] in Germany and statistics are readily available.

MARGINAL WAGE TAXATION

The marginal rate of wage taxes including social insurance contributions is 39 per cent in the lowest wage group (BAT X);[17] it increases up to wage group BAT IVb (for unmarried employees), where it reaches the highest observed value of 58.7 per cent. Then the marginal rate t^m declines, because the limit for compulsory health insurance has been reached.[18] In the next four wage groups the marginal rate increases, until in wage group BAT Ib the limits for compulsory retirement insurance and unemployment insurance are reached.[19] Then the further increase in marginal rates is only due to the progression in the income tax.

Without a doubt the social insurance contributions have a slightly different character than taxes. This is true especially in the case of retirement insurance, where the benefit-principle plays a certain role. But with increasing burdens, this fine difference loses its importance.[20] Therefore it is likely that the reactions to an increase in social insurance contributions are similar to those which follow from an increase in income taxation.

Comparing the critical marginal tax rates of the self-employed and the effective marginal burdens (t^m) of the public service employees (especially in the case of unmarried employees)[21] shows that in the middle of the wage scale the effective marginal burdens are at times considerably higher.[22] At these high effective marginal rates a relatively high percentage of the self-employed will reduce or have already reduced their supply of effort. Therefore it seems likely that these high marginal rates have disincentive effects on the work supply.

TABLE 8.4

Average and Marginal Rates of Wage Taxes ($\bar{t}_w$, t_w^m)[a], of Social Insurance Contributions ($\bar{t}_s$, t_s^m)[b] and of their sum ($\bar{t}$, t^m) for the Gross Wages of Public Service Employees in the Federal Republic of Germany, 1979

Wage - Tax - Bracket I (Unmarried Employees)									
Wage Group (BAT)	Annual Gross Wages (in DM)	Annual Net Wages (in DM)	$\bar{t}$	$\bar{t}_w$	$\bar{t}_s$	t^m	t_w^m	t_s^m
I	70,167.87	39,143.87	0.442	0.337	0.105	0.511	0.511	—
Ia	61,596.58	34,902.58	0.433	0.314	0.119	0.497	0.497	—
Ib	57,018.24	32,599.24	0.428	0.299	0.129	0.487	0.487	—
IIa	51,700.22	29,811.22	0.423	0.281	0.142	0.581	0.476	0.105
IIb	47,080.13	27,774.85	0.410	0.262	0.148	0.567	0.462	0.105
III	46,826.76	27,670.68	0.409	0.261	0.148	0.566	0.461	0.105
IVa	43,339.51	26,116.99	0.397	0.245	0.152	0.554	0.449	0.105
IVb	37,942.95	23,642.35	0.377	0.217	0.160	0.587	0.417	0.170
Va	34,845.18	22,305.38	0.360	0.201	0.159	0.565	0.395	0.170
Vb	33,814.15	21,836.55	0.354	0.195	0.159	0.555	0.385	0.170
Vc	30,930.36	20,502.80	0.337	0.178	0.159	0.526	0.356	0.170
VIa	30,404.38	20,244.58	0.334	0.175	0.159	0.522	0.352	0.170
VIb	28,670.44	19,387.08	0.324	0.165	0.159	0.502	0.332	0.170
VII	25,906.55	17,882.95	0.310	0.150	0.160	0.463	0.293	0.170
VIII	23,620.98	16,609.58	0.297	0.140	0.157	0.429	0.259	0.170
IXa	22,883.75	16,158.59	0.294	0.135	0.159	0.415	0.245	0.170
IXb	22,083.21	15,669.61	0.290	0.131	0.159	0.401	0.231	0.170
X	21,213.90	15,130.10	0.287	0.128	0.159	0.390	0.220	0.170

TABLE 8.4 (continued)

Wage - Tax - Bracket III/O (Married Employees, No Children)								
I	71,519.61	48,805.61	0.318	0.214	0.104	0.408	0.408	—
Ia	62,948.32	43,566.32	0.308	0.190	0.118	0.371	0.371	—
Ib	58,369.98	40,467.98	0.304	0.177	0.127	0.346	0.346	—
IIa	53,201.96	37,289.96	0.299	0.162	0.137	0.315	0.315	—
IIb	49,227.34	34,570.86	0.298	0.157	0.141	0.391	0.286	0.105
III	48,178.50	33,897.94	0.296	0.148	0.148	0.382	0.277	0.105
IVa	44,691.25	31,607.13	0.293	0.141	0.152	0.355	0.250	0.105
IVb	39,294.69	27,915.37	0.290	0.131	0.159	0.325	0.220	0.105
Va	36,196.92	25,883.76	0.285	0.125	0.160	0.390	0.220	0.170
Vb	35,534.44	25,463.44	0.283	0.123	0.160	0.390	0.220	0.170
Vc	32,217.88	23,356.32	0.275	0.116	0.159	0.390	0.220	0.170
VIa	31,691.80	23,015.84	0.274	0.114	0.160	0.390	0.220	0.170
VIb	29,957.96	21,920.56	0.268	0.109	0.159	0.390	0.220	0.170
VII	27,494.07	20,342.47	0.260	0.101	0.159	0.390	0.220	0.170
VIII	24,908.50	18,683.94	0.250	0.091	0.159	0.390	0.220	0.170
IXa	24,171.27	18,183.11	0.248	0.087	0.161	0.390	0.220	0.170
IXb	23,370.73	17,709.77	0.242	0.083	0.159	0.390	0.220	0.170
X	22,501.42	17,100.46	0.240	0.080	0.160	0.390	0.220	0.170

[a] Marginal tax rates t_w^m calculated from income tax regulations for 1979.

[b] Marginal social insurance contribution rates on normal income increases (not, for example, on holiday pay).

Source: Petersen (1979b, Appendix Tables 9, 10 and 11).

Figure 8.1
One Person Household

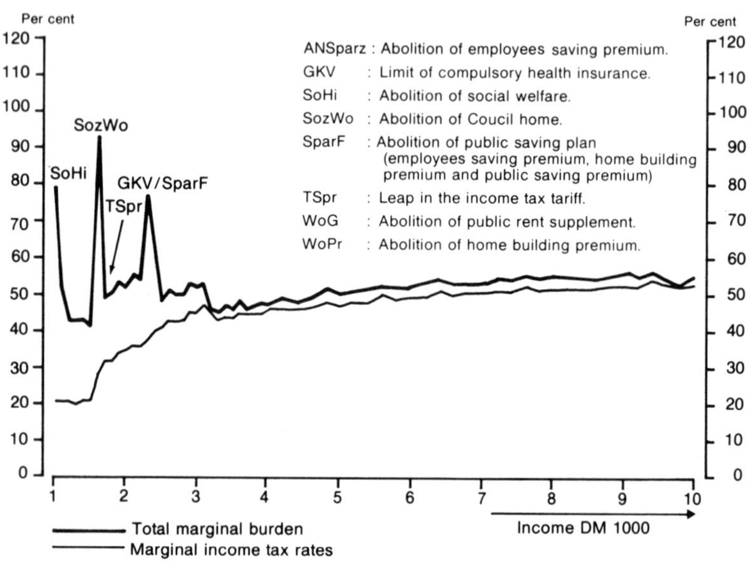

Source: Karrenberg and Kitterer (1979)

For Protestants and Roman Catholics the church tax has marginal rates between 2 per cent on low incomes and 5 per cent on high incomes.[23] The marginal tax rate of indirect taxes to gross income has been estimated by Karrenberg and Kitterer (1979, p. 130) at between 8 per cent in the lower (up to a gross income of DM 2500 monthly) and 1 per cent on the higher income brackets (about DM 8000 monthly). If one adds these marginal tax rates to the marginal rates of wage taxes and social security contributions, in the wage group BAT IVb the marginal burden of all taxes including social security contributions reaches almost the maximum of 70 per cent of gross income.[24] Naturally the marginal rates of indirect taxes are less noticeable to taxpayers, but international cross-section analyses have shown that the "imperceptibility" of indirect taxes disappears with an increasing tax burden.[25]

If additional transfers to households are taken into consideration, which would overextend the topic of this paper, one can observe combined marginal tax and transfer rates, which are considerably higher than 100 per cent—because of uncoordinated income brackets and the

Figure 8.2
Two Person Household

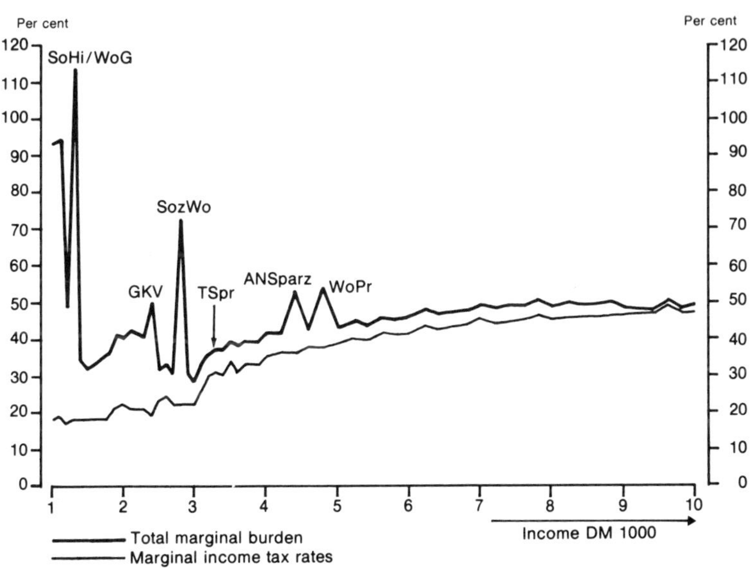

Source: Karrenberg and Kitterer (1979)

sudden abolishment of transfer payments. Figure 8.1 shows the course of such combined marginal rates over the entire income scale for one-person households and Figure 8.2 shows the corresponding rates for a two-person household (with only one salary earner). The examples above should make it clear that disincentive effects on the work supply are likely to exist within present-day tax and transfer systems—especially for wives—and that the disincentive effects in Germany are particularly strong in the lower and middle income brackets. If critical reactions have not yet taken place, one must still be very careful with further increases of the marginal rates of income taxes as well as social security contributions. The negative impact of taxation on the work supply is likely limited to overtime work, because the nominal number of hours which salary earners work is fixed by collective bargaining agreements. But negative impacts on morale at work and especially impacts on additional illicit (non-taxed) work as well as on the do-it-yourself movement are possible. If effective, the underground (barter) economy might grow faster than the market economy.

IMPACT OF TAXATION ON SAVINGS AND INVESTMENTS

There are only a few empirical studies on the impact of taxation on the supply of work. The same is true for studies on the impact of taxation on savings of the private sector. It is difficult enough to determine whether or not taxation changes the supply of work, let alone to determine in which direction the marginal propensity to save could be influenced.[26] In low earnings brackets, where the income effect dominates, the marginal propensity to save is low and the effects on saving depend on the extent to which the additional tax burden could be compensated for by additional work supply. If full compensation is possible, it is likely that savings will be constant; if not, savings will decline, because taxpayers will want to maintain their consumption standard.

In the income brackets where the substitution effect dominates, it is possible that, as the result of additional illicit work or do-it-yourself activity, savings will be kept constant; otherwise, if the consumption standard is just maintained, savings will decline. It is nearly impossible to estimate these different effects because a micro-model of the taxpayer's behaviour does not yet exist. Therefore we can only estimate some rough development trends with regression analyses, using simple macro-data from the German National Accounts Statistics.

To shed light on the relationship between the savings of private households and taxation, total taxes have been divided into two groups: taxes on private households and taxes on the corporate sector. The taxes on private households are (1) wage taxes, (2) value-added taxes, (3) excise duties, (4) import levies, and (5) employee contributions to the social insurance system. With this definition of taxes on private households it is assumed that no shifting has occurred, or, using Musgrave's (1959, p. 230) terminology—that effective incidence is the same as impact incidence.

The ratio of taxes on private households to employee gross income has been computed from the German National Accounts Statistics. This ratio (TPH)[27] has been correlated with the growth rate of real savings for private households $\dot{S}$:

$$(1)\quad \dot{S} = a + b\,TPH$$

Estimating the regression equation over the whole sample period yielded:

$$(2)\quad \dot{S} = 62.657 - 1.528\,TPH$$

$$F = 3.938;\ \bar{R}^2 = 0.140;\ DW = 1.1817;\ N = 18.$$

F is the F-test value, $\bar{R}^2$ the adjusted R squared, DW the Durbin-Watson-test and N the number of cases. The F-test value is significant at 10 per cent, and the DW-test rejects serial correlation. The adjusted R squared shows that a weak negative correlation exists between the growth rate of savings of private households and the tax ratio TPH. Dividing this ratio into a ratio of taxes on private households excluding social security contributions TPH_T and a ratio of the social security contributions of employees TPH_{SOC} to gross income of employees, gave the results:

$$(3)\quad \dot{S} = 63.736 - 2.074\ TPH_T$$
$$F = 2.629;\ \bar{R}^2 = 0.083;\ DW = 1.722;\ N = 18.$$

$$(4)\quad \dot{S} = 52.163 - 1.792\ TPH_{SOC}$$
$$F = 3.728^*;\ \bar{R}^2 = 0.132;\ DW = 1.987;\ N = 18.$$

The multiple regression for both components yielded:

$$(5)\quad \dot{S} = 14.521 + \underset{(0.675)}{2.101\ TPH_T} - \underset{(3.413^*)}{7.212\ TPH_{SOC}}$$
$$F = 3.208^*;\ \bar{R}^2 = 0.197;\ DW = 2.172;\ N = 18.$$

where F-test values of the coefficients are given in parentheses; asterisks indicate coefficients statistically significant at the 10 per cent level. Interpreting the results of equations (3) to (5): There is some evidence of a weak negative correlation between the growth rate of private household saving and social security taxes, whereas there is no significance for a corresponding correlation between private savings and the taxes on private households; the sign changes as well from the simple to the multiple regression equation.[28]

CAUTION NEEDED

There are several reasons to consider these estimates with great care. Not the least of these is the fact that all other relevant variables, which might have an impact on private household savings, are included in the error term.[29] But as stated above these results should only be interpreted as trend results; even so, however, some speculations can reasonably be made.

The impact of taxation on private investment is discussed among others by Roskamp (1959, p. 258–332), who analyses the influence of different tax exemptions favouring capital formation in the post-war period (1948–1957) in Germany. The combination of high marginal income tax rates with numerous tax exemptions (especially depreciation allowances) led to high investments in this period.[30] During the following decade marginal tax rates were lowered and tax exemptions were partially abolished.

Another attempt to estimate the effects of changes in the tax system on private investments with a macroeconomic tax model[31] has been made by Beckmann and Uebe (1970). The Wissenschaftlicher Beirat beim Bundesministerium der Finanzen (1967) made the proposal to increase direct taxation (income taxes, corporate income taxes and inheritance taxes) by about DM 5 billion and to lower indirect taxation by the same amount. Beckmann and Uebe (1970, p. 12–13) estimated that an increase in the profit tax rates of about 5 per cent would lead to a strong decline in investments[32] and cause a decline in economic growth, similar in magnitude to the decline in economic growth resulting from the recession of 1967 in Germany. But the result is predetermined by the investment function used, and by a causation chain which leads from profit taxation via investment to economic growth.

In later studies, for instance, a study of the "Institut Finanzen und Steuern" (1978) simple time series of the development of investment and corporate taxation have been compared without using any model. The "Institut Finanzen und Steuern" (1978, p. 95) observed that for the years up to 1977: "The analysis of the long-termed development of investment makes it obvious that the annual growth rates of investments are declining permanently. The high growth rates of tax yield are leading to 'fiscal drag' effects on economic growth." Therefore strong changes within the system of corporate taxation were considered necessary.

It is obvious that, up to now, retained profits have been taxed at relatively high rates. In an international comparison the Institut der deutschen Wirtschaft (1979, p. 3) observed the highest tax rates on retained profits for corporations in Germany,[33] but in this comparison the effect of the capital gains taxes in countries such as the U.K. and U.S. has been neglected. For the years following 1977 we again have relatively high positive growth rates for private investments,[34] despite the fact that no substantial changes have been made in tax legislation for retained profits.

To focus more clearly on the relations between private investment and taxation we use a relatively simple approach. The taxes on the corporate sector are (1) taxes on incomes of entrepreneurial activities and wealth, (2) corporation income taxes, (3) other taxes on corporations, (4) occupation taxes, (5) payroll taxes,[36] (6) real-estate taxes,[37] and (7) employers' contributions to social security insurance. It is also assumed that no shifting has occurred, the worst-possible-situation for the corporate sector.

The ratio of taxes on the corporate sector to gross income on entrepreneurial activities and wealth[37] (TCW) has been correlated with the growth of the real private investments I:

$$(6)\quad \dot{I} = a + b\ TCW$$

Estimating the regression equation over the whole sample period yielded:

$$(7)\quad \dot{I} = 24.879 - 0.345\ TCW$$
$$F = 2.377;\ \bar{R}^2 = 0.071;\ DW = 1.276;\ N = 18.$$

The ratio TCW has been divided into a ratio for taxes on the corporate sector TCW_T and a ratio for employers' social security contributions TCW_{SOC}. The regressions gave the results:

$$(8)\quad \dot{I} = 13.687 - 0.284\ TCW_T$$
$$F = 0.373;\ \bar{R}^2 = -0.036;\ DW = 1.181;\ N = 18.$$

$$(9)\quad \dot{I} = 10.757 - 0.287\ TCW_{SOC}$$
$$F = 1.483;\ \bar{R}^2 = 0.026;\ DW = 1.230;\ N = 18.$$

The multiple regression for both components yielded:

$$(10)\quad \dot{I} = 27.145 - \underset{(0.807)}{0.416\ TCW_T} - \underset{(1.881)}{0.332\ TCW_{SOC}}$$
$$F = 1.137;\ \bar{R}^2 = 0.015;\ DW = 1.337;\ N = 18.$$

The F-test values are not statistically significant. The $\bar{R}^2$ values are extremely low, so it appears that negative correlations do not exist. This is not very surprising, if one looks at the development of the ratio TCW_T in the sample period.[38] (It has been relatively constant.) The ratio TCW_{SOC} has nearly doubled since 1960, but the negative signs in equations (8) and (9), are not significant either. If further variables were added, stronger correlations might be possible. However, if tax shifting is taken into consideration, the opposite results could occur.

III. IMPACT OF THE TAX SYSTEM ON ECONOMIC GROWTH

The question which will be discussed in this section is: what connection exists between the average tax rate and economic growth? As in the regressions above, for the following analyses we use simple macro-data from the German National Accounts Statistics.[39] Economic growth is measured here as the annual growth rate of the real gross national product $\dot{Y}_R$.[40] The equation which will be tested is:

$$\dot{Y}_R = a - c\,T$$

where T indicates the macroeconomic average tax rate (including social security contributions). With this equation we only test the maximum influence of taxation which is theoretically possible; all other relevant variables are incorporated into the error term. Therefore the following analyses should be interpreted as trend results.

For the sample period from 1951 to 1982[41] the corresponding regression equation gave the result:

$$(11)\quad \dot{Y}_R = 21.983 - 0.469\,T$$
$$F = 14.595;\ \bar{R}^2 = 0.305;\ DW = 1.466;\ N = 32.$$

where the F-test is significant at 1 per cent, and the Durbin-Watson-test (DW) rejects serial correlation. The adjusted R squared ($\bar{R}^2$) shows that a weak negative correlation exists between growth rate and average tax rate in Germany over the sample period.

The yield elasticity of the tax system during the most recent years and high nominal and real growth rates of income have caused the strong increase in the average tax rates in spite of some autonomous tax reductions (see Neumark, 1979). This growth has—because of different yield elasticities of the various taxes—some consequences for the tax structure. The direct average tax rate, the average tax rate of the social security contributions[42] as well as the ratios of these taxes to total taxation considerably increased during the sample period. In contrast, the indirect average tax rate as well as the share of indirect taxes in total taxation declined.

DIRECT AND INDIRECT TAXATION

Therefore the total average tax rate has been divided into shares of direct and indirect taxation (TDIR and TIND) and social insurance contributions (TSOC) to gross national product.[43] Estimating the regression equations gave these results:

$$(12)\quad \dot{Y}_R = 15.230 - 0.929\,TDIR$$
$$F = 12.387;\ \bar{R}^2 = 0.269;\ DW = 1.436;\ N = 32.$$

$$(13)\quad \dot{Y}_R = -29.484 + 2.612\,TIND$$
$$F = 15.603;\ \bar{R}^2 = 0.320;\ DW = 1.633;\ N = 32.$$

$$(14)\quad \dot{Y}_R = 13.879 - 0.795\,TSOC$$
$$F = 12.387;\ \bar{R}^2 = 0.290;\ DW = 1.401;\ N = 32.$$

The simple linear regression equations are all significant; a weak negative correlation can be observed between both the direct average tax rate (TDIR) and the average rate of the social insurance contributions (TSOC) and the growth rate, whereas there is a positive correlation between the indirect average tax rate (TIND) and the growth rate.

Estimating the multiple regression equation over the whole sample period yielded:

$$(15)\quad \dot{Y}_R = -20.117 - \underset{(0.40)}{0.389\,TDIR} + \underset{(1.51)}{2.126\,TIND} + \underset{(0.03)}{0.118\,TSOC}$$

$$F = 5.126;\ \bar{R}^2 = 0.285;\ DW = 1.615;\ N = 32.$$

Only in the case of the average rate of the social security contributions does the sign change, however, the values of the F-test (in parentheses) are not significant.

Compared to the linear regression with the total average tax rate (see equation (11)), the adjusted R squared deteriorated. In the sample period, a negative correlation is likely between the direct average tax rate and the growth rate for Germany.

Considering the aggregated disincentive effects of taxation on the supply of effort (see Beenstock, 1979, p. 10), it seems likely that, especially when secular inflation is accompanied by real economic growth, the phenomenon of "fiscal drag" exists (see Neumark, 1979, p. 197). In the case of Germany this "fiscal drag" effect was mostly caused by direct taxes; the fact that indirect taxation is less noticeable to the citizens than direct taxation likely leads to less growth retarding pressure. But—as international cross-section analyses have shown—as indirect taxation increases it, too, is correlated with declining growth rates.[44]

IV. REDISTRIBUTION EFFECTS OF THE TAX SYSTEM

The ability-to-pay principle as well as the redistribution principle of taxation are seen particularly in progressive income taxes, the most important progressive taxes in the German tax system. Figure 8.3 shows the progressive tax rates as well as the exemption regulations for all levels of income in the wage-tax-bracket I (unmarried salary earners) measured by the yield elasticity.* Figure 8.4 shows the corresponding

* Elasticity is defined as the numerical relationship of change between two different variables. For example, the Yield Elasticity of Tax, with respect to Income (Et,y) is defined as:

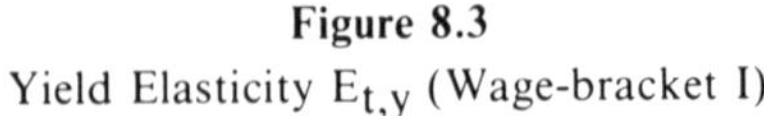

Figure 8.3
Yield Elasticity $E_{t,y}$ (Wage-bracket I)

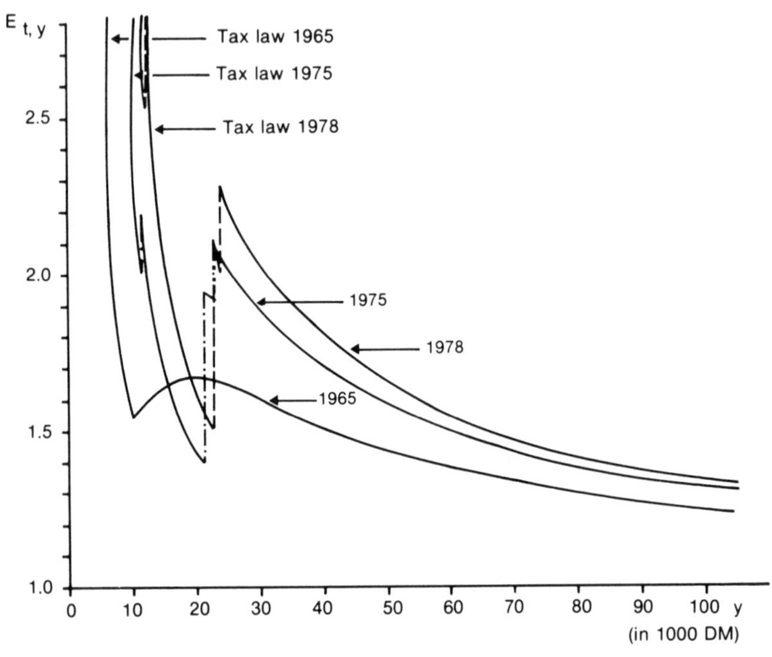

Source: Author's Computations

rates measured by residual income elasticity. It is obvious that the lower and middle income brackets are sharply graduated by the income tax and that with the tax reforms this graduation has been increased with the exception of some small income areas.[45]

The redistribution effect of the income tax is dependent on the residual income elasticity and the distribution of the individual gross incomes (y). We have estimated the redistribution effects for the wage tax and the assessed income tax for the years 1965, 1968 and 1971 with an income and wage tax model.[46] For the tax laws of 1975 and 1978 a simulation model of the wage tax has been used to estimate their redistribution effects.[47]

$$\text{Et,y} = \frac{\text{per cent change in tax revenues}}{\text{per cent change in incomes}}$$

Et,y in ordinary language, describes the per cent change in tax revenues which result from a given per cent change in incomes. – ed.

Figure 8.4

Residual Income Elasticity $E_{y^n,y}$ (Wage-bracket I)

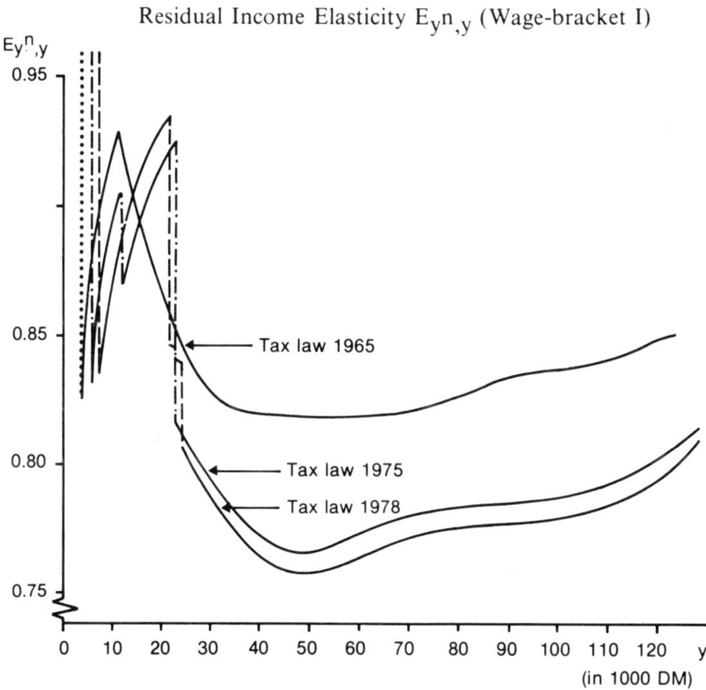

Source: Author's Computations

In Table 8.5 various Gini coefficients** are given. If the distributions of gross income y and net income y^n are compared, it is obvious that the redistribution effects of wage taxes and of assessed income taxes are relatively small. For the wage tax the redistribution effect ($y - y^n$) increases slightly from 1965 to 1971, whereas for the assessed income tax the redistribution effect declines slightly from 1965 to 1971.

Table 8.6 shows the Gini coefficients for gross income (y) and net income (y^n) in the wage tax bracket I for six consecutive simulation periods ($t = 0,1,\ldots, 5$); the gross income distribution for 1974 ($t = 0$) has been extrapolated by 10 per cent for each period.[48] As for the wage tax in Table 8.5 the redistribution effect ($y - y^n$) increases with an increase in income, but the differences in the redistribution effects of the different tax laws are very small.

** A Gini coefficient of 1.0 indicates absolute (income) equality: each member of society has exactly the same amount (of income) as every other. A Gini coefficient of 0 indicates absolute (income) inequality: one person has all (the income) and no one else has any. – ed.

TABLE 8.5

Gini Coefficients for Gross Income (Y), Tax Exemptions (E), Taxable Income (X), Tax Yield (T), and Net Income (Y^n) for Wage Taxes and Assessed Income Taxes

	Wage Tax						Assessed Income Tax		
	Basic Tariff			Splitting Tariff					
	1965	1968	1971	1965	1968	1971	1965	1968	1971
Y	0.351	0.372	0.371	0.312	0.273	0.271	0.520	0.477	0.412
E	0.382	0.382	0.320	0.474	0.219	0.188	0.299	0.251	0.204
X	0.337	0.367	0.391	0.251	0.301	0.302	0.578	0.542	0.462
T	0.560	0.570	0.543	0.493	0.481	0.422	0.785	0.748	0.652
Y^n	0.333	0.352	0.348	0.297	0.254	0.251	0.453	0.413	0.351
$Y - Y^n$	0.018	0.020	0.023	0.015	0.019	0.020	0.067	0.064	0.061

Source: Petersen (1977, Tables 27 and 42).

TABLE 8.6

Gini Coefficients for Gross Income (Y) and Net Income (Y^n) in the Wage-Tax-Bracket I for Six Consecutive Simulation Periods and the Income Tax Laws of 1965, 1975 and 1978

	1965 Income Tax Law			1975 Income Tax Law			1978 Income Tax Law		
t	Y^a	Y^n	$Y-Y^n$	Y^a	Y^n	$Y-Y^n$	Y^a	Y^n	$Y-Y^n$
0	0.383	0.353	0.030	0.383	0.355	0.028	0.383	0.355	0.028
1	0.383	0.352	0.031	0.383	0.353	0.030	0.383	0.353	0.030
2	0.383	0.350	0.033	0.383	0.350	0.033	0.383	0.350	0.033
3	0.383	0.349	0.034	0.383	0.348	0.035	0.383	0.348	0.035
4	0.383	0.348	0.035	0.383	0.345	0.038	0.383	0.345	0.038
5	0.383	0.346	0.037	0.383	0.342	0.041	0.383	0.342	0.041

[a] 1974 Distribution.

Source: Petersen (1981a Tables 2, 3 and 4).

THEORY AND PRACTICE

On examining the German income tax system as a whole, it becomes obvious that a redistribution effect exists in principle. However, in practice, this effect is rather small. In the case of direct taxes (income taxes) the redistribution effects are obvious: income is distributed more equally after taxes than before. But the very existence of redistribution effects (in the same direction) in the case of indirect taxes is unproven. This is a controversial question among German economists. Bedau and Göseke (1977, p. 381) estimated a nearly even distribution of the indirect tax burden (for 1974), *i.e.,* no redistribution at all. In their view, this resulted due to the value-added tax rate which is lower (6.5 per cent instead of 13 per cent) on basic necessity items. But they observed a slight increase in the average indirect tax rate from 13.2 per cent for monthly incomes of DM 1000 to 13.7 per cent for monthly incomes between DM 3000 and DM 4000. For higher incomes the average tax rate declined as well for incomes over DM 7000 monthly, the average tax rate was smaller than for low incomes.

Although the negative distributional consequences of levies on ("necessity") goods and services have been more or less mitigated since Lassalle's famous discourse on "Indirect Taxes and the Situation of the Working Classes" (1863), as Neumark (1981) states: "The fact remains that such levies are indisputably regressive and have a particularly unjust impact on families with a large number of children." This can also be seen from the research of Karrenberg and Kitterer (1979, p. 130) cited above; they find that the marginal rate of indirect taxes declines from 7 to 8 per cent in the lower and middle income brackets to 1 to 2 per cent in the highest income bracket. Redistribution within the total German tax system depends on the redistributional effect of the indirect taxes. Direct taxes, especially West Germany's income taxes as estimated in Tables 8.5 and 8.6, have only a small redistributional effect. If indirect taxes are evenly distributed, then the redistributional effect is small for the total tax system. If one carries the arguments of Karrenberg and Kitterer (1979) and of Neumark (1981) one step further, the distribution would be either the same before and after taxes or quite possibly the distribution could even be more skewed toward the rich after taxes.

Reynolds and Smolensky (1978, p. 75) observed a decline in the redistributional effects of income taxes in the United States after World War II. A similar development has taken place in Germany. The estimates above show that Tullock (1971) is doubtlessly correct when he assumes that most redistributions only shift the tax burden within the middle income-groups. This is particularly true today as the lower and middle income brackets are taxed with a degree of progression, which formerly only existed for relatively high incomes.

V. IMPACT OF INFLATION ON THE TAX SYSTEM

In the sections above we have discussed the impacts of the tax system on economic development. But many of the problems discussed above are connected to—if not the consequence of—the impacts of the secular inflation on the tax system, especially on the progressive income tax.

We shall consider only the overall impact of inflation on fixed exemptions and tariff regulations for personal income taxation. This is called "kalte Progression" ("cold progression") in German.[49] This effect in particular caused the strong increase of income tax revenue in the decade 1965 to 1975, when income tax laws were held constant. The lower and middle income brackets were especially stricken with inflation, because in these categories progression is very sharp (see Figures 8.3 and 8.4).

Income tax statistics are only available in West Germany at three year intervals. For these assessment years we estimated the effects of inflation on wage taxes as well as on assessed income taxes, using a tax simulation model.[50] The difference between tax revenue without indexation and with full indexation (that is: indexation of exemption regulations as well as of the income tax tariff) represents the inflationary share of tax revenue (see Table 8.7). In the assessment years different rates of inflation were measured by the German consumer price index.[51] As prices increased, the inflationary share of tax revenue rose sharply, especially in the case of the wage tax. This gives a broad hint that the employees who are only taxed on wages (those who usually earn less than those whose entire income is taxed), are greatly concerned about the "kalte Progression."

TAX REFORM

In 1975 there was a more dramatic income tax reform, which yielded a loss in revenue of about DM 15 billion that year. But this amount was not enough to compensate for the inflationary effect of 1974 alone (see Table 8.7). Since 1975 secular inflation has led to further increases in tax revenue. Table 8.8 shows some estimates for the period 1974 to 1980 based on the cash tax revenue. If one (counter-factually) assumes that with the income tax reform of 1975 a full compensation of the inflationary effects has been reached, the consumer price index—on which the deflator for indexing is based—is set at 100 per cent for 1974. The inflationary income tax revenue increased from DM 5 billion in 1975 to DM 27.2 billion in 1980; total inflationary income tax revenue amounts to about DM 90 billion for the period 1975-1980, whereas the income tax cuts in 1977/78 and 1979 led to reductions in the tax yield of only about DM 20 billion.

TABLE 8.7

Income Tax Revenue Caused by Secular Inflation

Year	(1) Total Wage Tax Revenue Without Indexation[a]	(2) With Indexation[a]	(1) - (2)[a]	(1) - (2) / (1) (per cent)
1965	14.606[b]	13.957	0.649	4.4
1968	18.743	16.921	1.822	9.7
1971	39.783	34.411	5.372	13.5
1974	68.103	52.807	15.296	22.5
	Total Assessed Income Tax Revenue Without Indexation	With Indexation		
1965	14.821	14.593	0.228	1.5
1968	15.701	14.926	0.775	4.9
1971	25.437	22.887	2.550	10.0
1974	29.047	24.759	4.288	14.8
	Total Income Tax Revenue Without Indexation	With Indexation		
1965	29.427	28.550	0.878	3.0
1968	34.444	31.847	2.597	7.5
1971	65.220	57.298	7.922	12.2
1974	99.150	77.566	19.584	20.2

[a] All figures in DM billion.

Source: Petersen (1979c, Tables 4a - 4c).

In spite of a stagnation in economic growth in the period 1975 to 1978, the income tax yield vigorously increased during that period. As the result of a sharply graduated income tax and a secular inflation accompanied by stagnation ("stagflation"), the "built-in flexibility" does not lead to automatic tax reductions and therefore to expansive effects on economic activities; on the contrary, income taxes create "fiscal drag" to further economic growth, as we have seen. It is also obvious that the increasing disincentives on the supply of effort as well as the reductions in the redistributive effect of income taxation are at least partly consequences of the inflationary income tax increases.

TABLE 8.8

Additional Income Tax Revenue Caused by Inflation 1975-1980 (Estimates)

Year	(1) Consumer Price Index	(2) Total Income Tax Revenue (DM Billion)	(3) Inflationary Income Tax Revenue (DM Billion)	(4) Additional Income Tax Revenue (Per Cent)
1974	100.0	98.8	—	—
1975	106.6	99.2	5.0	5.0
1976	110.6	111.5	7.8	7.0
1977	114.7	126.3	12.6	10.0
1978	117.8	139.9[a]	16.8	12.0
1979	122.6	153.1[b]	20.7	13.5
1980	129.3	164.9[b]	27.2	16.5

[a] Estimated without the changes in the 1978 Income Tax Law.

[b] Estimated without the changes in the 1979 Income Tax Law.

Source: Calculated from Bundesministerium der Finanzen (1979).

Instead of implementing a systematic adjustment scheme for income taxation, politicians did nothing. After ten years they began initiating haphazard and unsystematic income tax reductions, which favoured random and changing groups of taxpayers. Avoided was a total and equitable compensation of the inflationary effects on the income tax. It is also obvious that—had indexation been implemented—a total change in economic policy would have been necessary: income tax rates would have been increased, or growth rates of public expenditures would have declined.

VI. SOME IMPLICATIONS FOR TAX POLICY

1. Briefly summarizing the results: There is some empirical evidence that the disincentives of the tax system, especially on the supply of work, have grown in importance. In the cases of savings and especially investments, "many modern economists tend to overrate the significance of taxes" (Neumark, 1981), especially if tax-shifting is taken into consideration.
2. There is some empirical evidence that the increasing shares of direct taxation in gross national product as well as in total taxation have led to growth retarding pressure. But a strong relationship between taxation and economic growth as expressed in the "Laffer curve," which seems to gain increasing popularity in Anglo-American countries, cannot be observed for Germany.[52] Therefore, it is impossible to give a precise maximum average tax ratio or marginal tax rate which represents the limit, where further increases become counter-productive.

   Growth retarding forces are much more involved in the innumerable and very complicated details of tax laws. In Germany, for instance, the investment in shares is discriminated against, because dividends are taxed at source with corporation taxes and dividend taxes, whereas interest payments on mortgages, fixed-interest bearing bonds and other monetary investments are not so treated. Here we have a "publicly accepted toleration of tax evasion" on interest payments, with far reaching consequences for allocation. For many years investments in—as Giersch (1973) calls it "Betongold"—and similar property were taxed at higher rates than investments in productive assets. Not only inflation but also tax laws led to the result. It is important that these "excess burdens" for productive assets must be avoided.
3. There is some empirical evidence that the redistributive effect of the German tax system has declined since World War II, since today nearly all citizens are covered by income taxation, including the lower income brackets, and these areas have sharply graduated tax rates. The increase of the maximum marginal income tax rate from

53 per cent to 56 per cent in 1975 had no positive effect on redistribution. Doubtless, the Meade Commission was correct in claiming that extremely high marginal tax rates are very problematic, because they contribute little to vertical equity, and may well have significant disincentive effects on the supply of effort (Meade, 1978, p. 308).

4. Many of the problems connected with taxation only occurred because politicians did nothing about the distortions caused by inflation. Rather, they welcomed the additional inflationary tax revenue, and used it for further increases in public expenditures. The consequence was that at least for a time, inflation accelerated. This process yielded not only a declining money illusion but also an increasing "tax awareness" (or declining "tax illusion").
5. Therefore it seems senseless to substitute indirect for direct taxes to try to lower the growth retarding pressures. With an increasing share of indirect taxes, their imperceptibility disappears. Just as money illusion decreases with an increasing rate of inflation, so "indirect tax illusion" falls with a rising share of indirect taxes. Beyond this, indirect taxes (as well as the expenditure tax) promote the movement "back to barter," because do-it-yourself and other "underground" transactions become more lucrative.[53]
6. With an adjustment scheme for the impact of inflation on income taxes (*i.e.*, indexation) many problems would be diminished. Politicians would be forced to openly increase tax rates, if they want to increase public expenditure. But then taxpayers' resistance to taxation will likely reduce public expenditures.
7. An inflation adjustment scheme for income taxes will reduce progression, because purely nominal income increases would then be taxed proportionately. A reduction of marginal income tax rates, especially in the lower and middle income brackets, is necessary in order to avoid further strengthening the disincentive effects and the growth of the underground economy.[54] Naturally, the "green," "back to nature," and "back to barter" movements always have some sympathetic followers, but if these attitudes become accepted by most of the members of society, they destroy its very economic foundations.
8. An inflationary adjustment scheme as well as a reduction of marginal income tax rates could be financed by abolition of the various direct government subsidies.[55] Also advisable is the harmonization of the tax and transfer system through an integration of social concepts into the income tax system. This can lead to a widening of the tax base and avoid cumulative side effects of different kinds of transfer payments. As well, higher than 100 per cent combined tax-transfer rates can be ended. In this way the principle of "vertical

equity" can be better realized. A comprehensive income tax base lends the financial scope for diminishing tax progressivity, and especially for reducing the disincentive effects in the lower and middle income brackets. It also leads to a redistributive effect which is more efficient, because redistribution avoids transferring money from one pocket to the other—the most important effect of the present tax and transfer system. A "trade-off between equity and growth" as the consequence of progressive (income) taxation will still remain, but with a more finely tuned tax and transfer system the negative implications of the "trade-off" could be reduced.

NOTES

1. If not otherwise noted, the macroeconomic average tax rate (or more precisely the average tax ratio) is defined in the following as the relation of total taxation (including social security contributions) to gross national product (GNP). The aspects of the nearly simultaneously increasing ratio of public debt to GNP are not handled in this paper.
2. See, *e.g.*, Brunner (1978), Beenstock (1979).
3. Details about the tax structure and a list of the single taxes of the German tax system are given in Table 8-A1 in the Appendix.
4. See, for instance, Wales and Woodland (1979) and the literature cited there.
5. See, *e.g.*, Beenstock (1979).
6. Among these Strümpel (1966) and Engelhardt (1968).
7. See Petersen (1977; 1979b). The income tax reductions in 1975, 1977/78 and 1979 did not change this situation; a corresponding assertion can be made for the income tax reduction planned for 1981.
8. See Koch (1978).
9. This question was posed for two cases: an increase of 10 per cent corresponding to an absolute increase in the tax yield of DM 20 per worker per month and, because this was a relatively small absolute increase, an increase of 100 per cent of the average tax rate corresponding to an absolute increase of DM 200 to DM 400.
10. Adding veracity to the findings, the relatively small reaction of the tax consultants proves that they are the group with the best information about taxation.
11. They were derived as answers to the question: "It is often argued that a further increase of the tax burden would lead to a strong decline in the supply of effort. How would you react?" (The answers "others" and "no answer" are responsible for the failure of the responses to add up to 100 per cent.)
12. The effective average tax rates result from other questions.
13. There are two possible explanations: (1) the lawyers have a high sensibility to taxation without precise information; (2) the growth rates of their supply of effort have already declined. See Koch (1978).
14. For this comparison one has to recognize that in 1975 the maximum marginal tax rate of income taxes was increased from 53 to 56 per cent.

15. This does not include the civil servants (Beamte), who do not pay social insurance contributions in Germany.
16. In the private sector salaries are perhaps somewhat higher.
17. This marginal rate as well as all marginal rates in Table 8.4 exclude the employers contributions to social insurance.
18. In 1979 the limit was at DM 3000 monthly; at this amount the maximum compulsory premium (employee contribution) amounted to DM 195 (6.5 per cent of gross wages).
19. In 1979 the limit was DM 4000 monthly; at this amount the maximum compulsory premium (employee contribution) for retirement insurance amounted to DM 360 (9 per cent of gross wages) and for unemployment insurance, DM 60 (1.5 per cent of gross wages).
20. In this respect Messere (1978, p. 204) observed "the erosion, if not yet the complete collapse of the insurance myth."
21. The same burdens are given for married employees, when husband and wife earn equal amounts.
22. Naturally the self-employed can pay voluntary premiums for private or public retirement insurance, but these premiums are not directly tied to their gross incomes.
23. The church tax amounts to 9 per cent of the income tax yield (in some German states 8 per cent).
24. The separate marginal rates are:
    (1) wage taxes - 41.7 per cent,
    (2) social insurance contributions - 17.0 per cent,
    (3) church taxes - 3.8 per cent,
    (4) indirect taxes - 7.0 per cent.
25. See Petersen (1981b). In Germany the discussion of the tax burden has become a popular topic for the mass media.
26. See, *e.g.,* Musgrave (1959, p. 268–272).
27. Since no distinction is made between pensioners, entrepreneurs, and employees in the statistics, it is impossible to determine the indirect taxation for employee households alone. Therefore the ratio TPH is too high and the results presented here only indicate tendencies.
28. The implementation of time lags shows that with a time lag of up to three years signs stay negative. Using 5-year moving averages leads partially to an increase in $\bar{R}^2$ values.
29. If shifting is taken into consideration, which has been excluded from these analyses, other results might occur. For example, as suggested in an OECD Study (1978, p. 83) labour unions might attempt to use wage tax increases as an excuse for higher monetary wages.
30. A similar combination seems to apply today in the U.K., according to a publication of the Institut der deutschen Wirtschaft (1979). Compared to Germany the U.K. must be a "depreciation paradise," but it seems that this combination does not work as well as in the post-war period in Germany.
31. The basic model used is the one created by van der Werf for the Planning Office of the Netherlands.
32. Albach (1970) reached similar results using microeconomic appraisals.
33. The combined tax rate of corporation taxes on retained profits (56 per cent) and of occupation taxes on profits (6.15 per cent at an average collection rate of 325 per cent when taking into consideration the deduction

allowance of occupation taxes for corporation taxes) amounts to 62.15 per cent; see Institut der deutschen Wirtschaft (1979, p. 3).

34. In 1974 and 1975 there were high negative growth rates.
35. This tax was only levied in some German communities. This tax was abolished in 1980.
36. Taxes on private property are included.
37. Private property is included as well.
38. See Table 8-A3 in the Appendix.
39. See the critical remarks about this kind of analysis above.
40. See Table 8-A2 in the Appendix.
41. The statistics for 1979–1982 have been extrapolated from the National Accounts Statistics using data from public program planning and the last estimate of tax revenue.
42. The increase in social security contributions was caused by increases in social security rates by government and social insurance institutions.
43. Following the definition of the German National Accounts Statistics.
44. In Sweden (which has the highest average tax rate of all OECD member countries) there is a relatively significant negative correlation for direct as well as indirect taxation; see Petersen (1981b). Some international comparisons of growth rates and tax ratios are given in Table 8-A4 in the Appendix. This table shows that Germany has middle ranks for real growth rates as well as for the tax ratios compared to the other OECD member countries.
45. Since the last reform of the income tax tariff in 1979 once more we have an accelerated progression in the first area of direct progression.
46. Because of important differences in tax statistics, wage and assessed income taxes cannot be combined.
47. See Petersen (1977, pp. 139–218).
48. For a discussion of the method, see Petersen (1979a).
49. "Kalte Progression" is defined as an increasing individual average tax rate resulting from purely nominal income increases without the implementation of an adjustment scheme. Naturally, there are special problems connected with the taxation of profits and interest; but especially in the case of profit taxation there are numerous regulations within the German income tax law which make it possible for firms to become more or less resistant to inflation. See, for instance, Petersen (1977, pp. 67–91). Estimations similar to those of Feldstein and Summers (1979) are not available for Germany.
50. See Petersen (1977).
51. The deflator for indexation was 1.033 in 1965, 1.105 in 1968, 1.226 in 1971, and 1.480 in 1974.
52. See Petersen (1981b).
53. Especially in the case of personal progressive expenditure taxes.
54. Formerly disincentives on high incomes were most frequently discussed; today they are less important, perhaps because of the numerous possibilities for high income earners to avoid taxes or to gain from tax expenditures.
55. Here one only has to mention the numerous articles written about the "comprehensive tax base."

REFERENCES

Albach, Horst. *Steuersystem und unternehmerische Investitionspolitik,* Wiesbaden: Gabler (1970).

Albers, Willi. "Umverteilungswirkungen der Einkommensteuer," *Öffentliche Finanzwirtschaft und Verteilung II,* Berlin: Duncker & Humblot (1974) 69–144.

———."Einkommensbesteuerung, III: Statistik." Handwörterbuch der Wirtschaftswissenschaft, 2:240–47 (1980).

Albrecht, Dietrich. "Subventionen, Problematik und Entwicklung," *Schriftenreihe des Bundesministeriums der Finanzen,* No. 25 Bonn (1978).

Beckmann, Martin, and Götz Uebe. *Makroökonomische Untersuchungen der Auswirkungen von Steuersystemänderungen,* Wiesbaden: Gabler (1970).

Bedau, Klaus-Dietrich, Gerhard Göseke. "Die Belastung der privaten Haushalte mit indirekten Steuern," *Wochenbericht des Deutschen Institus für Wirtschaftsforschung,* 44:377–84 Berlin (1977).

Beenstock, Michael. "Taxation and Incentives in the UK." *Lloyds Bank Review,* No. 134:1–15 London (1979).

———, A. Gosling. *Taxation, Incentives and Government Revenue in the U.K.,* London: London Business School (1979).

Blöcker, Marianne, Hans-Georg Petersen. "Eine vergleichende Analyse der deutschen Einkommensteuertarife von 1958, 1965 und 1975 unter Einbeziehung des Progressionsgrades," *Public Finance,* 30:3:347–65 The Hague (1975).

———, "Zur Problematik der 'heimlichen' Steuererhöhungen," *Deutsche Steuerzeitung,* 65:20:397–98 Bonn (1977).

Boskin, Michael J. "Taxation, Saving and the Rate of Interest," *Journal of Political Economy,* 86:2:S3–S27 Chicago (1978).

Brunner, Karl. "Reflections on the Political Economy of Government. The Persistent Growth of Government," *Schweizerische Zeitschrift für Volkswirtschaft und Statistik,* 114:3:649–80 Bern (1978).

Buchanan, James M. and Richard E. Wagner. *Democracy in Deficit: The Political Legacy of Lord Keynes,* New York, London: Academic Press (1977).

Bundesministerium der Finanzen, *Finanzbericht 1980,* Bonn (1979).

Engelhardt, Gunther. *Verhaltenslenkende Wirkungen der Einkommensteuer,* Berlin: Duncker & Humblot (1968).

Feldstein, Martin S. and Lawrence Summers. "Inflation and the Taxation of Capital Income in the Corporate Sector." *National Tax Journal* 32:4: 445–70 (1979).

Giersch, Herbert. "Indexklauseln und Inflationsbekämpfung," *Kiel Discussion Papers* No. 32 (1973).

Goode, Richard. *The Individual Income Tax,* Revised Ed., Washington, D.C.: The Brookings Institution (1976).

Institut der deutschen Wirtschaft, *Steuern: Hemmschuh für Wachstum und Leistung,* Köln (1978).

——— Steuerliche Investitionsförderung in fünf Industrieländern. *Beiträge zur Wirtschafts-und Sozialpolitik,* No. 73 Köln (1979).

Institut "Finanzen und Steuern," *Steuerliche Massnahmen zur Investitionsförderung,* Brief 177, Bonn (1978).

Jüttemeier, Karl-Heinz, Konrad Lammers, Klaus-Werner Schatz, Enno F. Willms. *Auswirkungen der öffentlichen Haushalte auf sektorale Investitionsentscheidungen im Industrie-und Dienstleistungsbereich,* Forschungsauftag des Bundesminsters für Wirtschaft, Kiel (1977).

———, Konrad Lammers. "Subventionen in der Bundersrepublik Deutschland," *Kiel Discussion Papers,* No. 63/64 Kiel (1979).

Karrenberg, Hanns, Wolfgang Kitterer. "Die Grenzbelastung von Arbeitnechmerhaushalten bei steigendem Einkommen," *Mitteilungen des Rheinisch-Westfälischen Instituts für Wirtschaftsforschung Essen, 30:3:125*–50 (1979).

Kesselman, Jonathan R. "Non-Business Deductions and Tax Expenditures in Canada: Aggregates and Distributions," *Canadian Tax Journal* 25:3: 160–79 (1977).

Koch, Walter A. S. *Einkommensteuern und Leistungsanreize,* Habilitationschrift an der Wirtschafts-und Sozialwissenschaftlichen Fakultät der Universität Kiel (1978).

Maslove, Allan M. "The Other Side of Public Spending: Tax Expenditures in Canada," *Public Evaluation of Government Spending,* London: Butterworth (1979).

Meade, James E. (ed.). The Structure and Reform of Direct Taxation. *Report of a Committee chaired by Professor J. E. Meade,* London, Boston: Allen & Unwin (1978).

Messere, Ken. "Tax Levels, Structures and Systems: Some Intertemporal and International Comparisons," Horst Claus Recktenwald (ed.), *Secular Trends of the Public Sector,* Paris: Edition Cujas (1978) 193–210.

Musgrave, Richard A. *The Theory of Public Finance: A Study in Public Economy,* New York: McGraw Hill (1959).

Neumark, Fritz. "Wandlungen in der Beurteilung eingebauter Steuerflexibilität," *Kyklos,* 32:177–204 (1979).

———. "Comment on Hans-Georg Petersen's paper: *Taxes, Tax Systems and Economic Growth,*" Herbert Giersch (ed.), *Towards an Explanation of Economic Growth,* Tübingen: J. C. B. Mohr (1981) 348–353.

OECD. "Public Expenditure Trends." *Studies in Resource Allocation,* No. 5 (1978).

Petersen, Hans-Georg. "Ein Vorschlag zur Reform des Einkommensteuertarifs 1978," Finanzarchiv, N.F. 35:128–46 (1976).

———. *Personelle Einkommensbesteuerung und Inflation: Eine theoretisch-empirische Analyse der Lohn- und veranlagten Einkommensteuer in der Bundesrepublik Deutschland,* Frankfurt am Main: Lang (1977).

———. "Effects of Growing Incomes on Classified Income Distributions, the Derived Lorenz Curves, and Gini Indices," *Econometrica* 47:138-198 (1979a).

———, "Finanzwirtschaftliche Folgen einer Harmonisierung der Belastung von Arbeits-und Alterseinkommen mit öffentlichen Abgaben," *Kiel Working Papers* No. 93, Kiel (1979b).

———. "Simulationsergebnisse über die Wirkungen einer Indexbindung des Einkommensteuersystems," *Finanzarchiv,* N.F., 37:50-72 (1979c).

———. "Some Further Results on Income Tax Progression," *Zeitschrift für Wirtschafts- und Sozialwissenschaften,* 100:45-59 (1981a).

———. "Taxes, Tax Systems and Economic Growth" Herbert Giersch (ed.), *Towards an Explanation of Economic Growth,* Tübingen: J. C. B. Mohr (1981a) 313-347.

Reynolds, Morgan, Eugene Smolensky. "Why Changing the Size Distribution of Income through the Fisc is Now More Difficult: Hypotheses from U.S. Experience," Horst Claus Recktenwald (ed.), *Secular Trends of the Public Sector,* Paris: Edition Cujas (1978) 69-83.

Roskamp, Karl Wilhelm. *Economic Growth, Capital Formation, and Public Policy in West Germany 1948 to 1957,* University of Michigan (1959).

Statistisches Bundesamt, Volkswirtschaftliche Gesamtrechnung, Wiesbaden 1950-1979.

Strümpel, Burkhard. "Steuermoral und Steuerwiderstand der deutschen Selbständigen," Ein Beitrag zur Lehre von den Steuerwirkungen, Köln: Westdeutscher Verlag (1966).

Tullock, Gordon. "The Charity of the Uncharitable, *Western Economic Journal* 9:6:379-92 (1971).

Wales, Terence J., A. D. Woodland. "Labour Supply and Progressive Taxes," *The Review of Economic Studies,* 46:85-95 (1979).

Wissenschaftlicher Beirat beim Bundesministerium der Finanzen, Gutachten zur Reform der direkten Steuern, *Schriftenreihe des Bundesministeriums der Finanzen,* Vol. 9 Bonn (1967).

STATISTICAL APPENDIX

TABLE 8-A1

Shares of Single Taxes to Total Tax Revenue

Taxes	Revenue of Single Taxes to Total Tax Revenue in Per Cent										
	1970	1971	1972	1973	1974	1975	1976	1977	1978	1979[1]	1980[1]
1. taxes on income and wealth	53.3	54.0	55.6	58.1	60.0	58.7	59.7	61.8	59.9	58.5	57.8
among them taxes on											
—income	40.7	41.5	43.1	45.6	47.5	46.3	47.2	49.0	47.9	46.9	47.9
—wealth	4.7	4.3	3.8	3.5	3.5	3.7	3.8	3.9	3.5	3.1	2.8
—business	7.9	8.2	8.7	9.0	9.0	8.6	8.7	8.9	8.5	8.5	7.1
2. taxes on wealth transactions	1.4	1.4	1.3	1.1	1.0	1.1	1.3	1.0	1.0	1.1	1.1
3. taxes on income spending	45.3	44.6	43.0	40.7	39.0	40.3	39.0	37.2	39.1	40.4	41.1
among them											
—sales taxes	25.4	25.6	24.3	22.5	21.8	22.8	22.2	21.4	23.4	24.9	26.2
—motor vehicle tax	2.5	2.4	2.4	2.2	2.2	2.2	2.1	2.0	2.0	2.1	1.9
—mineral oil tax	7.5	7.2	7.2	7.4	6.7	7.1	6.8	6.4	6.4	6.4	6.2
—customs	1.9	1.8	1.6	1.4	1.4	1.3	1.4	1.2	1.2	1.1	1.1
—others	8.0	7.6	7.5	7.2	6.9	6.8	6.5	6.2	6.1	5.9	5.7

[1] Estimate

Structure for the single groups:

Taxes on income	wage tax, assessed income tax, dividend tax, corporation tax.
Taxes on wealth:	wealth tax, land tax, equalization fees.
Taxes on business:	occupation tax, payroll tax.
Taxes on wealth transactions:	inheritance tax, realty transfer tax, stamp duty, capital movement tax.
Taxes on sales:	VAT, import levy, freight traffic taxes, premium tax.
Taxes on consumption:	tobacco tax, tax on liquors, champagne tax, beer tax, coffee tax, tea tax, sugar tax, vinegar tax, salt tax, tax on lighting materials, lottery tax, other local taxes.

Source: Bundesministerium der Finanzen (1979).

TABLE 8-A2

Growth Rates of Real Gross National Product $\dot{Y}$, Total Tax Ratio T, Direct Tax Ratio T_{DIR}, Indirect Tax Ratio T_{IND}, and Ratio of Social Security Contributions T_{SOC}

Year	$\dot{Y}$ (In Per Cent)	T (In Per Cent of Y)	T_{DIR} (In Per Cent of Y)	T_{IND} (In Per Cent of Y)	T_{SOC} (In Per Cent of Y)
1951	10.45	30.82	8.50	13.78	8.53
1952	8.89	32.12	9.47	14.26	8.39
1953	8.22	32.76	9.88	14.18	8.70
1954	7.44	32.29	9.50	14.05	8.74
1955	12.00	31.37	8.67	13.94	8.77
1956	7.29	31.51	8.85	13.80	8.86
1957	5.68	32.07	8.64	13.61	9.83
1958	3.73	32.14	8.36	13.28	10.50
1959	7.30	32.53	8.66	13.59	10.28
1960	9.02	33.03	9.24	13.77	9.19
1961	4.87	34.20	10.19	13.92	9.21
1962	4.42	34.61	10.49	13.87	9.38
1963	2.98	34.79	10.59	13.81	9.50
1964	6.63	34.44	10.60	13.69	9.27
1965	5.54	33.81	9.96	13.56	9.37
1966	2.53	34.28	10.13	13.43	9.76
1967	- 0.13	34.63	10.00	13.76	9.86
1968	6.50	34.33	10.25	13.00	10.06
1969	7.89	36.32	10.69	14.14	10.43
1970	5.88	35.57	10.73	12.84	10.89
1971	3.34	36.36	11.24	12.75	11.19
1972	3.65	36.95	11.01	13.00	11.74
1973	4.91	39.25	12.59	12.87	12.52
1974	0.35	39.67	13.01	12.38	12.90
1975	- 1.75	39.05	11.96	12.24	13.48
1976	5.28	40.44	12.78	12.28	13.97
1977	2.55	41.71	13.75	12.45	14.11
1978	3.52	41.14	13.01	12.73	14.14
1979	4.36	40.89	12.68	12.85	14.07
1980	1.50	41.19	12.93	12.79	14.10
1981	1.00	41.77	13.38	12.72	14.13
1982	2.50	42.61	14.22	12.68	14.21

Source: 1950-1978, Statistisches Bundesamt (1950-1979). 1978-1982, Estimates.

TABLE 8-A3

Growth Rates of Real Savings for Private Households $\dot{S}$, and the Ratios TPH, TPH_T, and TPH_{SOC} and the Growth Rates of Real Private Investments $\dot{I}$, and the Ratios TCW, TCW_T, and TCW_{SOC}

Year	$\dot{S}$	TPH	TPH_T	TPH_{SOC}	$\dot{I}$	TCW^a	TCW_T	TCW^a_{SOC}
1960	4.59	33.53	25.29	8.25	7.00	54.30	35.73	18.57
1961	10.56	33.88	25.87	8.01	6.50	58.58	39.10	19.49
1962	- 0.44	34.04	25.96	8.08	2.70	61.38	40.77	20.61
1963	19.55	34.07	26.00	8.07	- 1.10	63.37	41.65	21.72
1964	21.87	34.65	26.59	8.06	9.30	59.69	39.27	20.42
1965	16.68	33.84	25.73	8.11	5.70	58.21	37.46	20.76
1966	- 2.28	34.05	25.72	8.33	1.30	60.18	37.96	22.22
1967	- 2.05	35.27	26.76	8.51	- 6.40	58.47	36.59	21.88
1968	16.98	35.29	26.45	8.85	3.50	56.27	34.68	21.59
1969	15.19	37.66	28.49	9.18	10.90	62.01	38.42	23.59
1970	6.42	37.57	28.34	9.24	10.60	54.24	30.23	24.00
1971	2.57	38.19	29.05	9.14	7.80	55.98	30.16	25.82
1972	14.93	38.10	28.69	9.41	4.50	61.26	32.51	28.74
1973	- 3.30	39.36	29.55	9.81	0.30	68.90	37.15	31.75
1974	8.34	39.00	29.22	9.78	- 13.20	70.72	37.06	33.66
1975	5.17	38.59	28.27	10.32	- 4.50	67.48	33.42	34.06
1976	- 9.05	39.92	29.07	10.86	6.50	70.80	35.81	34.99
1977	- 5.12	40.61	29.62	10.99	5.50	73.14	38.54	34.60
1978	2.38	40.90	29.87	11.03	6.00	72.60	37.57	35.03

[a] Social security contributions of public employees included (for "Beamte" only fictitious contributions).

Source: Statistisches Bundesamt (1960-1979).

TABLE 8-A4

Mean Real Growth Rates of GNP/GDP and the Tax Ratios T, TDIR, and TIND, and the Shares of Direct TDIR/T, and Indirect Taxation TIND/T to Total Taxation for OECD Member Countries (1965-1977)

	$\dot{Y}_R$ (MEAN)	RANK No.	T (MEAN)	RANK No.	TDIR[a] (MEAN)	RANK No.	TIND (MEAN)	RANK No.	TDIR/T (MEAN)	RANK No.	TIND/T (MEAN)	RANK No.
Australia	4.49	10	26.71	17	20.17	15	6.54	19	75.44	3	24.56	21
Austria	4.54	8	36.90	5	21.19	13	15.70	2	57.36	19	42.64	5
Belgium	4.10	12	36.55	7	24.72	6	11.83	9	67.24	12	32.76	12
Canada	4.90	6	30.92	14	20.02	16	10.89	11	64.59	14	35.41	10
Denmark	3.55	17	38.84	4	24.18	7	14.66	4	61.94	15	38.06	9
Finland	4.08	14	35.08	9	21.34	11	13.75	6	60.49	17	39.51	7
France	4.58	7	36.23	8	22.08	10	14.15	5	60.84	16	39.16	8
Germany	3.58	16	34.30	11	23.87	8	10.44	13	69.41	10	30.59	14
Greece	6.22	3	24.07	19	12.21	21	11.86	8	50.55	22	49.45	2
Ireland	3.78	15	31.11	12	15.50	18	15.61	3	49.65	23	50.35	1
Italy	4.10	12	31.08	13	20.28	14	10.80	12	65.04	13	34.96	11
Japan	8.00	1	19.98	22	14.57	19	5.41	23	72.55	7	27.45	17
Luxembourg	2.96	19	36.59	6	28.70	3	7.89	17	78.20	2	21.80	22
Netherlands	4.33	11	41.42	2	30.42	1	11.01	10	73.31	6	26.69	18
New Zealand	2.84	20	28.72	16	21.33	12	7.39	18	74.04	5	25.96	19
Norway	4.51	9	41.29	3	24.74	5	16.55	1	59.87	18	40.13	6
Portugal	5.70	4	22.39	20	12.08	22	10.31	14	53.85	21	46.15	3
Spain	5.45	5	18.56	23	12.62	20	5.94	21	67.46	11	32.54	13
Sweden	2.47	22	42.56	1	30.30	2	12.25	7	70.88	9	29.12	15
Switzerland	2.48	21	25.18	18	18.96	17	6.21	20	74.80	4	25.20	20
Turkey	6.70	2	20.22	21	11.32	23	8.90	16	55.13	20	44.87	4
United Kingdom	2.23	23	35.01	10	24.99	4	10.03	15	71.28	8	28.72	16
United States	3.38	18	29.02	15	23.52	9	5.50	22	81.01	1	18.99	23

[a] Social security contributions included.

Source: Petersen (1981b, Tables 2 and 7).

COMMENT

Herbert Grubel

Dr. Petersen's paper very ably summarizes the existing stock of knowledge about the effect of taxation on the supply of work effort, savings and investment and income distribution in Germany in the post-war period. He also analyzes the effects of tax incidence and of inflation on the level of taxation.

In general, the results of the studies he reviews are consistent with and reinforce those made of other countries' tax systems in the same theoretical tradition. Thus, in Germany it is difficult to establish that the tax system has had an important aggregate influence on the supply of labour and economic growth as a function of capital accumulation, but it is clear that the income equalization effects have been disappointingly small and that inflation has led to sharp increases in government revenues and expenditures.

I found of particular interest the results of the surveys of German writers concerning income and substitution effects. This confirms long established theoretical preconceptions held by economists. Whatever the shortcomings of surveys, in this case they have resulted in valuable information obtainable in no other way.

While I can find no faults with Petersen's review of the German studies, I must confess to a certain scepticism about their results. Introspection and casual observation of other people suggests to me that the effects of taxation on work effort, growth and income distribution may well be larger than has been discovered in the studies reviewed by Petersen. The reason for this state of affairs seems to be flaws in our conceptual apparatus. We may well need some new theoretical and empirical approaches that allow us to go beyond the orthodox measures.

In the following I will discuss briefly and quite superficially some possible new approaches to the study of the effects of taxation. This may lead to a revision of the conventional results.

CONSIDERING THE TYPE OF EXPENDITURES

Assar Lindbeck in his contribution to this volume speculates that reactions to increased taxes are largely influenced by the benefits received from the government expenditures made with the tax revenues. For example, my savings for retirement will be lower if a marginal increase in my taxes entitles me to an actuarially equivalent retirement benefit. There is no need for me here to elaborate on Lindbeck's brilliant general statement of the problem and his taxonomy of effects.

Instead, I would like to discuss a different type of effect induced by some of the expenditure programs. This leads to reduced work effort and savings, which I believe should be added to the effects noted by Lindbeck. Thus, government expenditure programs in the form of alleged public insurance like unemployment compensation, medical care, retraining programs and retirement pensions inevitably are accompanied by the phenomenon of moral hazard. This phenomenon generally manifests itself as a greater incidence of the hazard and therefore as an increased "need" for the benefits of the insurance scheme. This higher frequency of need, moreover, is a decreasing function of the degree of coinsurance by the insured. For example, the higher are unemployment benefits relative to wages, medical insurance payments as a proportion of the total cost of illness and retirement benefits as a fraction of the cost of living, the greater are the induced effects of the government programs on unemployment, frequency of illnesses and private poverty in old age.

Given these effects, we should in principle be able to show that they induce a reduction in work effort through an increase in the natural rate of unemployment and greater frequency of sickness leaves, and a fall in savings through increased average propensity to consume out of after-tax incomes. In addition, the overall allocational efficiency of the economy is reduced. Citizens now consume more of the services priced at a marginal cost of zero than they would if these services were priced at their true marginal social cost.

In sum, the preceding considerations suggest that the induced overconsumption of unemployment, leisure, job search, and medical services (these have been found to be quite substantial by some researchers) should be added to the estimates of the reduction of work effort and efficiency created by the package of tax-financed public insurance programs.[1] Similarly, as Martin Feldstein[2] has shown, there must be a reduction in overall social savings as private individuals reduce their savings in expectation of government benefits financed through their tax payments. (This holds true to the extent that the government does not use in real capital formation revenue collected for retirement pensions).

THE MIX OF OCCUPATIONS AND INVESTMENT

All choices of occupations and investment involve risk. As the modern theories of finance and human capital indicate, the greater the risk, the greater is the average rate of return needed in order to compensate the workers and investors for the disutility of the risk. Assume that yield and risk patterns are in equilibrium in an economy with zero (or proportional) taxes on income. And then consider the imposition of a progressive tax on income. It is clear that this is equivalent to cutting off the upper end of the distribution of expected returns. This is especially true the more risky is the occupation or investment. As a result, the supply of people and savings is initially reduced for the riskier and increased for the less risky occupations and projects. A general adjustment of returns later raises the average yield in the riskier projects, but the average cost of the output produced by these occupations and industries has to rise. Given a downward sloping demand curve for their output, employment and investment in these industries is reduced.

Under these conditions there is a reduction in overall welfare, assuming that the initial pre-tax mix of occupations and investment was optimal. However, there may well be additional effects on work effort and growth. For we must assume that the more risky jobs allow discretionary variation in effort (*i.e.*, entrepreneurial and professional work) and that risky but successful investments are those that often lead to technological breakthroughs and spurts in growth. Under these assumptions, the progressive tax system can lead to a reduction in work effort and real economic growth even though there is no evidence that work effort in the low-risk occupations has decreased or overall investment has fallen. The negative impact of the tax system is hidden by changes in the occupational mix, promoting civil service and low-skilled occupations at the expense of professional and entrepreneurial occupations. I believe that many observations about conditions in different countries made by several authors lend general support to my hypothesis.

REGULATION AS A FORM OF TAXATION

In Petersen's, as well as all of the other papers, I missed a discussion of the effects of regulation as a form of taxation on efficiency and effort. The German draft of young people for military service is a special form of taxation and causes inefficiencies and therefore reductions in economic growth. Persons with potentially high social productivity in civilian occupations are forced into several years of relatively low productivity employment. Rent controls in Sweden, Canada and many other countries represent a tax on wealthholders and lead to many well-known distortions and inefficiencies. These laws reduce real economic growth rates for given rates of growth of labour and capital.[3] The list of such taxes implicit in regulation is quite long and includes widespread agricultural programs, controls over the marketing of drugs, transportation services and many others.

PROBLEMS OF INCOME INEQUALITY

Studies of the effects of progressive income taxation and transfer payments on the equality of the income distribution (including the ones on German conditions reported by Petersen) typically find little reduction in inequalities through time. This, in spite of increasingly greater progressivity of the tax structure and increased transfer payments.There is a difficulty, however. These studies may be highly misleading, since they don't take account of socially acceptable influences on the degree of inequality observed at different points in time. For example, using family incomes, between 1960 and 1980 there has been a very large increase in the proportion of families with two and more income earners. This has taken place in almost all Western countries. As a result, there has been a large increase in families with high incomes. Therefore the observed degree of inequality of incomes has risen. Yet, that source of income inequality is not one that most social architects concerned about equity either want to, or, without severe effects on incentives, can eliminate.

There are many other such socially acceptable or even desirable influences on income distributions. Consider, for instance, the 65 year-old person who inflates upper decile numbers because he has a high income from work and from the assets accumulated for use and decumulation in the following year. Also, numerous students entering the labour force in fall every year inflate the number of people in the low-income deciles. These phenomena do not at all require corrective actions to maintain what in most people's view is an equitable income distribution.

In sum, I am suggesting that intertemporal studies of the income distribution effects of tax expenditure and transfer programs should first purge the raw data of these influences on private income before they apply the standard estimating techniques.

SUMMARY AND CONCLUSIONS

In conclusion, let me emphasize that the preceding suggestions for the extension of the scope of studies on the impact of taxation on work effort and capital formation are not to be construed as a criticism of Petersen's fine paper. Instead, they represent a suggestion to broaden the approach to the study of the important subject he discussed, in the hope that such broadening will lead to new insights, better understanding of the past and, perhaps more important, better economic policies.

NOTES

1. See Grubel H. and M. Walker (ed.). *Unemployment Insurance: Global Evidence of Its Effects on Unemployment,* Vancouver: The Fraser Institute (1978).
2. Feldstein, M. "Social Security, Induced Retirement and Aggregate Capital Accumulation," *Journal of Political Economy,* 82:5:905-26 (1974).
3. See *Rent Control: A Popular Paradox,* Vancouver: The Fraser Institute (1975).

DISCUSSION

Edited by: Walter Block

Assar Lindbeck began the informal discussion of the German tax system by commenting on redistribution effects and labour-leisure allocations. "Professor Petersen suggests that redistribution effects are very small for both wage taxes and assessed income taxes. I understand that in those estimates the government spending financed by taxes, such as transfer payments, is not included. But I think this very misleading. If we are going to discuss the redistribution effect of taxes, I think we really have to include the expenditures side too, for reasons I stated earlier in my previous intervention. If you look at Sweden, for instance, it would seem that the main redistribution effect is connected with the fact that taxes are taken from "everybody," and that transfers are paid to the lower decile. This creates a large difference between the distribution of factor income and the distribution of disposable income. But that is largely because of the way the expenditures, not the taxes, are distributed.

"My second point is that it is difficult for people in the short run to change their working time because this is regulated by bargaining and legislation. In the long run, however, bargaining and legislation respond to the incentive system. We see how labour unions increasingly try to bargain for higher living standards in the form of shorter working hours; we see how governments, through the political process, increasingly give people extra leisure; for instance people can stay home with their children, sick relatives, or for so-called adult education, etc. This means that people get outlets to take more leisure by exploiting these various social programs which provide subsidized leisure. I think that if we take a longer-term perspective, the possibilities of varying leisure are much greater because of the effects through bargaining and political decision making."

This provoked a discussion between Lindbeck and Zane Spindler. Said the latter: "I'm sympathetic towards this long-run effect that Assar pointed out, but do you have any idea of how one might determine whether that comes from the tax system, or whether it is a result of the operation of the simple income elasticity on the demand for leisure?" Replied Lindbeck, "No. that's a very difficult issue; I really don't know. You should expect that when people pay 60–80 per cent marginal tax rates in a country, it is quite tempting to take out additional compensation in the form of shorter working hours. The explanation is probably *both* rising income in society *and* the substitution effect of taxes toward leisure. It's an ambitious research program to try to disentangle the effects."

Continued Spindler, "I'd like to raise a minor technical point about the estimations which might bias the coefficient for the average tax rate upwards; that is, they might allow the estimations to indicate that taxes have a lesser impact on the growth rate than they might in fact have. This question deals with the composition of the dependent and the independent variable here. The way I interpret it, the dependent variable could be rewritten as change in income in the private sector plus change in income in the government sector divided by income in both the private and government sector. The independent variable is income in the government sector divided by income in the private sector plus income in the government sector. When there is an increase in income in the government sector, that is, in the average tax rate, there is also an increase in the measured growth rate of gross domestic product. So I would think that probably a more accurate indication of the effect of taxes on growth might come from looking at the growth rate for the private economy as a function of taxes relative to the income of the private economy."

Lindbeck then set out his analysis of incentives, and was joined in this discussion by several other participants:

Lindbeck: "There is a possibility that economists are underestimating the incentive effects. This is because they are so elusive and so multi-dimensional. Our methods of analysis might be simply too blunt to register them. I don't think we are entitled to say that the effects are small—or large for that matter—simply because we do not have methods sophisticated enough to analyze the effect.

"Moreover, incorrect analysis of the income effect will hide the essence of the issue, for instance when people are asked whether they work less or more because of taxes. In such cases they certainly include both the income and substitution effects because they most likely assume a *ceteris paribus* change in the tax rate; they probably do not take account of the fact that they get back the money in some other ways which tend to cancel the income effect.

"Suppose the government takes $1,000 from me and gives it to another person. There is a positive income effect on me because I have to work more, but a negative one on the other person. The question is, 'What is the net of these two income effects which go in the opposite direction?'

"This discussion is confused. First of all there is a positive income effect on those who pay the tax and a negative income effect on those who receive the payment. The net income effect on labour supply incorporates *both* of these. However, I regard these income effects as irrelevant from an efficiency point of view, because they do not create disincentives. They do not create wedges between factor costs or rewards to individuals. We don't treat lump sum taxes and lump sum transfers as an efficiency problem. Why then should we treat the income effect of taxation as an efficiency problem? There is no reason for this whatsoever."

Grubel: "Consider this negative income effect. If the $1,000 that is taken away from me goes to my father whom I used to have to support in his old age, then I'm no worse off than I was before. Therefore, I think the point that Lindbeck made is very important. We have to be careful in specifying when we ask these questions about the effects."

But Walter Block disagreed. Said he, "Although Professors Lindbeck and Grubel may not see it this way, I think that one point we can see more clearly than other people is the importance of distinguishing between public and private goods. When you consider private goods like razor blades or lipstick or bicycles or perfumes, stockings, radios or TVs, the ordinary private goods, we know that when a person spends money for them it is evidence that he values these things more than the money he had to pay. But if you take public goods like jet planes or parks, schools, limousines, roads, planning services, zoning, civil service, the connection is by no means so clear. We, as economists, cannot definitively say that whenever a dollar gets spent on a public service that there is some citizen that values this service more than the cost of it. Therefore we must be cautious in accepting the view that there is an exact offset between the income effect on taxpayers and the income effect of those who receive gifts, goods and services from government. As well, I think if this distinction is made more clearly we could perhaps make a case for less public services and, *i.e.,* less taxes.

Spindler: "The thing that one should pay attention to in some of these studies is that they do measure temporary equilibrium adjustment proceeds which may have balancing interventions to counter the change in taxes. For instance, an increase in the marginal rate of taxation may lead to an increase in the non-taxable advantages that are given to workers. The result is that there is no change in labour supply so that these counter adjustments may make it appear like nothing has changed with respect to a change in the tax rate when in fact there has been a change."

De Vany: "I want to point out that it is not theoretically correct to discuss an income effect as a pure income effect, given the way the government redistributes income. It is typically the case that relative prices are affected as well. For example, consumption of government services are basically time-intensive types of commodities. When one reallocates the production of resources from money-intensive to time-intensive ones, there are effects on relative prices. We should, therefore, be very careful about discussing pure income effects. For, in fact, most of these transfers affect relative prices and, therefore, induce both income and substitution effects in and of themselves. For example, consider a program which subsidizes medical service, but which also makes medical service more time-intensive relative to that provided in a private program. This is a program which will induce both income and substitution effects. What we call the income effect is really a reduction in the work effort required to efficiently consume the new, now more time-intensive commodity bundle offered on the supply side. I don't think we have the theoretical analysis well in hand here at all."

Charles Stuart: "I would like to make a couple of comments about the regressions of growth rate on tax rate. In particular, I think I see an area where future research can refine these sorts of results. The problem I see arising with this very simple regression is that there are a number of alternative hypotheses which can explain the results that, essentially, growth rates seem to be negatively correlated with the rate of taxes. There is, of course, the tax disincentive hypothesis, which is what we've been discussing here. There is also, given in the results before us, some possibility that what we're really observing is growth rates falling over time as Germany rebuilds after the war and its technology becomes more up-to-date and on a par with the technology existing in other developed countries.

"I think it is important in the future when we do this sort of study on the impact of the tax system on growth rates, that we have a more specific model which would hopefully allow us to separate out these different hypotheses. If we really are interested in capturing the disincentive effects, we should be focusing on marginal instead of average tax rates. Now it could be the case that the average and marginal tax rates lie in a constant relation so that no econometric problems actually arise. But it would be more natural to make the analysis in terms of marginal rates since it is marginal rates which influence incentives.

"I would also like to comment on the point made by Spindler. We should look at the private sector of the economy and at how taxes have influenced the private sector. This should net out the public sector from the regressions. But there is a problem. If taxes increase, and the government starts spending and funding for the public sector increases, that is going to draw resources away from the private sector. We are going to change the mix of the private and public sectors in the economy. Regardless of whether there is a disincentive effect, if we had netted out the public sector from the growth in income, we would have observed the results now before us. There is a bias, in other words, toward observing a disincentive even when none exists.

"On the other hand I am sympathetic toward Professor Spindler's comments as regards how the public sector should be included. I think there is definitely a difficulty with how the public sector should be treated, simply because it is evaluated in the national income accounts at its factor costs, not at market price."

Edgar Feige: "I just want to add to Professor Stuart's possible alternative hypothesis regarding that regression because I was also drawn to it when I read the Petersen paper. Our official GNP statistics might simply be systematically understated as a result of shifting resources into the unobserved sector. Obviously, higher tax rates would provide the incentive to do that. If so, I'm delighted by this German result because it is in fact very consistent with independent results I found for the United States. So I would bank on that hypothesis as one that should at least seriously be considered."

Herbert Grubel: "The more I look at the studies the more I find evidence for the simple picture that so many people have about the influence of the tax structures. The tax levels in Britain are the symbol of a country where the tax system has caused so many difficulties. Germany, on the other hand, is one that had a more rational tax structure. This may have been greatly responsible for the great economic success of Germany in post-war years. I'm beginning to worry whether, in fact, the tax system can explain very much of this phenomena."

Professor Petersen concluded our analysis by replying to several of the participants, "I totally agree with Professor Grubel that we need other models for estimating the effects of taxation on effort. We especially need behavioural models. But I am not very optimistic. The formulation of such models is very difficult and often such models – to use a quotation of Jack Wiseman's – are 'like garlic cheese repackaged as boursin.' I also totally agree with Professor Lindbeck that we need information concerning the incidence of the total public budget (including the expenditure side, especially transfer payments). We have some studies about this topic in Germany, but up to now the results are a function of the presuppositions of the authors, and today I see no solutions to that problem.

"I agree with Professor Stuart that we must focus upon the marginal tax rates, not the average. Up to now we have had problems deriving macroeconomic marginal rates. But this also applies in microeconomics. Marginal rates are of specific interest. The ratio between marginal and average tax rates is crucial; this yield elasticity is the most important measure that can be used to judge the effects between rising incomes and the increasing tax burden. At the same average tax rates, there can be very different marginal tax rates. For tax reform we should choose the tax schedules with the lowest marginal rates which are possible at the corresponding average rates. Tax schedules with lower yield elasticities will also decrease the disincentives which are built into our current tax systems.

"With regard to my regression results I will only say that they are extremely simple. They are only a very first attempt; we have to build more complex models with more variables and we have to recognize different structures of GNP. I am not very optimistic about future research on this topic because it is very difficult to judge the productivity of the public sector and how much of our real growth is due to the private sector.

"We must also be aware that the same marginal tax rate structure works quite differently in different countries; the influences are especially dependent on the specific attitudes of the taxpayers. In Europe we distinguish between German-type and Roman-type countries; the tax morality is very different. In Italy and France, for example, people have very strong reservations about direct taxation, especially in the form of income tax. This is perhaps a consequence of the decisions made during the French revolution. Indirect taxes were favoured because the French people were afraid of the 'inquisition fiscale' which is connected with income taxation. I think that today's attitudes in the Roman-type countries are still influenced by this choice made during the 18th and 19th centuries. Beyond that, the effects of the tax system on the attitudes of taxpayers are especially dependent on the efficiency of the fiscal administration. In Germany, for instance, the taxpayers have to make a financial 'strip-tease' before our fiscal administration. This seems to be impossible in other countries. When we discuss the effects of marginal rates on effort, we must recognize these different attitudes of taxpayers in the different countries."

CHAPTER 9

A GENERAL DESCRIPTION OF THE ITALIAN TAX SYSTEM

Sergio Ricossa

I. PRINCIPAL FORMS OF TAXATION

The main components of the Italian tax system are:

-the progressive personal income tax
-the proportional corporation income tax
-the value-added tax
-social security contributions

International comparisons show that the Italian tax system has the greatest reliance on social security contributions as a proportion of total taxes paid. It ranks only eleventh out of twelve major industrial countries in terms of taxes on income and wealth (see Statistical Appendix, Table 9-A 1). This is the consequence of the choice, made in fascist times, of financing an extended social security system by means of special contributions instead of through general taxes.

Italian social security contributions are mainly paid for by employers, as a percentage of wages. Assuming no shift in incidence, this is to the benefit of Italian employees. The cost of labour is thus higher than it would otherwise be, especially when trade unions are strong. But this has deleterious effects on employment. For this reason, there is a growing demand for changes in the social security laws. As a matter of fact, in recent years the burden has shifted somewhat from special contributions to general taxes, and more of this is expected in future.

Adding all taxes to social security contributions, the Italian tax ratio is still well below 40 per cent of gross domestic product. This again places Italy eleventh out of twelve, this time in terms of total taxes as a percentage of GDP (see Table 9-A 1). But tax ratios are misleading. Exactly the same political effects may be caused by quite different political actions resulting in quite different tax ratios. For example, Italy has a widespread system of rent control, which is outside the fiscal system.

However, this is equivalent to a special tax on houses and land, even if the government budget does not record it as such. When phenomena such as these are taken into account, Italian government expenditures as a percentage of national income are well in line with those of the other industrial countries. What is different is how expenditures are financed. Italy prefers public debts to taxes.

INFLATION TAX

Inflation may also be interpreted as a tax on liquidity and on money savings. A 15–20 per cent rate of inflation has characterized Italy in recent years, and the nominal rate of interest on bonds and bank deposits has ranged between 10–15 per cent. The *real* rate of interest is thus negative and yet tax is levied against interest "earnings" despite the fact that they are negative. Only interest on central government bonds are free from taxes (this is perhaps one of the most relevant cases of "tax expenditures" in Italy). Of course, Italian banks are subject to strict regulations preventing any effective competition on the rate of interest. As well, all the principal banks are nationalized.

One may be puzzled as to why savings have not been entirely eradicated under such a system. One answer is "money illusion." Also, the habit of saving appears to be very strong in most families, especially in the older generations. It is not easily changed because of the urgent wish to accumulate a reserve of wealth and liquidity for future needs. The Italian social security system does not give retired people assurance that their working life standard of living will be maintained. So public pensions are supplemented, as far as possible, by private savings, even if losses are incurred. According to the Italian law, however, national savings cannot be invested abroad (except under special licenses).

INVESTMENT LIMITATIONS

What of the alternatives to savings? Savers are thus compelled to accept the domestic situation. There is a very strict rent control on houses and land properties, which practically wipes out any proprietor's investment. Stock prices are now well below the 1960 level, in spite of the continuous depreciation of the 1960 lira because many big companies are not in a position to pay regular dividends. Suffering as they are from heavy trade union attacks and other misfortunes, a certain number of manufacturing companies are actually on the brink of failure. The Italian stock exchange is thus despised by national investors, and its activity is moribund. The purchase of gold and diamonds is either illegal, or subject to punitive taxes. Most Italian families seem to think that the best way to save is to lend money to public institutions only, or to keep money at hand in bank deposits.

Public institutions are quite eager for the money, which is then partly channelled to the private companies in need.

BRACKET CREEP

Since the Italian progressive income tax is not indexed, any increase of nominal incomes due to inflation is considered a real gain, and taxed at a higher marginal rate. The same applies to capital gains: the original or historical value of assets on the books is not allowed to be adjusted according to the diminishing purchasing power of money with very few exceptions. Most of the difference between the current value and the original or historical value is thereby taxed. The fisc thus profits from inflation both directly and indirectly. Corporations suffer as taxpayers; on the other hand, they are favoured as debtors when they borrow at a sufficiently low real rate of interest.

Another point needs to be stressed. The Italian tax is relatively burdensome compared to other countries with regard to incomes above the subsistence level. Such a computation shows that this revised tax ratio is higher in Italy than in any country with a more developed economy.[1]

SOME COMPARISONS

An interesting international comparison refers to a standard family: a wage earner (the husband), his wife (without income), and two children. For all family incomes up to 30 million lire (about 30–35,000 dollars per year) the income tax ratio in Italy is higher than in West Germany, and France; but below that of the United Kingdom. However, if we add social security contributions to the income tax, the total tax ratio as a percentage of family income is higher in Italy than in the U.K., West Germany and France (the three leading countries in Western Europe). Nominal income tax rates are relatively low in Italy, but deductions from taxable incomes are also usually much lower than abroad. The Italian family's situation is further deteriorated by social security contributions, which are a maximum in Italy. True, most of them are actually charged to the employer, not the wage earner, but there may be some incidence shift. While the income tax is progressive everywhere, social security contributions are proportional. They are regressive in Germany and France (not in Italy and the U.K.) because of the existence of ceilings in collected contributions per worker ("massimali") (see Statistical Appendix, Table 9-A2).

The total tax ratio for the standard Italian family is about 30 to 40 per cent of gross family income, roughly comparable to expenditures on food. Taxes are greater than family expenditures on shelter, 10 to 20 per cent of income, and much larger than expenditures on clothing, usually less than 10 per cent of income (see Table 9-A3). The standard family receives public services and allowances in exchange for taxes and social security contributions. But there is a widespread dissatisfaction with the quality and quantity of benefits, while the costs are strongly lamented. It is extremely difficult, moreover, to obtain a clear overall picture of who gains and who loses.

THE UNDERGROUND ECONOMY

One reason for this is the popular practice of tax "avoision." It is estimated that only half the Italian national income comes under the scrutiny of the fiscal authorities. This is shown by comparing the tax accounts with the national income accounts, which are published by the Italian Central Institute of Statistics (quite independently of the fiscal authorities). As well, we must keep in mind that the *official* national income is perhaps 10-15 per cent lower than the *actual* national income. The Central Institute of Statistics is unable to record the output of the "submerged economy" which employs about 5 million workers, either full-time or part-time. However, this figure is no better than a mere guess based on unofficial sample surveys. For example, in 1976 taxable income as declared for the progressive income tax was 45,674 billion lire; at the same time, net national income at factor cost was officially 115,794 billion lire. Of course, not all taxable incomes are subject to the progressive tax, but most of them are. In any case, there is a huge gap between 45,674 and 115,794 billion lire. Moreover, the 115,794 billion lire is certainly an underestimate of actual net national income. The actual figure may be nearer to 130,000 billion lire (see Table 9-A4).

If only half of the Italian national income is taxed, the other half is concealed by either legal avoidance and/or by illegal evasion. No reliable information is available on the relative importance of actual evasion and avoidance. However, the expectation is that evasion is particularly serious in small business firms, for independent workers, and for holders of a second job, etc. It concerns income taxes as well as the value-added tax and other indirect taxes. Bribery of tax officials is not unknown. Until recently, the income of independent workers was subject to higher tax rates—in order to offset their presumed larger evasion. The Supreme Court has now repealed this questionable piece of legislation. Unfortunately, there remain on the books many other questionable, complex, elaborate and uncertain tax regulations. These give rise to a very large number of cases slowing down the entire court calendar. As a result, most Italian taxpayers do not know how much they will actually pay on past incomes—even many years after incomes were earned.

II. HISTORICAL PATTERNS

The post-war period shows a clear trend toward more reliance on income taxation, and away from indirect taxation. This pattern became more significant after an important tax reform introduced in 1972–1973. The number of Italians subject to the progressive income tax increased from 4.8 million in 1973 to 22.8 million in 1974. This stupendous jump does not mean that the money volume of tax payments also quadrupled. It rose by much less, since many "new" taxpayers were already paying a *non-progressive* income tax. The reform unified the two taxes into one progressive income tax. However, tax evasion was reduced for two reasons: 1) more severe penalties for new cases, and 2) amnesty for past violations when the persons involved regularized their position as taxpayers.

Excluding social security contributions, direct taxes on all kinds of income and wealth increased from about 30 per cent of total tax payments at the beginning of the 1970s to nearly 50 per cent by the end of the decade. This is the result of both a changed political will, and the mechanical play of inflation. As the marginal rates of progressive taxation are seldom changed to comply with the declining purchasing power of money, inflation submits nominal incomes to higher and higher tax rates. We have already seen that even negative real incomes may be taxed as a consequence. Another result is that most incomes eventually rise above the minimum cut off point and become taxable, even when the equivalent purchasing power was exempt in the past. Poor people, thus, especially suffer from inflation.

INDIRECT TAXATION

Indirect taxation is often considered inappropriate or no more than a second best alternative in comparison with direct taxation. It is seen as socially unfair when it cannot discriminate against rich people. And yet a great deal of fiscal revenues still come from this source. The Italian value-added tax, which may be considered as a tax on consumption, has widely differing rates according to the particular goods in question. For example, necessities are taxed at zero or low rates, and luxuries are subject to higher tax rates up to 35 per cent of their prices. But evasion increases as the rates go up. The maximum 35 per cent rate would otherwise effectively prohibit virtually all trade in luxuries. It is not clear, then, that the Italian value-added tax, despite the politicians' intentions, is a progressive tax.

Another remarkable trend concerns the financing of public expenses. Until the middle of the 1960s, about 90 per cent of those expenses were covered by taxes. Recently, the proportion has been reduced to about 70 per cent. At the same time, net borrowing by the public sector increased from 1–3 per cent of net national income to 10–15 per cent yearly (see Table 9-A5). The deficit of the government budget in Italy is now quite abnormal with regard to the international standard: the latest estimate for 1979 puts it at 40,000 billion lire, or 16.2 per cent of national income. This is a record unparalleled in the Western world: in absolute terms, it is even larger than the U.S. deficit. Even worse, most of the deficit is not devoted to public investments, but to current consumption. Under these conditions, public debt accumulation, which amounted to about 45 per cent of GDP at the beginning of the 1970s, had reached nearly 70 per cent by the end of the decade.[2] Such a heavy debt load must lead either to heavily increased tax deferrals or to a sustained and ever-accelerating inflation. Of course, thanks to the deterioration of the value of money, this debt accumulation is far greater in nominal than in real terms. But the growth of its share in the national income fills the future with concern. To keep down the rate of interest, the government is obliged to maintain a loose monetary policy: the money circulation is currently expanding at 20–25 per cent each year, which is utterly incompatible with any slowdown of inflation.

AN INSOLUBLE PROBLEM?

Nor will even a successful fight against tax evasion solve this problem. A stricter enforcement of tax laws is under way, and heavy penalties (including prison) are now inflicted for fiscal crimes. Tax inspectors have been given additional powers. But any progress in this direction is likely to cause damage to the private economy and to render any long-term advantages dubious. It is commonly recognized that, after 1969, the fastest developing sector of the Italian economy, apart from the public sector, is the so called "submerged sector," *i.e.,* those small businesses which are best able to avoid fully paying governmental request for excessive tax revenues. These companies are also most able to elude the most rapacious demands of the trade unions. This is such a serious problem that many large companies can no longer continue in business without the help they receive from the government. The paradox is that punitive fiscal measures are followed by government grants to firms which otherwise would collapse under the too heavy burden. Public money is thus pumped in and out of the production process without any clear assessment of its side-effects. However, the result surely is a progressive weakening of free private enterprise in Italy. The ultimate result will have to be in the direction of a non-market economy under centralized state control.

III. IMPACT OF THE TAX SYSTEM

What we have just said with reference to firms may be generalized to families. Considering public revenues together with public expenditures, it is impossible to prove if and to what degree the tax system has been redistributive in Italy. This is the emphatic conclusion reached by all recent studies of this issue. We may quote, for example, Antonio Pedone, Professor of Economic Policy at the University of Rome: "Measuring the redistributive effectiveness of the Italian tax system is actually impossible so far as data are available. On the one hand, the statistical material on personal income distribution before taxes are levied is uncertain and fragmentary. On the other hand, the effective allocation of the fiscal charge to the various income classes is not officially published, nor is any useful information for computing it."[3]

Since high incomes often result from independent work or overtime, "out-of-office," second job dependent work, their recipients are able to avoid and evade taxes to a significant degree. If Italy had a proportional personal income tax, instead of the progressive income tax actually in operation, the flat-rate tax able to collect the same revenue would be in the range of 10–15 per cent. It would be below 10 per cent of earned income, if avoision could be completely barred. This proves that progressive marginal rates of 80 or 90 per cent have very little importance for public revenues. In Italy as elsewhere, rich people have the regrettable habit of being few in number, and the richer they are the fewer are their numbers (see Table 9-A6).

Estates and gifts are also subject to progressive taxation. Yet, rich people are able to transfer their great wealth from one generation to another by using legal and illegal stratagems of tax avoidance. Progressive taxes on cars are of moderate importance. Yet, even here rich people can escape high taxes by purchasing two or three small cars instead of one big (and expensive) one.

SMALL EFFECTS

The redistributive consequences of the progressive direct taxes are thus rather small. They may easily be cancelled by the regressive characteristics of other programs such as indirect taxation.[4] Since 1945, income inequality in Italy has actually manifested a downward trend. But this is not due to fiscal causes. It is chiefly the natural tail end of rapid economic development and a lower unemployment rate up to 1969. After 1969, the economic boom dissolved. This was due to a more aggressive trade union policy which wiped out profits in big companies.

As well, there was a deteriorated international situation. Trade unions succeeded temporarily in increasing wages, particularly those of unskilled workers. But this was without any regard to productivity and sales. So they contributed to a reduction in income inequality. But the cost was a general slump in profits—which eventually reversed this effect.

When public expenditures are considered together with revenues, it becomes even more difficult to assess the amount of income redistribution carried on by the government. Many prices are regulated by the government, and numerous commercial activities are subsidized. As a result, it is impossible to conduct a rational cost-benefit analysis. There is a feeling that the middle classes gain most, but that there are wide disparities even here. As Professor G. Stigler once said of political goals, "we do not know how to get there. . . . We do not know the relationship between the public policies we adopt and the effects these policies were designed to achieve." This is particularly true in Italy, a country with a weak statistical organization and unstable governments, where public policies are often distorted by communist trade union interferences.

RENT CONTROL

Undoubtedly, public policies and trade unions aim at more equality; yet, they do so with discordant emphases, and operate in the dark, since real effects are seldom checked. For example, rent control is enacted on the assumption that property owners are richer than tenants.[5] Of course, the reverse may actually be true. In any case, it provokes a slowdown of new housing construction for rent, and thus hurts new families wishing to rent a house, particularly families who cannot afford to purchase.[6]

What is more, the Italian public targets are themselves contradictory. Public sponsored lotteries and subsidies for concerts and ballets are all anti-egalitarian. But the most conspicuous contradiction is financial aid to big business, or artificial protections against competition. This helps the rich, to the detriment of the poor. Large fortunes have been accumulated in private hands thanks to protectionism, at the expense of taxpayers and consumers. Large fortunes are still accumulated in private hands thanks to protectionism in spite of declining corporate profits, since market success is no longer necessary for acquiring great wealth.

THE REAL FUNCTION OF TAXES

The impact of taxes on the improvement of general welfare, social justice or equality is dwarfed by the more prosaic task of providing money to politicians for the mere exercise of power for power's sake. Public money, in the Italian experience, is increasingly spent according to the worst criteria of "public choice." It is used to establish and maintain privileges for the politicians themselves, their bureaucracy and for allied social groups. The Italian political parties are supported by public money. In addition to the legal grants they are entitled to receive, their members and clients benefit from the expansion of politics into the economy. This implies the continuous shift from the economic market to the political market: satisfying private consumers is becoming less and less important than satisfying the government and its allied parties. The main opposition party, the communist party, is itself strongly in favour of the state economy. It collects a share of grants the taxpayers are compelled to give, and has a say in all political decisions through its members of parliament and, to an even higher degree, its trade unions.[7]

A former Italian minister, Professor Siro Lombardini, has summarized this phenomenon as follows: "the workers' welfare will depend more and more on public consumption and less and less on private consumption; in such a way that the economic market is becoming obsolete, since public consumption must be the responsible choice of the whole community."[8] Of course, this community making responsible choices outside the market does not exist. What Professor Lombardini really means is that politicians do exist who will eagerly make choices on behalf of the entire community. But this causes a serious loss of efficiency in the private sector of the economy, and an even greater loss in the economy as a whole, where the public sector squeezes out the private sector. "Crowding out" effects are commonly observed in Italy. Private production, no longer rewarded according to its productivity in the economic market, prospers or declines according to political criteria. But these are far removed from price-and-quality competition which can alone guarantee efficiency. Public production is even more monopolistic, and completely disregards customers' wants.

COERCIVE SOCIALISM

The long-term incidence of taxation is thus particularly destructive of the industrial mix and of the overall efficiency of the economy. Savings and investments are reduced in some measure by heavy taxation, but, worse than that, they are channelled in political directions in opposition to the free choices of private consumers. The same applies to the labour supply. This may be welcomed by those with a collectivistic bias. But the complete collapse of the free market economy in Italy will not help the average citizen of Italy. On the contrary, coercive socialism endangers both economic efficiency and political freedom.

The Italian government is not only the actual owner of a number of industries, it also generously aids ailing private industries. However, public aid always has political strings which reduce managerial independence. Nearly all Italian political parties are fond of applying the Latin motto: *Protego ergo obligo* (Protecting means obliging). The final result of these fiscal excesses will be a socialist society in which the whole of the economy is under political control. The government itself is nothing but a tool or instrument for achieving that far reaching result in a subtle, surreptitious way. This is the Italian lesson in a nutshell.

NOTES

1. See G. Parravicini, *La pressione tributaria e finanziaria,* in P. Scaramozzino (editor), *Studi in onore di Libero Lenti*, Milano (1979). The computation considers an income per capita net of: i) those incomes which do not flow to families; ii) non-taxable family incomes; iii) a fixed income which covers consumption at the subsistence level.
2. See A. Martino, *I danni dello statalismo,* in *Atti del convegno su lo Stato nell'economia di domani*, Milano (1980).
3. From A. Pedone, *Evasori e tartassati*, Bologna (1979). The gap is partially filled by a publication of the ministry of finance: Ministero delle finanze, *Analisi delle dichiarazioni dei redditi delle persone fisiche presentate nel 1977,* Roma (1980).
4. This is also the tentative conclusion of Giuseppe Sobbrio's econometric research. See his *Un criterio di misurazione della progressivita del sistema tributario nel 1974,* in E.Gerelli and M.Vitale (editors), *E' fallita la riforma tributaria?,* Milano (1979).
5. D. Gale Johnson
6. See *Rent Control: Myths and Reality,* ed. Walter Block & Edgar Olsen, Vancouver: The Fraser Institute (1981).
7. Local governments are often in the hands of the communist party. Their finances derive largely from the general (national) taxes, which are collected by the central government and then distributed to local governments according to law.
8. S. Lombardini, *Oltre la crisi,* Bologna (1979).

STATISTICAL APPENDIX

TABLE 9-A1

Tax Comparisons in Twelve Major Industrial Countries (1975)

Total Taxes as % of GDP		Taxes on Income as % of Total Taxes		Social Security Contributions as % of Total Taxes	
1. Netherlands	47	1. Denmark	59	1. *Italy*	46
2. Sweden	46	2. Sweden	50	2. France	40
3. Norway	45	3. Canada	48	3. Netherlands	38
4. Denmark	43	4. U.S.A.	44	4. W. Germany	34
5. Belgium	41	5. U.K.	44	5. Belgium	32
6. Austria	39	6. Norway	41	6. Austria	29
7. France	37	7. Belgium	40	7. U.S.A.	24
8. U.K.	37	8. Netherlands	35	8. Sweden	19
9. W. Germany	35	9. W. Germany	34	9. Norway	19
10. Canada	34	10. Austria	26	10. U.K.	18
11. *Italy*	32	11. *Italy*	22	11. Canada	10
12. U.S.A.	30	12. France	18	12. Denmark	1

Source: OECD, *Revenue Statistics of OECD Member Countries*, Paris 1977.

TABLE 9-A2

Tax Ratio[a] in Selected Western European Countries as % of Family Income

Family income (b) (000 Dollars Per Year)	France	W. Germany	U.K.	Italy
1	30	23	8	34
5	30	26	24	36
10	29	30	27	38
15	26	30	28	40
20	26	27	30	43
25	26	27	33	44
30	26	27	36	45

(a) Income taxes and social security contributions
(b) Wage earner (husband), wife (no income), and two children

Source: F. Reviglio, *L'imposta sul reddito delle persone fisiche;* in E. Gerelli and M. Vitale (editors), *E' fallita la riforma tributaria?*, Milano 1979.

TABLE 9-A3

Family Expenditures in Italy (1977; Billion Lire)

Total family consumption (including indirect taxes)	113,269	(100%)
of which food	39,846	(35.2%)
clothing	10,313	(9.1%)
shelter	14,358	(12.7%)
All taxes (including taxes which are not directly charged to families)	60,772	(53.9%)
of which social contributions	25,579	(22.8%)
personal income tax	10,098	(9.0%)

Source: Instituto Centrale di Statistica, *I conti degli italiani*, Roma 1978.

TABLE 9-A4

Official and Unofficial Income Estimates in Italy (1976; Billion Lire)

	GDP at Market Prices	Net National Income at Factor Cost
Official standard estimate (a)	143,849	115,794
Official estimate as revised according to EEC suggestions	156,657	128,711
Unofficial estimates (b)		
low guess	160,000	130,000
high guess	170,000	135,000

(a) In the present study, official standard estimates are used, unless otherwise specified.
(b) Our estimates from a survey of the Italian current literature.

Source: Isco, *Quadri della contabilita nazionale italiana*, Roma 1979;
A. Martino, *Another Italian Economic Miracle?*, unpublished paper.

TABLE 9-A5

Public Finance in Italy as % of GDP

Year	1960	1965	1970	1975	1978
Government expenditures	33.0	37.0	37.3	49.5	49.2
Taxes and social security contributions	29.2	30.8	31.0	32.3	35.8
Other revenues	2.9	2.3	3.2	2.6	2.0
Net borrowing	0.9	3.9	3.1	14.6	11.4

Source: A. Pedone, *Evasori e tartassati*, Bologna 1979

TABLE 9-A6

Personal Progressive Income Tax in Italy (1976)

Income Per Person (Million Lire Per Year)	Taxable Income (Billion Lire)	Taxes (Billion Lire) Gross	Net (a)
0 - 1.38	3,659	370	24
1.38 - 3	6,722	674	220
3 - 4	6,837	712	386
4 - 5	7,064	794	516
5 - 6	4,982	611	449
6 - 7.5	4,296	589	478
7.5 - 9	2,628	505	351
9 - 11	2,350	403	363
11 - 13	1,505	283	263
13 - 15	1,040	212	200
15 - 17	830	181	172
17 - 19	672	154	148
19 - 22	786	189	183
22 - 25	562	142	139
25 - 30	617	165	161
30 - 35	373	105	103
35 - 40	250	74	73
40 - 50	292	91	90
50 - 60	189	63	62
60 - 80	201	72	71
80 - 100	110	42	42
100 - 125	68	27	27
125 - 150	40	17	17
150 - 175	27	12	12
175 - 200	16	7	7
200 - 250	19	9	9
250 - 300	14	7	7
300 - 350	8	4	4
over 350	19	9	9
Total	45,674	6,424	4,587

(a) In Italy, some deductions refer to the gross tax, instead of income.

Source: Ministero delle finanze.

COMMENT

Zane Spindler

In this comment, I would like to amplify a theme which has been touched on by Sergio Ricossa, using data from recent OECD *Economic Surveys* and a recent article by Sergio Gambale.[1] As Ricossa's paper implies, and the title of Gambale's paper announces, public finance in Italy is in severe crisis—a crisis that has been developing, virtually unabated, throughout the 1970s.

The existence of this crisis is more clearly exposed by data on the public sector deficit and by the growth of public sector debt as a means of *current* finance. During the 1970s the public sector borrowing requirement (see Table 9.1) expanded from *14 to as much as 31 per cent* of the government budget and from *4 to as much as 16*[2] *per cent* of gross domestic product. Net issues of government bonds in the capital market have generally covered around half of the government's borrowing requirement (although it has gone as high as 90 per cent in 1977 and as low as 22 per cent in 1974) and these issues have been placed mainly with banks and financial institutions. The rest of the borrowing requirement has been covered by an expansion of the monetary base. Despite attempts by the Bank of Italy to keep monetary aggregates within target (mainly at the expense of private sector borrowing), the money supply and total domestic credit have grown at rates of around 20 per cent. Naturally, inflation has proceeded at a similar pace.

Occasional changes in deficit finance might be due to current economic conditions—as in 1974–1975—and, thus, to induced and planned stabilization budget activity. However, the major upward trend in deficit finance is definitely due to redistributional budget activity—and, to a lesser extent, allocational budget activity—which arose from social welfare legislation of the late 1960s to mid-1970s. This legislation, and its application, has turned Italy into a "transfer economy" that uses "deferred taxes," in the form of public debt, and "inflation taxes," in the form of money creation, as a *normal* component of its public revenue.

INTERNATIONAL COMPARISONS

Such a view of Italian public finance has some interesting consequences with respect to measurement of the impact of the fisc—especially, in relation to other OECD countries. On the basis of a traditional public finance view, Italy seems to bear a relatively low tax burden. But in the "Italian view," Italy bears a burden, relative to GDP, that is approximately the same as that of the United Kingdom (this is second only to

TABLE 9.1

Public Sector Borrowing Requirement

Item	1970*	1971*	1972*	1973	1974	1975	1976	1977
Billion lire, current prices	2,247	3,336	4,085	5,761	5,531	13,816	10,092	15,126
including social security				5,235	5,992	16,647	13,323	17,043
Per cent of budget	14.2	18.2	19.7	22.4	15.0	30.6	18.8	21.9
including social security				13.7	11.3	24.9	16.8	17.2
Per cent of GDP	3.9	5.3	5.9	7.0	5.4	12.0	7.0	8.7
including social security				6.3	5.9	14.5	9.3	9.9

* Figures for these years were not available for social security accounts.

Source: OECD Economic Survey — Italy (various issues) Statistical Annex: Table F

Sweden among OECD countries). If deficit finance is treated as a form of taxation, it is more appropriate to consider total expenditure[3] as a measure of burden (as implied by Ricossa, p.2) rather than total tax revenue. However high, effective marginal tax rates on "recorded" private activity and/or the "recorded market" medium of exchange have driven economic activity into the non-recorded "underground" market and non-market sectors. This has occurred to the extent that "only half of Italian national income comes under the scrutiny of fiscal authorities" (as Ricossa asserts). Given this, the tax burden relative to measured and unmeasured GDP is substantially lower. A meaningful comparison of real tax burdens among OECD countries would require comparable information on the underground and non-market economies of other OECD countries.

There have been a number of attempts during the 1970s to increase revenues from traditional tax sources and to gain financial control. New taxes, such as VAT have been introduced (1973), official tax bases have been extended, tax rates on existing direct taxes (income and social security contributions) have been increased (1977), precollection of taxes has been accelerated (1977–1978) and complete indexing of the income tax system was avoided (although there was a partial inflation correction in 1975). To a certain extent these measures have apparently been met by increased evasion and avoidance. Nevertheless, they have also led to an increase in revenues from explicit tax sources – both in nominal and in real terms. In 1978, for example, central government revenue increased by 19 per cent over the previous year, while the inflation rate was in the range of 12 per cent. Unfortunately, central government expenditures accelerated at an even more rapid rate than tax revenues – 38 per cent over the same period.

GOVERNMENT EXPENDITURE AND DEFICIT FINANCE

Typically, during the last decade, automatic and discretionary changes in public expenditure have outpaced automatic and discretionary changes in public revenue from explicit taxes – necessitating deficit finance. The driving force behind expenditure growth is the almost continuous legislative and administrative revisions of the pension system, the health system and the financing system for public enterprises and local authorities (local government). Besides introducing indexing of pensions (1971) and wages of government workers, these revisions have generally reduced or eliminated any cost-minimizing incentives. As a result, they have substantially broadened the scope for the operation of "moral hazard."[4] Given the resulting institutional structure, time and inflation lead to an automatic and inevitable growth in government expenditure which is frequently augmented by further discretionary expenditures.

Considering the tax and expenditure system together, then, there appears to be built-in instability rather than built-in stability. A deficit that leads to inflation leads to an indexed increase in transfers and wages, an increase in tax avoiding activity and, as a result, to further increases in the deficit.

A deficit may be considered equivalent to taxes, albeit in a hidden or deferred form. If so, then the effective revenue system of the public sector is determined by legislative and administrative decisions that set expenditures as well as by those that set explicit taxes. That is, given the government budget constraint, there is a necessary connection between the tax system and the expenditure system—in practice. The Italian experience provides an extreme lesson about the consequences of not paying explicit attention to that connection. Whether Italian fiscal authorities have learned that lesson is not yet clear. While a "new deal" in public budgeting was initiated in a recent three year (1979–1981), comprehensive budget plan, the most recent data indicates continuing budget deficits and inflation in the 20 per cent range.

OUTLOOK IS BLEAK

Without a successful implementation of balance and control, the prospects for the Italian *Public* Economy are bleak. While the public sector will continue to grow in nominal terms, (as denoted in lire), it may not grow in real or relative terms. The lire and lire-denominated government debt will rapidly depreciate in value. With such depreciation, deficit finance will increasingly fail to provide sufficient command over the real resources needed to meet expenditure commitments. This, in turn, will continue to erode the legitimacy and power of the state.

The unofficial, unmeasured private economy will continue to expand and stable foreign currencies (particularly the Swiss franc) will unofficially replace the lire as the relevant Italian medium of exchange or store of value. Private enforcement will continue to replace public enforcement as a means of security of persons and property. As a result, the Total Italian Economy—the public economy, the measured private economy and the unmeasured private economy—may even remain relatively healthy. But because of the increased transaction costs and other inefficiencies involved with unofficial economic activity, actual economic activity will fall far below potential.

In an important sense, the private market will move to correct government failure. However, because of the constraints imposed by government failure (particularly those aimed at preventing a private market response) the private market may not be able to provide as productive and efficient response as if government failure had not occurred.

The remedy for this public malaise may be found by returning to some simple concepts from traditional (pre-Keynesian) public finance

—namely, the benefit principle of expenditure *and* taxation and (its operational expedient) earmarked taxes. The Wicksellian system of requiring expenditure legislation to specific explicit tax finance and made subject to a "qualified majority" vote (for an increase—a qualified minority vote for a decrease) would be most effective in re-establishing *democratic* fiscal control. Its operation could be simplified by adopting a simple tax system employing proportional rates on broadly specified (income, expenditure and/or VAT) bases.[5]

Such a simplification would allow a given proposed expenditure to be "financed" by a proposed change in a proportional tax rate. Fiscal illusion would be decreased and fiscal responsibility increased by such a system. Unfortunately, in Italy, as in many modern, representative democracies, there does not appear to be a mechanism to bring about such a simple public good as responsible control of the Public Purse.

NOTES

1. Sergio Gambale, "The Crises in Public Finance in Italy," *Banca Nazionale del Lavoro*, March (1979) pp. 73–90.
2. The latter figure given for 1978 by Gambole, p. 73.
3. Which for 1976, relative to GDP, was 46.5 per cent, 46.8 per cent and 49.4 per cent for Italy, U.K., and Sweden, respectively (Source: OECD Economic Survey-Italy (1979) p. 53).
4. For an econometric analysis of this for local financing see G. Brosio, D.N. Hyman and W. Santagata, "Revenue Sharing and Local Public Expenditure: The Italian Experience, "*Public Choice*" 35 (1980) 3–15.
5. Modern incidence studies tend to show that progressive rates on certain taxes have not resulted in progressive tax systems while they have resulted in disincentive effects for official economic activity. Most redistribution of real income has occurred on the expenditure side of the government's budget. Given this, progressive taxes do not have much to recommend them and probably should not be retained in modern tax systems.

DISCUSSION

Edited by: Walter Block

Only two main topics of discussion followed the presentation of the study of Italy. The first, which dealt with the role of intellectuals in the aggrandizement of the government, was begun by Herbert Giersch: "What is the role of intellectuals, and the role of economists in particular, in connection with the general expansion of the government sector over time and of the international differences in tax systems, taxation, and government expenditure? In Germany, for example, since 1861 when Wagner's law was passed, there has been a secular increase in the government sector. There has been some wishful thinking behind it because Wagner belonged to the group of 'chair socialists' and he thought there was a general tendency for the state to take over more and more private activities, including those which were performed by the family. But when I look at the post-war development, I think the increase in the government sector must have something to do with tax policy.

"For with a built-in durability of public expenditures, and given the progressivity of the tax system, some trend expansion of the whole government sector seems inevitable. We talked about indexation of tax schedules with regard to inflation. But in a growing economy with a progressive tax system, one would expect an automatic increase in the share of taxes in national income.

"So far we have considered several countries; also relevant are the different attitudes of economists and especially of public finance economists in the many countries. How well are Italian public finance economists aware of what has been going on? When did the attitude which I heard all throughout this paper become widespread in Italy? It is important that we discuss this if intellectuals are to have a leading function in the roll-back of government expenditure. Otherwise, this movement may not start. Of course, I always thought of public finance economists as being to their countries what business economists are for firms. That is, they try to expand their particular calling in order to create more effective demand for their own services. But this is a side issue. We have reached a critical stage, and Italy in particular seems to be an example of this. So the question is, what do economists in general think about it?"

With a clarion call for discussion such as this, it was inevitable that the other participants would take up the challenge. In what followed a spirited, multi-dimensional and wide-ranging discourse took place.

Sergio Ricossa: "The recent plan adopted by the Italian government is based on a maximum estimate of the deficit and of total borrowing. These figures cannot be exceeded but there is no limit to increasing them year after year. There are also many other ways to arrive at any level of expenditure that the government wishes, ways which respect the law superficially but really cheat it. As to the question put by Professor Giersch, Keynes is no longer followed in Italy by my colleagues. Most of the Italian intellectuals now share moral sentiments which can be labelled 'austerity.'

"'Austerity,' unfortunately, may be translated as 'more public consumption and less private consumption.' But more public consumption means more taxes. We are forced to this extreme because there is no direct financial chain connecting families and production. The families are no longer willing to save and lend money to private productive enterprise because it is completely distorted by political interference. So the government is willing to collect the money from families and individuals and then to give businessmen the money which would not otherwise have been forthcoming. Finance experts in Italy quarrel about what kind of taxes must be laid. There is practically no exchange of ideas about the convenience of reducing government expenditures."

Herbert Grubel: "I'd like to follow up on the important point Professor Giersch raised because I feel we are brought together by a common concern over where the taxation systems of our countries have gone and what we might do about it. In order to get a handle on this, it is very useful to understand how it came about. However, I would stress in contrast to Professor Giersch, the development of the idea that increased government services are something society can afford as it becomes richer. It is sort of an income elastic demand for greater income equality, greater pension provisions, health care, and so on.

"I think economists and intellectuals, unfortunately, have played a great role in engendering this idea. In so doing, they have paved the way for ever-increasing government programs. They thought—here is a problem, so let us go out and create a program to solve it; we must raise taxes to pay for it and thereby fix it. This has led to unexpected negative consequences; to costs that were simply not anticipated by the partial equilibrium approach of these individual programs.

"What we have now, as evidenced by the scholars in this room, is a beginning of understanding and recognition that the costs of doing these things are much greater than we had anticipated. I wonder whether there is any recognition in Italy that perhaps the attempt to deal with many of the so-called shortcomings of the free enterprise system is perhaps not ideally resolved by the government because of the problems you are now discovering?"

James Buchanan: "I also want to follow up on Professor Girsch's question. Knowing a little bit about the Italian setting and the public finance setting in particular, it seems to me that amongst all the countries here represented, historically the Italian economist has been far more realistic about the government than economists in other countries. And we can see that coming through in Professor Ricossa's paper. They have never been under the sort of romantic illusions about the benevolence of the state found elsewhere. You find this all the way back for centuries. The Italian economists have been very realistic—at least a certain substantial proportion—and particularly about finance economy. They have no illusions whatsoever about the state. And yet we find in fact that Italy is, if anything, in worse shape than other countries. I think that the lesson, probably, is that we ought to be very skeptical about economists having real input into tax finance decision making, or any real effect on it."

Zane Spindler: "Let me reply to the point that has been raised by Professor Giersch. I was impressed when I looked at the actual provisions that had been put into effect with respect to the Italian pension scheme. It favourably compares with pension schemes in the United States. At roughly the same time, across a number of industrial countries, we see virtually the same types of programs regardless of the conditions in the individual countries. This raises the question of whether these schemes have naturally arisen from the population as part of consumer demand—or are they in fact imposed by the intellectuals who are privy to this common knowledge that is published in journals as to what the 'in-vogue' scheme will be this year? If so, once they are put in place, they will generate all of these adverse consequences which haven't been anticipated by the intellectuals who have analyzed this in a vacuum."

Alan Walters: "Well, I know next to nothing about Italy, but as I hear it from Professor Ricossa, this sounds very much like Britain in many respects. I had heard much of this story before, but what struck me here was the increasing politicization of the overt, as distinct from the underground economy. And those economies which I've observed which have had such a very rapid and ubiquitous politicization have not lasted very long. They went down the drain with great rapidity. The important point was that it created such tensions in society. It was a matter of life and death whether or not your party was in power. There are many economies like this, which I have seen around the world, where politicization has gone on and on—and they have all come apart. Their power has been disposed from the barrels of guns. In no time at all they've disintegrated—usually with very rapid inflation, a great deal of social unrest and often military takeover and turmoil. One recent example is Chile. There is tremendous politicization of the whole of economic life there. Nevertheless, the politicization was such that it exploded and generated a military takeover.

"Can I go back to the role of the economists here? It seems to be quite different in Italy from that in Britain. British economists, generally speaking, have applauded this takeover activity. They have regarded it quite rightly as a bonanza for themselves, and many people warm seats in the House of Lords who have indeed egged-on this socialization of the economy. There is no doubt that it does wonders for the economic profession in Britain, until recently, when I think it can be claimed we've been found out. All is lost now. The Emperor really is a fat slob with no clothes at all.

"I'm puzzled really. I'd like Professor Ricossa to explain how Italy has gone limping along like this. I think I can explain how Britain came limping along. But now there's a person wielding a fairly sharp axe to the government sector, and she keeps her power straight while she does it too. Well, I can't see this occurring in Italy and I wondered whether Professor Ricossa would explain my difficulty in seeing what's happening there."

Assar Lindbeck: "Maybe the explanation for Italy is that the public bureaucracy is so inefficient it cannot disturb the private sector."

Alan Walters: "That I agree with, but why do they exist side by side? How can it go on for so long? In other societies I've heard it's broken down. In Chile it certainly broke down, in Argentina it did, and Uruguay is a very sad case as well."

Sergio Ricossa: "We have a lot of troubles, of course, we have the red brigades and so on. But, as you said before, civil servants are not very productive. Part of this may be because they have a second job. The official work time is from eight in the morning to two in the afternoon. That actually means from nine-thirty to mid-day. Then the whole afternoon is free for a second job. So, everybody is happy because there is a lot of money going around. Families are forced to give their money to the state. Business firms receive the money at half the market rate of interest because the other half is paid by the government, so they are very glad. Of course, not any kind of businessman can receive that money. But those who are faithful to the government parties or the powerful opposition parties receive lots of money. So everyone who really counts is happy."

Assar Lindbeck: "Is this a stationary state or must this system head somewhere?"

Sergio Ricossa: "Twenty years ago I used to say, 'We are at the end of our story.'"

Herbert Giersch: "But it didn't happen under Einaudi. Did it start under Einaudi when he was President?"

Sergio Ricossa: "The story began in 1960–1961, when we started with the first government including the Socialist Party. Einaudi died in 1961 if I remember correctly. So it was the end of one era and the beginning of another."

Herbert Grubel: "I heard a sociologist say that the great distinctive feature of Italian life is the strength of the family unit."

Sergio Ricossa: "No longer. The old Italian family perhaps, yes, but the new families, no."

Assar Lindbeck: "But if you look at the GNP growth rate figures from Italy in the post-war period they look quite nice, like the German."

Sergio Ricossa: "Up to 1969."

Assar Lindbeck: "Well the 1970s are not so bad compared to other European countries."

Edgar Feige: "But they have made arbitrary adjustments of 10 per cent increases to GNP for four years running in the statistics office simply to reflect this growth in the unobserved sector. Those adjustments, I understand, are totally capricious and arbitrary so you cannot trust Italian GNP data for anything."

The second topic engendered by the Italian study had to do with the underground economy.

Robert Clark: "I would like to ask a question of fact in relation to Professor Ricossa's paper. He says, 'It is estimated that only half the Italian national income comes under scrutiny by the fiscal authorities.' Are you referring to total personal income or gross national product or gross domestic product?"

Sergio Ricossa: "I am referring to Table 9-A5. I am comparing facts and figures with net national income at factor cost which seems to me the best basis for a comparison."

Robert Clark: "I'll just give you the Canadian figure for purposes of comparison. In 1977 the net income reported by all taxpayers to the government was 75 per cent of total personal incomes as estimated by Statistics Canada. That certainly tends to support your view. There's a great deal that doesn't get reported in Italy."

Sergio Ricossa: "Yes there is, definitely."

Edgar Feige: "Were those comparable concepts or was that a comparison of personal income with adjusted gross income? I ask because those are quite different concepts in the United States. It takes major adjustments to make those figures comparable. That sounds high to me for Canada."

Robert Clark: "They're quite stable. I have them for several years if you want to see them."

Edgar Feige: "I'd love to."

Sergio Ricossa: "But I estimated the net national income at factor cost. I increased it by 10–15 per cent because of the submerged sector of the economy. Perhaps the Canadian statistics are not corrected in that regard."

Edgar Feige: "Is that over and above the official corrections at 10 per cent?"

Sergio Ricossa: "Yes, above."

Michael Walker: "I have a technical question for Professor Ricossa. There has been increasing attention given in North America to the idea of a consumption tax in the hope that we could thereby avoid a lot of the difficulties we have with income taxation. I note in your paper that you, almost in a throwaway line, suggest that the progressive consumption tax in Italy is widely evaded. I just wondered how it is that the tax is evaded? You would think this would be fairly difficult, unless both the retail agents and the consumers collude to evade it. How is it typically done?"

Sergio Ricossa: "This is because there is a collusion between sellers and those buyers who are willing to evade taxes; old customers and so on."

Michael Walker: "Does that imply that the estimates of retail sales volumes are all distorted?"

Sergio Ricossa: "To some extent, yes. A quite recent law obliges each restaurant customer to leave with a fiscal document. He is liable to be arrested if he is found without the document within a radius of 400 yards approximately from the restaurant. But of course nobody is there to check if you have the bill or not, because the restaurants are so numerous and the policemen are so few. Evasion is largely practised also because tax rates are sometimes so high that some branches of trade would disappear if the law had always to be respected; the consumption tax is sometimes as high as 35 per cent.

"According to Professor Hayek, 'It is a feature of modern democracy.' In a country such as Italy where democracy is feeble, it is quite evident that the system is not working well. In other countries with a stronger democratic system the wrongs are not so visible, but they are there and they may explode at any moment. I fully agree with Professor Hayek in believing that only radical change in our old system of democracy can stop the trend we are considering now in public finance."

CHAPTER 10

RECENT DEVELOPMENTS IN THE JAPANESE TAX SYSTEM

By Keimei Kaizuka

This study supplements a paper written with J. Pechman which reviewed the features and the development of the Japanese tax system since the Second World War.[1] That paper evaluated the role of taxation in the rapid growth of the Japanese economy. Since it was written in 1974, the Japanese economy has undergone a considerable change, and the fiscal system has been forced to adapt to a new situation. The chief aim of the present study is to trace the process of the adaptation of the Japanese tax system to the new economic situation. It examines whether there have been any changes in the main features of the Japanese tax system.

THE TRANSITION IN THE ECONOMY

In order to trace the recent development of the tax system, it is important to understand the change in the Japanese economy because the changes in the economy have a substantial impact on the fiscal system. This is true even though in the long run the way the fiscal system works has, in turn, an influence on the performance of the national economy through disincentives or incentives on private saving, private investment and work efforts.

Before the oil crisis in 1973 and 1974, the Japanese economy enjoyed a very high rate of economic growth. However, in 1974 the Japanese economy recorded a zero rate of growth. Ever since then, the economy has shown less growth than in the period before 1974 (see Table 10.1). Whereas the increase in the price indices have not differed greatly in the two periods, this is not so for the growth rates of GNP in nominal and real terms.

It will be left to economic historians to explore the intricacies of the slowdown in economic growth. Here only two factors need be mentioned. One is the expansive monetary policy adopted by the Bank of Japan. In 1971 and 1972 the rate of increase in money supply (M2) was about 25 per cent. This monetary policy caused price indexes to rise in late 1972 and 1973. (The WPI rose by 22.7 per cent in fiscal 1973).

TABLE 10.1

Changes in the Economy[a] (%)

	Nominal GNP	Real GNP	CPI	WPI
1965 - 1974	17.4	9.3	8.5	6.5
1974 - 1978	12.3	4.1	10.3	5.8

[a] All figures are the average rate of annual change for each index (in fiscal years).

Source: Economic Planning Agency, *Annual Report on National Accounts* (1980).

The other factor was the doubling of oil prices between 1973 and 1974. This pushed up import prices by 66.2 per cent in 1974. The combination of these two factors forced the Bank of Japan to adopt an extremely tight monetary policy in 1974 and 1975. The rates of increase in the money supply (M2) were held to 11.5 per cent in 1974 and 14.5 per cent in 1975. The Bank of Japan continued its tight monetary policy until inflation was reduced to the single digit level. The prolonged tight monetary policy and the fear of future oil price increases depressed business expectations, and resulted in a severe depression from 1975 to 1977. As a result of these sharp fluctuations in prices and output, caused mainly by policy adjustment (mal adjustment!) the growth trend of the economy was altered in a downward direction in 1974. This turned into what Japanese economists have called a "more stable economic growth path."[2] The transition to the new phase has had a substantial impact on fiscal balance.

THE EFFECT ON FISCAL BALANCE

Figure 10.1 traces the growth in central government expenditure and tax revenue in general account between 1965–1978. The gap between expenditure and tax revenue (this corresponds roughly to government bond issue) has catapulted since 1974. The biggest gap occurred in 1975. Tax revenue was decreased in that year, which reflected zero rate of growth in the previous year. The same tendency is observed in other industrialized Western countries, but the size of fiscal deficits is probably largest in the Japanese case. Even though there are difficulties of international comparison of fiscal deficits because of institutional differences, Table 10.2 shows that the degree of increase in deficits in Japan is substantial compared with other major countries. Japan's

Figure 10.1
Gaps Between Expenditure and Tax Revenue.

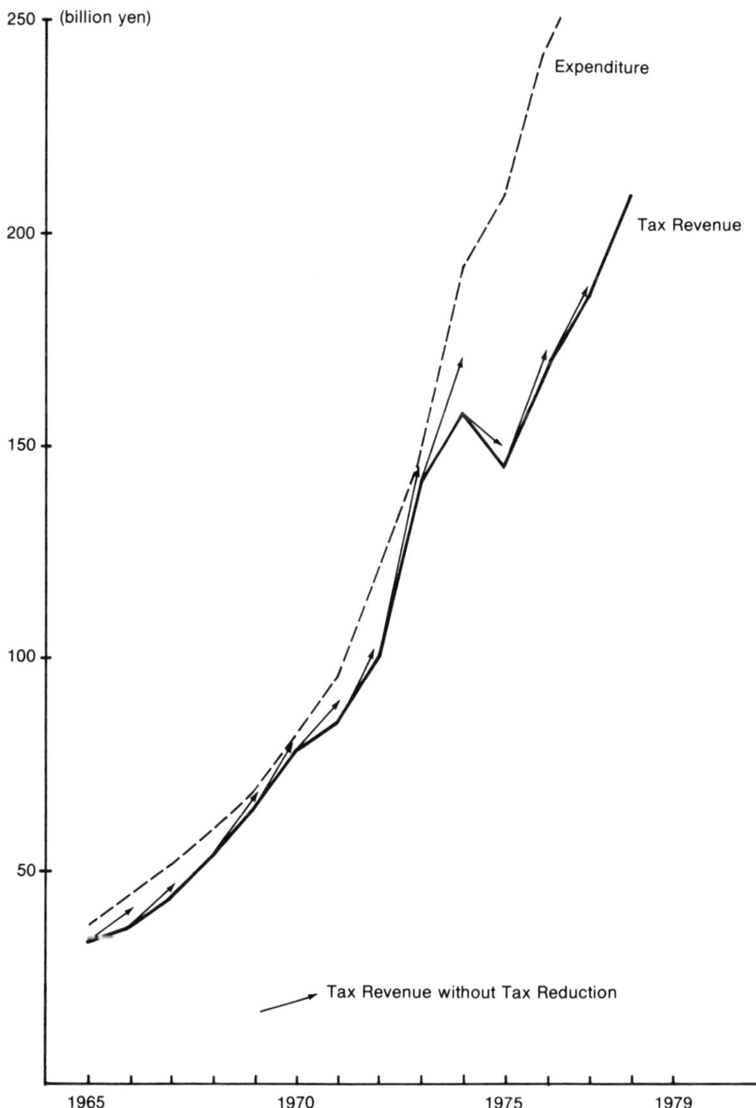

Source: Computed on basis of data from the annual issues of Tax Bureau, Ministry of Finance, Zasei shuyō sankō shiryōshū (Principal Reference Data for the Tax System).

TABLE 10.2

Ratio of Deficits to Expenditure (%)

	Japan	U.S.	U.K.	West Germany	France
1971	12.4	10.9	-8.8	1.5	-0.1
1972	16.3	10.1	2.9	3.6	-2.1
1973	12.0	6.0	8.7	2.2	-2.6
1974	11.3	1.7	12.1	7.1	-7.9
1975	25.3	13.9	18.4	19.2	12.2
1976	29.4	18.1	14.2	15.9	6.4
1977	32.9	11.2	11.9	12.7	5.6
1978	31.3	10.8	16.3	13.7	7.2
1979	35.4	5.6	—	14.0	5.9

Source: Japan, *Budgetary Statistics* (1979)
U.S., *The Budget of the U.S. Government*
U.K., *Financial Statistics*
West Germany, *Finanzbericht* (1980)
France, *Statistiques et Etudes Financieres*

average annual deficit increased by more than 20 per cent, while other countries showed a gain of only about 10 per cent. After declining in 1975, tax revenue increased during 1976–1978. However the growth of tax revenue was below that of public expenditure. This partly reflected an increase in public investment and an expansive fiscal policy.

Although Keynesian economics gradually became the academic orthodoxy in post-war Japan, the budgetary authorities have been reluctant to use fiscal instruments as tools for stabilization policy. In particular, the use of tax rates as an anti-cyclical weapon has been avoided. Even during the 1974–1977 depression, the budgetary authorities were rather inactive in implementing expansionary fiscal policy. They were reluctant to cut taxes and also hesitated to expand public investment. Finally, in 1977, an expansionary expenditure policy was adopted. Therefore, a substantial part of the large deficit seems to be due to the response of tax revenue to slower growth.

The question of whether large deficits are harmful to the economy has been debated between economists and the Ministry of Finance. Although a group of younger economists recently joined the camp of the Ministry of Finance, the debate is expected to continue. In any event, the authorities have tried to re-establish fiscal discipline even during the recession. An increase in tax revenue has been the major policy aim since 1975.

TABLE 10.3

Year-to-year Elasticity of the Central Government Tax System, 1972–1979[a]

Fiscal Year	All Taxes	Individual Income Tax	Corporate Income Tax	Inheritance Tax	Other Taxes
1972	1.40	1.81	0.96	3.21	1.25
1973	1.82	2.46	2.42	0.09	0.75
1974	1.03	1.50	1.50	-0.15	-0.07
1975	-0.66	0.69	-2.89	2.36	0.61
1976	1.19	1.09	1.04	0.19	1.53
1977	1.15	1.43	1.46	0.98	0.65
1978	1.33	1.59	0.85	1.64	1.56
1979	1.77	2.65	2.01	0.05	0.97

[a] Elasticity is the ratio of the percentage change in tax liabilities to the percentage change in gross national product. The calculations are based on estimated tax receipts before the annual tax reductions.

Source: Computed on basis of data from the annual issues of Tax Bureau, Ministry of Finance, *Zeisei shuyŏ sankŏ shiryŏshū* [Principal Reference Data for the Tax System].

INCOME ELASTICITY OF THE TAX STRUCTURE

During the high growth period the most prominent feature of Japanese tax policy was the annual tax reduction, made possible by the high income elasticity of revenue. At that time, Pechman and I maintained that the Japanese had not discovered a new formula for a high-elasticity income tax and wrote, "It is only necessary to combine high rates of growth of money income with relatively high exemption levels and moderately progressive rates to achieve an elasticity as high as 2.0."[3] Since 1974, the rate of growth of money income has slowed down, so we can judge whether our view is correct or not. Table 10.3 shows year-to-year elasticity of the Central Government Tax System in Japan, and we can clearly see that the elasticity of individual income tax was lower in the years 1974–1978 on the average. (Compare Table 10.3 with Table 10.4.) Average elasticity of individual income tax decreased from 1.77 (1955–1971) to 1.49 (1974–1979). So it is possible to say that the high elasticity of tax revenue is to a certain extent due to high growth rates of nominal income. This is true even though there may be other features of personal income tax which might contribute to the high elasticity.

With increasing deficits in fiscal balance, we could not expect a

TABLE 10.4

Year-to-Year Elasticity of the Central Government Tax System in Japan, by Type of Tax, 1955–1971

Fiscal Year	Elasticity*				
	All Taxes	Individual Income Tax	Corporate Income Tax	Inheritance Tax	Other Taxes
1955	0.35	0.75	-0.12	2.27	0.28
1956	1.37	1.28	2.42	2.18	0.96
1957	1.49	1.28	2.84	1.19	0.94
1958	0.12	1.06	-2.48	0.50	1.33
1959	1.24	1.25	1.36	1.16	0.83
1960	1.64	2.12	2.45	1.27	0.99
1961	1.31	2.14	1.27	1.37	0.95
1962	1.06	2.97	1.02	3.48	0.09
1963	0.92	1.66	0.54	2.00	0.76
1964	1.22	1.98	1.05	1.07	0.89
1965	0.60	2.13	-0.23	2.85	0.19
1966	1.01	1.52	0.92	1.57	0.66
1967	1.28	1.56	1.53	0.89	0.91
1968	1.33	1.91	1.22	1.11	0.99
1969	1.34	1.90	1.45	1.83	0.81
1970	1.44	2.07	1.51	2.14	0.80
1971	1.01	2.43	-0.05	4.78	0.52
Average, 1955-71	1.22[b]	1.77	0.98	1.86	0.76

a. Elasticity is the ratio of the percentage change in tax liabilities to the percentage change in gross national product. The calculations are based on estimated tax receipts before the annual tax reductions.

b. Weighted average based on yields of various taxes in fiscal 1971.

Source: Pechman, Joseph A. and Keimei Kaisuka. "Taxation" in *Asia's New Giant,* Washington, D.C.: The Brookings Institution (1976).

chance of annual tax reduction such as in the high growth period when the government hesitated to incur bigger deficits. Thus, a prominent feature of Japanese tax policy—annual tax reduction—has disappeared with the shift to slower economic growth. Actual tax policy since 1974 is characterized by tax increase rather than tax reduction. Table 10.5 shows estimated annual tax changes in recent years, where except in 1975 and 1977, tax increases have been implemented.

TABLE 10.5

Estimated Annual Tax Changes in Japan, Fiscal 1975–1980 (Billions of Yen)

	National Taxes										
	Individual Income				Corporation Income						
Fiscal Year	Total	Exemp-tions	Rates	Special Tax Measures	Total	Rates	Special Tax Measures	Other Direct Taxes	Indirect Taxes	Local Taxes	Total
1975	-186	-221	0	35	-6	0	-6	-298	118	-467	-839
1976	0	0	0	0	115	0	115	0	268	35	418
1977[b]	-441	-616	0	175	110	0	110	0	112	-53	-272
1978[b]	-228	-300	0	12	49	0	29	0	447	78	262
1979	88	0	0	80	218	0	218	0	329	182	809
1980	22	22	0	0	371	0	371	0	10	213	605

[a] These estimates of the effect of the tax actions are based on the official economic projections included in the annual national budget. This effect is estimated on the assumption that the tax revision had been enacted at the beginning of the year.

[b] Includes a supplementary tax cut in 1977 and 1978.

Source: Tax Bureau, Ministry of Finance, the annual issues of *Zeisei shuyō sankō shiryōshū* [Principal Reference Data for the Tax System].

CURTAILMENT OF SPECIAL MEASURES

Another feature of the Japanese tax system is wide use of tax incentives. Unfortunately, there is no compilation comparable to the comprehensive list of tax expenditures published annually in the United States. However, we can use the revenue cost of the provisions of special measures as an estimate. This covers a substantial part of tax expenditure. On this basis, the range of tax preferences is being reduced. In 1976, Pechman and I stated that "there is no more reluctance now than in the past to use tax devices to promote new national objectives."[4] In recent years, however, the approach of the Tax Bureau has changed considerably. It is now eager to curtail access to special measures, especially with regard to corporate income taxation. This pattern has been accelerated due to large fiscal deficits. The government thought it needed a substantial tax increase in order to lower deficits. It believed that in order to realize the tax increase, the curtailment of special measures was vital from the political point of view (in order to overcome objection to tax increases).

From 1973 to 1980, almost all of the special measures relating to corporate income tax were curtailed. Some of them were abolished outright. Most have subsequently been revised and given favourable treatment. The treatment of depreciation is a case in point.

Increased initial depreciation of acquisition costs for important industries was abolished in 1976. This privilege was also abolished for equipment used in large cities (gas supply equipment and equipment of privately owned railroads).

The case of tax-free accounting reserves for inventory losses also illustrates the trend. In 1973 the limit of the tax-free reserves to total inventories was 4 per cent. This has been lowered successively to 3 per cent in 1974, 2.7 per cent in 1976, 2.4 per cent in 1977, and to its present level of 2 per cent in 1978. Another example is the treatment of increased initial depreciation for the equipment of small and medium sized businesses. This initial depreciation percentage has been lowered from 25 per cent of total acquisition cost in 1973 to 16.6 per cent in 1976 and to 14 per cent in 1980.

The curtailment on the special measures on personal income tax is not very significant. However, there were several improvements in this area. The Special Tax Measurement Law permits separate taxation on interest and dividend income, at a rate of 25 per cent (1973). This rate was raised to 30 per cent (in 1976) and again to 35 per cent (in 1978). The measure allowing the deduction of 72 per cent of medical fees attracted wide attention because of physicians' conspicuously high income. And in 1979, the top bracket of the graduated income tax system was reduced from 72 per cent to 52 per cent.

TABLE 10.6

Comparison of Estimated Revenue Loss from Special Tax Measures and Tax Revenue, Fiscal 1966 - 1979[a]

	Revenue Loss from Special Tax Measures (Billions of Yen)			Per Cent of Revenue Loss to Tax Revenue		
Fiscal Year	Total Income Tax	Individual Income Tax	Corporate Income Tax	Total Income Tax	Individual Income Tax	Corporate Income Tax
1966	242	162	80	11.4	14.9	7.8
1967	250	163	87	9.6	12.6	6.7
1968	278	176	103	8.7	10.6	6.4
1969	350	219	131	8.7	10.9	6.5
1970	425	245	179	8.5	10.1	7.0
1971	522	294	228	9.6	10.2	8.9
1972	572	339	233	8.5	9.1	7.8
1973	633	405	228	6.4	7.6	5.0
1974	706	439	267	6.3	8.2	4.6
1975	772	468	204	8.0	9.0	5.0
1976	734	500	234	6.7	8.0	4.8
1977	811	583	228	6.7	8.9	4.1
1978	862	670	192	6.3	8.8	3.2
1979	881	655	232	5.3	7.1	3.1

[a] Individual and corporate tax revenues, from Tax Bureau, Ministry of Finance, *An Outline of Japanese Taxes*, 1979 (Tokyo, 1974), revenue loss from special tax measures, from data presented to the Tax Advisory Commission by the Tax Bureau.

AN IMPORTANT IMPROVEMENT

Probably the most important improvement in the personal income tax is abolition of separate taxation on interest and dividend income. This will be implemented in 1984. It is expected that in 1984, except for tax exemption of capital gains on securities, the basic structure of personal and corporate income tax will be improved from an equity viewpoint. However, there still remain various special measures which favour specific economic activities.

Reflecting these tendencies, estimated tax loss from special measures has declined relative to income tax revenues. It can be seen from Table 10.6 that the tax loss from special measures has declined from about 11 per cent in the mid-1960s to 6 per cent in 1974. Especially important was the revenue loss from special measures in the corporate income tax. It declined from 8 per cent to 3 per cent of corporate income tax revenue in the corresponding years. The importance of special measures related to export promotion and foreign investment declined sharply in 1972, and continued at a very low level afterwards (see Table 10.7). In the early years, special measures included under corporate income tax were for promotion of business saving and investment. But as the 1970s drew to a close, the importance of this category declined.

The Japanese tax system was well known (or notorious!) for its frequent use of tax expenditure measures (or their abuse!). In the joint paper we could not find evidence demonstrating the effect of tax preferences on economic activities. We could only mention the undesirable consequences of eroding the tax base. Table 10.8 shows that the proportion of actually-used to legally-permitted depreciation deductions was higher in 1978 than in 1970. This can be interpreted as an index which shows increased use of tax preference by corporate business.

Even though tax preferences were curtailed, there were a few instances where measures were adopted, and the scope of existing measures were extended. In 1978, temporal tax credit for purchase of equipment for energy saving, prevention of pollution, and for small and medium-sized firms was implemented. This was done in order to promote fixed private sector investment in the short run. This marked the first occasion that special tax measures were adopted as an instrument for stabilization policy.

INTRODUCTION OF SALES TAX

There are two methods of reducing the huge fiscal deficits. One is to cut expenditure and the other is to increase taxes. The fiscal authorities have adopted the latter method, and plan to introduce an entirely new tax, a variant of the value-added tax. As Table 10.9 shows, the main source of tax revenue for the central government is the income tax.

TABLE 10.7

Percentage Distribution of the Estimated Revenue Loss from Special Tax Measures, by Type of Incentive, Fiscal Years 1968–1979

Fiscal Year	Promotion of Individual Saving and Investment	Promotion of Business Saving and Investment	Promotion of Exports and Foreign Investment	Other
1968	55.2	23.0	13.3	7.3
1969	50.3	22.5	14.0	13.2
1970	42.2	23.9	17.5	16.9
1971	39.9	42.7	13.3	17.4
1972	40.2	40.2	4.4	19.6
1973	43.7	35.2	1.2	20.9
1974	42.2	36.7	2.3	20.9
1975	43.3	29.3	4.0	27.2
1976	39.3	31.1	2.7	29.2
1977	42.9	27.1	2.4	30.0
1978	45.4	24.1	2.1	33.1
1979	47.9	25.6	2.2	26.4

Source: Unpublished data to the Tax Advisory Commission by the Tax Bureau of the Ministry of Finance.

Even though indirect tax amounts to about 30 per cent of the total, it does not include a general sales tax.[5] The present indirect taxes are composed of customs, liquor, and commodity taxes which were originally levied chiefly on luxury goods. The post-war tax system was proposed by the commission headed by Professor C. Shoup, and was designed as a comprehensive income tax system. Actually, in the years following, this system eroded into a partial income tax. Recently, the erosion of the tax base has been reversed to some extent. Therefore, if a general sales tax is introduced, the main structure of the Japanese tax system will be affected. In spite of the eagerness of fiscal authorities, the plan to introduce a general consumption tax (which was expected to yield fifty thousand billion yen) was temporarily shelved when the liberal Democratic Party was almost defeated at the general election in the fall of 1979.[6] The Ministry of Finance has, however, not abandoned the idea. Instead, it is waiting for an appropriate opportunity to revive the plan.

In the U.S., proposals for adopting the value-added tax have attracted wide attention. The substitution of income tax with VAT was actually carried out in the U.K. Since the underlying systems of both

TABLE 10.8

Use of the Special Tax Measures by Corporations by Size of Corporation, Fiscal 1970 and 1978

Size of Corporations in Millions of Yen of Paid-in Capitals	1970		1978	
	Legally Permitted Deductions Under the Special Tax Measures Actually Used	Total Depreciation Accounted for by Special Measures	Legally Permitted Deductions Under the Special Tax Measures Actually Used	Total Depreciation Accounted for by Special Measures
Less than 1	96.7	3.5	82.2	1.8
1 - 5	94.1	5.5	87.9	2.4
5 - 10	92.3	7.1	86.0	3.5
10 - 100	88.4	7.2	86.9	3.7
50 - 100	90.4	9.5	77.2	4.6
100 - 1,000	78.2	6.6	78.6	1.9
1,000 - 5,000	61.9	9.1	86.2	2.6
5,000 - 10,000	43.2	10.1	86.4	1.9
10,000 and over	61.6	16.5	58.7	3.4
All corporations	66.8	10.4	74.5	3.0

Source: National Tax Administration Agency, Hojin kigyo no jittai [Sample Survey of Corporate Business (1972, 1980)].

TABLE 10.9

Distribution of Revenues of the Japanese Central Government, by Major Tax Sources, Fiscal 1974–1980

Fiscal Year	Individual Income	Corporate Income	Indirect	Death and Gift
1974	34.0	38.0	26.1	1.9
1975	37.8	29.4	30.7	2.1
1976	37.0	28.7	32.5	1.9
1977	35.7	30.2	32.2	1.9
1978	33.4	34.1	30.7	1.8
1979	37.1	29.5	31.7	1.7
1980[a]	37.0	30.5	30.9	1.6

[a] Estimates based on initial budget data.

Source: The annual issues of Tax Bureau, Ministry of Finance, *Zeisei shuyô sankô shiryôshû* [Principal Reference Data for the Tax System].

countries are income tax oriented, it is interesting to compare Japan with the U.S. and the U.K. The case for introducing VAT in the place of the income tax is usually justified for two reasons.[7] First, the introduction of VAT encourages private saving and is beneficial for capital accumulation. Secondly, a general consumption tax is equitable from the viewpoint of spending power over the entire lifetime. This is in contrast with equity in the short period in the Haig-Simons sense. In the Japanese case, the promotion of private saving is not an important policy objective, for the saving ratio of households is distinctly higher than in any other industrialized Western country. Thus a VAT is not required for the promotion of private saving. The justification on the ground of lifetime equity is not raised by public finance specialists in Japan.

HORIZONTAL EQUITY

The Japanese sales tax avoids the administrative defect and the burdensome character of the income tax, especially that of the personal income tax. But there still remains the problem of equity between salaried workers and other income earners. This holds especially for farmers and other unincorporated business. Although it is difficult to assess underestimation of taxable income in unincorporated business from statistical data, it is widely believed that the tax burden of unincorporated business is low compared to salaried workers. This is essentially a problem of tax administration. A more accurate assessment of taxable income could be achieved by more stringent tax administration, particularly by adopting a system of numbering taxpayers. However, the tax administration has not tackled this problem squarely. The majority of salaried taxpayers oppose tax increases. They would rather reluctantly accept the introduction of a sales tax in spite of its regressivity. This is because the present income tax is not administered equitably; incentives to contribute a fair share of taxes are thus discouraged. However, even if the income tax were administered equitably, there still remains the problem of tax illusion. Taxpayers feel less burdened by the sales tax compared with the individual income tax.[8]

CONCLUSION

This paper has concentrated on re-examining two features of the taxation system: the tremendous elasticity of the individual income tax, and the widespread use of special tax measures. Since 1974, the importance of these features has faded. The high elasticity of individual income tax has been greatly reduced, mainly due to slower economic growth. Further, although there are still elaborated tax preferences, the curtailment of special measures has decreased their significance. These developments essentially reflect the adjustment of the fiscal system to the transition to a new phase of the economy.

NOTES

1. Joseph A. Pechman and Keimei Kaizuka, "Taxation" in *Asia's New Giant: How the Japanese Economy Works,* Washington: The Brookings Institution (1976).
2. For example, see M. Yoshitomi, *Conditions to Break Through Stagnant Japanese Economy: Examination of Transition Period*, In Japanese, Toyokeizaishimposha (1978).
3. *Op. cit.,* p. 351.
4. *Op. cit.,* p. 354.
5. Nor does the local tax system include a general sales tax.
6. The Tax Advisory Commission, *Report on the General Consumption Tax,* September (1978).
7. For example, The Institute for Fiscal Studies, *The Structure and Reform of Direct Taxation,* London: George Allen & Unwin (1978).
8. See J.M. Buchanan, *Public Finance in Democratic Process,* University of North Carolina Press (1967), Chap. 10.

COMMENT

Donald Daly

I should like to make some suggestions in order to widen the perspective and to place the Japanese tax system in a broader context of fiscal and monetary considerations. The increased importance of small business during the 1970s and the limited coverage of this dynamic element in the Denison-Chung[1] and Caves-Uekusa[2] models, may warrant some expansion here, with special emphasis on the tax aspects:

- Could some attention be given to the factors on the expenditure side, as Figure 10.1 and Table 10.1 suggest more rapid increases in expenditures than GNP, reversing the similarities of the previous two decades or so?
- Related to this is the size of the budget deficit in the last half of the 1970s, and how it was financed. How important were the changes in the Bank of Japan holdings? What was the monetary expansion of the period?
- In light of the price inflation in the early 1970s (which has become much more modest from 1975 to 1978 or so), would it be helpful to include some discussion of inflation as a tax, as was done in some of the other country studies?

LIMITED OBJECTIVE

Professor Kaizuka's paper has a more limited objective than most of the papers in this volume. He had co-authored a chapter with Professor Joseph Pechman on taxation for the Brookings volume *Asia's New Giant.*[3] The present paper updates six tables from the earlier study (or about one-third of them), and discusses some of the implications. Japanese experience is an interesting and important example to consider, as the experiences are different in magnitude from those of many other countries.

Table 10.2 (a new table) shows the ratio of deficits to government expenditures running about 30 to 35 per cent for the last four years. This is the *largest* deficit of any country represented here—and in the entire world as well. This is an important point, and I will consider later why it has happened and its implications for Japanese economic growth during the later 1970s.

A second important point is that the ratio of taxes and government expenditures to GNP in Japan continue to be one of the *lowest of any* of the countries we are considering. Table 10.10 showed tax revenues as a per cent of GNP, but a comparable table on expenditures would

TABLE 10.10

Tax Revenues as a Per Cent of Gross National Product, by Source, Selected Countries, 1972[a]

Country	Tax Source						
	Individual Income	Corporate Income	Payroll	Goods and Services[b]	Property	Death and Gift	Total
Norway	12.5	1.1	12.4	18.7	0.9	0.1	45.7
Denmark	21.4	0.9	3.5	16.8	2.0[c]	0.2	44.8
Sweden	18.5	1.7	9.9	13.4	0.3[c]	0.1	43.9
Netherlands	11.7	2.8	14.7	11.7	0.8[c]	0.2	41.8
Austria	8.4	1.6	12.1	14.2	0.7	0.1	37.0
Germany	10.1	1.7	12.4	10.8	0.9	0.1	36.0
France	4.0	2.1	14.8	14.3	0.5	0.2	35.8
Belgium	9.6	2.6	10.6	12.0	0.0	0.3	35.2
United Kingdom	11.1	2.5	6.1	10.3	3.9	0.8	34.7
Canada	11.6	3.6	3.0	11.5	3.5	0.2	33.5
Italy	4.0	2.3	12.1	12.2	0.3	0.2	31.1
United States	9.4	3.1	5.7	5.5	3.7	0.6	28.1
Australia	9.3	3.8	1.0	8.2	1.4	0.5	24.3
Switzerland	8.1	1.9	5.6	6.8	1.4[c]	0.3	24.1
Japan	5.4	5.1[d]	4.1	5.1[d]	1.0	0.4	21.1

a. Includes national and local taxes.

b. Includes sales, value-added, and excise taxes, taxes on imports, exports, and transfers of property and securities, and other transactions taxes paid by enterprises.

c. Includes net worth taxes.

d. The Japanese enterprise tax levied by the prefectural governments is included in the corporate income tax and excluded from the tax on goods and services.

Source: Pechman, Joseph A. and Keimei Kaizuka. "Taxation" in *Asia's New Giant*, Washington, D.C.: The Brookings Institution (1976).

also be helpful when the deficit has become so large. It might also be useful to include tables on tax revenues and expenditures to GNP for Japan and some other OECD countries.

A third important development is that the Japanese are moving to narrow and eliminate some of their previous tax incentives and subsidies. As active participants in the last two multilateral tariff conferences, they have also sharply reduced tariff and non-tariff barriers to trade. This is partly related to the increased influence of the Ministry of Finance, and to a reduction of the role of The Ministry of International Trade and Industry (MITI) (with different policy emphases) during the 1970s. The Japanese are moving toward a more neutral tax policy domestically and to a more open policy internationally. Paradoxically, Japan is following the Canadian Carter Commission tax philosophy, while Canada is moving in the other direction.

A RESEARCH PROGRAM

There are a few specifics about the Japanese tax system that Professor Kaizuka might be able to clarify:

1. What proportion of the working population pay personal income taxes? Is this much different for employees in small and large firms and establishments?
2. The paper discusses the size of the Japanese budget deficit in recent years and the desire of some of the finance officials to see it reduced. (Methods suggested include changes in the rates and coverage of the personal income tax, or the introduction of a value-added tax.) Does the author feel that the size of the deficit has been undesirably large or insufficiently stimulative for the circumstances of Japan in the late 1970s? There is also no discussion of how it has been financed. Are the holdings of the Bank of Japan and the implications for monetary policy an important consideration in the support for tax increases?

Comparisons of the changes in government expenditures since 1973 (in Figure 10.1) and the changes in nominal GNP (in Table 10.1) are of interest. They suggest that the rates of increase in government expenditure have been more rapid than in GNP for the first time in about twenty years. This seems to merit more discussion and emphasis as a factor in the size of the budget deficit. Are there differences in the rates of growth on transfer payments, expenditures on current goods and services and capital expenditures?

The high income elasticity of the personal income tax was central in the elasticity of the whole Japanese tax structure. There were frequent increases in exemptions and reductions on rates that were introduced

TABLE 10.11

Estimated Annual Tax Changes in Japan, by Type of Change, Fiscal Years 1950–1974[a] (Billions of Yen)

	National Taxes										
	Individual Income				Corporate Income						
Fiscal Year	Total	Exemp-tions	Rates	Special Tax Measures	Total	Rates	Special Tax Measures	Other Direct Taxes	Indirect Taxes	Local Taxes[b]	Total
1950–53	-386	-272	-86	-28	-25	31	-56	16	-138	-46	-580
1954	-31	-29	0	-2	-3	0	-3	-3	20	-26	-43
1955	-53	-23	-13	-18	-12	-14	2	0	-1	-7	-73
1956	-23	-23	0	0	14	0	14	0	7	12	11
1957	-110	-40	-85	15	22	-2	24	0	20	-12	-81
1958	-6	0	0	-6	-22	-20	-2	-3	-6	-20	-57
1959	-23	-28	-12	17	-4	0	-4	0	20	-8	-16
1960	0	0	0	0	0	0	0	0	7	-12	-5
1961	-56	-38	-23	5	-40	0	-40	0	19	-13	-90
1962	-50	-25	-23	-2	-1	0	-1	-2	-62	-40	-156
1963	-67	-32	0	-35	13	0	13	0	4	-18	-68
1964	-75	-66	0	-8	-59	-5	-54	-5	19	-56	-174
1965	-65	-92	0	26	-57	-28	-28	-1	7	-9	-124
1966	-158	-101	-53	-4	-99	-50	-49	-15	-39	-53	-364

TABLE 10.11 (continued)

	National Taxes										
	Individual Income				Corporate Income						
Fiscal Year	Total	Exemptions	Rates	Special Tax Measures	Total	Rates	Special Tax Measures	Other Direct Taxes	Indirect Taxes	Local Taxes[b]	Total
1967	-93	-142	11	38	-30	0	-30	-3	32	-19	-113
1968	-125	-135	-11	*	*	0	*	0	57	-21	-89
1969	-183	-142	-41	*	2	0	2	0	*	-95	-276
1970	-289	-173	-131	15	75	97	-22	0	8	-97	-302
1971	-415	-286	-107	-22	12	0	12	-7	93	-87	-403
1972	-32	0	0	-32	31	0	31	-12	9	-98	-103
1973	-375	-335	0	-40	27	0	27	-40	10	-146	-524
1974	-1,783	-1,467	-260	-56	352	424	-72	0	316	-113	-1,228

* Reduction of Y500 million or less.

a. These estimates of the effect of the tax actions are based on the official economic projections included in the annual national budget. This effect is estimated on the assumption that the tax revision has been enacted at the beginning of the year. The 1971 figures include the effect of tax changes in the budget at the beginning of the fiscal year and of a supplementary tax cut enacted in October 1971.

b. Includes prefectural and municipal governments.

Source: ibid.

between 1950 and 1974 (see Table 10.11). From 1972 to 1979 the elasticity of the personal income tax averaged 1.45, compared to 1.93 in the eight preceding years. The paper seems to emphasize the slower growth in money GNP during the latter part of the 1970s as the major reason for the decline in elasticity. However, the simulations of different growth rates in money incomes with the Japanese pattern of exemptions did not show any large variations in elasticity (see Table 10.12). For example, a 15 per cent rate of growth yielded an elasticity of 1.82 (without income splitting), while a 12 per cent rate of growth gave rise to a measurement of 1.77, only slightly less. The average elasticities in the eight years after 1972 were almost .50 below the average of the eight preceding years. It seems quite unlikely that the slower growth rate in money income can explain the lower level of elasticity, when the simulations showed only such small effect.

INCOME TAX ELASTICITIES

The estimate of the year-to-year elasticities for the individual taxes, and for all taxes combined, is based on changes in individual tax collections in relation to GNP. In 1975, a sharp drop in corporate profits tax collections occurred (reflecting the sharp drop on corporate profits, while GNP continued to rise). The magnitude of the drop was due to the permanent employment practice, the high burden of fixed costs, and to falling sales and production. As well, the attempt to expand the Japanese share of the world market for manufactured products cut into profit margins.

Let me provide an alternative interpretation. Professor Petersen's paper (pp. 283–319) charts the tax elasticity for one individual at alternative levels of income, and personal exemptions, assuming a progressive marginal tax rate. He shows how persistent inflation reduces elasticity—unless exemptions are either indexed (as in Canada) or increased frequently, as in Japan.

The elasticity for all taxpayers is a weighted sum of these alternative elasticities; taxes payable are the weights. If many taxpayers have incomes close to the permissible deductions, the whole tax system will have a high elasticity for income changes. If many individuals have incomes well above exemptions and high levels of taxable income, the personal income tax system will have low elasticity. When the Japanese exemptions were adjusted to income increases (as they were from 1950 to 1974—see Table 10.11), the tax system continued to have a high revenue elasticity. (The indexing of the Canadian exemptions permits a continued high elasticity in this country). When incomes continue to go up (even though at a slower rate), but exemptions remain unchanged, the elasticity of the personal income tax declines. This interpretation

TABLE 10.12

Elasticity of the U.S. Federal Individual Income Tax with Per Capita Exemptions of $750 and $1,060, and with and without Income Splitting, at Selected Income Growth Rates, 1974

	Elasticity[a]		
Annual Income Growth Rate (per cent)	Exemptions of $750 Per Capita, with Income Splitting	Exemptions of $1,060 Per Capita, with Income Splitting	Exemptions of $1,060 Per Capita, without Income Splitting
5	1.52	1.61	1.67
10	1.60	1.70	1.77
15	1.62	1.74	1.82
20	1.65	1.77	1.86

a. Elasticity is the ratio of the percentage change in tax liabilities to the percentage change in personal income less transfer payments.

Source: ibid.

also explains the higher elasticity in 1979, for exemptions in Japan were increased with the supplementary tax cuts of 1977 and 1978.

ECONOMIC GROWTH

Let us now consider some possible explanations for the recent slowdown in Japanese economic growth. The Keynesian growth model is of interest in this regard. As we know, government expenditures have grown more rapidly than GNP in Japan during most of the 1970s. Furthermore, budget deficits were very large. In discussions at a conference in Tokyo in April 1976, Hugh Patrick and other U.S. participants strongly encouraged the Japanese to follow a policy of active fiscal stimulus.[4] The volume of exports by Japan also expanded vigorously—about double the previous peak in volume by 1978. This involved a significant increase in relation to domestic production and GNP, and an enlarged part of the world market for manufactured products. The tendency for Japanese manufactured exports to increase during periods of slack and slow growth has appeared in each such a situation since World War I, and is not just a special case during the mid-1970s. But with such stimulus from exports, government expenditures and a budget deficit, it is hard to satisfactorily explain the slower growth from a Keynesian model.

A monetarist model actually gives better results. In the early 1970s the rate of monetary expansion was up to 20 to 30 per cent per year in 1971 and 1972, and this was cut by late 1973 to roughly 10 per cent. A short, sharp recession occurred. The adjustments were mainly in terms of hours worked and output per man hour, not increased unemployment (the experience in North America during the same period). Since 1975, the rates of increase in domestic prices and labour costs per unit of output have returned to the pre-1969 period rather than to the rapid increases of the first half of the 1970s. A check on the rate of monetary expansion led to a sharp reduction in price inflation and the recession was short-lived.

Professor Kaizuka decided to leave the explanation of the slowdown in economic growth to the economic historians. However, this phenomenon had been predicted by the Denison-Chung Brookings study as far back as 1975. They distinguished between the growth factors that seemed to be sustainable into the 1980s, and those that were not. Their warnings that the growth rate would slow down in Japan even though it would continue above North American levels have stood the tests of the last five years well.[5] On the other hand, Dr. Kanamori at the Japan Economic Research Center and others have had to revise downward their medium term projections on each successive re-working.

AN ALTERNATIVE MODEL

However, one new element seems also to be relevant in Japan. This is the interpretation introduced by Edgar Feige,* which emphasized U.S. data. We can see this pattern in the data describing the productivity slowdown, and it seems to reflect some of the same underlying tendencies regarding the hidden economy. Since 1975 employment in large establishments has declined in manufacturing industries. This has been accompanied by big increases in employment in smaller establishments. The tax treatment of this sector is generous, and salaries to family employees are permitted in unincorporated businesses.[6] The limited employment opportunities in large establishments has meant a larger absolute and relative increase in employment in small establishments, at incomes that will be lower over a lifetime than in large establishments. Productivity levels in manufacturing are still well below the previous 1973 highs among small establishments, while they are up substantially in the large establishments. This is especially important when it is recalled that about 65 per cent of employment in Japanese manufacturing is in establishments employing less than 300 employees. My article in *Canadian Business Review* on Japanese manufacturing[7] deals with the productivity slowdown since 1973.

---

* See Chapter 2 above—ed.

In summary, the monetarist and supply-oriented models throw considerable light on the timing and direction of the slowdown in Japanese growth. This took place in spite of a major increase in exports, and a budget deficit in Japan that may be unique in size for an industrialized country during the 1970s. Japanese growth was very strong before 1973 while taxes and expenditures were fairly stable ratios of GNP; the growth rate was slower during the latter part of the 1970s, in spite of a significant fiscal stimulus. Japan thus provides some parallels but also some contrasts with the experiences of other economically advanced countries.

In light of the large and increasing importance of small business in Japan (in wholesale and retail as well as manufacturing) and the continued tax encouragements to small business, it is probable that the unobserved portion of small business has increased even more than can be discerned from the data available. The large number of small establishments and the high turnover are likely to make it difficult for full statistical reporting.

NOTES

1. Edward F. Denison and William K. Chung. *How Japan's Economy Grew So Fast,* Washington: The Brookings Institution (1976), Chapter 12, "Can the Growth Rate be Sustained?," 114–127.
2. Richard E. Caves and Masu Uekusa. *Industrial Organization in Japan,* Washington: The Brookings Institution (1976).
3. Joseph A. Pechman and Keimai Kaisuka. "Taxation" in Hugh Patrick and Henry Rosensky, eds., *Asia's New Giant: How the Japanese Economy Works,* Washington: The Brookings Institution (1976) 317–382. The chapter was essentially finished in 1974, so it does not reflect the subsequent severe recession and the more moderate nature of the subsequent growth in productivity and real output and the associated large budget deficit and its financing. Many of my comments relate to the interpretation of these developments and to place them into a broader international perspective.
4. Hugh Patrick. "What the Japanese Economy Needs Now: Moderation and Stimulus" in Hisao Kanamori, ed., *Recent Developments of Japanese Economy and Its Differences from Western Advanced Countries,* Tokyo: Japan Economic Research Center (1976) 101–105.
5. *Op. cit.,* Denison-Chung.
6. *Op. cit.,* Pechman-Kaisuka, p. 335.

DISCUSSION

Edited by: Walter Block

The discussion surrounding the presentation of the Japanese tax system was especially evocative, given the recent successes of this nation's economy. Whether, and if so, to what degree, the Japanese tax code could take credit for these occurrences was a theme that underlay much of the interchange of ideas.

Specifically, however, the deliberations flowed along several well marked channels. First, the question of high marginal tax rates was taken up. Based on probing questions from Douglas Auld and Alan Walters, it was determined that the highest marginal tax bracket in Japan is 92 per cent. However, pointed out Assar Lindbeck: "I think that when we mention the 92 per cent marginal tax rate, it's important to clarify that most people have marginal tax rates of only, maybe 15 per cent, 20 per cent, 25 per cent in Japan. That 92 per cent is for an extremely small group and it probably accounts for people with expense accounts. So, I think, you wouldn't expect so much distortion when so very, very few people have high marginal tax rates, as compared to Europe."

Herbert Grubel insisted that: "Very high marginal tax rates have all kinds of distortionary effects. There is a famous story that went the rounds in Britain several years ago about why there are such a large number of Rolls-Royces there. It is because it is just very cheap to drive a Rolls-Royce given the high marginal tax brackets in effect. I wonder whether, in Japan, there are very strong evidences of distortion introduced by this sort of thing. I know about the misuse, in some sense, of all the expense accounts by corporations, but are there other things? Is this of any concern to the public? And, to what extent has the basic ethos of the society, the consensus ethos, prevented the negative effects of this high marginal tax rate from manifesting themselves?"

Keimei Kaizuka disagreed, "Not from the viewpoint of an economist. I can say that people like to see this type of thing, fringe benefits and other types of expense accounts, it means prestige. The use of expense accounts, a car with a chauffeur and so on, that exists, but as an economist I do not favour it. I am, rather, against this type of abuse."

In Herbert Grubel's view, "High progressivity explains why all that income is spent in the form of payments to Geisha girls."

At this point, the discussion became chaotic, with several voices insisting that payments to Geisha girls were not necessarily economically distortive.

The chairman, Alan Walters, attempted to "rule out all discussion of Geisha girls" but was less than fully successful. Said Edgar Feige: "My point is related, I'm afraid. In terms of how the Japanese GNP accounts are actually constructed, number one, do they have independent estimates from both the income side and the product side? Number two, what would be your conjecture as to the effect on the published statistics themselves of a dramatic growth in the direction of in-kind payments through corporate perks? That would obviously show up as an increase in expenses, a reduction in corporate income. So the income side could be significantly biased downward by that kind of a move. Is there independent estimation from the product side which might show up in a statistical discrepancy? If so, are you aware of any changes in the statistical discrepancy which would indicate that over time?"

Keimei Kaizuka: "Well, recently we adopted a new system on national accounts. Table 10.1 was taken from this. We call it S.M.A. accounts and these accounts approach, as you mentioned, from the expenditure side and also from the production side. Old theorists were different I think, old estimates were different, but the new system features estimates of the expenditures for the expense account. We call it consumption expenditure outside household."

The next train of thought concerned income tax elasticities. This did not generate quite the exuberance of the previous topic, but was also of great interest to the participants:

Lawrence Smith: "I just wanted to follow up on something Professor Daly actually dealt with, individual income tax elasticities. I wonder whether you have any breakdown as to the components attributable to real growth, inflation, and the change in tax exemptions that took place. It seems that all of those things were intermixed during the last few years. Perhaps that can explain why it's so high in the years 1978 and 1979."

Hans-Georg Petersen: "I want to make a technical point on Table 10.3. I think negative elasticities are only possible if tax revenue is not corrected by tax rate changes (because of tax reforms), and this is the case in Table 10.3. What Professor Kaizuka has estimated are "ex-post elasticities" and these are less constant than the "ex-ante elasticities" as demonstrated by Professor Daly. I think if Professor Kaizuka makes tax estimates with such "ex-post elasticities" he will be seriously incorrect. We have such experiences in Germany where our tax estimators used such "ex-post elasticities." Therefore, I think, it is better to use the "ex-ante elasticities" as described by Professor Daly."

Alan Walters: "I think the danger is, of course, that you get big errors as those numbers get smaller, and uninflationary slump conditions where the numbers may be very small indeed. The errors in it magnify enormously the calculation of the ratio."

Donald Daly: "Could I just add a sentence of clarification? The elasticities are calculated on the basis of percentage change in GNP as the base on which everything is compared with, and the percentage change in the tax collections, year over year. In certain cases, there are certain taxable categories such as a corporate income, where the corporate profits dropped like a stone, even though GNP had gone up. This sort of result is attained because of the use of a different pattern of the tax base compared to GNP."

Keimei Kaizuka: "Professor Pechman and I did a simulation of this in an earlier paper comparing elasticities in the United States and Japan. We tried to take into account differences in the exemption level, in the growth rate and the different systems of splitting income. We concluded that the rate of growth affects the elasticity. As Professor Daly mentioned, higher levels of exemption affect the elasticity as well. So, I partly agree with Professor Daly because the three components are important to explain a higher elasticity of tax revenue."

This section ended with a dispute over the importance of the elasticities:

Armen Alchian: "Why bother about the tax elasticity of income? What's the point of it all? I'm puzzled. Why are we talking about that number? Maybe you've got an answer for me, but if someone can tell me why that number is of any interest whatsoever, I shall appreciate it."

Assar Lindbeck: "One question is, did you define the elasticity as the relation between the tax base and the tax revenues? You can say that it's an expression of how much the individual can change his economic situation by changing his base, for instance, by increased effort. You should then take the elasticity of disposable income with respect to the tax base."

Armen Alchian: "But that's for every person separately and this overall data has no relevance."

Assar Lindbeck: "You must look at this figure completely disaggregated with respect to GNP. I guess the only reason for looking at aggregate figures would be some over-simplified macro-model where you want to help the authorities to have some approximate idea about what happens with a budget balance when the economy grows. But, again, I think you really should disaggregate to the different tax bases, otherwise it's a very poor approximation."

Next, the discussion turned to the Arab tax of Japan.

Assar Lindbeck: "If you look at the chart of the deficit it is interesting to notice that it starts to emerge in 1973, 1974, and 1975. That was when the oil price shock hit. National income account analysis would say that what happened was simply that the Arabs put a tax on the Japanese population by some 3 per cent of GNP. The private savings, household savings, and business savings weren't changed.

Then you needed a deficit in the public sector to counter-balance the "oil tax" and this is what happened. The deficit in the public sector simply means that the Arabs took over the tax functions of the Japanese government to the extent of 3 per cent of GNP. If you include the oil price increases as a sales tax on the Japanese population, you just have to record the 'tax receipts' to the Arabs rather than to the Japanese government."

Block disagreed with this analysis. "I wanted to dissent from Assar Lindbeck's equation of taxes and prices as expressed in his view that the Arabs were taxing Japan, in effect, because of the increased oil price. Perhaps, for some limited purposes, it is proper to look at it in this way. But I think it important to stress the difference between prices and taxes. Conflating prices and taxes is supportive of the idea that government is just one more institution, indistinguishable from any other in the marketplace. But it is important to make the point that government is a unique institution in society. Therefore, we have to keep taxes and prices at least conceptually distinct. Government, after all, is the only institution which can derive its revenues through force. It and it alone is thus above and beyond the vicissitudes of the profit and loss system which reigns in every other business institution. In this regard, I also object to calling taxicab prices tariffs. For we must also distinguish between a tariff, which is an interference with trade, and a price, which is part and parcel of the market system. And while I'm on this philosophical point, I feel compelled to mention another convention beloved of public finance theorists. I refer to an almost universal practice of using 'equality' and 'equity' as synonyms. It seems that many people look at these two terms as the same, and I would just like to point out that they are not.

"If they were synonyms, then every time a poor person stole from a rich person equity would be enhanced. There is more *equality* in such cases, but not more equity. I think equity is equivalent to fairness or justice. Thus if it is wrong to steal, and it is, then such activity *decreases* equity, even if it increases equality.

"Equality is a perfectly well understood English word. Why don't public finance theorists use this word when they really mean equality? Why must they resort to 'equity,' with its normative implications?

"I can think of only one reason: the wish to convince others of the moral appropriateness of equality, without the bother of cogent ethical arguments."

The session ended with several questions being put to the author of the study of Japanese taxation, and his replies:

Armen Alchian: "Let me ask a question of Professor Kaizuka. What was the Japanese tax structure like prior to World War II? Was it very similar to this or, in what respect was it spectacularly different from what it is now? The reason I ask is to find out about, and also to cast cold water on, the idea that the advice of westerners had a major influence on the Japanese tax system.

Keimei Kaizuka: "The difference is mainly in the personal income tax. We didn't have separate income tax brackets before the war, and the income tax rates were much lower then."

Armen Alchian: "I see. From where did Japan obtain most of its revenue? What tax did they use more, that they do not use now?"

Keimei Kaizuka: "Customs taxes, commodity taxes, and also excise taxes."

Robert Clark: "I'd like to ask a question which is really in two parts. First, why is it that Japan has not had a general sales tax up to the present time? The second question is – in moving toward a sales tax, why does the Japanese government favour a value-added tax as compared with other forms of sales tax?"

Keimei Kaizuka: "In respect to the first question, it's very difficult to answer. Maybe there is a historical reason. We have never had a general sales tax. It could be said that we are not accustomed to such a type of taxing. That's the only answer I could give. In respect to the second question, Japan's government believes the dominant type of general tax is the VAT. This is simply because they see that many countries have adopted this system and they think it is rather efficient compared with other types of sales tax. I think this is the reason."

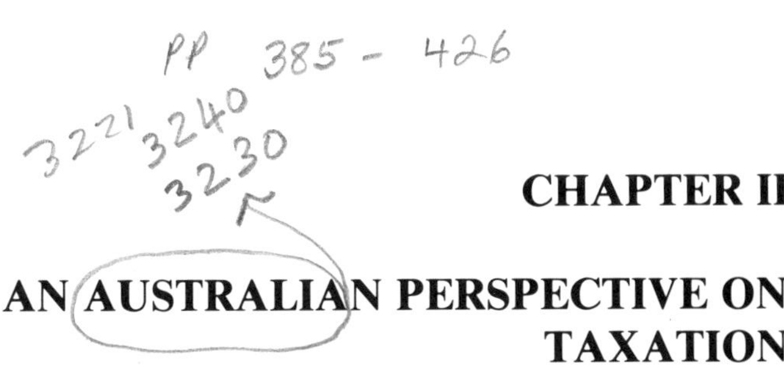

CHAPTER II

AN AUSTRALIAN PERSPECTIVE ON TAXATION

Malcolm R. Fisher

'I often think it's comical,
How nature always does contrive,
That every boy and every gal,
That's born into the world alive
Is either a little Liberal,
Or else a little Conservative.'

Iolanthe-by Sir W. S. Gilbert

* * * * * *

I. INTRODUCTION

Sir William Gilbert through his deft pen made a characteristic insight not only on the Britain of his time but on western-type democracy today, not least in Australia. Of course we might express it in different reference terms, distinguishing parties that at least to a degree support with some enthusiasm freedom of enterprise and endeavour, for which we reserve the reference term—liberal, and ones that embrace centralized decision-taking with strong paternalist or socialist sympathies—and to which I assign the term conservative. (North Americans would put the reference the other way around!) The one group supports vigorous expansion of the private sector, the other that of the public sector.

The free enterprise enthusiast thinks that every endeavour within the public domain should be justified on pragmatic grounds. He generally fights shy of principles but is instinctively supportive of decentralized decision-taking. He would try to limit public sector endeavour to the provision of what economists have named "public goods"—those goods and services in joint usage in consumption, that are not exclusive by person either in demand or in supply. The balance are classed as private goods and services, those for which generally some exclusive provision can be made, though sometimes at a cost. Of course most goods and services come in shades of grey. But the free enterpriser would want the publicness of activities to be clearly demonstrated. For example, defence, internal order, and the formulation and administration of law would clearly be justifiable under this head. If services such as these were organized privately, individuals could "free ride:" capture the benefits, and escape payment.[1]

The individual recipient of public goods is thus not willing to pay for the service until he is assured that others, who cannot be excluded from the service, are also contributing an appropriate share. The difficulty is that there is no way of determining a fair price for goods supplied in joint consumption. Payments are set by the taxing authority in lieu of any adequate pricing mechanism. But this leaves other questions unresolved. How is the total amount of resources to be assigned to the provision of the public good determined? The ultimate recipient is certainly concerned by the severity of his share of the tax measured against the desirability for him of the service. On this he finds it difficult to express a view or take protective measures. He can periodically express some form of blurred dissent through the ballot box. Alternatively, he can react by trying to accord to himself a "free ride" to the activity, not necessarily by refusing to pay taxes, but by taking a position where he is removed at least in part from the tax base.

THE FREE RIDER

The willing recipient of public goods objects to anyone else having a free ride. Likewise the unwilling recipient tries to secure a free ride for himself once taxing is resorted to as the means of financing the public goods. Much of the public finance literature has failed to explicitly note this symmetry in the "free rider" problem. For accuracy, "free" should be interpreted as graded, or discriminatory charging, including a zero impost.

The free enterpriser may object to the size of the provision of the service and to the proportionate share of the cost he is assigned. He may express this concern through his private sector activities, for it is from these that his taxes will be drawn to a substantial degree.

Governmental activity, however, has by no means been confined to public goods. The paternalist-socialist maintains that the working of a competitive decentralized system has weaknesses. Some of these are attributable to coalitions of persons being able to act in restraint of trade, some to sheer size of operations in individual hands. Others are due to inability to exclude third parties from undesirable effects from productive operations, as in the polluting of a stream with factory waste. The free enterpriser might retort that these market "imperfections" arise directly from interventions already made by the governments. State monopolies, regulatory agencies, licensing boards, to mention but a few, are cases in point. Such matters are hotly debated and recently the argument has been extending to criticisms of our presently held views of the competitive process itself.[2]

It is often argued that the distribution of personal claims upon resources is a historical accident and that therefore the state should use its powers of control to amend the distribution in more desirable directions. Those control measures would include taxing and spending through the budget. But we must recognize that the choice is essentially normative and that the "best" way can never be prescribed. The free enterpriser may also reply that the fluency of change in a decentralized economy can quickly shift cohorts from one claimant range to another – "clogs to clogs in three generations" as our nineteenth century forebears claimed at a time of apparently more uneven distribution of incomes – and that this implicit target, and performance, may be very difficult to better through public sector intervention.

ECONOMIC STABILITY

Should the state use its powers to promote more regular activity and development than the private sector market offers on its own account? This view gained considerable support as a result of the experiences in the Great Depression and the contemporary writings of economic philosophers, principally, Lord Keynes, on the powers of State intervention to promote economic stability. Fiscal and monetary flows, it was argued, should be used by government to reduce the severity of slumps and the overstimulus of booms. This would not only benefit output but also employment.

Looking back on post-war experiences, the free enterpriser notes the tremendous expansion of the public sector. But after post-war reconstruction was complete, he feels less sure about the degree of stabilization attained and the degree of innovation and general competitiveness engendered. The current anti-tax mood has probably been fostered by dissatisfaction with government performance in this regard.

With government expansion into any economic sphere, a whole range of vested interests develop. The substantial growth, and present day size, of the public sector has created an organized, and often very able group of administrators who can only envisage substantial personal loss from any curtailment of their roles. The public sector is one where empire building is easily induced and where the level of accountability, almost by definition, is low. It is inconceivable that departments of state can ever go bankrupt. None of the traditional inducements for promoting work performance operate. No alternatives of note have been produced to fill the void. Governmental parties may come and go, but the powers of the civil service to maintain the status quo, or even extend their domain, are very substantial. They constitute a formidable barrier against any reversal in the balance of public-private sector activities. Legislators, of course, derive their rationale and public appeal from action in this area. The size of, and the spread of activities in the public sector are easily used to bolster their time in office. The private sector thrives on the ability to identify, to separate, to exclude, and to match performance against cost. In contrast, the public sector thrives on an ability to confound and delimit powers, to separate performance from cost in areas well removed from strict public goods categories. Detection of low performance and failure becomes difficult and attacks can be deflected. Since the public sector engages in a wide range of activities it is always easy to claim that a shortfall in performance under some heads is more than compensated for by achievements in others. Since performances are often unassignable and untestable, the task of rolling back public sector activity becomes difficult.

If the free enterpriser finds curtailing public activities too difficult to confront directly by persuasion and vote he naturally turns to other routes open to him. In many cases, these consist of a search for a free ride so that more and more of the costs of the public activities are borne by those who find them attractive or less objectionable. In this way, the people at large are encouraged to scrutinize the civil service more carefully. This may indeed be the only appropriate competitive action now open.

TAX BASE

Economists tend to argue that the tax base should be as comprehensive as possible, and that general taxes should be preferred to specific taxes. In this way there is less interference with market choice. But in the presence of a large public sector (whose domain extends beyond public goods provision) the individual member of the community may indeed have a preference for particular taxes such as tobacco and liquor if he is a virtual abstainer. Not only would he improve his direct position, but he, joined by sufficient others, could through a combination of particular taxes and aided by a sufficiently complex pattern of taxing incomes, shift the burden to others. To this extent they will find a means by which to build up hostility to the intensity of public sector provision in general.

Thus it can be argued that acceptance of the case for a broad tax base and for the adherence to general taxes may give an individual more efficiency in the small but deny it to him in the large by leaving the public sector virtually intact. Reaction patterns can be quite complex.

People who endeavour to avoid tax will be reluctant to see some public expenditure streams curtailed whilst the public sector itself makes highly directed responses to any efforts to curtail its activities. For example, the pruning of expenditures in Britain under Margaret Thatcher has led public authorities to curb items that cause most inconvenience, such as public lavatory provisions, and to leave unmolested other items of more immediate appeal to legislators and bureaucrats. If society could ever reach the point where there was unanimity on social goals and the way to attain them then such concern with the tax base and the forms of taxes would be irrelevant. But this is to deny that through such means governments will be able to reach differing expression of desired goals within a comfortable margin of tolerance. Since the much-derided distribution criteria of the private sector are being amended by governments on their own equally arbitrary distribution criteria, it is mere wishful thinking to assume that there is a socially acceptable trade-off position in the long run.

EXPENDITURE PATTERNS

This discussion may seem tangential to our main interest – the nature of the tax system – but it seems difficult to give meaning to concern with the size, and distribution, of taxes save in relation to expenditure patterns, in size and distribution. At the simplest level, help to industry through tax reduction has a different effect on the size of the public sector than when the aid is given through subsidies. The argument is pursued at a more intense level where money for family allowances, health and education is taken in taxes, fed through an intermediary, government, and back again in similar amounts, when priced, to the same taxed persons. Instead, such services could be better confined to those really in need. In this way the distribution system becomes increasingly blurred, tests the tax base, induces expanded activity of free riders, helps empire building in government departments and, from the free enterprise viewpoint, is inimical to efficiency.

Gilbert got it right. The divide runs deep, deeper than professional writers have allowed. For choices as to optimal tax structures are not, and cannot be, independent of patterns of social preference between private and public goods provision. Curiously, the most highly regarded current theorizing in this area confines discussion to private goods, which compounds the problem![3]

Taxation may be regarded as justified in terms of intended public expenditure. But the norms that determine public expenditure levels and content have still to be settled. The tax base will be sensitive to the size of the public activity and its distribution by category. This may enhance or retard the growth of national product. The content of items in the national product is all important both for efficiency and distributional considerations. But the nature of these components can be legitimately questioned by members of the community both through their ability to organize in the decentralized sector and through their powers to persuade and vote in ways that may alter government policies. We look for a clearcut criterion where there is none for the choosing: this should caution us when we are presented with formulae appropriate to ideal tax systems.

In this chapter we examine the Australian tax system, its extent, composition, and incidence. We suggest some considerations that may be relevant in an across-country exchange of experience.

The procedure followed is to set out the present situation showing the composition and scale relative to national income of tax provision at federal, state and local levels and to describe the patterns of taxes and exemptions in some detail (Parts II and III). Then we draw a postwar picture of the evolution of the taxation system in Australia (Part IV). Finally we discuss the nature of incidence, and some of the more central features of the working of the tax system in Australia (Part V), rounding off with some assessments for the future (Part VI).

II. THE TAXATION SYSTEM IN 1980

Australia has a federal system of government operating under a constitution, quite distinct from her parent country, the United Kingdom. Government consists of three main tiers, federal, state and local authority. As a taxing authority it will be immediately appreciated that the federal government dominates. State governments receive considerable revenues but many of them come in the form of grants, often tightly earmarked by the federal government.

Table 11.1 shows the distribution of tax receipts by important designated categories, expressed as proportions of total taxation raised by the combined public authorities in fiscal years 1979–1980. The most striking feature is the primacy of the income tax on individuals, with income taxes on companies as the third largest category. This would suggest a dominance of direct over indirect taxes, but care must be exercised in reaching that conclusion. Indirect taxes clearly are more fragmented by category.

Income tax is not levied by the states, being purely a federal impost. Property taxes, principally rates, are levied by the local authorities. The relative unimportance of capital taxes (estate, succession and probate) is noteworthy. To some extent the division of taxes by tier of authority is historic—indeed it was not until 1942 that the federal government came to dominate in the taxing of income. Table 11.2 shows the tax breakdown for 1979–1980.

TABLE 11.1

All Public Authorities: Taxation by Type of Tax
(Percentages of Total)

TYPE OF TAX	'48/49	'51/52	'55/56	'60/61	'65/66	'70/71	'71/72	'72/73	'73/74	'74/75	'75/76	'76/77	'77/78	'78/79	'79/80
Income Taxes															
—on individuals	37.0%	)	)	)	)	36.9%	38.4%	38.0%	40.0%	43.5%	43.2%	44.5%	45.0%	43.4%	45.1%
—on companies	13.6	53.4%)	49.6%)	47.9%)	50.6%)	16.6	15.5	15.0	14.7	13.7	12.2	11.7	11.8	10.6	9.8
Estate, gift, Probate & Succession Duties	2.9	2.2	2.9	2.9	2.7	2.6	2.2	2.2	1.9	1.6	1.5	1.4	1.3	1.0	0.6
Customs Duties	11.8	)	)	)	)	5.4	4.8	4.8	4.4	4.7	4.9	5.1	4.6	4.9	5.0
Excise Duties	11.6	20.7)	22.1)	21.3)	20.3)	12.2	12.4	11.8	11.3	9.7	10.9	10.0	10.1	13.0	14.2
Sales Tax	7.2	9.2	9.5	10.3	7.4	7.4	6.9	7.1	7.1	6.5	6.6	6.7	6.5	6.0	5.7
Primary Production Taxes	—	—	—	—	—	0.3	0.3	0.3	0.5	0.8	0.5	0.6	0.7	1.0	—
Payroll Tax	3.7	3.6	3.9	3.6	3.2	3.1	4.0	4.2	4.9	5.7	5.5	5.3	5.3	5.2	5.1
Property Tax	4.7	4.3	5.4	6.6	6.8	5.9	5.7	5.7	5.1	5.1	5.2	5.2	5.2	5.1.	5.6
Liquor Taxes	—	0.4	0.6	0.5	0.5	0.5	0.5	0.5	0.4	0.4	0.5	0.5	0.5	0.5	0.5
Taxes on gambling	2.6	1.2	0.8	0.6	1.5	1.5	1.5	1.6	1.5	1.6	1.6	1.6	1.6	1.2	
Taxes on Ownership & Operation of Motor Vehicles	1.9	2.0	2.5	2.9	3.4	3.0	3.1	3.2	2.8	2.5	2.6	2.6	2.7	2.7	2.3
Stamp Duties, not elsewhere included	1.3	1.2	1.6	2.2	2.2	2.8	2.6	3.3	3.2	2.2	2.6	2.7	2.6	2.7	2.7
Other Taxes, Fees, Fines etc.	1.6	1.8	1.2	1.1	1.4	1.9	2.0	2.2	2.2	1.9	2.1	2.1	2.1	2.1	2.2
Taxation as a percentage of G.D.P.	24.1	27.3	22.3	23.1	24.6	26.0	26.6	25.7	27.0	29.2	29.9	30.1	29.9	28.9	29.9

Source: Australian Bureau of Statistics, Public Authority Finance and Australian Official Yearbook.

TABLE 11.2

All Public Authorities: Outlay and Receipts by Level of Government, 1979–1980 ($ Million)

	Commonwealth Authorities	State Authorities	Local Authorities	All Public Authorities
OUTLAY				
Expenditure on goods and services —				
General public services --				
General administration, n.e.c.	1,012.7	889.6	520.1	2,422.4
External affairs	144.7	—	—	144.7
Law, order and public safety	198.1	1,290.7	—	1,488.8
General research	258.9	—	—	258.9
Defence	2,786.4	—	—	2,786.4
Education	283.4	6,035.5	12.4	6,331.3
Health	565.7	3,362.2	52.6	3,980.5
Social security and welfare	324.6	226.2	48.8	599.6
Housing and community amenities -				
Housing	- 3.5	283.2	10.6	290.3
Community and regional development	41.1	97.7	44.3	183.1
Protection of the environment	14.6	369.8	279.0	663.4
Community amenities	1.2	1.7	20.8	23.7
Recreation and culture	312.3	242.5	384.7	939.5
Economic services -				
Agriculture, forestry and fishing	164.9	654.8	5.5	825.2
Mining, manufacturing and construction	99.2	168.7	17.9	285.8
Electricity, gas and water supply	7.7	1,647.9	237.4	1,893.0
Transport and communication	1,349.7	1,725.7	742.9	3,818.3
Other economic services	381.5	272.2	48.0	701.7
Other purposes	- 0.6	2.0	19.4	20.8
Total expenditure on goods and services	7,942.6	17,270.0	2,444.4	27,657.0

TABLE 11.2 (continued)

RECEIPTS AND FINANCING ITEMS				
Receipts —				
Taxes, fees, fines, etc. -				
Income tax -				
Individuals	15,040.1	—	—	15,040.1
Companies (b)	3,501.5	—	—	3,501.5
Estate, gift, probate and succession duties	48.9	171.4	—	220.3
Customs duties	1,628.8	—	—	1,628.8
Excise duties	4,965.3	—	—	4,965.3
Sales tax	1,864.8	—	—	1,864.8
Payroll tax	12.4	1,694.8	—	1,707.2
Primary production taxes and charges	278.3	—	—	278.3
Property taxes	16.5	310.9	1,339.2	1,666.6
Liquor taxes	2.1	174.7	—	176.8
Taxes on gambling	—	565.7	—	565.7
Taxes on ownership and operation of motor vehicles	7.8	764.0	0.2	772.0
Stamp duties, n.e.i.	6.9	993.4	—	1,000.3
Departure Tax	18.4	—	—	18.4
Fees from regulatory services	48.7	60.8	43.7	153.2
Other taxes, fees, fines, etc.	111.9	528.1	17.0	657.0
Total taxes, etc.	27,552.4	5,263.7	1,400.1	34,216.2
Income from public enterprises	992.9	663.6	200.4	1,856.9
Property Income -				
Interest received -				
From the States and the Northern Territory	1,375.6	—	—	(c)
Other	184.7	593.5	109.9	888.1
Land rent, royalties, dividends	48.7	435.4	—	483.2
Grants from the Commonwealth Government -				
For current purposes	—	9,079.6	—	(c)
For capital purposes	—	1,565.8	—	(c)
Direct grants from Commonwealth Government to local authorities	—	—	17.3	(c)
Grants from State authorities	—	—	587.2	(c)
Grants from local authorities	—	52.3	—	(c)
Total receipts	30,154.2	17,653.0	2,314.9	37,444.4

Source: Australian Offical Yearbook.

Clearly we shall have to devote most of our attention to income taxes because of their dominance in the structure and the likelihood that much public resentment is likely to be focused upon them. We shall examine the taxes by tier starting with the local authorities, and then turn to state governments and the federal authority.

LOCAL AND REGIONAL AUTHORITIES

Local authorities receive grants from federal and state authorities but far and away their main source of income is rates levied on property. Local authorities are empowered to deal with the construction and maintenance of (local) roads, streets, and bridges, water sewage and drainage systems, health and sanitary services, supervision of building. As well, they control the administration of regulations relating to items such as weights and measures, slaughtering, and dog registration, and may extend into the provision of transport facilities, electricity and gas, hospitals and charitable institutions, parks, recreation grounds, swimming pools, libraries, and museums. Their powers are defined by the state legislature with some supervisory powers accorded to the federal government. Water and sewerage, covered by separate rates, are often placed under separate authorities.

Next come the States—New South Wales, Victoria, Queensland, South Australia, West Australia and Tasmania, in order of size of population. In 1979 they were joined by the Northern Territory. The Australian Capital Territory (ACT) comes under the federal domain. The states provide their own central governments but in many cases have created statutory bodies or other organizations in which they have a controlling interest. Unfortunately, itemizing these categories within the state fiscal aggregates is not practicable in every instance.

The states derive their receipts in part from subventions from the federal government, in part from direct levying of imposts and in part from the issue of federal government bonds the proceeds of which are assigned to the states. The dominance of grants in 1979–1980 is a notable characteristic (Table 11.3).

TAX CATEGORIES

The considerable spread by type of impost is also noteworthy. There is however heavy dependence on payroll taxes and on taxes on the operation and ownership of motor vehicles. Gambling taxes from poker machines are significant in N.S.W. Some of the states have abolished or are in the course of abolishing estate and succession duties. This move was led by the initiative of Queensland, a state of great resource potential, but also, because of its climate, an attractive retirement location. Stamp duties, partly falling on cheques, on financial instruments

TABLE 11.3

Outlay, Receipts and Deficit of State Budgets ($ Million)

	1979-80
Receipts —	
Taxation —	
Estate taxes	171
Liquor taxes	175
Lottery taxes	316
Racing taxes	227
Stamp duties, n.e.i.	993
Land taxes	290
Motor taxes	764
Pay-roll tax	1,694
Other taxes) Fees, fines, etc.)	634
Total taxation	5,264
of which —	
Indirect taxes	4,703
Direct taxes, fees, fines, etc.	561
Other receipts —	
Interest, rent, royalties and dividends	1,029
Grants from Commonwealth	10,645
Grants (precepts) from Local authorities	52
Total other receipts	
Total receipts	17,653

Source: Australian Official Yearbook.

such as insurance policies and premium renewals, share and property transactions, are also significant.

For state public enterprises it is only possible to set out their incomes and the advances made to them:

	1975–76	1977–78	1978–79
Gross Income of Public Enterprises	914	1204	1363
Depreciation	282	380	417
Net Advances from State Budgets	611	432	329

The distribution of receipts of state governments by major expenditure categories is set out in Table 11.4. We should note the significance of the specific purpose grant, very common in Australia, whereby the federal government in transferring funds to the states also stipulates how they are to be deployed. Very strict federal control applies to

TABLE 11.4

Outlay, Receipts and Deficit of State Budgets ($ million)

	1979-80
Outlay —	
Net expenditure on goods and services —	
Final consumption expenditure —	
Law, order and public safety	1,391
Education	6,035
Health	3,362
Social security and welfare	226
All other	731
Total	11,645
Capital expenditure —	
Expenditure on new fixed assets —	
Education	620
Health	286
Social security and welfare	12
Roads	1,026
All other	1,058
Total	3,002
Increase in stocks	65
Total capital expenditure	3,067
Total net expenditure on goods and services	14,712
Purchases of existing assets (net)	6
Transfer payments —	
Cash benefits to persons	309
Grants to State non-budget authorities	167
Grants to Local authorities	587
Interest paid	2,240
Subsidies	112
Grants for private capital purposes	65
Total transfer payments	3,481
Total expenditure	18,193

Source: Australian Official Yearbook.

roads. Education through universities remains under the federal authorities. N.S.W. and Victoria are not allowed to obtain grants for special financial assistance on their own application. Most grants for specific purposes are closed-ended, though health provisions under Medibank have been open-ended in that extra provisions made in the states may attract parallel financing from federal funds, especially for state hospitals. The relative importance of open-ended grants has been declining.

The balance of tax receipts accrues directly to the federal government. This spread of taxation by tiers and associated expenditures shows the heavy dependence of the states on federal funding (vertical imbalance). A distribution of direct receipts and grants by individual states would show substantial horizontal imbalance also.

PERSONAL INCOME TAX

Assessable income includes all income, other than exempt receipts derived directly or indirectly from Australian sources plus in the case of residents, earnings from abroad. Certain other items are also subject to tax, although gifts, legacies, profits from the sale of property other than that purchased for trading, lottery winnings and capital gains are exempt.

Expenditure incurred in producing assessable income or in carrying on a business is allowable as a deduction provided it is not of a capital, private, or domestic nature. Special deductions are forthcoming for trading losses in previous years, bad debts, depreciation, annual rates and land taxes, gifts to various institutions, and one-third of amounts paid on call to afforestation companies operating in Australia. Certain further deductions are made in respect of capital spending incurred in mining operations and with primary producers. Special tax deductions are granted to people living in isolated zones of a very sparsely populated, and often arid country.

In Australia income is assessed by individual, not by household. Certain maximum allowances are made as a deduction from income for a spouse or housekeeper, but if the dependent derives separate net income the deduction is reduced. This means that for working wives there is no deduction. No deduction is given for children. Family allowances for each dependent child under 16, or full-time student, are paid by the Government from general revenues. This is an example of "universal redistribution," which is often merely recirculation, less administrative costs.

A REBATE SCHEME

In addition, Australia offers a quite complicated concessional rebate scheme. This consists of a fairly modest deduction in tax over and above a general deduction available without qualification. The minimum deduction under this head is set at $533. Concessional rebate claims in excess of $1,590, the rate on which $533 as rebate of tax was determined, are eligible for deduction of about one-third of the accrued aggregate (that is, at the rate for the lowest tax bracket). The component items include life insurance and superannuation fund payments to a maximum of $1,200, education expenditure on self or children with a limit of $250 per person, rates on property with a limit of $300, medical, dental, optical, and funeral expenses in excess of those recovered from medical insurance funds, and calls paid to afforestation companies. Apart from unusually large medical bills only afforestation schemes offer much room for exploitation of these concessional deductions. Many persons will indeed have only a few items under these categories and yet receive the general rebate. Thus the provision contains a marked discontinuity effect.

Rent interest and dividends are taxed at the same rate as earned income, the charges being levied equally on assessable net income from all sources. Pensions are taxable as are scholarships in many cases and lump sum payments on retirement. Lump sums bear tax on 5 per cent of the total receipt at the rates applicable when they are aggregated in assessable net income. There is also an estimate of the value to an employee of use of an employer's car incorporated in assessable income, and payments by employers on behalf of an individual's health funds are similarly treated. Income from partnerships is assigned by partner. For those who do not operate private health funds of approved type, a health levy is charged each year. But members of approved health funds are exempted. Housing loan interest is no longer deductible for tax, as from 1980, and has been limited to people with low incomes in any event for some years. There is no notional rent on owner-occupied housing in incomes calculations, but subject to the peculiar workings of the concessional rebates system, rates on owner-occupied property up to a value of $300 are deductible. The specific maxima applicable to individual items in the concessional category have not been raised for quite a number of years.

TAX SCHEDULES

Income that is assessable bears tax according to the following schedule:

Income in Year	*Tax on taxable income*
0–$ 3,893	Nil
$ 3,893–$16,607	Nil plus 33.07% for each $1 in excess of $3,893
$16,608–$33,215	$4,205 plus 47.07% for each $1 in excess of $16,608
$33,216–and over	$12,022 plus 61.07% for each $1 in excess of $33,216

This yields the following pattern for average and marginal rates of tax:

Taxable Income	Tax Payable	Average Rate	Marginal Rate
$	$	$	$
5,000	366	7.3	33.07
10,000	2,020	20.2	33.07
15,000	3,673	24.5	33.07
20,000	5,802	29.0	47.07
25,000	8,155	32.6	47.07
30,000	10,509	35.0	47.07
35,000	13,111	37.5	61.07
40,000	16,165	40.4	61.07
50,000	22,272	44.5	61.07
80,000	40,593	50.7	61.07

Salary and wage earners have the bulk of their tax commitments deducted regularly from pay. Those with $400 or more from other sources have to pay provisional tax before the final payment becomes due. This was introduced so that the revenue did not suffer unwarranted delay in receipts.

Averaging for tax purposes is permitted up to a maximum of 5 years to primary producers whilst actors and artists are assessed on normal incomes plus a third of the abnormal.

INCOME TAX ON COMPANIES

These general income tax arrangements apply to both private and public companies. Income for the purposes of this tax should be equivalent to the change in the value of the property rights of the company over the defined income tax year. This means that it should cover gross revenue minus all associated expenses of production, including an amount in the form of depreciation to cover the equivalent cost of replacing capital at the end of the year to the level that was held at the beginning, so as to maintain capital intact. As well, there is a deduction for any loss in the value of inventory held over the year (or addition for any gain in the value of inventory over the year), replacement costs of inventory now being lower (higher).

Of course, the taxable base in practice only secures an approximation to this ideal. Problems arise with depreciation for which there is no conceptually best method for accumulating the sums required – prior to the undertaking of the actual replacement. For the taxpayer, the more rapid the depreciation the better because the present value of the aggregate of deductions for depreciation will then be as high as possible. This is so, provided that the taxable income stream is sufficiently positive to incur tax at the same rate throughout, and that tax rates are not expected to change. In Australia two alternative rates for depreciating assets have been allowed – the diminishing value and the prime cost method. These have been applied to historical cost of the asset, not replacement cost, an effect which becomes more deleterious to firms the higher the rate of inflation. The diminishing balance method gives more rapid write-offs in earlier years but lower ones in later years. This is usually preferred, the more so the greater the rate of innovation in equipment, for obsolescence receives no allowance under existing tax arrangements.

L.I.F.O./F.I.F.O.

With stock valuation there is also a choice of methods – F.I.F.O. (First in First out) or L.I.F.O. (Last in First out). There is little to choose between them when prices remain stable. But when prices escalate L.I.F.O. reduces measured profits whilst under falling prices F.I.F.O. has that effect. Australia uses F.I.F.O. With the recent persisting inflation profits have been overstated for tax purposes, as the tax is borne on nominal levels not on "real" ones.

Interest on borrowed funds is treated as a legitimate business expense but dividends on share capital are not.

Many companies, anxious to gain and retain labour at a time when marginal tax rates on income are high (and there is pressure from governmental authorities to hold down pay increases) offer their employees benefits in kind. These are generally tax deductible. Cheap loans for housing, provision of cars and health insurance, recreational facilities, and entertaining benefits are amongst these. Some of these are gradually being brought into charge under personal income tax, others still remain unassessed.

Company tax is assessed on the net income obtained as indicated above and bears a proportionate rate of 46 per cent for both public and private companies. Earlier there were graduated rates but these have been abandoned as they had induced income splitting. Private companies are however charged a higher rate of tax than public companies if they fail to distribute at least 30 per cent of their profits to shareholders. The justification for this is that in its absence there would be an inequity created as between sole traders and partnerships and private companies. This would arise from the differential between company tax at 46 per cent and the marginal income tax rate of over 60 per cent which would induce profit retentions in private companies. The tax imposed for excess retentions is at the rate of 50 per cent. It would seem however that if there is the case for this differential penalty on private companies it should also apply to public companies.

DOUBLE TAXATION

The central features of corporate tax levied under the so-called "classical method" are well known. The company is a separate legal entity and is for this reason thought to be as appropriately taxable as persons. This means that individuals who receive dividends are in effect taxed on these dividends when received as personal income. But they have earlier suffered through a reduction in net profits, and hence presumably in net dividend payout, through the levy of company income tax. This is the so-called "double" taxation of dividends. On retained profits such tax payments are really deferred. The differential created between current and deferred payouts leads, other things equal, to an appreciation in share values at the time of the tax imposition. This is induced by the fact that the increase in share valuation is not taxed, whether the shares are sold or retained by individuals, as there is no capital gains tax. The effects thus become capitalized, and no net gains are available to subsequent purchasers of the shares.

The tax also causes a differential in costs of borrowing, since debt streams are cheaper than equity. This serves to increase the debt-equity ratio of the companies. For both these reasons, the tax cannot be said to be neutral in its effects on resource allocation.

In the recent inflation, the bleeding of companies through the method of valuation of income has necessitated hasty actions to offset the additional burden. These have taken the form of greater allowances for stock valuation and the introduction of investment allowances, a form of accelerated depreciation. Both have been operated in a staccato manner and have been substantially reduced recently as rates of inflation have moderated somewhat. The adjustments, very rough and ready, have in no sense conformed to any sensible indexation pattern.

THE REAL WAGE GAP

Of course investment allowances and accelerated depreciation could have been introduced in part with other ends in view. In Australia a sizeable "real wage gap" was created in the mid-1970s when wage rates, especially those in the public sector in the first instance, were raised. Firms felt the squeeze on profits. With labour becoming relatively much more expensive, they shifted their labour-capital mix in favour of capital. The government probably decided to encourage this as a means of reducing the sharp slide in profits.[4]

An argument often advanced for the retention of company tax is that this is the only effective way that foreigners' profits from a wide range of activity in Australia can be assessed. In this way the alternatives, interest and dividend withholding taxes, can be avoided.

Uncertainty as to the incidence of the company tax clouds our analysis. Is the tax borne by the entrepreneur-owners, is it borne by shareholders in general, or is it borne by the general populace through higher products prices? If it is borne by the first group it is inimical to innovation and risk-taking. If it is borne by the last group then consolidation within a general income tax framework would seem to be sensible, save for any desire to explicitly tax foreigners. As far as shareholders in general are concerned, transactions in shares once the tax is imposed, or augmented, will take place at market prices, discounted by the capitalized tax expectations. (This is because the advantages to individuals of reducing tax on incomes by purchasing shares have already been discounted.)

The question of tax reform whether within the dual structure, or by shifting to a different form of taxation overall, such as the expenditure tax, is too big a subject to embark on here.

III. INDIRECT TAXES

Most of the taxes under this heading could be described as particular rather than general in character.

EXCISE DUTIES

This tax is levied by the federal government on beer, spirits, tobacco, gasoline, petroleum, and liquid petroleum gas. There are a few other minor items. A notable omission is table wine, of which Australia is now a large producer. All of these are taxed at a specific rate, which tends to be reviewed at each budget, and periodically changed, often by large amounts. These taxes do not automatically keep pace with inflation. But over time some attempt is made through discontinuous jumps to adjust for this, a particularly sharp rise was last imposed in 1978. The general rate on spirits runs at the level of $19 per litre of alcohol, while that for cigarettes is $24.75 per kilogram.

The levies on crude oil and crude oil pricing have been changed dramatically in the last few years and deserve more than the summary treatment we can here accord them. Australia produces about 65 per cent of its oil from domestic fields which were opened up as late as 1967, and are still being extended. There are known to be very workable deposits of oil shale in the country and there is still hope that oil in substantial quantities may be forthcoming from the Gulf of Carpentaria in Northern Queensland. For the five years from 1970 to 1975, crude oil producers received the import parity price prevailing in 1968. Thus, this did not reflect the quadrupling of oil prices secured through OPEC in 1973–1974. An excise levy of $2 per barrel was imposed in late 1975 and the government introduced a distinction in the price to be paid per barrel for old and new oil. Old oil received a very minor increase and refiners paid this plus the levy of $2.

New oil was defined as that discovered after 1975. By choice of date this excluded the rich basin in Bass strait. It was to be paid the import parity price of 1975, $8.90, less the levy, and refiners would bear this plus the $2 levy. In 1977 the levy was raised to $3 and new oil was exempted entirely. From that date pricing on old oil was changed. Producers were given import parity prices minus the levy for an annually increasing proportion of production, or 6 million barrels whichever was the greater. This applied to each new field, or development within a field. The proportion was initially set at 10 per cent, and was to rise annually to reach 50 per cent by 1980.

In 1978 the government decided to raise the price paid by refiners to the import parity level for *all* domestic crude oil. But the same phasing in arrangements was retained. The levy on controlled oil was increased to bridge the difference between the import parity price and the price paid to producers, but the levy on parity priced oil was left at $3. From June 1979 the levy on new oil and on expansions in old oil fields was raised to $6.75 per barrel. This amounted to $3 plus 75 per cent of the increase in import parity price when the field produced between 2 million and 15 million barrels. At greater production levels the levy is set at $3 plus the increase in import parity price—which leaves the return to producers at 1978 levels. From January 1980 the price paid to producers was adjusted by either the consumer price index or the import parity price, whichever had risen less.

To summarize: in recent years the price paid to producers for old oil field development has been allowed to rise to a degree, but import parity pricing to refiners has been secured on all oil by the use of a graded levy. This reaches as high as $16 on controlled oil. The government has hence enjoyed a lucrative expansion in revenue from oil, the yield from oil and liquid petroleum gas combined having risen from $476 million in 1977–1978 to an estimated $2,057 million in 1979–1980. At a time when the government was trying hard to meet a proclaimed sharp re-

TABLE 11.5

ASIC* Code	Description	IMPORTS AND EXPORTS: Imports as % of Domestic Sales (1968-69) 1972-73	Imports as % of Total Imports by Manufacturing Industries (1968-69) 1972-73	Exports as % of Turnover (1968-69) 1972-73	Exports as % of Total Exports by Manufacturing Industries (1968-69) 1972-73	ASSISTANCE: Average Nominal Rate on Output % 1969-70	Average Effective Rate % 1969-70	Gross Subsidy Equivalent $m 1969-70	Net Subsidy Equivalent $m 1969-70
	CLOTHING AND FOOTWEAR								
	Knitting Mills								
2411	Hosiery	(3.7) 1.8	(0.06) 0.03	(0.4) 5.8	(0.01) 0.01	46	79	21	17
2412	Cardigans and pullovers	(6.0) 7.9	(0.10) 0.12	(0.1) 0.1	(0.01) —	42	74	21	15
2413	Knitted goods n.e.c.	(13.7) 25.1	(0.34) 0.87	(1.7) 1.4	(0.09) 0.06	36	37	25	15
241	Total knitting mills	(8.5) 15.6	(0.49) 1.02	(0.8) 0.8	(0.11) 0.07	41	79	n.a.	47

TABLE 11.5 (continued)

	Clothing								
2421	Womens and girls blouses and frocks	(3.2) 10.9	(0.06) 0.24	(0.5) 0.5	(0.03) 0.02	49	87	26	19
2422	Womens and girls outerwear n.e.c.	(6.1) 10.7	(0.08) 0.16	(0.1) 0.1	(..) ..	54	111	20	15
2423	Mens and boys trousers and shorts; work clothing	(3.4) 5.9	(0.05) 0.10	(0.6) 0.9	(0.03) 0.03	66	152	29	22
2424	Mens and boys suits and coats; waterproof clothing	(3.4) 6.7	(0.05) 0.07	(2.3) 3.3	(0.09) 0.06	59	112	21	16
2425	Underwear, nightwear, shirts and infants clothing n.e.c.	(4.4) 9.5	(0.12) 0.26	(0.7) 1.1	(0.06) 0.05	54	116	44	31

* Australian Standard Industrial Classification

Source: Australia-Committee to Advise on Policies for Manufacturing Industry. Policies for the Development of Manufacturing Industry. (The Jackson Report) Canberra AGPS 1975.

duction in the budget deficit, this proved the revenue creator which enabled it to meet the target.

SALES TAXES

Three rates of tax apply: 2½ per cent, 15 per cent and 27½ per cent. These are levied on the wholesale price of goods. Items falling into the heavily taxed categories are:

	%
Jewellery, furs	27½
Motor cars and station wagons	15
Photographic equipment	27½
Sporting and travelling equipment	27½
Furniture and white goods	15

CUSTOMS DUTIES

Australia is a high tariff country. Protection has been an integral part of government programmes since the beginning of the century. Today, support for the policy derives from the belief that it ensures job protection. This applies to many in the clothing and footwear industries, whose jobs would be threatened by emerging Asian low-cost suppliers. In recent years quotas on entry of these goods have been imposed as well. But in general the tariff has been the principal weapon of protection. Effective rates have generally been regarded as very high by international comparison. An enquiry of 1976 into Australian manufacturing (The Jackson Report) shows that the high rates of effective protection are due to high nominal rates imposed both on goods and factors (see Table 11.5).

INDEXATION OF TAXES

In 1977 Australia gained some publicity for being the first of the western democracies to introduce indexation of various nominally expressed deductions and allowances in connection with her personal income tax. The indexation adjustment is announced just before the deductions for the new fiscal year come into force and influence the regular tax deductions from pay. In the first two years these indices followed closely the movements in the consumer price index. But in 1978–1979 the government offered only half indexation. Unfortunately in 1978–1979 the government ended the year with a large domestic deficit. They decided, amidst outcry, to continue an income tax surcharge (now incorporated in the figures quoted) that had been levied half way through the year. Curiously, the public outcry was much louder against the surcharge being allowed to continue into the new year, despite the government's insistence that it would be temporary, than it was against indexation being halved. For 1979–1980 indexation has been discontinued, and for 1980–1981 something approaching half indexation was offered. This early attempt at honest government seems to raise doubts as to whether an electorate supports it. It is yet to be seen whether it will be restored.

There is no indexation on the company income tax. As we have emphasized, the excise duties are specific but adjusted only periodically and in large jumps. This ill-accords with the notion of indexation.

MISCELLANEOUS TAXES

Gambling taxes apply to racing, especially totalizator activity lotteries, and poker machine takings and are levied *ad valorem*. They are collected by the states.

Taxes are imposed upon the issue of driving licences, upon the issue and renewal of motor vehicle registrations, and the associated third party cover insurances. As well, there are certain other taxes on road transport together with contributions for road maintenance. These imposts accrue to the States.

Across the states the payroll tax is fairly uniform at 5 per cent. The chief variation is the minimum level of payroll before tax is liable. Even this is hard to determine because of the use of the graduations but roughly it is $60,000–$150,000.

The principal source of state income on alcohol is licences for trading in Liquor.

Stamp duties are the second largest source of state income. When coupled with the rather similar duty on motor vehicles, it comes close in size to the tax collections on payroll. The duties on financial instruments and share transactions usually amount to about .2–.3 per cent, on property 2 per cent. Both are *ad valorem* on the contract price.

A land tax is levied on freehold and crown lands, unless the sites are used for owner-occupied residence or primary production. Graduated rates of tax are levied on unimproved value. The maximum rate in N.S.W. is reached at $130,000 at the rate of 2.4 per cent

There is a rich assortment of primary production charges. For example wool transactions are taxed at 8 per cent, and there are charges on dairying, tobacco, honey, poultry etc., of a specific nature.

Estate and succession duties have been discontinued by the federal government and by Queensland. Certain other states have undertaken to follow suit in the next fiscal year. Estates passed to widows in N.S.W. bear no tax.

TABLE 11.6

Income Tax Contributions by Income Groups, Australia 1976–1977

Classification by Numbers Quintile	% Contribution to Total Tax
Highest	47.4
Second	20.4
Third	17.8
Fourth	10.2
Lowest	4.2
TOTAL	100.00

Classification by Incomes Quintile	% Contribution to Total Tax
Highest	30.2
Second	16.5
Third	25.0
Fourth	16.8
Lowest	11.5
TOTAL	100.0

Source: Author's calculations, based on data drawn from Report of the Commissioner of Taxes.

RATES

These are levied on land values on formulae that differ by state. The revenue accrues to the local authorities. Unimproved capital value is the most usual base, but site value which includes capital costs involved in improving the land is also used. Annual rental value of property with improvements is occasionally employed .

The rates are set annually by each council (on a proportionate basis) and the total collected is closely related to the council's estimated expenditure.

SOME OVERALL PATTERNS

Table 11.6 shows Income Tax Liabilities by income groups as a percentage of income in the fiscal year in 1976–1977.

Table 11.7 shows Income Tax Contributions by Income Groups as a percentage of total tax in the fiscal year 1976–1977.

These calculations are based on the tax allowances of all kinds to

TABLE 11.7

Income Tax Liabilities by Income Groups, Australia 1976–1977

Classification by Numbers Quintile	Net Tax (as % of Net Income)
Highest	30.0
Second	21.4
Third	18.9
Fourth	15.4
Lowest	8.7
Classification by Incomes Quintile	**Net Tax (as % of Net Income)**
Highest	33.3
Second	24.6
Third	21.1
Fourth	18.3
Lowest	12.2

Source: Author's calculations, based on data drawn from Report of the Commissioner of Taxes.

which the various income groups are entitled and are based on their prevailing rates of tax. The data, drawn from the Commissioner of Taxes, report is based on their calculations of the distribution of income.

The following three tables draw on information collated in the Household Expenditure Survey of 1975–1976 and enable us to depict income tax paid in relation to other major categories of household expenditure by designated demographic and occupational groups at that time. They refer to the latest year for which such a breakdown of expenditure is available.

IV. THE POST-WAR PATTERN OF TAXATION

Table 11.1 above contains a distribution of tax receipts by proportionate shares drawn from alternative tax bases. It covers a large range of post-war years with a continuous picture for the 1970s. However, not incorporated in the table is the recent change from income tax deductions for family composition to a system of family allowances which do

TABLE 11.8

Selected Expenditure Items as a Percentage of Average Weekly Income of Households with Employee (a) Head of Household by Occupation (b) of Head, Australia

Expenditure Items	Occupation of Head of Household				
	Professional Technical, Administrative, etc. (c)	Clerical & Sales (d)	Tradesmen Production Process Workers, Labourers	Other Employees	All Households with Employee Head
Food	11.7%	13.3%	15.6%	14.5%	13.9%
Alcohol & Tobacco	3.3	4.0	5.5	5.2	4.5
Clothing & Footwear	5.6	6.6	6.5	5.5	6.1
Housing	11.1	12.2	9.5	10.9	10.7
Rent Payments	2.5	3.4	3.4	4.4	3.3
Mortgage Payments (e)	5.1	5.4	3.7	3.1	4.3
Rate Payments	1.0	1.2	1.1	0.9	1.1
House Insurance	0.2	0.2	0.2	0.2	0.2
Repair & Maintenance	1.5	1.2	0.8	1.8	1.2
Housing Payments for other dwellings	0.7	0.7	0.3	0.6	0.6
Transport & Communication	14.1	14.9	15.9	16.0	15.2
Income Tax	16.7	13.1	12.2	12.5	13.8
Average Weekly Income ($)	334.28	255.46	244.81	239.33	266.88

(a) Those workers who are wage and salary earners in their main job.
(b) Occupation was coded only for 'employees' on the basis of their main job.
(c) Professional, technical & related workers; administrative, executive and management workers.
(d) Includes book-keepers, typists and shop assistants.
(e) Includes both principal and interest components of any housing loan repayments. Excludes payments of a capital nature.

Source: Australian Bureau of Statistics Household Expenditure Survey 1975/1976.

TABLE 11.9

Selected Expenditure Items as a Percentage of Average Weekly Income of Households with Two Adults and One Child by Household Income, Australia

Expenditure Items	Weekly Household Income						
	Under $80	$80 & Under $140	$140 & Under $200	$200 & Under $260	$260 & Under $340	$340 or More	All Households with Two Adults & One Child
Food	51.4%	25.0%	17.4%	14.0%	13.1%	7.3%	14.1%
Alcohol & Tobacco	12.8	6.4	5.9	4.0	5.5	5.6	4.7
Clothing	12.2	5.4	7.6	5.9	7.8	3.7	6.3
Housing (e)	21.2	15.5	16.4	12.7	11.2	6.1	12.0
Transport & Communication	39.8	20.7	18.5	17.5	12.2	3.4	14.8
Income Tax	10.9	9.2	12.4	14.0	14.6	14.7	13.6

(e) Includes both principal and interest components of any housing loan repayments. Excludes payments of a capital nature.

Source: Australian Bureau of Statistics Household Expenditure Survey 1975/1976.

TABLE 11.10

Selected Expenditure Items as a Percentage of Average Household Income of Households with Head of Household Aged 30-44 Years and 45-65 Years, by Household Income, Australia

Expenditure Items	Weekly Household Income													
	Under $80		$80 & Under $140		$140 & Under $200		$200 & Under $260		$260 & Under $340		$340 or More		All Households	
	Age of Household Head		Age of Household Head		Age of Household Head		Age of Household Head		Age of Household Head		Age of Household Head		Age of Household Head	
	30-44 Years	45-65 Years	30-44 Years	45-65 Years	30-44 Years	45-65 Years	30-44 Years	45-65 Years	30-44 Years	45-65 Years	30-44 Years	45-65 Years	30-44 Years	45-65 Years
Food	70.3%	38.7%	30.6%	21.5%	20.8%	19.2%	17.0%	15.5%	14.5%	13.8%	10.8%	11.3%	15.8%	14.7%
Alcohol & Tobacco	15.5	6.9	8.1	6.3	5.9	4.9	3.4	5.1	4.2	4.8	3.1	4.1	4.4	4.7
Clothing & Footwear	19.8	11.3	9.6	7.1	6.5	7.4	5.4	6.7	6.8	6.9	5.6	6.1	6.6	6.7
Housing	37.0	19.1	19.5	14.6	14.2	9.5	13.2	7.0	11.5	6.9	8.2	5.4	11.6	7.4
Transport & Communication	34.5	20.5	20.2	18.3	16.9	16.8	11.4	14.4	16.0	16.1	12.1	14.1	14.8	15.3
Income Tax	10.0	2.8	8.2	9.9	11.0	11.5	9.8	12.7	13.6	13.5	17.3	15.9	14.1	13.7

Source: Australian Bureau of Statistics (ABS) Household Expenditure Survey 1975-1976.

not bear tax. For ideal comparability there should thus be a deduction related to family composition taken from income tax and total tax receipts for the last 3 years.

The sheer dominance of the personal income tax and its proportionately increasing importance is the most striking feature. The virtual demise of capital taxes is also noteworthy. Indirect taxes are rather more difficult to assess for they comprise customs, excise duties, sales tax, taxes on motor vehicles, stamp duties, gambling, and even payroll tax. For 1979–1980 this would bring the combined proportion up to 36 per cent. Indeed, if property taxes and liquor licences are added in, it climbs to 43 per cent. Thus if we take note of the spread of indirect taxes across a whole range of tax bases, the sheer dominance of the personal income tax evaporates. But when income taxes of persons and companies are combined, the statement that direct taxes dominate indirect cannot be denied. This conclusion was much less clearcut before 1965. The recent growth tax, the crude oil levy, comes under the heading Excise taxes. Company taxes seem to be on a declining trend, as a proportion of total taxation.

On the bottom line of the table we show the total tax take as a proportion of gross domestic product. This is the figure that is quoted in OECD publications. Since the early 1960s the trend has been upwards, with sizeable jumps in the mid 1970s when the new Labour government decided to extend the public sector though we may notice the moderateness of the fall since then. Water, gas, electricity, and in recent years telecommunication, are excluded from these figures.

Outlays of Public Authorities as proportions of GDP are as follows:

	Federal	State & Local	All Public Authorities
1969-70 to 1972-73 (Aver)	24.7	16.8	31.8
1973-74	24.7	16.7	31.8
1974-75	29.7	19.6	37.4
1975-76	30.8	20.3	38.2
1976-77	30.4	20.1	38.4
1977-78	31.1	20.9	39.7
1978-79	29.8	20.4	38.3
1979-80	29.1	20.0	37.8

Source: Budget Papers 1981-1982.

(Note that transfers between sectors have been netted out of the final column.) The Public Authority overall deficit has risen from 1.6 per cent in 1973–1974 to as high as 6.0 per cent in 1977–1978 and was 4 per cent in 1979–1980. These deficits have been financed by issue of federal debt to the public and to banking institutions in Australia, with some borrowing from abroad.

Until the mid-1970s income taxes were graduated across 29 steps with the marginal tax rising from zero to 66.7 per cent for virtually all years from the early 1950s.

The disentangling of transfer expenditures for a long series of years would be a major task. But we do know the transfer payments of the combined public authorities and can express them as a proportion of gross domestic product for the last ten years. These rise from 14 per cent in 1969–1970, to 22 per cent in 1978–1979. There was a big rise from 16 to 19 per cent in 1974–1975 and a more gradual upward trend thereafter. This estimate covers cash benefits to persons, grants to states, interest paid, subsidies, and transfers overseas. Of the 3 per cent rise between 1974–1975 and 1978–1979, .5 per cent is accounted for by interest paid on accumulating debt at the higher interest rates gradually prevailing.

SHORT AND LONG RUN TAXATION

In raising funds to finance its activities, government basically has three sources: taxation, inflation and issue of public debt. (which includes the possibility of borrowing from abroad from time to time). The main sustained source is normally taxation. Major shortfalls tend to be met by the issue of bonds. Under such circumstances, these are often taken up by the banks, thereby adding to the money supply. The 1975–1983 Australian government inherited the inflationary experience of the pre-1975 period. It has tried to curb such issue of debt to the banks. However, the Prime Minister in 1978 came to grief through the simultaneous pursuit of this aim and the inconsistent policy of lowering interest rates at a time of increasing world pressures on interest rates. Something had to give, and it was the money supply on that occasion which was allowed to expand. This interfered with the policy of reducing the domestic rate of inflation. Whether this lesson has been learned by the new Labour government remains to be seen.

Assume, then, that the main source of funding is to be taxation. Existing taxes must be able to carry the strain, or be adjusted. The main adjustments would include strengthening the tax base on which rates are levied and increasing or regrouping the rates themselves. The tax base can never be perfect in a world where the individual can preserve an element of discretion. Even if all gambling activity of an organized type is taxed, there is still no way of effectively taxing private gamblers. In like manner, all officially recorded income may in principle be subject to tax, but a lot of it might be created through transactions (involving money transfers) that can never be fully checked upon – except perhaps in a police state. Often the more precise the definition of the tax base, the more clear become ways in which the tax may be avoided. Then taxes will be borne mainly by those for whom the utility derived from taxable activity exceeds the payoff from transferring to non-taxable endeavour sufficiently to outweigh the additional costs. Of course there may also be deliberate evasion. In this case, utility estimates will have to be qualified to allow for the probability of discovery and conviction and the expectations as to the punishment if detected.

TAX EVASION NEVER PAYS?

Beyond a certain point, the easier it is to evade taxes the less likely is one to be punished as the courts and the prisons would be kept too busy! These problems are most manifest in relation to income and wealth taxes. Hicks has drawn attention to the analytic elusiveness of the income concept.[5] This suggests the great difficulty in securing a reliable and stable tax base. Man is a strange creature. Even though he may share the social aims of the governments he helps to elect, he does not wish to bear more than the absolutely enforced proportion of those costs himself. He is therefore by nature a tax shifter.

There are two canons of taxation. According to one, taxes should be based "on ability to pay"; according to the other "equality of sacrifice" should be the criteria. Whichever is used, taxation has implications for individuals that infringe upon their personal preferences. As such, fiscal aims are expressed through sophisticated variations in deductions for family composition and size, for size of income, and for its composition. The individual finds ways of shifting across designated classes in order to lighten his tax obligations. In Australia, specially favourable tax treatment is given to those who hold life insurance policies. So this induces a greater proportion of the populace to hold such policies than would occur otherwise. Australia has no tax on capital gains. Instead, it has a steep marginal tax on income. So there is strong inducement to take receipts disproportionately in the form of capital gains. Likewise, there is no tax on the family, only on individuals. Thus each household has an inducement to bolster the tax bearing income of the less well paid at the expense of the more well paid, since they bear different rates at the margin. Further, it is advantageous to set up family trusts and dispose of claims on wealth to low-income earning members of one's family. However, these arrangements must be made inviolable.

NO TAX NEUTRALITY

In these ways adjustment takes place to a prevailing pattern of taxes. The eventual outcome may or may not bear a close relationship to the original aims of the government as to distribution of tax burdens and patterns of after-tax incomes. In Australia very often the result has differed from intentions. Much effort has been devoted to the reframing of tax legislation to outlaw various forms of organization or to reverse the swing of actual tax incidence between sections of the community. But this further legislative provision involves qualifications greater than at the previous round. Those who find it possible to gain by shifting the impact of taxes will be induced to work all the harder to do so. This is especially true of the well-to-do, who can afford to pay for the best advice to this end. This is essentially a no-win situation for a government. Such policy would not be pursued so hard if unrealistic egalitarian aims were not so deeply entrenched. In circumstances such as these, governments need to lower, not increase taxes. Only in this way can they retain more people within the tax contributing range and reduce the benefits from tax economizing search directly. A reduction in qualifications, deductions, and allowances are more likely to achieve this.

TAX INCIDENCE THEORY

The incidence of taxation has been the central and most difficult part of the public finance literature. Incidence theory asks whether those on whom the taxes were levied were the ultimate bearers. This discussion assumes an unequivocal definition of the tax base. One aim is to determine whether commodity taxes fell on firms' profits or on households through higher prices for consumer goods.

This theory is highly developed although it has proved very difficult to test and many of the central features are still questioned. Shifting between tax classes is really a corollary of that theory and so in a sense should be the endeavour to gain exclusion from the tax base. But these subjects have been touched upon only briefly if at all. This is partly because it is only in the last 10–20 years that tax burdens have been moving into the magnitude where that becomes a really profitable activity. Ideally the term "incidence" should cover both of these aspects. Few books have given these new aspects detailed treatment though especially good exceptions include Kay and King,[6] and the taxation monographs of the IEA[7]

The main patterns of taxation eventually become clear, and people adjust to them to the best of their ability. Future transactions between sellers and buyers then take place on the assumption of their continuance. The effects of taxation, favourable or unfavourable, thus become capitalized into prices, incomes, and earnings. Purchasers after capitalization would suffer windfall losses from any rectifying changes taking place in taxation structures. In contrast, those who originally benefitted from the pattern of imposts before capitalization will have escaped the counter-attack to secure redress. This is a source of inequity of no little magnitude.

UNANTICIPATED TAX CHANGE

When households and firms face an unexpected change in tax policy, the tracing of incidence, both short and long run, begins afresh. We assume people seek the best ways of economizing on the burdens of tax, with the relative utility of doing so balanced against cost. Within the dynamic phase of such changes it should be possible empirically to determine something about the incidence of the varying taxes. People will in principle reveal where the incidence of the tax falls—if they escape the tax they will make no adjustments—in the direction of their tax alleviating adjustments.

The difficulty is that such tax adjustments are often introduced to provide a corrective to certain developments in the economy that the government desires to reduce, eliminate or foster. It may be difficult to unscramble the one effect from the other. Sometimes they may pull in opposite directions, sometimes they may be reinforcing. Yet essentially this approach should prove a more fruitful way of making an empirical check on incidence than the rather peripherally related studies from cross-section analysis and time series that economists have used. Such studies cannot take cognizance of the fact that there are now many more trading, but non-tax paying, members of the community than there were some years ago.

EMPIRICAL INCIDENCE STUDIES

The empirical analysis of incidence is in a less satisfactory state than the theory itself, although the latter must share some of the blame. It has been customary in this field to draw upon the theory of the consumer and the income and substitution effects of a change in wages. Statistical studies rely on times series or cross-section analysis. Much use has been made of the latter. Here, hours of work have been correlated against wage rates of a range of people at a given time. Even with maximum care as to control for other influences, there is no way in which such studies can throw light on the income and substitution effects of that theory. If wage rates for people of a given skill differ, it must be because of differences in non-pecuniary conditions or imperfections. Yet these are excluded from the theory being tested. This is a fundamental criticism that never seems to be grasped. Using such information one may be able to devise a test of pecuniary versus non-pecuniary effects but no one has done so yet. Only one good argument is needed to undermine an approach and this will suffice.[8]

But there is more. Since the question of incidence relates to movements between taxed and untaxed sectors, it would be strange if this could be empirically tested without drawing information from each of the sectors directly. And one would have to be very subtle indeed to derive the effects from surrogate markets. Moreover, the identification problem here is a real one. Demand effects cannot be ignored. It is not clear whether the New Jersey experiments and the married women's participation analyses,[9] two alternative sources of income and substitution effects, can survive the first criticism but if they can then the second criticism becomes the damaging one.

It is also important to appreciate that traditional analyses of incidence do not directly handle transactions not included in the cash nexus. Fortunately the extension is straightforward.

All transactions are based on contracts. Some may be informal, and verbal, others formal, and legally enforceable. Conventionally economists have based their theories on the latter though they have ignored the costs of this provision. The taxing authorities have secured the tax base on such legally enforceable contracts but as taxes have been growing in severity the attractions of informal contracts have relatively increased. Self-insurance can become an economic proposition. Activities undertaken can still be legitimate and not imply evasion of taxes, though tax pressure on legitimate activities can make the risks of illegitimate activities the more worth running. We should recognize that goods can be transacted at alternative prices, ones which allow for the contract to be legally enforceable, ones that do not. This point can be easily handled within a "characteristics" approach.[10]

A DIFFERENT METHODOLOGY

An alternative method of proceeding is to recall that activities are selected both for their pecuniary and their non-pecuniary advantages. As Marshall would say, people select activities where the "net advantages" are strongest.[11] In the labour market we may select leisure-oriented skills in the organized market, and may do so the more avidly, the higher is the tax rate on incomes. For example we may select jobs that give satisfaction within the job or that offer associated non-pecuniary benefits such as appealing work conditions and facilities. Or again, in-kind but non-taxable benefits exclusive to an individual recipient may be available. This is analogous to the selection from a portfolio of bonds of those with low nominal money interest and prospect of capital gain (where the latter, when realized, bears less tax).

When worktime is deducted from total time available, the residual is described as leisure time. But leisure time is also subject to gradations. Just as we may speak of leisure-oriented market skills, we may speak of market-oriented leisure skills. But such skills may not be presented in ways that involve formal contractual agreements. Do-it-yourself activity such as painting, building patios and swimming pools at home come under this head. One may also do work of this type for others where exchange is effected either through barter, or through money transfers by unenforceable contracts. Normally such exchanges lie outside the taxable base, for to operate otherwise would exact too high a price in search, surveillance and control. Yet the higher the taxes imposed upon the tax base the more are individuals induced to resort to market-oriented leisure skills. The more likely is government, threatened with reductions in its tax take, induced to pay the heavy cost of monitoring.

WORK AND LEISURE

There is no sharp dividing line between work and leisure. The spectrum is a reasonably continuous one.[12] We can follow Becker's classification system[13] and assume that each activity involves a goods component and a time component. Playing golf requires clubs and time on the greens. Time components assigned to engaging in exchange or interaction with other persons attract rates of reward. These will differ according to quality in skill, and perhaps vary between the formal and informal sectors.

In the formal sector allowance must be made for the fact that a contract exists. This very act renders the arrangement subject to outside scrutiny and thus to possible imposition of tax. Moreover the contract will include explicit or implicit requirements to perform up to a given standard, and in default to make good the work. That is to say the wage payment contains a risk premium. Thus, to the extent that the charge is borne by an employing firm it becomes a factor constraining levels of employment and/or market rates of pay. With informal work patterns, tax is not borne by the buyer (at least overtly) and risks may or may not be borne by the individual worker. Where work is performed for a firm whose time of active trading will extend beyond that of the employee's commitment to it, some of the risk will be borne by the firm. Hence the firm must weigh up the advantages and disadvantages of formal contracts.

Where continuity in trading is unimportant, the individual can ignore the risk. There seems to be no way through which the demander of this service can enforce even an informal agreement. Where continuity in trading is important to the individual, such risks must be borne at least in part through self-insurance, privately arranged insurance or private contract (a dangerous signal that tax is being avoided).

Formal contracts offer certain advantages. For example, workers' compensation and the terms of a marketed (or government) contract may be the cheaper deal, quality for quality. Activities within the market have to be weighed carefully in respect to all their components in assessing the advantages and disadvantages both relative to one another and to any extra-market activities. Over a relevant taxing period there will be an intimate connection arising in their relative "prices."

Insurance, tax, and other differential costs will influence at the margin relative rates of return. Such relative rates of return will settle at the point where there is no advantage to any individual in regrouping. The pressures, of course, can arise also from the side of demand (through subcontracting perhaps). The price of non-marketed labour in a skill is constrained within definable limits, with respect to the price for the parallel marketed skill, a point that is very often not mentioned in the avoision literature, where one often gets the impression that the situation is open-ended. This interrelationship between the informal and formal market we shall now show in a simplified case drawn from the labour market. We envisage a world with no tax on labour where a competitive market for a skill establishes a relative price for labour at the intersection of Marshallian market demand and supply curves. A tax on market work is introduced that is an *ad valorem* tax on this rate. (This is rather akin to a proportional income tax and makes our essential point without bringing in the complexities that arise when marginal differ from average rates.) The tax now elicits the same supply of labour as before provided the after-tax wage rates are unaffected. This occurs if the within-market rates of exchange between pre-tax pay rates and labour supplies are given by the curve S′S′, higher and to the left of SS, the curve that applied before taxes were introduced (see Figure 11.1). The equilibrium pre-tax wage rate is now P′N′ and the post-tax rate is RN′ less than PN. At this rate N′N less labour is employed than before. But, more importantly, there are now inducements emanating from both sides of the market to encourage contracting in an untaxed sector. At the rate of RN′ or anywhere between P′N′ and RN′ demanders may be willing to contract in the untaxed sector and reduce labour costs, provided other costs such as those affecting their reputation as suppliers and the risks of dealing are thought sufficiently small. At most, N′N″ would-be buyers could transfer to the untaxed sector. (There could be more if some in the range ON′ could become disentangled with the development of the alternative market.)* Similarly, at any rate between PN and P′N′ in the untaxed sector portion of the

*Both SS & S′S′ could be affected.

Figure 11.1

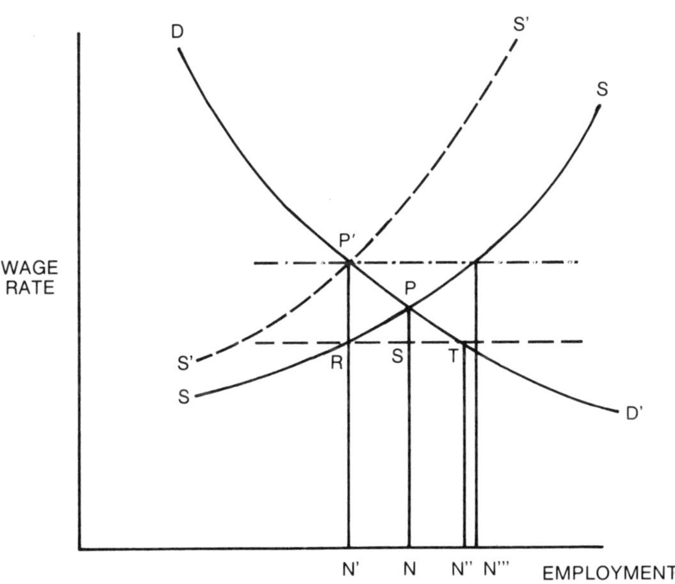

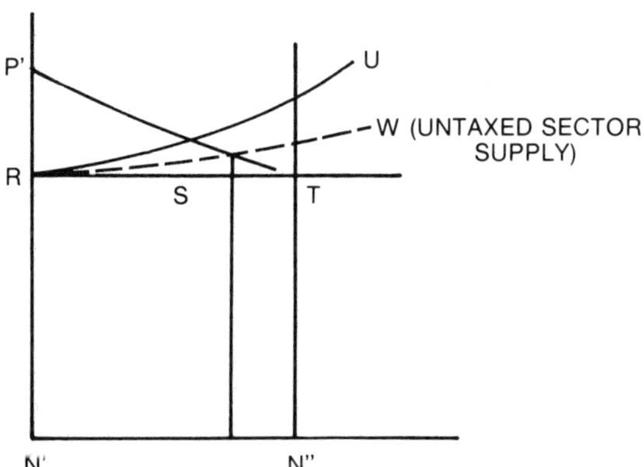

Enlargement showing effects
after creation of untaxed sector.

would-be suppliers, NN‴ might be induced to enter if the risks and other associated costs, including those involved in greater search for jobs and loss of goodwill with respect to quality, are sufficiently small. Further, some of the range of potential suppliers ON′ may wish to transfer—who knows how people will react when they are presented with opportunities that were closed before.

A CAUTION

One must be careful with the argument here. Before taxes were introduced people were assumed to prefer the pattern of formal agreements to all types of informal arrangement. Thus the opening up of an untaxed sector does not provide better opportunities than were originally available. In fact, the choices are now narrower and inferior—Adam Smith's advantages of specialization are indeed impaired. But the untaxed sector may offer benefits over and above those now available in the taxed market sector. So all would-be demanders and suppliers must inevitably re-think their positions. Our own verbal and geometric account under-represents this point.

Wage rates in the untaxed sector will lie between RN′ and P′N′. They will be lower, the more elastic is the supply of labour to the untaxed sector, and the more inelastic is the demand for the goods proffered by the untaxed sector.

Of course, we have ignored income effects. If these are large and normal in pattern, suppliers will tend to offer more labour in the taxed sector. The dominance of the substitution effect depicted in our diagram may mask differences in income effects between those who would remain with the taxed sector and those who would transfer out of it. Such lower rewards in the taxed sector would curtail profitable opportunities in the untaxed sector.

Throughout we have confined discussion to a one-skill economy. Where there are many skills, both market and non-market, the imposition of taxes may influence selections according to the relative weight of pecuniary and non-pecuniary components in the pay packet.

MINIMUM WAGES

It should now be clear that there are bounds on the deviation of the untaxed sector rate of pay from that applicable in the taxed sector. The actual band may be wider than the one shown above because of complicating circumstances. We can illustrate this point with the enforcement of a minimum wage rate above market-clearing levels—although the argument would carry over in part to the case where there is some cyclical unemployment. The after-tax wage rate will be the minimum wage rate pre-tax less the amount of tax. The higher rate of pay both pre-and post-tax which arises as a direct consequence of the imposed minimum will help those who still hold jobs, but not those who are unemployed. Hence queueing for jobs in the untaxed sector could increase. Indeed this sector is likely to have already been established even before the onset of high taxation. For the imposition of the minimum wage gives displaced workers an incentive to look for ways round this obstacle to employment. This argument, moreover, could be used for any form of regulatory activity. It is merely one example of the old theory of "black markets." But the compounding of tax and regulatory control can augment this effect. It can drive down the wage rate in the untaxed sector and encourage participation in this market. This is likely to occur, unless demand transfers are sufficiently strong.

The central point of our argument is that in equilibrium net rates of non-monetary and monetary reward, in combination, must equate for every individual who participates in market or leisure activity, however compounded, that he undertakes. Tax avoision does not offer open-ended returns. But this does not imply that the returns in the untaxed sector may not be great and heavily utilized. To what degree they are utilized in any given situation is an empirical question.

Casual observation about the growth and size of untaxed markets has been much derided. But this must be accepted against viable alternatives. That casual observation, which was widely endorsed, is revealed preference—and is the best information currently available. Still unclear, however, is whether the importance of such untaxed markets is to be assigned to taxing policy, to regulatory policy, to general adversity and disequilibrium in recession or to a combination of these factors. This is a much more relevant question, although the separation of influences will be difficult. Avoision activity may be more important for low and high income earners than for those in the middle ranges. The first group encounters steep marginal rates of tax as soon as income rises above the exemption level. Those in the top ranges must contend with the highest marginal rates of tax. They have the drive and the means to avail themselves of the most sophisticated tax advice. People in the middle classes find it more difficult to engage in activity outside the contractual area without making very large career readjustments.

V. TAX INCIDENCE

Theory talks about the incidence of each tax in isolation, as we have tended to do in the last section. But public finance theorists also tell us that incidence cannot be judged without also considering the taxes reduced or eliminated because of the new impost (or the increased public expenditures). Hence, a comprehensive picture is needed for empirical work.

In Australia there have been two such studies.[14] Both look at the problem of incidence, and treat all taxes and subsidies simultaneously. (Each, unfortunately, follows custom and avoids the non-taxed sector.)

These studies conclude that income tax is the most progressive of the taxes in Australia. Indeed, that it is really the only one. Indirect taxes are regressive; this means that state and local taxes are especially so. Excise taxes fall most heavily on the middle income ranges. The general conclusion is that taxes in 1975–1976, the year of the study, were proportional over the income range as a whole with the sole exception of the extremes.

On avoision various attempts at estimates have been summarized by Groenewegen.[15] In October 1978 Mr. E. Risstrom of the Taxpayers Association estimated that the revenue loss on personal income tax through evasion and avoidance was 8 per cent of collections. In April 1979 the federal treasurer stated that a sum equal to 70 per cent of that amount was tied up in known tax avoidance schemes. Reference to an unofficial report of the Treasury in May 1979 quoted a cost to the Treasury of $3000 million—a figure several times that quoted earlier. Finally, attention is drawn to the large difference in rates of growth in tax collections from salary and wage earners on the one hand and the self-employed together with those with business and property income on the other.

My own observations point to very large untaxed activity in the small buildings and maintenance area (there has been a marked recession in major building for several years which may have swelled labour supply for this purpose). The proliferation of tax accountants and advisers, and now television programmes on this topic, suggest widespread concern about tax. Presumably this indicates the degree of activity to curtail tax commitments.

VI. CONCLUSION

From a wide-ranging survey it is not easy to derive general conclusions. Heavy income tax, especially when accompanied by high marginal rates, dampens effort and incentives. It forces ingenuity away from conventional productive enterprise and associated innovation. It channels entrepreneurial creativity into tax saving, and into less efficient and less specialized enterprise (the underground economy). For this reason there is some advantage in a proportional income tax. A proportional tax of only 22–25 per cent would capture prevailing levels of income tax revenue in Australia. This would be of special benefit to higher income groups. For lower incomes, the position is less certain as there is a threshold problem.

Given this difficulty, it could be better to work for a somewhat lower and telescoped marginal set of rates, in the hope that the *effective* tax can be improved. The difficulty is that avoidance action, once resorted to, is built into people's behaviour patterns and would be more effectively curbed under the former proposal.

Even those who attach significance to the retention of the present relative levels of public expenditure may see merit in these simplifications.

But for those who would reduce the relative significance of public expenditure such changes would seem to be an integral requirement. This is the best way to restore a sizeable but equitable tax base within a market-oriented economy, one from which exclusion is little sought and through which market specialization and development may be fostered.

NOTES

1. The control of the money base would normally be similarly assigned, although there have been some recent reservations on this. Hayek, F.A., *Choice in Currencies,* IEA Occasional paper (1977).
2. Fisher, M.R. "Professor Hicks and the Keynesians," *Economica,* 43:305–14, August (1976).
   Carlton, D.W. "Market Behaviour with Demand Uncertainty and Price Inflexibility," *American Economic Review,* 68:4:571–87 (1978).
   Kirzner, I.M. *Perception, Opportunity and Profit: Studies in the Theory of Entrepreneurship,* Chicago: University of Chicago Press (1980).
3. Mirrlees, J.A. "An Exploration in the Theory of Optimum Income Taxation," *Review of Economic Studies,* April (1971).
   DasGupta, P. and P. Hammond. "Fully Progressive Taxation," *Journal of Public Economics,* 13:2:141–54 (1980).
4. Fisher, M.R., F.H. Gruen, P.J. Sheehan, and D.W. Stammer. *Real Wages and Unemployment,* Sydney: Centre for Applied Economic Research No. 4, University of N.S.W.
5. Hicks. *Value and Capital,* Oxford: Oxford University Press, Chapter 14 (1939).
6. Kay, J.A. and M.A. King. *The British Tax System,* Oxford: Oxford University Press (1978).
7. Seldon, A. (ed.) *Tax Avoision,* London: IEA Readings 22 (1979).
8. Fisher, M.R. *The Economic Analysis of Labour,* London: Weidenfeld and Nicolson (1972) pp. 248–9.
9. Cain, G. and H.W. Watts. *Income Maintenance & Labour Supply,* New York: Academic Press (1973).
   Mincer, J. "Labour Force Participation of Married Women," *Aspects of Labor Economics,* Lewis, G. (ed.), Princeton: Princeton University Press (1963).

10. Lancaster, K. J. "A New Approach to Consumer Theory," *Journal of Political Economy,* 74:2:132–57 (1966).
Becker, G. S. "Crime and Punishment: An Economic Approach," *Journal of Political Economy,* 76:2:169–217 (1968).
11. Marshall, A. *Principles of Economics,* 8th Edition, Book VI. London: Macmillan (1920).
12. Fisher, M. R. *Wage Determination in an Integrating Europe,* Leiden: Syjthoff (1966) Chapter 1.
13. Becker, G. S. "A Theory of the Allocation of Time," *Economic Journal,* 75:299:493–517 (1965).
14. Bentley, P., D. J. Collins, and N. T. Drane. "The Incidence of Australian Taxation," *Economic Record,* 50:132:489–510 (1974).
Warren, N. A. "Australian Tax Incidence in 1975–1976: Some Preliminary Results," *Australian Economic Review,* 3rd Quarter, (1979).
15. Groenewegen, P.D. *The Challenge of Tax Reform,* Economic Papers, Sydney, November (1979) p.79.

COMMENT

Thomas J. Courchene

INTRODUCTION

Let us begin by focusing on the interaction between federalisms and tax systems. The starting point of the analysis is the set of figures in Table 11.2 of Professor Fisher's paper. The Australian federal authorities, for 1976–1977, collected $19.8 billion of the $24.8 billion total government tax revenue, or 80 per cent of total revenues. In terms of outlays, however, the federal level accounted for only 32 per cent of the $20 billion total. This implies a tremendous degree of "vertical imbalance" in the Australian federation – the access to tax revenues by the Australian states falls well short of their constitutional spending authority. And as Tables 11.3 and 11.4 point out very clearly, this shortfall is bridged by a set of intergovernmental grants – from Table 11.3, $9.6 billion of the states' total revenues of $14.5 billion (for 1978–1979) comes in the form of grants from the commonwealth. Therefore, the first area I wish to discuss is the manner in which federal nations handle the problem of vertical imbalance, and with what impact. Indeed, one could extend this to the "intergovernmental" transfers that exist in unitary states (from the central government to the local authorities).

Thus far, most of the analysis in the various papers addressed the set of incentives embodied in the tax systems, and how they impact on the private sector. The focus on a sub-national tier of governments introduces another actor into the scene: What are the incentives in the tax or fiscal regime that impinge on the behaviour of this junior tier of governments? I shall argue that the manner in which the problem of vertical balance is addressed does indeed make a great deal of difference to things such as overall expenditure growth (and, therefore, average and probably marginal tax rates) and the degree of tax and fiscal harmony across the various nations.

A MAXIM

Let me begin with what I believe should be a maxim of intergovernmental finance: we are unlikely to end up with an efficient fiscal system if the level of government responsible for the spending authority is not also responsible for raising the revenue. Assar Lindbeck points out that local government spending in Sweden has been increasing by leaps and bounds because the central government was and is footing the bill. Until recently at least, much the same could be said of many local governments in Canada. This holds particularly with respect to education, where the local boards made the expenditure decisions and the provincial governments provided the funds.

Fisher points out that the bulk of the Australian intergovernmental transfers are not only specific (*i.e.*, conditional) but are closed (*i.e.*, not open-ended). The conditionality of these grants means they are geared to the preferences of the Commonwealth, not to those of the individual Australian states. In the limit, of course, a sophisticated set of conditional grants can emasculate federalism. There is little difference between redesigning the constitution to transfer these functions upward to the federal government and implementing a set of conditional grants which in effect force the states to administer these monies in a manner dictated by the centre.

OPEN-ENDED GRANTS?

Whether these intergovernmental grants are open-ended or not is also critical. Canada's experience with its 50 per cent open-ended, cost-sharing, interprovincial transfers for health care and post-secondary education come quickly to mind. Because of cost-sharing the provinces were in effect spending 50-cent dollars. This naturally channeled additional provincial expenditures to these areas, and the grants were open-ended as well. Not surprisingly, from the inception of this scheme until 1977 (when the grants were converted into quasi-unconditional form and the open-ended feature was removed) Canada witnessed a tremendous expenditure growth in these areas. In effect, the federal government's expenditures on these functions were determined in the ten provincial capitals. This is but another example of the general principle that the non-coincidence of the expenditure and revenue-raising authorities will generate excess spending. It also illustrates the contention that in assessing the impact of the tax system on the economy, one cannot leave out the set of incentives that impinge on the junior tier of governments.

Another example. Until recently, legislated minimum wages in most of Canada's "have-not" provinces were higher than the minimum wage in more prosperous Ontario. This, too, is a feature of the Canadian environment that in my opinion cannot be explained without reference to the tax-transfer system. Consider the province of Quebec. For many years it has had the highest minimum wage on the North American continent, let alone in Canada. This does not make economic sense, but it occurs because the provinces do not bear the full cost of their economic decisions. When greater unemployment results because of this higher minimum wage, Ottawa runs to the rescue with greater equalization payments, with unemployment insurance transfers (regionally differentiated so that citizens in high unemployment areas can collect benefits for longer periods) and with one-half of any welfare costs. Moreover, because of high levels of unemployment, Quebec can then lobby successfully for even greater tariff protection for its labour-intensive industries.

Quebec's minimum wage enactment causes great economic harm. That, however, is their right under the Constitution. But to allow that province to pass off the economic costs of such a decision, via Ottawa, is to remove an automatic safety device. If the social costs of this legislation had to be borne in Quebec, this might reduce the incentive to retain it.

And this phenomenon applies to other cases. The tax system can impact on individuals with respect to such things as work effort, channels through which they save and invest, the tendency toward resorting to the underground economy, etc. Each creates a corresponding set of incentives on the behaviour of the junior level of government which can be crucial.

INTERNAL TAX HARMONIZATION

There is another set of issues relating to the interaction of taxation and federalism. This concerns internal tax harmony or, more generally, the degree to which the domestic market can be characterized as an internal common market. Let us focus first on the behaviour of central governments and their ability to impose geographically differentiated taxes. The Australian Constitution (Section 51 [iii]) states: "The Parliament shall. . . have power to make laws. . . with respect to taxation; but not so as to discriminate between states or parts of states." The restraint on the Commonwealth goes beyond limiting its taxation freedom. Section 99 provides that "The Commonwealth shall not, by any law or regulation of trade, commerce, or revenue, give preference to one state or any part thereof over another state or any part thereof." In the United States the Constitution is not as restrictive on this issue. But there has developed a rather strong tradition that Washington should not interfere in regional development – whether this be by taxation or expenditure policies. In response to a recent call for federal intervention in regional problems, U.S. Senator Daniel Moynihan reflected this ingrained tradition:

> We must not politicize the question of relative regional growth or, for that matter, regional decline.... It would be contrary to the spirit of the constitution for the federal government to intervene in our economy to try to prevent the natural movements of capital and people from one state or region to another, if a free choice is made by those concerned. Such a restraint, surely, is imposed by the constitution on state governments by the interstate commerce clause. Certainly, the Federal government should not act in a manner forbidden to the states. The founders of this nation understood that our political freedoms and national stability very much depended on our becoming a single economy with the freest possible movement of capital and labour across state and regional borders. The Supreme Court more than once has had occasion to reaffirm that commitment.[1]

The Canadian federation is quite different. There is no constitutional roadblock to discriminatory federal taxation. On more than one occasion the federal government has incorporated in its overall tax system regionally discriminatory tax credits, and other policies, for such things as investment expenditure and R and D expenditures. But, in general, federal governments of federalisms do not go as far in this direction as the unitary states. The United Kingdom's system of regional employment premia and differentiated regional development is a case in point.

AN INTERNATIONAL COMPARISON

However, more important than the actions of the federal government are the tax and associated policies of the provinces or states. Here again the various federalisms differ considerably. The German and Australian federations have perhaps the most homogeneous tax systems. In Australia, this appears to be a matter more determined by custom than by constitution. The Australian states are free to mount their own income tax systems although none has yet done so. (Moreover, in great contrast to Canada, the fossil-energy-rich Australian states have not as yet made a tax grab for oil and gas rents. I suspect that this will change very soon.) At the other end of the spectrum are the Swiss with their so-called tax-jungle at the cantonal level. In between are Canada and the U.S. Canada is somewhat unique in that it has a very decentralized tax system (*e.g.*, one-third of personal income tax revenues accrue to the provinces) and also a rather harmonized tax system. Except for Quebec, all provinces adhere to the same definitions for income; the same exemptions exist at the provincial level as at the federal level. However, provincial tax rates do vary considerably. On the corporate side, there is more heterogeneity. Three of the largest provinces (Quebec, Ontario and Alberta) operate their own corporate tax systems. Although the prospects for this to degenerate into a Swiss-style tax jungle are clearly present, there is still a common formula for allocating the profits for multi-province enterprises. This is in stark contrast to the situation in the United States.

The American system is different for another reason. In those states that impose personal income taxes, taxpayers are allowed a write-off against federal personal income taxes. On the business side certain states have long been attractive—on tax grounds—as corporate headquarters.

A FEW PUZZLES

Several questions arise from all of this. What effect do these subnational policies (expenditures as well as tax) have on the incentive of individuals and corporations to migrate? Can one view these state or provincial measures as enhancing efficiency? Presumably this would follow from the model of "competitive federalism" espoused by James Buchanan and others. In the Canadian context, at any rate, with the current tendency toward a veritable flood of "province-building" or discriminatory tax and expenditure measures, the opposite question surfaces: at what point can or does competitive federalism degenerate into beggar-thy-neighbour federalism? The answer is far from clear. However, if one was to attempt to predict the future tax regime that will prevail in Canada, one of the most important determinants will be the outcome of this federal-provincial and interprovincial tax tug-of-war. With the recent rise in the number and types of barriers across the various U.S. states (not all on the tax side), this may be important for the allocative efficiency in the U.S. as well.

As an interesting aside, one should not jump to the conclusion that unitary states have unfettered domestic markets. Indeed, there is no provincial policy in Canada, nor I suspect in any other federal state, that inhibits internal migration as much as the housing policies of the local authorities in the U.K.

STATE CAPITALISM

There is another aspect of fiscal federalism that, in Canada at least, is going to have an immense impact on the viability of the private sector. This relates to section 125 of the constitution which, in effect, states that the crown cannot tax the crown. This means in practice that provincial ownership of business enterprises will typically escape federal taxation. Provincial government interest income (*e.g.*, from the $13 billion dollar Alberta Heritage Fund) thus escapes federal taxation. This gives a substantial incentive toward (provincial) government ownership. This is particularly the case in the Canadian context where federal-provincial relationships are, at best, rather strained.

A similar provision in the U.S. constitution makes municipal bonds tax exempt. Is there a similar feature in the Australian system which has comparable effects? Since both the U.S. and Australian constitutions have stronger provisions relating to state interference in interstate trade, this might provide one avenue for limiting state ownership. The Canadian constitution has much weaker provisions along these lines. State capitalism has therefore played, and will continue to play, a major role in the federation. And, as noted, underlying its growth is a tax rationale.

CONCLUSION

The thrust of my comments has been to argue that there is an aspect of the tax structure that has not received sufficient attention; namely, the range of incentives that exist between the different levels of government. This applies whether in a federal or unitary state. These incentives have a great deal to do with the overall size of government (and, therefore, the overall tax bill), the geographical location of people and enterprise within a nation, and the overall viability of the private sector.

As a final comment, let me raise an intriguing but I suspect unanswerable question. We have now reviewed the taxation systems of several countries. Is there anything that might allow one to predict what the tax system of a given country will look like? In other words, is there any degree of endogeneity of taxation systems? Presumably, factors such as history and cultural homogeneity and openness play some role. Initially, for federal nations at least, one might adopt a "constitutional determinist" view to federal tax systems. Certainly, the range of activities on the fiscal front allowed to the German, American, and Australian governments (at both levels) is somewhat circumscribed by their constitutions. Canada has more constitutional latitude. However, the constitution approach can only be carried so far. Consider the following example. In Canada, the provinces have had considerably more powers under the constitution (including judicial interpretation) than do the American states. However, suppose that there were only ten American states with the economic geography of the present Canadian provinces (*e.g.*, where two of the ten would hold between them, the majority of seats in the House of Representatives) and that the Canadian federation was composed of 50 provinces. Given the same constitutions, would the political economy of these two "redefined" federalisms conform to the present day structures in the U.S. and Canada? Or would the "redefined" U.S. states have a set of powers that resemble more those of the present Canadian provinces? I suspect that the latter is the more likely, *i.e.*, that constitutional interpretation is, to a degree, likely also to be endogenous.

Nonetheless, it would be intriguing if some enterprising scholar did attempt to investigate the degree to which the taxation systems of the various nations acquire predictable characteristics.

NOTE

1. Daniel P. Moynihan. "The Politics and Economics of Regional Growth," *The Public Interest,* No. 51 Spring (1978) p.7.

DISCUSSION

Edited by: Walter Block

Three major threads are discernable in the rich and varied verbal tapestry that followed upon the presentation of the Australian tax system. The first had to do with the methodological status of interviewing techniques, as a means of illuminating the incidence of taxation. It was Robert Clark who set off on this fascinating topic:

"What follows in terms of studies of incidence from the statement that people will, in principle, reveal where the incidence of the tax falls and the directions of their tax alleviating adjustments? Does that, for instance, suggest that personal interview studies are the most accurate way of arriving at information about incidence of personal income tax and, for that matter, other taxes?"

Malcolm Fisher: "My point there must be seen in context. Everything is relative. I was really downgrading the present state of the art in time series and cross section analysis. I did this in the course of my earlier delivery by saying that our casual observations, which I call revealed preference, are a much more reliable indicator than interviews. But, I don't know what the answer is.

"You mention specifically the personal interview. I'm very dubious about personal interviews. I think they have a place but I think you've got to know the underlying biases. I remember the National Plan in Britain in 1964. Firms were asked about their investment intentions. I've forgotten the direction of bias, I think they all tended to understate their intentions, but it was a powerful bias. This is usually encountered pretty quickly in the interview game, so I regard it as at best supplementary."

Alan Walters: "My recollection is that the National Plan interview question was, 'What would your investment plan be if the economy grew at 4 per cent per annum?' All of the respondents said, 'Splendid!' I think the only firms that behaved according to their plan were in the brick industry—which found itself with enormous over-capacity for the next five years. That's the interview technique for you."

Malcolm Fisher: "We economists think we've got these nice statistical exercises running, we think we can do all sorts of things, and we downgrade what the man in the street knows about the untaxed sector. What I'm trying to do is upgrade it, because our other record is pretty dismal."

Robert Clark: "But there is a distinction between asking people 'what would you do' in certain hypothetical circumstances that haven't happened, as compared with 'what have you done that would be different, as a result of taxes already in existence.' I think that the second does give a useful way of getting information."

Edgar Feige: "On this point of survey data and interview data, there was an interesting direct survey made in Oregon. A lawyer asked people directly about whether they obeyed tax laws. He had a remarkable 26 per cent negative admission response from the direct questionnaire.

"The I.R.S. recently conducted an opinion survey along similar lines, and there they used two response techniques. They asked the question directly with the assurance of complete anonymity. And they also used a randomized response technique where there are really two questions that the respondent is asked, and the interviewer does not know which question is being answered. But they know the sampling distribution of the two questions, so they can infer response rates. Those estimates revealed estimates which were between 62 per cent and 433 per cent higher on the questions in the randomized response technique used than in direct questioning.

"So, not only are there very significant downward biases of reporting on income questions, but there is also a tremendous variance in the degree of bias. It is very problematic.

"The other problem with direct questionnaires seems to be a growing confirmatory evidence of this phenomenon from changes in non-response rates to governmental questions. In 1967, I think, the non-response rates on the income question was 14 per cent. This is on the major current population survey which forms one of the basic components of the GNP accounts in the United States. By 1976, the non-response rate had risen to 26 per cent, and to that you have to add another 5 per cent for non-interviews. This is where they couldn't even find a person, or, if they did find them, there were reasons why they couldn't conduct the interview.

"So, we are talking somewhere in the order of magnitude of a 30 per cent to 32 per cent non-response rate on these sensitive questions. That means a tremendous amount of imputation required to fill in what are believed to be the incomes of the non-respondents. The interviewers do that but what those techniques yield is highly problematic."

Assar Lindbeck: "I would like to confirm what Professor Feige said about response rates. In Sweden in 1957–1958, we made rather comprehensive studies about savings and assets, using the interview technique, and the response rate was very high. But more recently, the Swedish government tried to make a new study, but the whole thing had to be cancelled because it was impossible to get answers."

The next question to be approached systematically by the participants had to do with housing, migration patterns, and values capitalized in land. It was begun by Professor Lawrence Smith: "Mine is really a conjunctal question, a preamble to our concern with taxes. We discussed monetary policy and rationales for holding interest rates down, and in that connection we talked about the percentage of home ownership being very large. With regard to the financing of home ownership in Australia, are mortgages short-term or are they long-term?"

Malcolm Fisher: "From my experience, they are reasonably long term. The interest rate adjusts within England. You'd call it the bank rate, the market rate."

Lawrence Smith: "So it's a floating interest rate. Then it has immediate effect, it's not a matter of capitalizing values?"

Malcolm Fisher: "At most, three or four months delay until the short-term rates seem to be stabilizing, then you get lower or higher levels."

Alan Walters: "Can I pick up a political point here? Why on earth didn't Australia just grant income tax exemption on the interest rate? Was that Smith's question?"

Lawrence Smith: "Well, it was whether there was any political pressures for that once rates started going up."

Alan Walters: "It seems to be a political way out, and not an unreasonable way out."

Assar Lindbeck: "Then you have to assess the income value of owning the home."

Alan Walters: "I can see the argument that all expectations about asset prices have been formed on the basis of non-liability. I prefer a crash economic program that is going to wheel in the Liberal vote. I can't see a better operation, I surmise we're wonderful."

Lawrence Smith: "Well, except that this plan didn't get that far in Canada. It won one election in 1980, but it didn't win the one eight months later in 1981."

Malcolm Fisher: "Alan Walters used a phrase which is very interesting and relevant to Australia, compared with the U.K. Australia was full of 'crash programs.' They shifted suddenly to an oil levy. Beer and wine, which is a domestic production, is not taxed, but spirits are, and the duties stay the same for several years. And then they are very quickly moved up by 50 per cent.

"I went downtown in a taxi shortly after this happened. The taxi driver was complaining about it. He made a very pertinent remark about Australians. He said, 'Oh, they're bellyaching in the pubs like mad!' but he said, 'Give them a fortnight and you won't hear another squeal.' I've lived in Australia now through three or four of those things and there's not another squeak after a fortnight. The people are very used to these crash changes, income tax surcharges and whatnot."

Armen Alchian: "The question you ask your students is, 'What's the effect of a tax?' Usually, the first answer is, 'nothing' because people adapt. Australia speaks the English language, so does Canada, so does the United States, so does England, and migration is pretty open, I think, among those four or five countries. What difference does it make what kind of taxing one country imposes? It all gets capitalized in land value. If people can move around among the various countries, like England, the United States, Canada, Australia and New Zealand, and it's an open economy, each one of them, what difference does it make to people what kind of tax you have in each country? It all gets capitalized in the land value."

Malcolm Fisher: "My own situation is a case in point, because I have recently migrated from England to Australia."

Armen Alchian: "So if the taxes are high in England, no matter, people move away until their salary is such that after the tax they come out the same as people living in Australia who pay a low tax, and the land values in England take a beating."

Thomas Courchene: "But even if it's perfectly capitalized it's got to be capitalized at one marginal rate."

Armen Alchian: "No."

Thomas Courchene: "It can't be equalized for everybody."

Armen Alchian: "I agree, it can't. . . "

Courchene: "The question is, at which margin is it capitalized."

Armen Alchian: "Yes, but they will still be different for marginal rates. Whether you're in a country A, B or C won't make any difference."

Malcolm Fisher: "I agree marginal rates are relevant, but one must be very careful. When I looked at the sums about moving from England to Australia I started at the traditional naive marginal rate and it was completely irrelevant to me because it's not *the* marginal rate. The marginal rate for migration is much nearer the average rate of tax between England and Australia. There is a dramatic difference in my case, between the average rates in the two countries which I had to do the sum on. The marginal rate on income is small beer in the context of that decision. It's still a marginal rate, but one must be careful of which margin and for what purpose."

Armen Alchian: "The moving margin is quite different from the margin."

Malcolm Fisher: "That's right."

Herbert Giersch: "I was puzzled about Mr. Fisher's introductory remark concerning specific taxes which allow migration from one country to another. If it stops with alcohol and cigarettes I'm in favour of it. But sometimes, they discriminate, and say, in effect 'Well, you shouldn't consume a luxury good and you should pay as much excise tax on that as on another.' So we finally end up with a sovereign which exerts a very strong influence on our preference, at least on what we consume, and this is not very different from the Soviet system."

Malcolm Fisher: "If I may say so, I supported that in my concluding remarks. It just goes to show the dangers of overstatement. What I really was attacking there was the modern group who want to broaden, comprehensively, the tax base on income inverted commerce. It seems to me, as someone who wants to lower the public sector, that I would rather live with roughly the present definition of income and try and move to a proportional tax rather than let these bureaucrats loose.

"It's a point that came up with Jim Buchanan's paper. Even if they offer us lower tax rates on this broader comprehensive tax base, times change and they will inevitably increase again. There's more opportunity for the individual who rejects the contribution of the public sector to opt out with a less general income tax arrangement."

Hans-Georg Petersen: "I would like to add something to what Professor Giersch has said. I think specific taxes have tremendous excess burdens as well as tremendous adverse consequences for allocation. Adam Smith formulated the quality principle of taxation, in contrast to the feudalistic and mercantilistic system, one with specific tax bases.

"And I want to say something in defense of the concept of a comprehensive income tax base. If such comprehensive tax base is noticeable for the single taxpayer, no "tax illusion" will be possible. Then, the resistance against tax (rate) increases would be strengthened. If government goes beyond certain limits, voters will react. And the minority has the freedom to vote by its feet or to escape into the underground economy. This is very important because it limits government revenues and the government public sector.

"This is why I oppose a total harmonization of the different tax systems within the European Community. If different tax systems exist, the systems are in competition with each other in the different regions. Thus the freedom to vote by one's feet remains."

Thirdly, there was an exchange between Professors Lindbeck, Fisher and Walters on the underground economy.

Assar Lindbeck: "Fisher said here that there is very little theoretical literature on the submerged or underground sector of the economy. However, there are some papers, for instance, about the choice between market activity, home activity and leisure. And the best theoretical article I have seen in the field is by an Israeli economist, Reuben Gronau. Gronau creates an international trade model with a transformation curve betweeen leisure and home work and then a trade line with a fixed price where one can trade on the market between leisure and market goods. Also, Abba Lerner wrote a very intelligent article in the early 1970s in the *American Economic Review* about the choice between taxed and non-taxed sector work. As always, Abba Lerner can, in a verbal analysis and small diagrams, reach as far as the later mathematical economists have done with optimum tax literature.

"There are also a number of articles on illegal activities, of course, in the Gary Becker tradition. Also the *Journal of Public Economics* has had many articles on the theory of tax evasion over the last five or six years. It is true that practically all optimum tax literature is concerned only with taxes to finance transfer payments. However, there are one or two articles concerning public goods. Stieglitz and Atkinson wrote one piece, but there is very little published on this subject. I agree with Professor Fisher that the literature is very narrow. It builds on utilitarian utility functions, where all individual utilities can be added. There is no room in the models for envy, for altruism, for entitlement, for principles of egalitarianism. There are identical utility functions for everybody, so it's a very narrow domain."

Malcolm Fisher: "Sometimes this literature introduces a bit of explicit cardinality, but nevertheless with a strong income redistribution drift."

Alan Walters: "It's best to regard it as a set of parables rather than relating to the real world."

Assar Lindbeck: "Yes, to do that is to prematurely use it for quantitative conclusions about the optimum rate. At first, this was very low. But later, writers have been able to push up the optimum margin rate to 60 per cent by trying hard."

Alan Walters: "That's an argument that it should be probabilistic, I believe. It's a very confusing field."

Malcolm Fisher: "I think that this theoretical literature needs watching. There's a tremendous ground swell in it, and the implicit assumptions there need to be made much more explicit. May I just add one point about the literature without being considered immodest; Professor Lindbeck mentioned Gronau. I think I was in the field in that area along with Reuben Gronau, about the same time as Gary Becker, and it really was derivative from their work in the 1960s, that I was applying here. Regarding your other references, I agree very much with your remarks on Lerner."

There was also a brief discussion of tax brackets between Professors Kesselman and Fisher that was of great interest.

Jonathan Kesselman: "I note in a table in Professor Fisher's paper that there are only three marginal tax rates used in the Australian system. This contrasts with the pattern in both Canada and the United States where there are more than a dozen such brackets. Many people feel that you need these fine gradations of marginal tax rates to get the right pattern of incidence in terms of income distribution. But it is quite apparent from the Australian example that you don't. In fact, even two rates would give you quite a good deal of effective average rate progressivity.

"I feel that this is noteworthy because of the reduction of incentives for taxpayer fiddling, (for example distorting the timing of incomes and deductions) that occur as the number of marginal rate brackets are reduced. Under what I would regard as the ideal system, there would be only one or two rates, a comprehensive tax base, and no exemptions. The relief of low-income people would be handled not through exemptions, but by a universal demogrant system to offset the taxes paid by low earners. This approach would also satisfy the goals of the negative income tax, without its apparent practical and technical shortcomings. Such a credit income tax potentially offers many advantages for tax simplification, as well as for improved taxpayer equity and economic efficiency."

Malcolm Fisher: "Now that we've got to three rates, it's a pity we didn't go on to one. But until about the time I came from New Zealand to Australia, there were more than three. But not long back, as I mentioned in this paper, there were twenty-nine brackets. It was a very fine gradation throughout the 1960s. But that has all been swept away."

INDEX